Ready® 3

PRACTICE AND PROBLEM SOLVING

Editorial Director: Cynthia Tripp
Cover Designer and Illustrator: Matt Pollock
Illustrator: Sam Valentino
Photography Credit: wk1003mike/Shutterstock (front cover background)

ISBN 978-0-7609-9224-1

North Billerica, MA 01862

45 44 43 42 41 40 39 38 37 36 35 34

BTS22

802381

Table of Contents

Family Letter available with every lesson.

Unit 4: Number and Operations—Fractions

Unit 5: Measurement and Data

Family Letter available with every lesson.

Unit 6: Geometry

Family Letter available with every lesson.

Dear Family,

This week your child is exploring the meaning of multiplication.

Multiplication involves working with equal groups of objects. For example:

3 groups of 2 shells is 6 shells in all.

Multiply: $3 \times 2 = 6$

The **product** tells how many in all.

The first **factor** tells how many groups.

The second **factor** tells how many in each group.

Your child is using arrays to show multiplication. An **array** is a set of objects arranged in equal rows and equal columns.

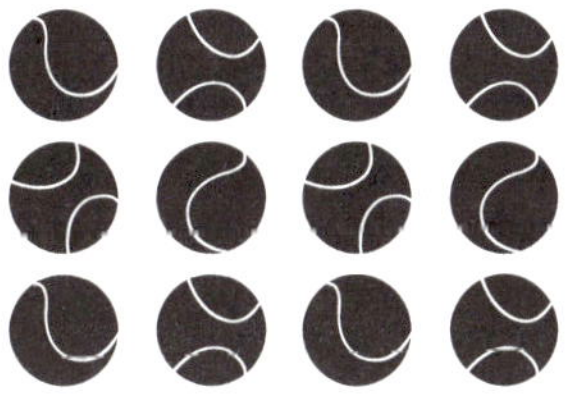

3 rows of 4 baseballs is 12 baseballs in all.

Multiply: $3 \times 4 = 12$

Invite your child to share what he or she knows about the meaning of multiplication by doing the following activity together.

NEXT

Multiplication Activity

Materials: 30 pennies or other small items and 4 to 6 small cups

- Ask your child to make 4 groups of 5 by putting pennies in cups.
- Using the pennies in the cups, complete this sentence:

_(4)_ groups of _(5)_ pennies equals _(20)_ pennies in all.

- Next, ask your child to remove the pennies from the first cup and arrange them in a row to begin an array.
- Have your child create the second, third, and fourth rows of the array with the pennies from the other three cups, as shown.
- Using the array, ask your child to multiply to find the total.

_(4)_	×	_(5)_	=	_(20)_
how many rows		how many in each row		total

Repeat this activity for equal groups of other sizes, such as 5 groups of 3, 2 groups of 4, or 3 groups of 6.

As your child becomes more familiar with the idea of multiplication, point out examples of multiplication in real life; for example, 3 groups of 2 socks shows $3 \times 2 = 6$.

Understand the Meaning of Multiplication

Name: ______________________

Prerequisite: How do you know if groups are equal?

Study the example problem showing equal groups and unequal groups. Then solve problems 1–6.

Example

Tell whether each picture shows equal groups.

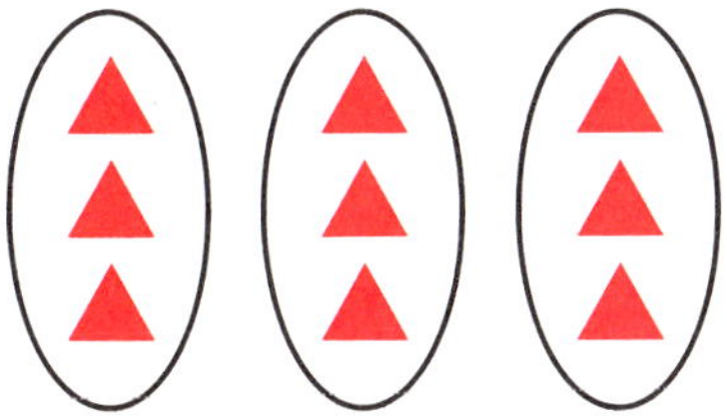

This picture shows equal groups.

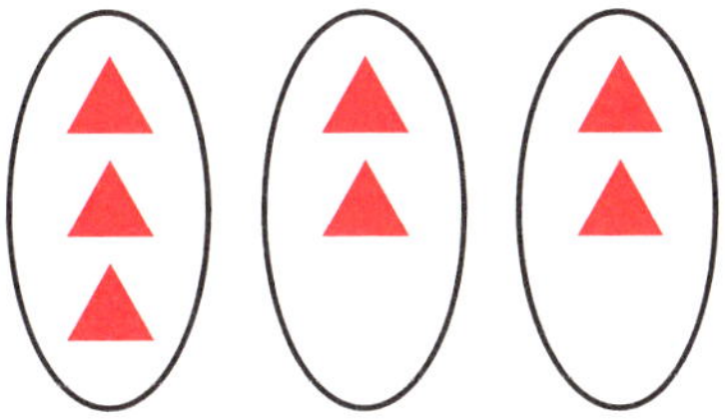

This picture shows unequal groups.

1 How many triangles are in each group in the first picture from the Example? ______

How many triangles are in each group in the second picture? ________

2 Why does the first picture show equal groups?

____

____

____

3 Look at the picture to the right. Does it show equal groups? How do you know?

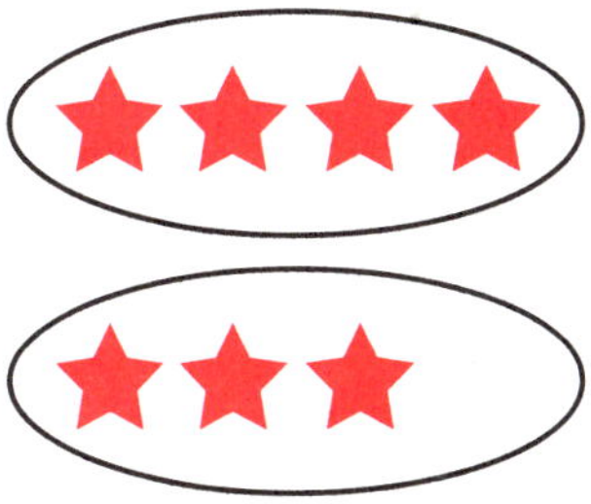

____

____

____

Solve.

4 Becky has 5 groups of apples. Each group has 2 apples. Use the rings below. Draw all the apples to show the equal groups.

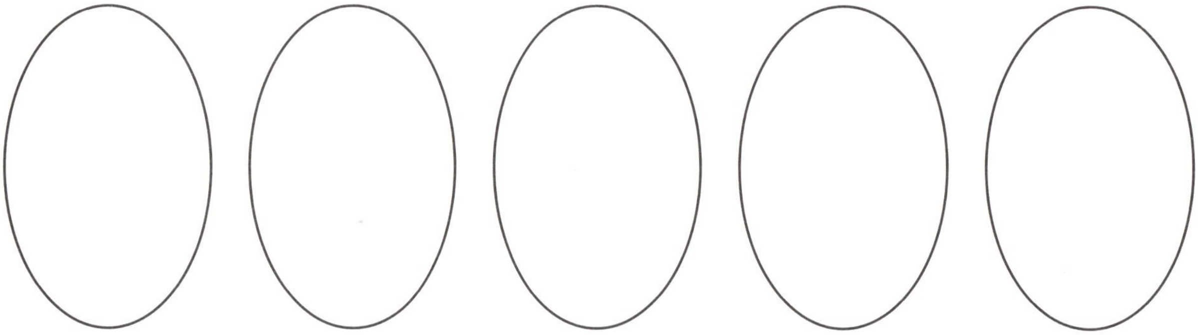

5 Mike has 3 shelves in his bookcase. Each shelf has 6 books on it. Mike drew an array to show how many books he has.

How many rows does the array have? ______

How many books are in each row of the array? ______

6 John earned 3 dollars 4 times.

Draw a picture to show this.

Fill in the blanks to complete the addition sentence that describes your picture.

______ + ______ + ______ + ______ = ______

Vocabulary

array a set of objects arranged in equal rows and equal columns.

Name: ____________________

Use Equal Groups to Think About Multiplication

Study the example problem showing a multiplication sentence to represent equal groups. Then solve problems 1–9.

Example

There are 2 leaves. There are 6 ladybugs on each leaf. How many ladybugs are there altogether? Write a multiplication sentence.

There are 2 equal groups of ladybugs. Each group has 6 ladybugs.

Multiplication sentence: $2 \times 6 = 12$

Use the picture below to answer problems 1–4.

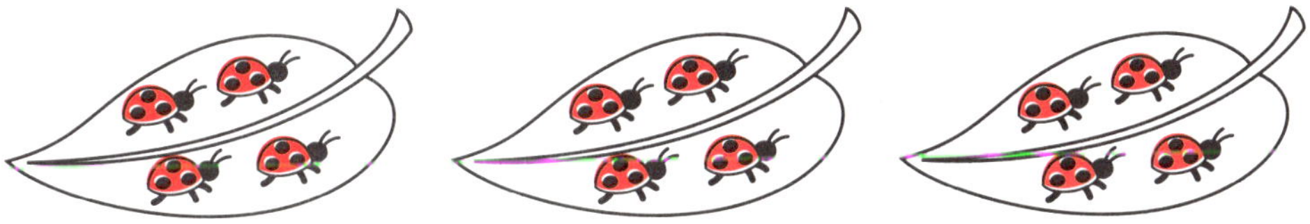

1 How many equal groups are there? ______

2 How many ladybugs are in each group? ______

3 How many ladybugs are there altogether? ______

4 Write a multiplication sentence about the number of ladybugs.

______ × ______ = ______

Solve.

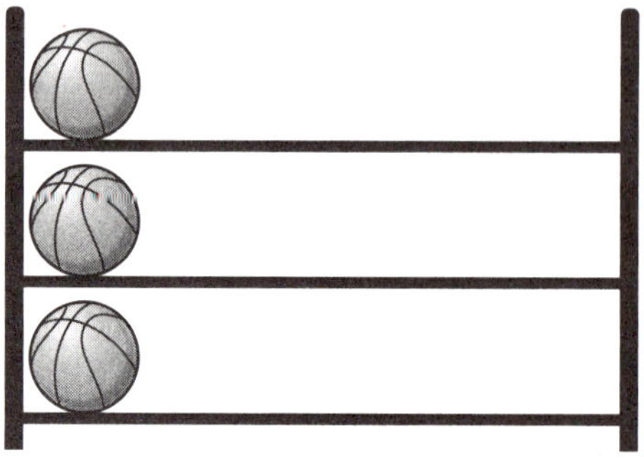

5 The basketball cart has 3 shelves. Each shelf can hold 5 basketballs. There is already 1 basketball on each shelf. Draw the rest of the basketballs to fill the cart.

6 Look at your picture of the basketballs on the cart. Think about the basketballs as an array.

How many rows are in the array? _______

How many basketballs are in each row? _______

How many basketballs are on the cart? _______

7 Fill in the blanks to represent the array of basketballs with a multiplication sentence.

_______ × _______ = _______

8 Write the multiplication sentence to represent the squares in the rectangle.

_______ × _______ = _______

9 Draw an array of square tiles to show $4 \times 6 = 24$.

Name: ______________________

Reason and Write

Study the example. Underline two parts that you think make it a particularly good answer and a helpful example.

Example

Casey drew a picture to show 4 × 7. He wrote:

My picture shows that 4 × 7 = 11.

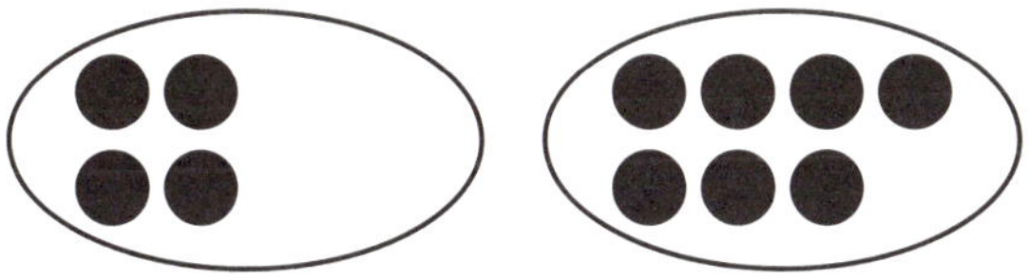

What did Casey do right? What did he do wrong?

Use pictures, words, and numbers to explain.

Casey drew loops to put models into equal groups. He knew that 4 and 7 were important numbers, but he modeled addition instead of multiplication. He drew a model for 4 + 7 instead of 4 × 7. He thought of 4 and 7 as addends instead of factors.

Casey should have shown 4 × 7 as 4 groups of 7 objects, so he needed to draw 4 loops with 7 objects in each loop. His drawing should look like this.

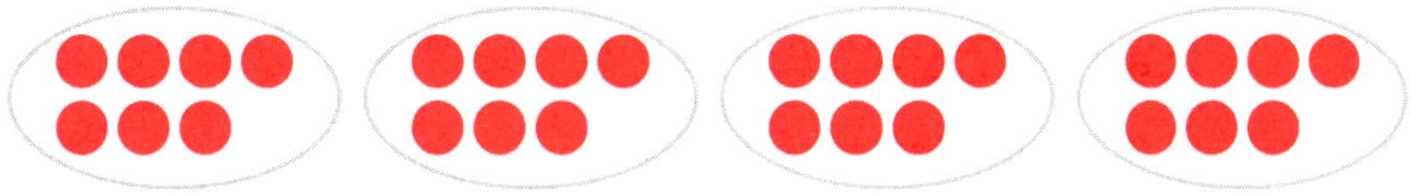

Then he would see that 4 × 7 = 28.

Where does the example . . .

- use a picture to explain?
- use numbers to explain?
- use words to explain?
- give details?

Solve the problem. Use what you learned from the example.

Jan found this picture of nests with eggs in them.

She wrote a multiplication sentence about the picture. She wrote:

$3 \times 5 = 15$

Explain what Jan did right. What did she do wrong?

Show your work. Use pictures, words, or numbers to explain your answer.

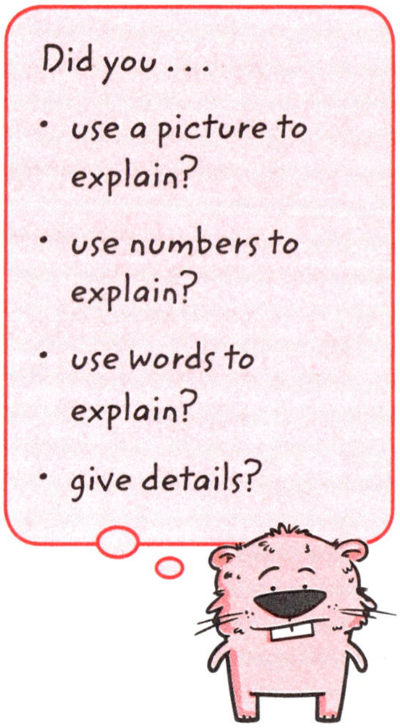

Dear Family,

This week your child is learning to use order and grouping to multiply.

He or she might see a problem like this one.

> Sam has 5 pencil boxes. Each box has 3 packs of pencils. Each pack has 2 pencils. How many pencils does Sam have?

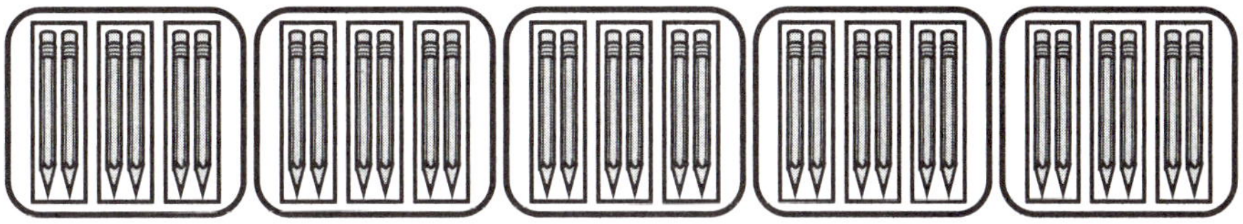

To solve, multiply 5 boxes × 3 packs in each box. That's 15 packs. Then multiply the 15 packs × 2 pencils in each pack. That's 30 pencils.

$$(5 \times 3) \times 2 \longrightarrow 15 \times 2 = 30$$

But what if you don't know how to find 15 × 2? Try changing the order. Multiply two different numbers first.

Multiply 3 packs × 2 pencils in each pack. That's 6 pencils in each box. Then multiply 5 boxes × 6 pencils in each box. That's 30 pencils. The parentheses in the problem below show which numbers you are multiplying first.

$$5 \times (3 \times 2) \longrightarrow 5 \times 6 = 30$$

Invite your child to share what he or she knows about using order and grouping to multiply by doing the following activity together.

NEXT

Activity to Explore Changing the Order of Factors

Materials: 24 pennies, or other small items

Do this activity with your child to demonstrate why changing the order of the factors in a multiplication fact doesn't change the product.

- Count out 12 pennies. Work together to arrange them in an array with 3 rows of 4 pennies in each row.

$3 \times 4 = 12$

- Then arrange the other 12 pennies in an array with 4 rows of 3 pennies in each row.

$4 \times 3 = 12$

- Try again with 2 rows of 6 and then 6 rows of 2.
- Discuss with your child, with questions such as these:
  - Does changing the order of the factors change the number of pennies?
  - Do you think this will always be true?
  - Does changing the order of the factors make either of the related multiplication facts easier for you?

Use Order and Grouping to Multiply

Name: ____________________

Prerequisite: Show Equal Groups with Multiplication

Study the example problem showing a multiplication sentence that represents a picture of equal groups. Then solve problems 1–7.

Example

Sophia has 2 groups of balloons.
Each group has 4 balloons.
Sophia has 2 groups of 4 balloons.
She multiplied to find how many balloons she has altogether.

$2 \times 4 = 8$

Use the picture below to answer problems 1–3.

Luke's Balloons

1. How many groups of balloons does Luke have? _____

2. How many balloons are in each group? _______

3. Write a multiplication sentence to show how many balloons Luke has.

   _______ $\times$ _______ $=$ _______

Vocabulary

multiplication an operation used to find the total number of items when you have equal-sized groups.

Solve.

4 Look at the picture.

How many groups are there? ______

How many dots are in each group? ______

Write a multiplication sentence for the picture.

______ × ______ = ______

5 Write a multiplication sentence for the picture.

______ × ______ = ______

6 Draw a picture that shows 3 × 6 = 18.

7 Mitch has 4 groups of 3 stamps. Draw a picture of the groups and write a multiplication sentence for the picture.

Multiplication sentence: ____________________

Name: ______________________

Use Order to Multiply

Study the example problem showing that the order of the factors doesn't matter when you multiply. Then solve problems 1–6.

Example

Paul has 3 groups of 2 coins. Jill has 2 groups of 3 coins. Who has more coins?

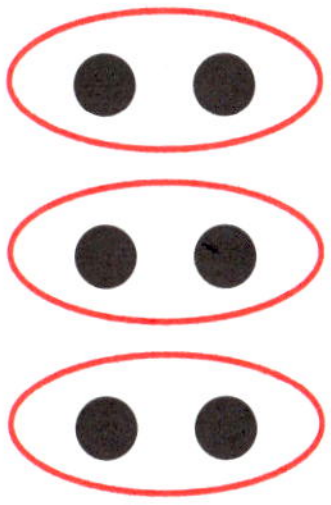

$3 \times 2 = 6$

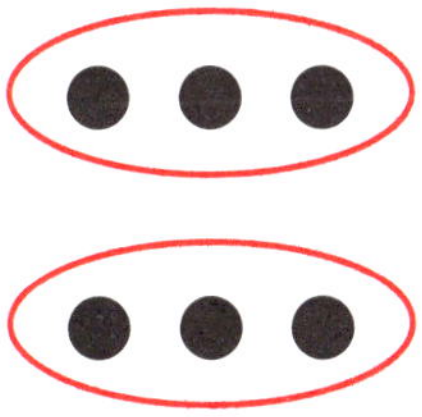

$2 \times 3 = 6$

Paul and Jill have the same number of coins.

1 For each picture, write how many rows there are and how many dots are in each row. Then write a multiplication sentence.

_____ rows

_____ dots in each row

_____ $\times$ _____ $=$ _____

_____ rows

_____ dots in each row

_____ $\times$ _____ $=$ _____

2 You know that $3 \times 9 = 27$. Explain how you know what 9×3 equals.

____

____

____

Vocabulary

factor a number that is multiplied.

$2 \times 5 = 10$

2 and 5 are *factors*.

product the result of multiplication.

$2 \times 5 = 10$

10 is the *product*.

Solve.

3 Daniel colored a grid to show $4 \times 6 = 24$. Color the other grid to show $6 \times 4 = 24$.

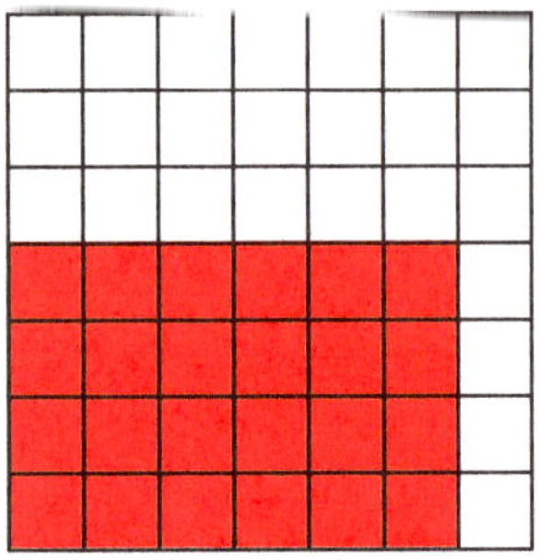

$4 \times 6 = 24$

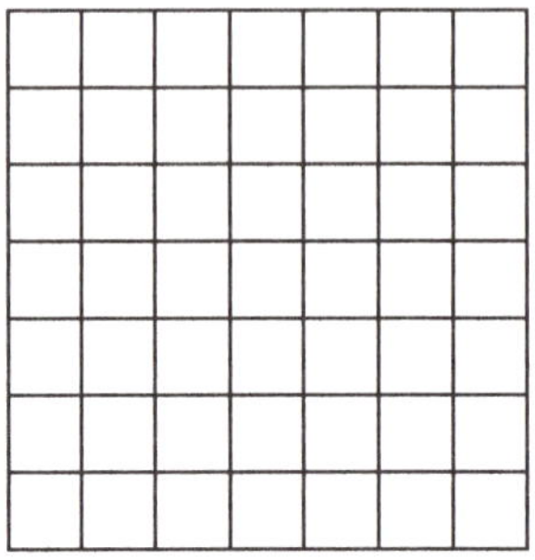

$6 \times 4 = 24$

4 Explain how you know there are the same number of colored squares in both arrays in problem 3.

____

____

____

____

____

5 This array shows $4 \times 3 = 12$. Draw an array that shows $3 \times 4 = 12$.

6 Avery has 3 baskets with 9 flowers in each basket. Ralph has 9 baskets of flowers. If he has the same total number of flowers as Avery, how many flowers does Ralph have in each basket? ______

Name: ______________________

Use Grouping to Multiply

Study the example showing how to use grouping to multiply. Then solve problems 1–9.

Example

Leo makes bracelets. Each bracelet has 5 beads. Leo puts the bracelets in bags. Each bag has 2 bracelets. He used 3 bags. How many beads did he use?

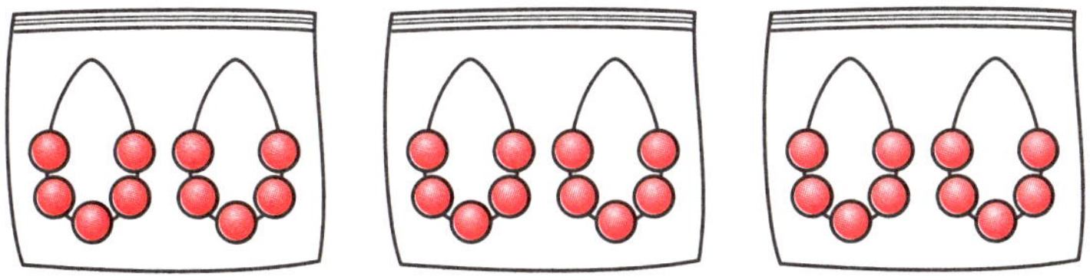

Leo wrote (5 × 2) × 3. He used parentheses to show what numbers he multiplied first.

Leo used 30 beads.

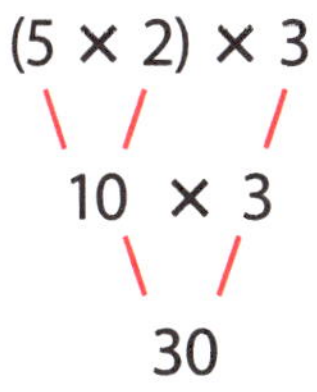

Use the following information to answer problems 1–5.

Kelly also made bracelets. The picture shows the bracelets Kelly made.

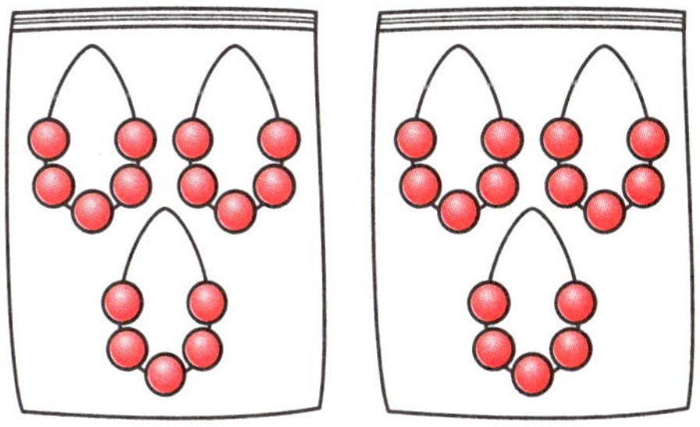

1. How many beads did Kelly put on each bracelet? ______
2. How many bracelets did Kelly put in each bag? ______
3. How many bags did Kelly use? ______
4. How many beads did Kelly use? ______
5. Write a multiplication sentence. Use parentheses to show which numbers you will multiply first.

   ______ × ______ × ______ = ______

Solve.

6 How would you group the numbers to solve $7 \times 2 \times 4$? Why?

____

____

____

7 Addison and Claire chose different ways to multiply $4 \times 5 \times 3$. Addison grouped the numbers like this: $4 \times (5 \times 3)$. She found $5 \times 3 = 15$. Then she multiplied 4×15 by adding $15 + 15 + 15 + 15$ to get 60.

Explain how Claire could have grouped the numbers to multiply. Show the steps she used to find her answer.

____

____

____

8 Show two different ways to group $8 \times 2 \times 3$. Then find the answer.

Solution: ______________________

9 Look at your work in problem 8. Which way of grouping is easier for you? Why?

____

____

____

Name: ____________________

Use Order and Grouping to Multiply

Study the example showing how to use order and grouping to multiply. Then solve problems 1–10.

Example

Rama changes the order and the grouping of numbers to make multiplication easier. What are two different ways Rama could multiply the numbers shown?

$(2 \times 4) \times 6$

8×6

48

$4 \times (6 \times 2)$

4×12

48

Use the numbers on the three number cubes to answer problems 1–4.

1. Order and group the numbers. Then multiply to find the product.

   _______ × _______ × _______ = _______

2. Order and group the numbers a different way. Then multiply to find the product.

   _______ × _______ × _______ = _______

3. Order the factors the same way you did in problem 2. Now, change the grouping with parentheses. Solve.

   _______ × _______ × _______ = _______

4. Which of these three multiplication sentences do you think is easiest to solve? Explain why you think so.

   ____

   ____

Solve.

5 Use the numbers 3, 5, and 2 as factors. Look at some of the ways the factors are ordered and grouped. Fill in missing numbers.

(3 × 5) × _____ = 30 (5 × 2) × _____ = 30 _____ × (3 × 2) = 30

6 Look at problem 5. Multiply the numbers in parentheses first, then fill in the numbers below.

(_____) × _____ = 30 (_____) × _____ = 30 _____ × (_____) = 30

7 Which of the three multiplication sentences in problem 5 is easiest to solve? Why do you think so?

____

____

____

8 Multiply the factors 9, 2, and 2. Choose an order, and use parentheses to show one way to find the product.

Solution: ______________________________________

9 Explain why you chose to order and group the factors the way you did in problem 8.

____

____

10 Multiply the factors 4, 2, and 5. Choose an order, and use parentheses to show one way to find the product. Then show the steps to find the product.

Solution: ______________________________________

Name: ______________________

Use Order and Grouping to Multiply

Solve the problems.

1 A box of yogurt cups has 5 rows with 3 cups in each row. Rose has 3 boxes of yogurt cups.

Write a multiplication sentence to show how many yogurt cups Rose has altogether.

(____ × ____) × ____ = ____

2 Show the easiest way for you to find the product of 2 × 7 × 5. Use parentheses to show how you grouped the numbers. Find the product.

Solution: 2 × 7 × 5 = ______

3 Which of these shows a way to order and group the factors 3, 5, and 6 to find the product? Circle all the correct answers.

A 3 × (5 × 6) = 3 × 30

B (3 × 6) × 5 = 18 × 5

C (5 × 3) × 5 = 15 × 5

D 6 × (3 × 5) = 6 × 15

Solve.

4 There are 3 students on a math team. There are 6 math teams. Each student has 2 pieces of scratch paper. How many pieces of scratch paper are there altogether?

Show your work.

Solution: There are ______ pieces of scratch paper.

5 Xavier knows $7 \times 4 = 28$. What other math fact does this help Xavier remember? Circle the letter of the correct answer.

A $3 \times 4 = 12$

B $7 + 4 = 11$

C $4 \times 7 = 28$

D $28 - 7 = 21$

Anna chose **B** as the correct answer. How did she get that answer?

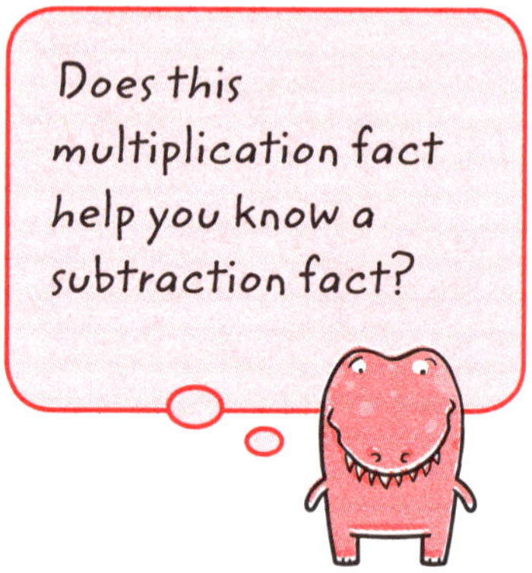

6 If you know that $7 \times 8 = 56$, what other fact does that help you know? Explain why.

Dear Family,

This week your child is learning to split numbers to multiply.

To solve a hard multiplication sentence, you can split one factor, or break it apart into smaller numbers, to make two easier multiplication sentences.

factor: a number that is multiplied

product: the answer to a multiplication problem

Pete planted 6 rows of carrots in his garden. Each row has 4 carrots. How many carrots did Pete plant?

Maybe you don't remember 6×4 but you do know 5×4 and 1×4.

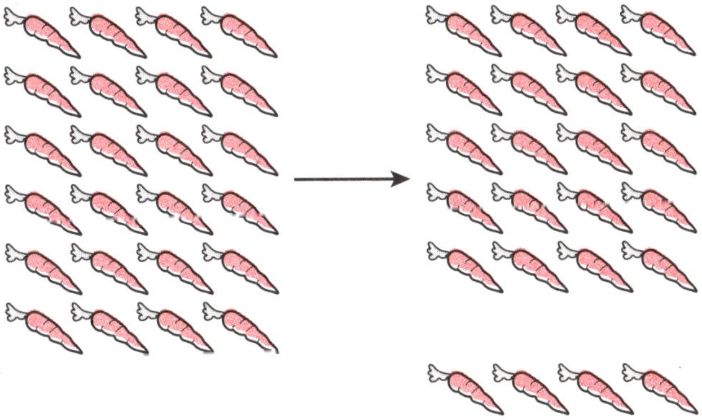

6 rows of 4 carrots is the same as 5 rows of 4 carrots and 1 row of 4 carrots.

$6 \times 4 = (5 \times 4) + (1 \times 4) = 20 + 4 = 24$

Invite your child to share what he or she knows about splitting numbers to multiply by doing the following activity together.

NEXT

Splitting Numbers Activity

Materials: 42 pennies or other small counters, a paper clip, a pencil, and this 2–7 spinner

Do this activity with your child to practice splitting numbers to learn multiplication facts.

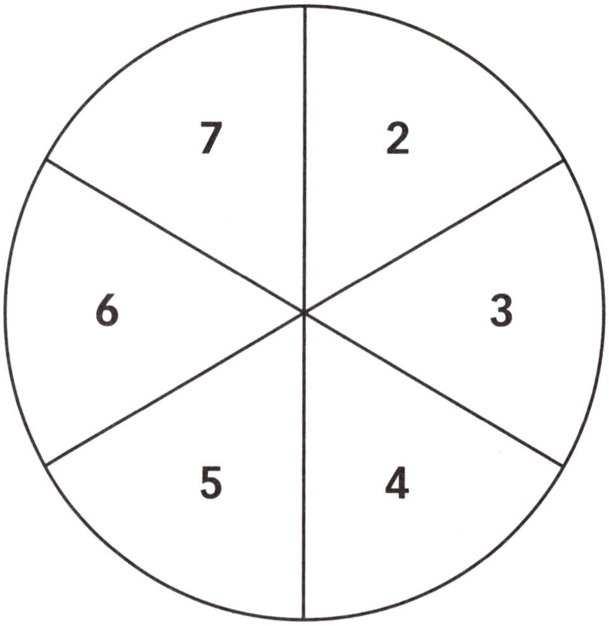

- Put the tip of the pencil through the paper clip at the center of the spinner.
- Have your child spin the spinner twice to determine the number of rows and columns in an array.
- Work together to build the array using the pennies.
- Have your child write the multiplication sentence shown by the array.
  For example: 7×5
- Ask your child to choose where to separate two rows in the array to show breaking apart a factor.
- Have your child write the two multiplication sentences he or she has made by breaking apart the rows in the array.
  For example: $(5 \times 5) + (2 \times 5)$
- Ask your child to find the two products, then add the products to find the answer to the original problem.
  For example: $25 + 10 = 35$
- Together, count the objects in the array to check the answer, then write the multiplication fact.
  For example: $7 \times 5 = 35$.

Lesson 3

Split Numbers to Multiply

Name: ____________________

Prerequisite: Show Multiplication as Equal Groups

Study the example problem showing a multiplication sentence for a picture of equal groups. Then solve problems 1–10.

Example

Elmo has 3 boxes of crayons.
Each box has 4 crayons.
Elmo's boxes show equal groups.
He can write a multiplication sentence to find the total.

$3 \times 4 = 12$ crayons

Shelly has 3 boxes of crayons.
The boxes have 4, 5, and 3 crayons.
Shelly's boxes do not show equal groups.
She cannot write a multiplication sentence to find the total. She has to add.

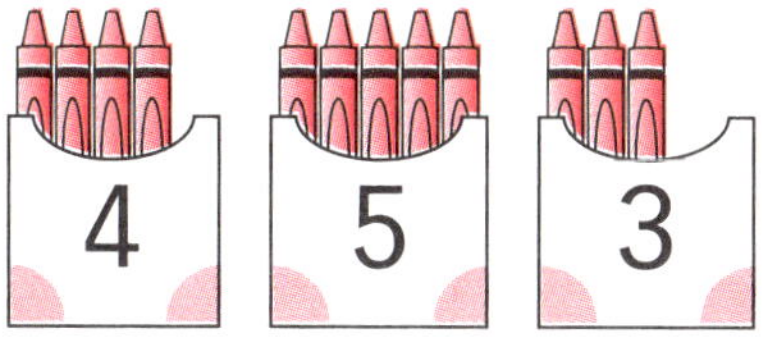

$4 + 5 + 3 = 12$ crayons

Use the picture below to answer problems 1–3.

Angie's crayons

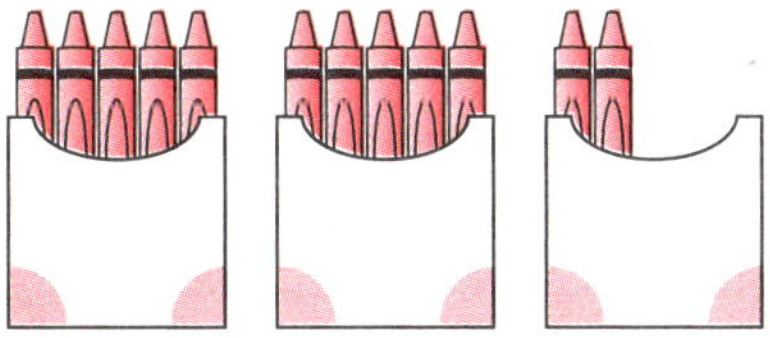

1 How many boxes of crayons does Angie have? _____

2 How many crayons are in each box? ____________

3 How many crayons does Angie have altogether? Can you write a multiplication sentence to find the total? Explain.

____

____

____

Solve.

Use the picture below to answer problems 4–6.

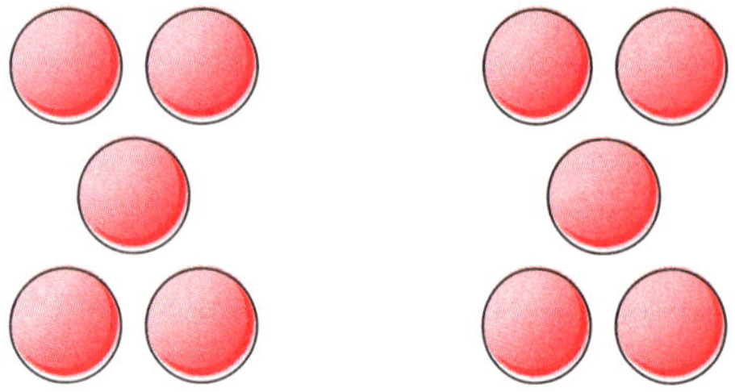

4 How many groups are there? _____

5 How many balls are there in each group? _____

6 Write a multiplication sentence to show how many balls there are altogether.

_____ × _____ = _____

Use the picture below to answer problems 7–9.

7 How many rows are in this array? _____

8 How many squares are in each row? _____

9 Write a multiplication sentence to show how many squares there are altogether.

_____ × _____ = _____

10 Draw an array for the multiplication sentence $2 \times 4 = 8$.

Name: ______________________

Break Apart Numbers to Multiply

Study the example problem showing how to break apart a number to multiply. Then solve problems 1–7.

Example

Owen has 8 bags of plums. There are 3 plums in each bag. How many plums does Owen have altogether?

$8 \times 3 = ?$

You might break apart the 8 into 4 and 4.

Multiply each part by 3.

Then, add the two products.
$12 + 12 = 24$.

So $8 \times 3 = 24$.

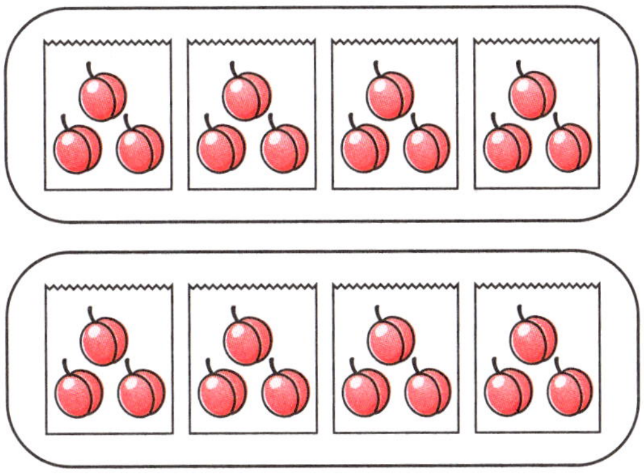

$4 \times 3 = 12$

$4 \times 3 = 12$

1 How many rows and columns are in the array? Fill in the blanks.

_____ rows and _____ columns.

2 Circle rows to break apart the array into two parts.

3 Write multiplication sentences to show the total for each part of the array.

_____ × _____ = _____   _____ × _____ = _____

4 How can you use your answer to problem 3 to find the product of 7 × 6? Explain.

____

____

____

____

Solve.

5 Draw a line to the pair of multiplication sentences that can be used to solve each problem.

$8 \times 4 = ?$	$5 \times 7 = 35$ $3 \times 7 = 21$
$3 \times 9 = ?$	$6 \times 5 = 30$ $6 \times 2 = 12$
$6 \times 7 = ?$	$3 \times 5 = 15$ $3 \times 4 = 12$
$8 \times 7 = ?$	$5 \times 8 = 40$ $4 \times 8 = 32$
$9 \times 8 = ?$	$5 \times 4 = 20$ $3 \times 4 = 12$

6 Draw an array to show 6×4.

7 Circle rows to break the array in two parts. Show how to use the parts to find 6×4.

Name: ____________________

Use Grouping to Multiply

Study the example showing how to break apart a factor to multiply. Then solve problems 1–7.

Example

Grace gives grapes to 6 friends. She gives each friend 7 grapes. How many grapes does Grace share altogether?

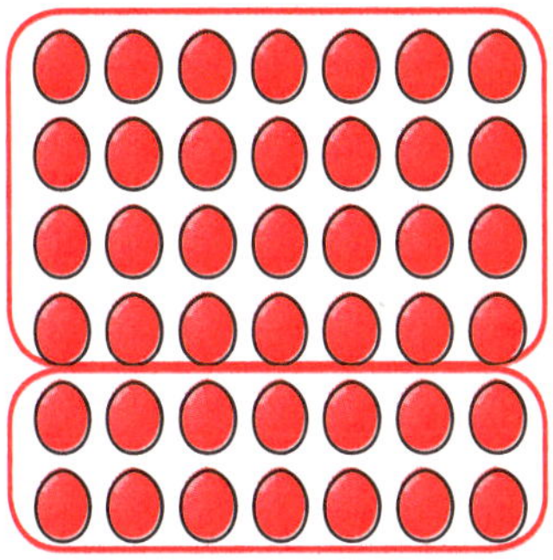

$6 \times 7 = ?$

You might break apart the 6 into $4 + 2$.

Multiply each part by 7. $(4 \times 7) + (2 \times 7) = ?$

Then, add the two products. $28 + 14 = 42$.

So $6 \times 7 = 42$.

Tony has 8 boxes of toy cars. Each box has 6 cars in it.

1 Write a multiplication sentence for this story.

_______ × _______ = ?

2 To help you find 8×6, you might break apart the 8 into 5 and 3. Write the two multiplication problems this would give you.

_______ × 6 = _______

_______ × 6 = _______

3 Add the two products in problem 2. How many toy cars does Tony have?

____

____

Solve.

4 Ron drew this array. What multiplication sentence can he solve using this array?

_____ × _____ = ?

5 Circle rows or columns to break the array into 2 parts. Then fill in the blanks to show how to use the parts to find the answer to problem 4.

6 × 6 = (_____ × 6) + (_____ × 6).

So, 6 × 6 = _____ + _____.

So, 6 × 6 = _____.

6 Write the multiplication sentence you solved in problems 4 and 5. How can you use that answer to find the product of 6 × 9? Explain.

_____ × _____ = _____

____

____

____

7 Draw a line from each box to the multiplication fact it could help you find.

	7 × 7 = 49
(2 × 5) + (6 × 5)	
	8 × 5 = 40
(2 × 8) + (5 × 8)	
	6 × 8 = 48
(2 × 7) + (5 × 7)	
	7 × 8 = 56

Name: ____________________

Break Apart Numbers to Multiply

Solve the problems.

1 Finn has 7 bags of marbles. Each bag has 3 marbles. Show one way to break apart the 7 to multiply. Then find the total number of marbles.

2 Tawny breaks apart 9 to solve 9×5. Show one way Tawny can do this. Then solve the problem.

3 Which of these are ways you can break apart a factor to solve 6×3? Circle all the correct answers.

A $3 \times 3 = 9$ and $3 \times 3 = 9$

B $4 \times 3 = 12$ and $2 \times 3 = 6$

C $6 \times 2 = 12$ and $4 \times 3 = 12$

D $6 \times 1 = 6$ and $6 \times 2 = 12$

Solve.

4 Sandy wants to multiply 7×5. She breaks apart the 7 into 4 and 3. What is Sandy's next step? Circle the letter of the correct answer.

A $7 \times 4 = 28$ and $7 \times 3 = 21$

B $7 \times 5 = 35$ and $5 \times 4 = 20$

C $4 \times 5 = 20$ and $3 \times 5 = 15$

D $4 \times 3 = 12$ and $7 \times 5 = 35$

Mitch chose **A** as the correct answer. How did he get that answer?

____

____

____

5 Tia solved 9×7 by breaking apart 7 into 5 and 2. Fill in the blanks to show how she did it.

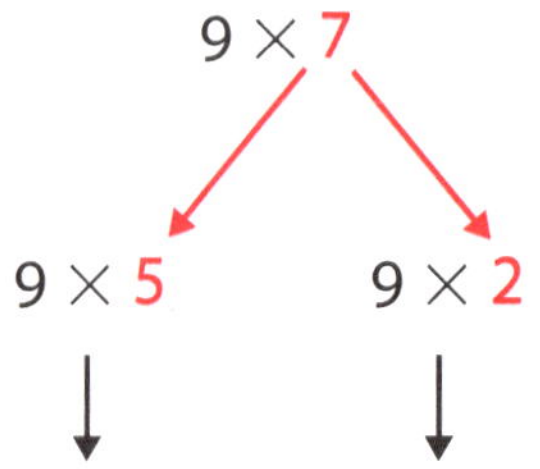

45 + _____ = _____

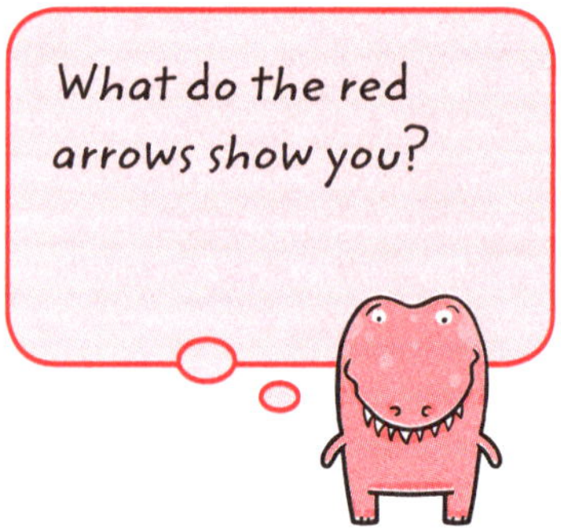

6 Look at problem 5. Show a different way to break apart factors to solve the problem.

Dear Family,

This week your child is exploring the meaning of division.

When you divide, you separate a group of objects into smaller, equal-sized groups.

You can use division to find the number in each group.

Betsy has 6 stickers. She puts the same number of stickers on 3 different pages. How many stickers are on each page?

The picture shows that 6 stickers grouped equally onto 3 pages is 2 stickers on each page.

Divide: $6 \div 3 = 2$.

Other times you know how many objects you want in each group, and you use division to find how many groups you can make.

Betsy has 15 flowers she wants to group into bunches of 5. How many bunches of flowers can she make?

If she puts 15 flowers into bunches of 5 she makes 3 bunches.

Divide: $15 \div 5 = 3$.

Invite your child to share what he or she knows about the meaning of division by doing the following activity together.

NEXT

Activity to Explore the Meaning of Division

Materials: 12 of one kind of item, such as socks, spoons, or coins

Help your child understand the meaning of division with this activity.

- Collect 12 of one item, such as socks.
- Have your child divide the 12 items into 3 equal groups. One way to approach this is to think about "dealing" the socks into 3 piles, one at a time, until all the socks are gone.
- Ask your child to tell what he or she did. For example, "I put 12 socks into 3 equal groups. Each group got 4 socks."
- Then ask your child to write or say the division sentence. *($12 \div 3 = 4$)*
- Then have your child divide the 12 items into groups with 3 in each group. Ask him or her to tell how many groups were formed, and write or say the division sentence.
- Repeat the exercise, dividing the 12 items into 6 equal groups, and then dividing into groups with 2 items each. Each time have your child describe what he or she did, and write or say the division equation.

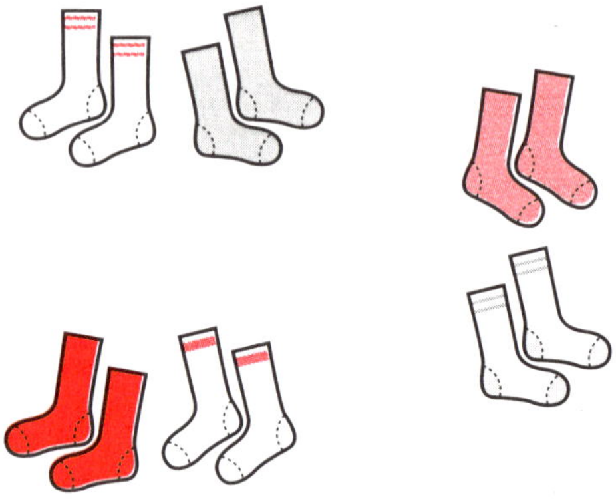

Lesson 4

Understand the Meaning of Division

Name: ____________________

Prerequisite: How can you make equal groups?

Study the example problem showing equal groups and unequal groups. Then solve problems 1–6.

Example

Caroline has 12 keys. She has 3 key chains.
She puts the same number of keys on each key chain.

Caroline puts 4 keys on each key chain.

1 Danny puts his keys on key chains.

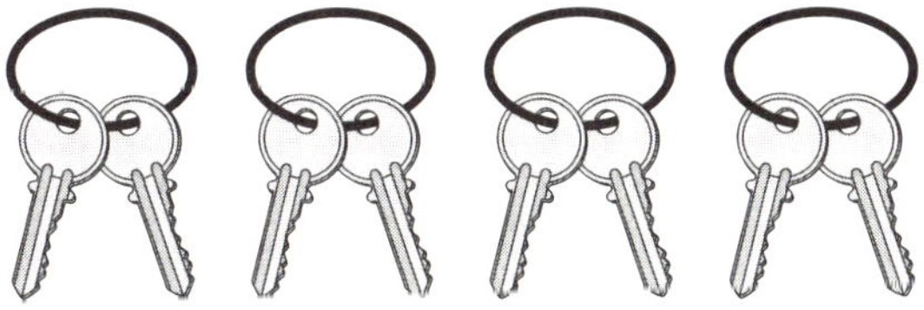

There are ______ keys in all.

There are ______ groups of keys.

There are ______ keys in each group.

2 Maren puts her keys on key chains.

There are ______ keys in all.

There are ______ groups of keys.

There are ______ keys in each group.

Solve.

3 Rita has 10 pens. She puts them in 2 boxes. Each box has the same number of pens. Draw Rita's pens in the 2 boxes.

4 Look at your drawing for problem 3. How many pens are in each box? ______

5 Explain how you could find the answer to problem 4 without using your drawing.

____

____

____

____

6 Fritz drew an array with 5 rows of dots. He drew 15 dots altogether. How many dots are in each row of Fritz's array? How do you know?

____

____

____

____

Name: ______________________

Use Equal Groups to Think About Division

Study the example problem with a division sentence that represents equal groups. Then solve problems 1–8.

Example

Emily picks 15 apples from her tree. She has 3 baskets. She puts an equal number of apples in each basket. How many apples does Emily put in each basket?

There are 15 apples in 3 baskets. Each basket has 5 apples.

$15 \div 3 = 5$

Use the picture of frogs on logs to answer problems 1–4.

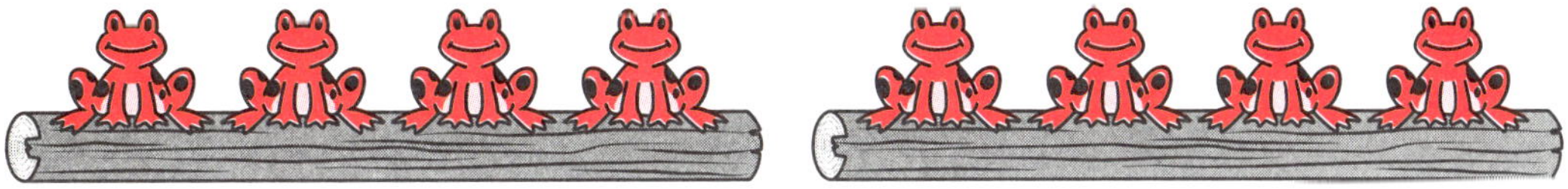

1. How many frogs are there in all? ______

2. How many logs are there? ______

3. How many frogs are on each log? ______

4. Write a division sentence about the 8 frogs in 2 equal groups.

   ______ ÷ ______ = ______

Solve.

5 A class has 20 students. The teacher divides them into teams of 4 students. How many teams are there? Draw a picture.

Solution: ______________________________

6 Parker said that the array of 18 rectangles shows the division problem 6 ÷ 3. What is her mistake?

____

____

____

____

____

7 Evan has 30 trading cards. He puts them in stacks that each have 5 cards. Write a division sentence to find the number of stacks.

_______ ÷ _______ = _______

8 Explain what each number in your division sentence from problem 7 represents.

____

____

____

____

Name: ______________________

Reason and Write

Study the problem. Underline the parts that you think make it a particularly good answer and a helpful example.

Example

Laura has 2 quilts. The quilts are made of cloth squares sewn together in an array.

- The red quilt has 24 squares, with 4 squares in each row.
- The blue quilt has 30 squares, with 6 squares in each row.

Which quilt has more rows of squares?

Use pictures, words, or numbers to explain how you got your answer.

Since the rows are all equal groups, I can use division to find out how many rows each quilt has.

Red quilt

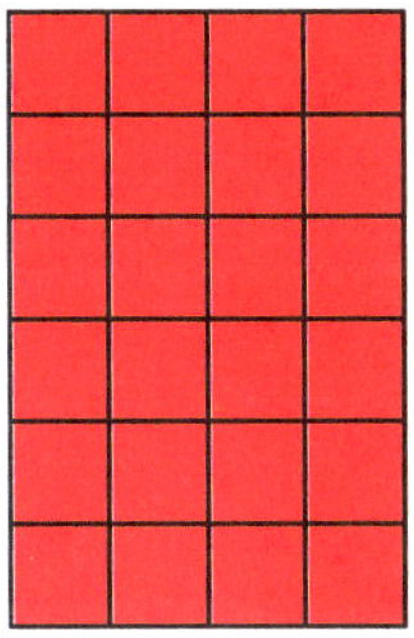

To find out how many rows the red quilt has I found $24 \div 4$. I know $4 \times 6 = 24$, so $24 \div 4 = 6$. The red quilt has 6 rows.

I checked my math by drawing a picture of a quilt with 4 squares in each row. I drew 6 rows, and that made 24 squares.

Then I found $30 \div 6$ to find out how many rows are in the blue quilt. I know $6 \times 5 = 30$, so $30 \div 6 = 5$. The blue quilt has 5 rows.

Blue quilt

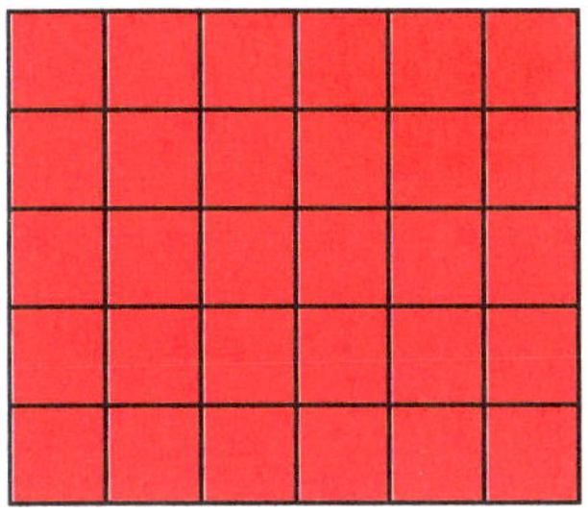

I checked my math by drawing rows of 6 squares. When I had drawn 5 rows, I had 30 squares.

Since the red quilt has 6 rows and the blue quilt has only 5 rows, the red quilt has more rows.

Where does the example . . .

- use numbers to explain?
- use words to explain?
- use pictures to explain?
- answer the question?

Solve the problem. Use what you learned from the example.

John is setting up chairs at tables for a party.
The round tables will have 6 chairs each, with 18 chairs altogether.
The square tables will have 4 chairs each, with 20 chairs altogether.
Are there more round tables or square tables?

Use pictures, words, or numbers to explain how you got your answer.

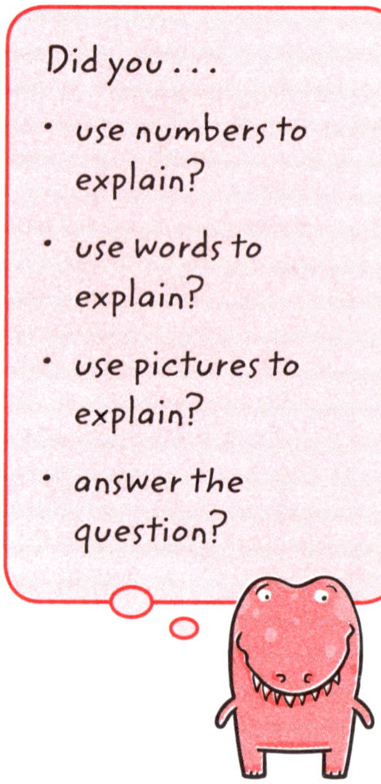

Dear Family,

This week your child is exploring how multiplication and division are related.

Multiplication and division can both describe problems where there are equal groups. Either one can be used to solve a problem like this:

> Lola buys 16 apples. She puts the same number of apples in 4 bags. How many apples does she put in each bag?

You know the total (16 apples) and the number of groups (4 bags). You need to find the number in each group.

A multiplication equation for the problem is

$4 \times \square = 16$

$4 \times 4 = 16$

A division equation for the problem is

$16 \div 4 = \square$

$16 \div 4 = 4$

Lola puts 4 apples in each bag.

Invite your child to share what he or she knows about how multiplication and division are related by doing the following activity together.

NEXT

Multiplication and Division Activity

Materials: a collection of 12 to 20 small items such as pennies, toothpicks, or toy bricks

Do this activity with your child to demonstrate how multiplication and division are related.

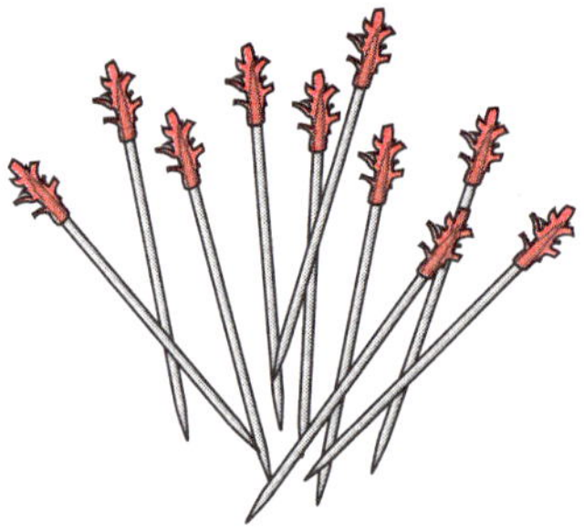

- Collect a set of small items such as toothpicks. Act out problems like the one below.
- For example, count out 10 toothpicks. Ask your child to consider the question, *How many toothpicks will be in each pile if I put these 10 toothpicks into 2 equal piles?*
- Ask him or her to write both a multiplication sentence and a division sentence for the problem.

  ($2 \times \square = 10$ and $10 \div 2 = \square$)
- Then have your child group the toothpicks into 2 equal groups to find how many are in each, and fill in the blanks in the number sentences above. ($2 \times 5 = 10$ and $10 \div 2 = 5$)

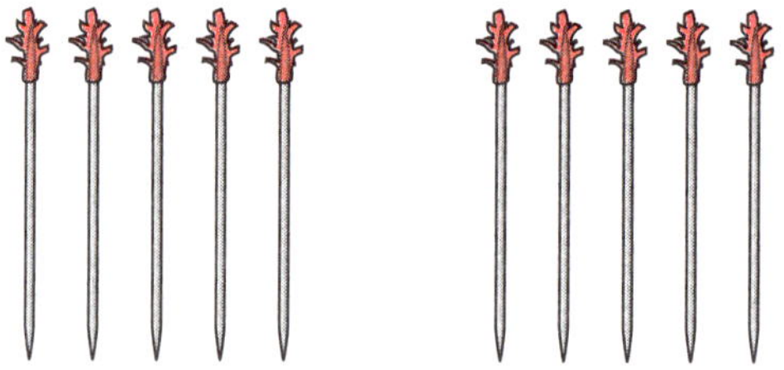

- Repeat, but invite your child to give you a problem. Write a multiplication sentence and a division sentence, and have your child check your work.
- After three or four examples, see if your child can talk to you about how multiplication and division are alike. Look for an understanding that both operations can represent equal groups.

Understand How Multiplication and Division Are Connected

Name: ____________________

Prerequisite: How do multiplication and division use equal groups?

Study the example showing a multiplication and a division sentence for equal groups. Then solve problems 1–9.

Example

2 groups of 5 fish

$2 \times 5 = 10$

10 fish put into 2 equal groups

$10 \div 2 = 5$

Fill in the blanks.

1 _____ groups of _____ birds

_____ × _____ = _____

2 _____ birds put into _____ equal groups

_____ ÷ _____ = _____

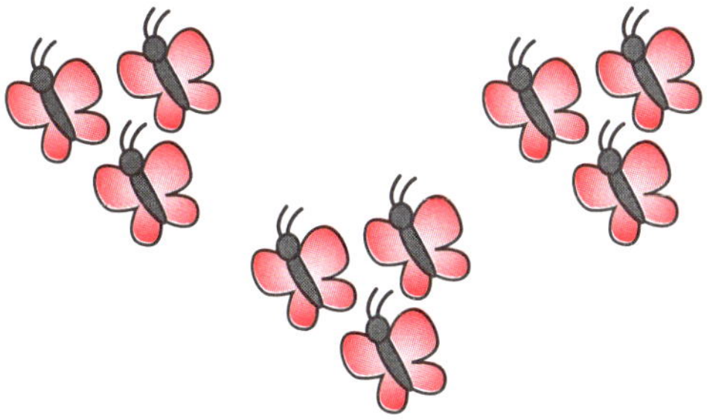

3 Write a multiplication sentence to describe the groups of butterflies.

____

4 Write a division sentence to describe the groups of butterflies.

____

Solve.

5 Which number sentences best show the arrangement of the cans of tennis balls? Circle your choice.

$6 + 3 = 9$	$9 \times 2 = 18$	$6 \times 3 = 18$
$9 - 3 = 6$	$18 \div 2 = 9$	$18 \div 6 = 3$

6 Look at the array. Multiply to tell how many in all.

$6 \times 3 =$ _____ or $3 \times 6 =$ _____

7 Draw a picture to show 15 cookies divided into 3 equal groups.

8 Write a division sentence for problem 7.

____

9 Write a multiplication sentence for problem 7.

____

Vocabulary

divide separate into equal groups.

array a set of objects arranged in equal rows and equal columns.

Name: ______________________

Explore How Multiplication and Division Are Connected

Study the example that shows one way to think about multiplication and division together. Then solve problems 1–13.

Example

Marta baked 15 muffins. She puts an equal number of muffins in 3 baskets.

She thinks, 3 times what number equals 15?

$3 \times ? = 15$

$3 \times \mathbf{5} = 15$

So, Marta puts 5 muffins in each basket.

1 Draw an array of 15 muffins in 3 rows.

2 How many muffins did you put in each row? _____

3 Fill in the blanks to write a division sentence for the array you drew.

_____ ÷ _____ = _____

Use the array to complete the number sentences.

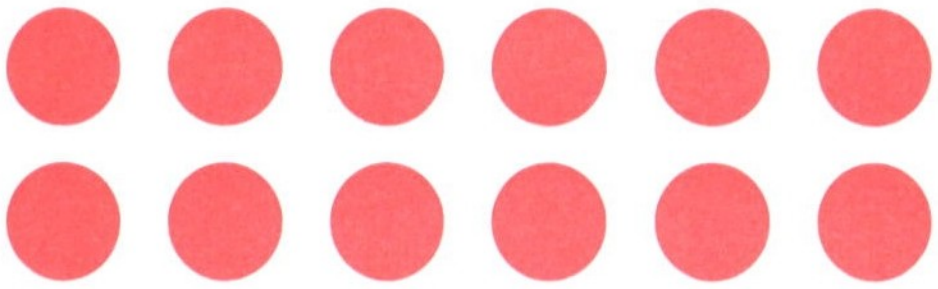

4 $2 \times$ _____ $= 12$ and $12 \div 2 =$ _____

5 $6 \times$ _____ $= 12$ and $12 \div 6 =$ _____

Vocabulary

divide separate into equal groups.

array a set of objects arranged in equal rows and equal columns.

Solve.

Use the numbers 3, 6, and 18 to write an equation for each problem.

6 There are 18 fish. Each bowl holds 6 fish.

What number sentence shows the number of bowls?

_____ _____ _____ = _____

7 There are 18 fish. An equal number of fish are in 3 bowls.

What number sentence shows the number of fish in each bowl?

_____ _____ _____ = _____

8 There are 3 bowls. 6 fish are in each bowl.

What number sentence shows the total number of fish?

_____ _____ _____ = _____

9 There are 6 fish in each bowl. There are 3 bowls.

What number sentence shows the total number of fish?

_____ _____ _____ = _____

This array shows that $6 \times 7 = 42$. Use this fact to complete the number sentences.

10 $6 \times 7 =$ _____ $7 \times 6 =$ _____

11 $6 \times$ _____ $= 42$ $42 =$ _____ $\times 6$

12 $42 \div 6 =$ _____ $42 \div$ _____ $= 6$

13 _____ $= 42 \div 7$ $7 = 42 \div$ _____

Name: ____________________

Reason and Write

Study the example. Underline two parts that you think make it a particularly good answer and a helpful example.

Example

This fact family has four facts.

$4 \times 3 = 12$	$12 \div 3 = 4$
$3 \times 4 = 12$	$12 \div 4 = 3$

Tell why there are four facts in this family. Is it true that there are four facts in every fact family?

Show your work. Use pictures, words, or numbers to explain your answer.

It is false. Most fact families have four different facts, but not all do. The picture below shows that you can turn the 4 × 3 rectangle on its side to make a rectangle to show 3 × 4.

4 × 3

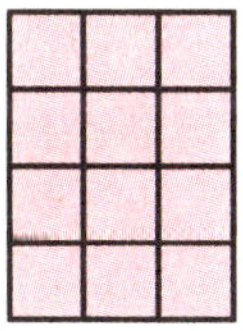

3 × 4

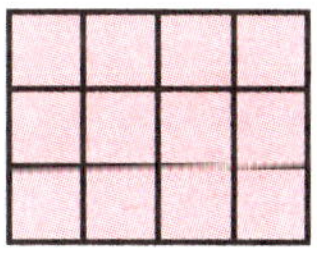

The two multiplication facts in this family are 4 × 3 and 3 × 4. Each multiplication fact has a division fact, so that's 4 facts in all.

But if both the factors are the same, there is only one multiplication fact. For example, 3 × 3 = 9. When you turn a 3 × 3 rectangle it on its side, it's still 3 × 3. It's not a new fact. The only related division fact is 9 ÷ 3 = 3. This family of facts has only 2 facts, so it is not true that every fact family has 4 facts.

3 × 3

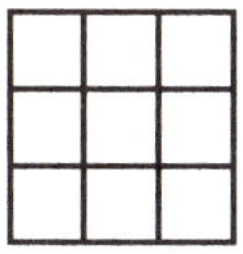

3 × 3

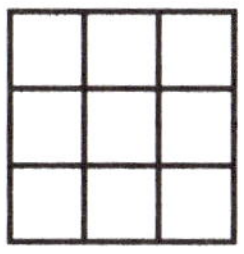

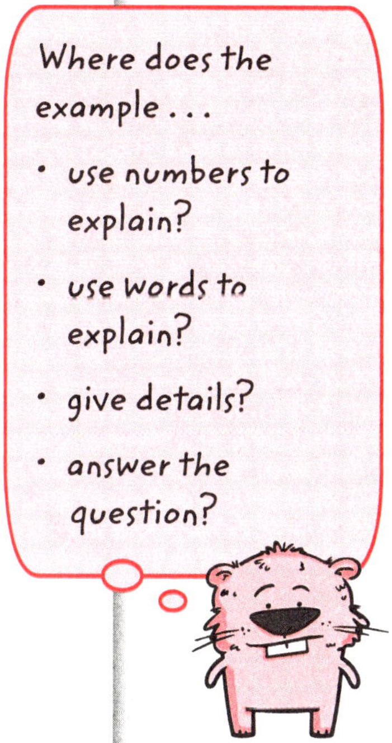

Solve the problem. Use what you learned from the model.

These are related multiplication facts.

$3 \times 5 = 15$	$5 \times 3 = 15$

Is it true that if you know two related multiplication facts, you can find two related division facts?

Show your work. Use pictures, words, or numbers to explain your answer.

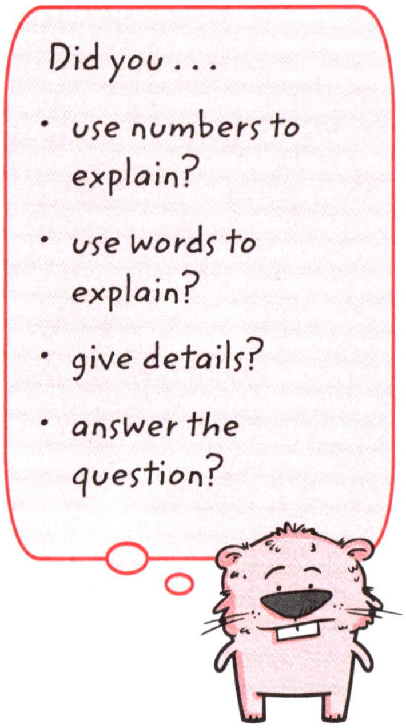

Dear Family,

This week your child is learning about multiplication and division fact families.

Fact Families are sets of related multiplication and division facts. Here is one example:

$3 \times 7 = 21 \qquad 7 \times 3 = 21 \qquad 21 \div 3 = 7 \qquad 21 \div 7 = 3$

Knowing about fact families can help you sometimes when you are trying to solve a problem. If you know the answer to any one of these, you know the answer to all of them.

$30 \div 5 = \square \qquad 30 \div \square = 5 \qquad 5 \times \square = 30 \qquad \square \times 5 = 30$

You might remember that $5 \times 6 = 30$. Then you also know $30 \div 5 = 6$, $30 \div 6 = 5$, and $6 \times 5 = 30$.

Your child may use a **multiplication table** to help learn multiplication facts.

This multiplication table shows all the facts up to 10×10. The numbers that are circled show that $5 \times 6 = 30$.

Invite your child to share what he or she knows about multiplication and division fact families by doing the following activity together.

×	**0**	**1**	**2**	**3**	**4**	**5**	**6**	**7**	**8**	**9**
0	0	0	0	0	0	0	0	0	0	0
1	0	1	2	3	4	5	6	7	8	9
2	0	2	4	6	8	10	12	14	16	18
3	0	3	6	9	12	15	18	21	24	27
4	0	4	8	12	16	20	24	28	32	36
5	0	5	10	15	20	25	30	35	40	45
6	0	6	12	18	24	30	36	42	48	54
7	0	7	14	21	28	35	42	49	56	63
8	0	8	16	24	32	40	48	56	64	72
9	0	9	18	27	36	45	54	63	72	81

NEXT

Fact Family Activity

Materials: scissors, index cards, and pencil (optional)

Play this game to practice recognizing facts that are in the same family.

Create fact family cards by cutting out the facts below, or by writing the facts on index cards.

- Each player chooses one of the single-number cards (42 or 56) and places it face-up in front of him or her. Shuffle the fact cards. Place them face-down in 2 rows with 4 cards in each row.
- Players take turns flipping over two cards.
  - If *both* the cards are in the same fact family as the number card, then the player keeps the cards.
  - If either of the cards is *not* in the same fact family as the player's number card, then put both cards face down in a discard pile.
  - Reshuffle the discard pile as needed.
- The first player to find the 4 cards that make a fact family that goes with his or her number card wins.

$8 \times 7 = 56$	$7 \times 8 = 56$	$56 \div 8 = 7$	
$56 \div 7 = 8$	$7 \times 6 = 42$	$6 \times 7 = 42$	
$42 \div 7 = 6$	$42 \div 6 = 7$	56	42

Multiplication and Division Facts

Name: ______________________

Prerequisite: Write Multiplication and Division Sentences

Study the example problem showing how to write multiplication and division sentences for arrays. Then solve problems 1–8.

Example

There are 12 eggs in the carton.
They are arranged in an array.

There are 2 equal rows.
There are 6 eggs in each row.

$2 \times 6 = 12$ $\qquad$ $12 \div 2 = 6$

1 Look at the division sentences from the box. Write two division sentences under each array.

_____ ÷ _____ = _____ $\qquad$ _____ ÷ _____ = _____

_____ ÷ _____ = _____ $\qquad$ _____ ÷ _____ = _____

Division Sentences

$20 \div 4 = 5$

$15 \div 5 = 3$

$15 \div 3 = 5$

$20 \div 5 = 4$

2 Write two multiplication sentences that could help you find the quotients in problem 1.

$4 \times 5 =$ _____

$5 \times$ _____ $=$ _____

Vocabulary

quotient the result of division.

Choose a multiplication sentence from the box for each story.

Number Sentences
$3 \times 5 = 15$
$20 \div 4 = 5$
$5 \times 4 = 20$
$15 \div 3 = 5$

3 Paige buys 5 packs of toys. There are 4 toys in each pack. How many toys are there altogether?

_____ × _____ = _____

4 Max has 3 bags. There are 5 toys in each bag. How many toys does he have altogether?

_____ × _____ = _____

Choose a division sentence from the box for each story.

5 Rodney shares 20 strawberries evenly with 4 people. How many does each person get?

_____ ÷ _____ = _____

6 Dan has 15 baseballs and 3 bags. He puts an equal number of balls in each bag. How many balls are in each bag?

_____ ÷ _____ = _____

Solve.

7 You know that $7 \times 8 = 56$. Use the numbers 7, 8, and 56 to solve related multiplication and division facts.

$7 \times 8 =$ _____ $56 \div 8 =$ _____

$8 \times 7 =$ _____ $56 \div 7 =$ _____

8 You know that $9 \times 6 = 54$. Use the numbers 9, 6, and 54 to fill in the blanks in these related facts.

$9 \times$ _____ $= 54$ $54 \div 6 =$ _____

$6 \times$ _____ $= 54$ _____ $\div 9 = 6$

Name: ______________________

Work with Division Facts

Study the example that shows how a drawing can help you understand division facts. Then solve problems 1–9.

Here is an array of 15 fish.

There are 3 rows with 5 fish in each row.

The fact family describes the array in different ways.

$3 \times 5 = 15$ $15 \div 5 = 3$

$5 \times 3 = 15$ $15 \div 3 = 5$

Write one of the facts from the list above that can help you answer each question.

1 How many fish are there altogether?

____

2 15 fish swim in 3 equal rows. How many fish are in each row?

____

3 15 fish swim in rows of 5 fish. How many rows of fish are there?

____

4 You know that $4 \times 9 = 36$. Write the whole fact family. Use the numbers 4, 9, and 36.

____ × ____ = ____

____ × ____ = ____

____ ÷ ____ = ____

____ ÷ ____ = ____

Vocabulary

multiplication and division fact family a group of related multiplication and division number sentences that use the same numbers.

Solve.

5 Sienna draws 18 squares in two equal groups of 9. Choose the division sentence her drawing shows.

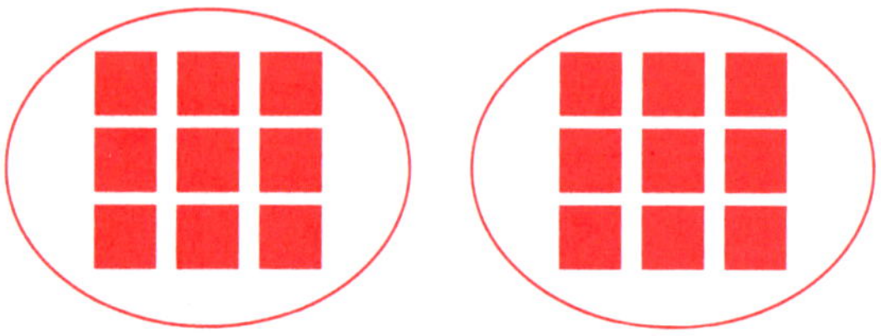

A 9 ÷ 3 = 3

B 18 ÷ 6 = 3

C 18 ÷ 2 = 9

D 6 ÷ 2 = 3

6 Write two different division sentences about the array.

_____ ÷ _____ = _____

_____ ÷ _____ = _____

Chee has 24 trading cards. He gives away all his cards to friends. He gives 8 cards to each friend.

7 Draw a picture to show Chee's cards in groups of 8.

8 Write two different division facts for the story.

__________________ and __________________

9 Write the multiplication facts that belong to the same fact family.

__________________ and __________________

Name: ______________________

Use a Multiplication Table to Solve Problems

Study the example that shows how a multiplication table can help you solve multiplication and division problems. Then solve problems 1–6.

Example

You can use the multiplication table to multiply or divide.

Look at the pink row of products for 4.
Look at the pink column of products for 6.

You can see how 6 × 4 = 24 is related to 24 ÷ 4 = 6 and related to 24 ÷ 6 = 4.

×	0	1	2	3	4	5	6	7	8	9
0	0	0	0	0	0	0	0	0	0	0
1	0	1	2	3	4	5	6	7	8	9
2	0	2	4	6	8	10	12	14	16	18
3	0	3	6	9	12	15	18	21	24	27
4	0	4	8	12	16	20	24	28	32	36
5	0	5	10	15	20	25	30	35	40	45
6	0	6	12	18	24	30	36	42	48	54
7	0	7	14	21	28	35	42	49	56	63
8	0	8	16	24	32	40	48	56	64	72
9	0	9	18	27	36	45	54	63	72	81

1 Write the fact family for the three numbers 6, 4, and 24.

_____ × _____ = _____   _____ ÷ _____ = _____

_____ × _____ = _____   _____ ÷ _____ = _____

2 Use the table or your fact family in problem 1 to fill in the missing numbers.

4 × _____ = 24   24 ÷ 6 = _____

_____ × 4 = 24   _____ ÷ 4 = 6

3 Find 21 on the table above. Use the table to fill in the missing numbers in this fact family.

7 × _____ = 21   21 ÷ 3 = _____

_____ × 7 = 21   21 ÷ _____ = 3

Vocabulary

multiplication and division fact family a group of related multiplication and division number sentences that use the same numbers.

Use the multiplication table to answer the questions.

×	0	1	2	3	4	5	6	7	8	9
0	0	0	0	0	0	0	0	0	0	0
1	0	1	2	3	4	5	6	7	8	9
2	0	2	4	6	8	10	12	14	16	18
3	0	3	6	9	12	15	18	21	24	27
4	0	4	8	12	16	20	24	28	32	36
5	0	5	10	15	20	25	30	35	40	45
6	0	6	12	18	24	30	36	42	48	54
7	0	7	14	21	28	35	42	49	56	63
8	0	8	16	24	32	40	48	56	64	72
9	0	9	18	27	36	45	54	63	72	81

4 What are the three numbers in the fact family for 28 ÷ 4? ______________________

Write the fact family.

_____ × _____ = _____   _____ ÷ _____ = _____

_____ × _____ = _____   _____ ÷ _____ = _____

5 What are the three numbers in the fact family for 6 × _____ = 42? ________________

Write the fact family.

_____ × _____ = _____   _____ ÷ _____ = _____

_____ × _____ = _____   _____ ÷ _____ = _____

6 What are the three numbers in the fact family for _____ ÷ 6 = 8? ________________

Write the fact family.

_____ × _____ = _____   _____ ÷ _____ = _____

_____ × _____ = _____   _____ ÷ _____ = _____

Name: ______________________________

Solve Problems with Multiplication and Division Facts

Solve the problems.

1 Circle the letter of the correct answer. Which fact can you use to solve $8 = 32 \div$ ______?

A $4 \times 8 = 32$

B $8 \times 8 = 64$

C $8 + 32 = 40$

D $32 - 8 = 24$

Anu chose **D** as the correct answer. How did he get that answer?

____

____

____

____

____

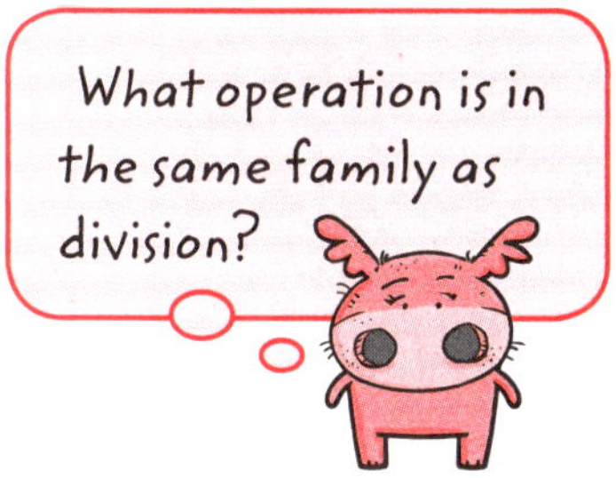

2 Mr. Smith is serving lunch. He has 30 carrot sticks to share evenly among 6 people. Which facts can be used to find how many carrot sticks each person gets? Circle the letter for all that apply.

A $3 \times 10 = 30$

B $30 \div 5 = 6$

C $6 \times 5 = 30$

D $30 \div 3 = 10$

E $30 = 5 \times 6$

3 Cross out the fact that is not in the same fact family as the others.

$2 \times 5 = 10$ $\quad$ $2 \times 10 = 20$ $\quad$ $10 \div 5 = 2$

$10 \div 2 = 5$ $\quad$ $10 = 5 \times 2$

Solve.

4 Write the fact family for these 3 numbers: 8, 9, 72.

____ $\times$ ____ $=$ ____   ____ $\div$ ____ $=$ ____

____ $\times$ ____ $=$ ____   ____ $\div$ ____ $=$ ____

If you know one fact, you can use it to find the other facts in a family.

5 Write the fact family for these 3 numbers: 5, 5, 25.

____

____

There is something different about this fact family.

6 Movie tickets cost $6 each for children. The Mendez family has 4 children. Which equation can you use to find out how much it will cost for the Mendez children to go to the movie? Circle the letter for the correct answer.

A $4 \times 5 =$ ____   **C** $4 \times 6 =$ ____

B $24 \div 4 =$ ____   **D** $6 - 4 =$ ____

What numbers will you need to find the total cost?

7 Russell has a box with 35 cat treats. He gives the cats 5 treats a day. Write a fact that can help him figure out how many days the box of treats will last.

I might skip count by 5s to figure this out.

How many days will the treats last? ____________

Dear Family,

This week your child is exploring patterns.

A **pattern** is a series of numbers or shapes that follow a rule to repeat or change.

In this addition table, there is a diagonal pattern that has all 6's in it.

+	0	1	2	3	4	5	6
0	0	1	2	3	4	5	6
1	1	2	3	4	5	6	7
2	2	3	4	5	6	7	8
3	3	4	5	6	7	8	9
4	4	5	6	7	8	9	10
5	5	6	7	8	9	10	11
6	6	7	8	9	10	11	12

This chart shows the addends used to make these sums of 6.

Addend	Addend	Sum
0	6	6
1	5	6
2	4	6
3	3	6
4	2	6
5	1	6
6	0	6

The rule for this pattern has two parts:

- The addends in the first column increase by one. These addends are along the left side of the addition table.
- The addends in the second column decrease by one. These addends are across the top of the addition table.

Invite your child to share what he or she knows about exploring patterns by doing the following activity together.

NEXT

Exploring Patterns Activity

Materials: red crayon or marker, Hundreds Chart

Explore patterns in the Hundreds Chart with your child.

- Have your child lightly color these numbers red: 5, 10, 15, 20, and 25.

1	2	3	4	5	6	7	8	9	10
11	12	13	14	15	16	17	18	19	20
21	22	23	24	25	26	27	28	29	30
31	32	33	34	35	36	37	38	39	40
41	42	43	44	45	46	47	48	49	50
51	52	53	54	55	56	57	58	59	60
61	62	63	64	65	66	67	68	69	70
71	72	73	74	75	76	77	78	79	80
81	82	83	84	85	86	87	88	89	90
91	92	93	94	95	96	97	98	99	100

- Together, look for and describe patterns you see in the numbers that are colored. (For example, the numbers form vertical lines in the Hundreds Chart. Also, the colored numbers alternate odd, even.)
- Ask your child what the rule is for coloring the next number red. (Color every fifth number, or skip count by 5's, or leave 4 white and color the next.)
- Ask your child to use his or her rule to tell what the next number in the pattern will be. (30) Have your child color all the numbers in this pattern red.
- Challenge yourselves to find other ways to describe the same pattern. There are usually several different ways to describe a pattern!

Understand Patterns

Name: ______________________________

Prerequisite: What patterns do you see when you skip count?

Study the example showing skip-counting by 2s. Then solve problems 1–7.

Example

What can you say about the numbers shaded pink?

- They show skip-counting by 2s.
- They are all even.
- You can figure out the next shaded number by adding 2 to 30.

1	2	3	4	5	6	7	8	9	10
11	12	13	14	15	16	17	18	19	20
21	22	23	24	25	26	27	28	29	30

1 Look at the example. What would be the next shaded number after 30? _____

2 In the chart below, circle the other numbers that would be shaded pink.

31	32	33	34	35	36	37	38	39	40

3 On the chart below, circle the numbers you say when you count by 5s.

1	2	3	4	5	6	7	8	9	10
11	12	13	14	15	16	17	18	19	20
21	22	23	24	25	26	27	28	29	30

Vocabulary

even number a number that can be divided into 2 equal groups.

odd number a number that cannot be divided into 2 equal groups.

Solve.

4 Circle the numbers you say when you skip count by 2s.

5 What are the next 3 numbers you would say when you skip count by 2s?

____

1	2	3	4	5
6	7	8	9	10
11	12	13	14	15
16	17	18	19	20
21	22			

6 Use these clues to figure out what number I am.

- You say my number when you skip count by 5s.
- My number is even.
- My number is greater than 15 and less than 30.

What number am I? ______

1	2	3	4	5
6	7	8	9	10
11	12	13	14	15
16	17	18	19	20
21	22	23	24	25
26	27	28	29	30

7 Use these clues to figure out what number I am.

- You say my number when you skip count by 3s.
- My number is not even.
- My number is in the 5th row.

What number am I? ______

1	2	3	4	5	6
7	8	9	10	11	12
13	14	15	16	17	18
19	20	21	22	23	24

Name: ______________________

Explore Number Patterns

Study the example that shows one way to think about a pattern. Then solve problems 1–6.

Example

Juanita has 6 bags with 10 beads in each bag. She puts the bags into 2 groups in different ways.

The table shows how many bags are in each group.

Group A	Group B
1 bag	5 bags
2 bags	4 bags
3 bags	3 bags
4 bags	?

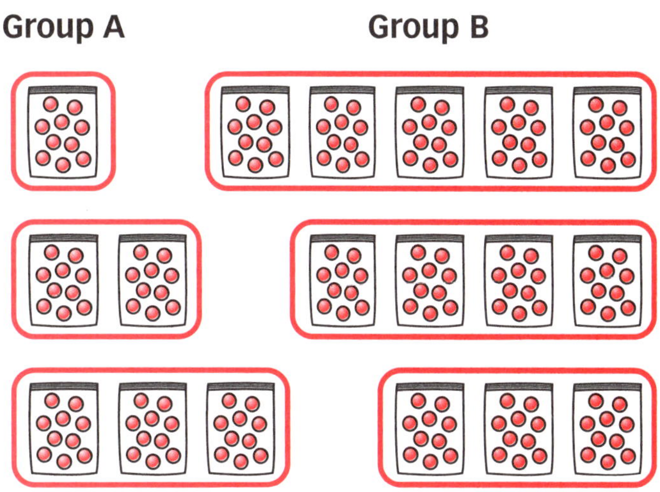

Juanita sees a pattern. When the number in Group A goes up by 1, the number in Group B goes down by 1.

1 Juanita made this table to show how many beads are in each group. Complete the table.

Group A	Group B	Total Beads
10	50	60
20		60
	30	60

2 Fill in the blanks to describe the pattern in the table in problem 1.

Group A ______ Group B = ______

Vocabulary

pattern a list of numbers or shapes that follow a rule, so what comes next in the list can be predicted.

Solve.

Chinzu has 35 beads. He ties 5 beads onto each string. He puts the strings of beads into 2 groups.

3 Circle the beads to show different ways Chinzu can put the strings of beads into 2 groups.

4 Complete the table to show how many beads are in each of the groups you made in problem 3.

Group A Beads	Group B Beads	Total Beads
5	30	35
10		35

5 Look at the table. Describe the pattern you see with the number of beads in each group.

____

____

____

6 If Chinzu moves 10 more beads into Group A, how many fewer beads will be in Group B? Explain how you know.

____

____

____

Name: ______________________________

Reason and Write

Study the example. Underline two parts that you think make it a particularly good answer and a helpful example.

Example

Tell how the numbers in Groups A and B are the same and how they are different. Then write these numbers in the correct places on the diagram. Tell why they belong where you put them.

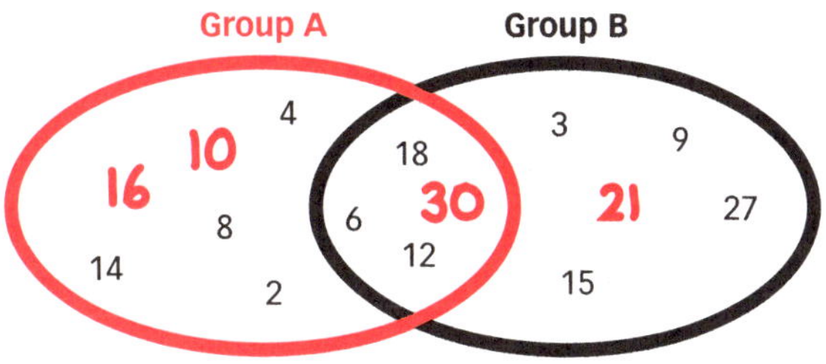

10	16	21	30

Show your work. Use pictures, words, or numbers to explain your answer.

I put all the numbers in both groups in order.

Group A: 2, 4, 6, 8, 12, 14, 18

Group B: 3, 6, 9, 12, 15, 18, 27

You can see all the numbers in Group A are even numbers. They show counting by 2s, with some missing. The numbers in Group B show counting by 3s, with some missing. You say 6, 12, and 18 when you skip count by 2s and by 3s. These numbers go in both loops.

I put 10 and 16 in Group A because they are even numbers. They are not in Group B because you don't say them when you count by 3s. I put 21 in Group B because you say it when you count by 3s. It is not in Group A because it's not even. You say 30 when you count by 2s and by 3s. It goes in both Group A and Group B, so it goes in the middle.

Where does the example . . .

- use a list to explain?
- use numbers to explain?
- use words to explain?
- give details?

Solve the problem. Use what you learned from the example.

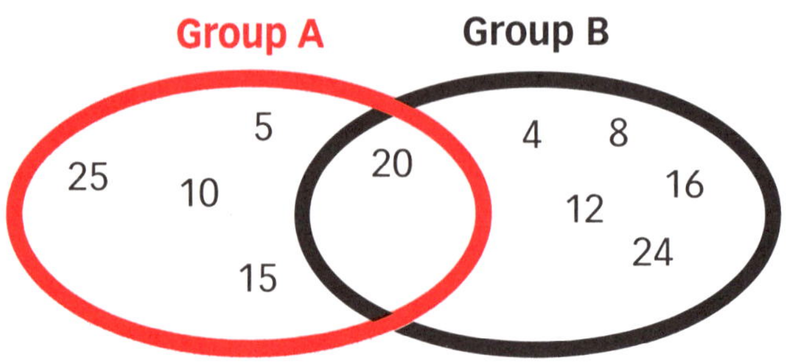

Tell how the numbers in Groups A and B are the same and how they are different. Then write these numbers in the correct place on the diagram. Tell why they belong where you put them.

28	30	40

Show your work. Use pictures, words, or numbers to explain your answer.

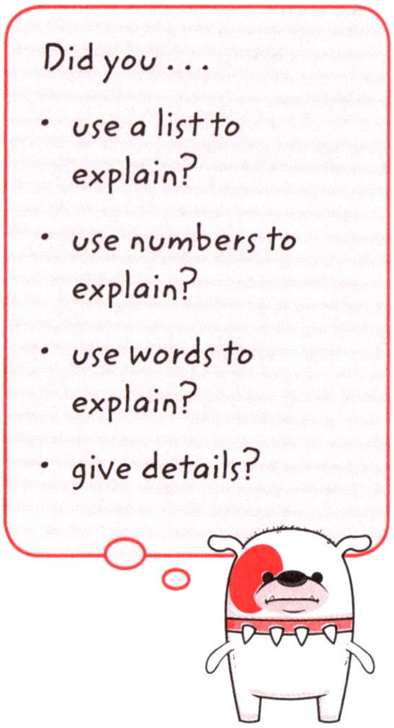

Name: ______________________

Fish for Factors!

What you need: Recording Sheet, 4 sets of Number Cards (3–9)

Directions

- Mix the cards on the table, face down. Each player takes 3 cards. You will use the numbers as factors. The goal is to make a product in each of the product groups on the Recording Sheet.
- Take turns. Play two factors that have a product from one of the product groups. Write the number sentence on the Recording Sheet. Set aside the two cards and draw two new cards.
- If you cannot make a product you need, ask the other player for a number. If the player has that number, use it with one of your numbers to make a product. Continue as described above. Each player draws a new card.
- If the other player does not have the number you ask for, your turn ends.
- The first player to write a number sentence for each Product Group wins.

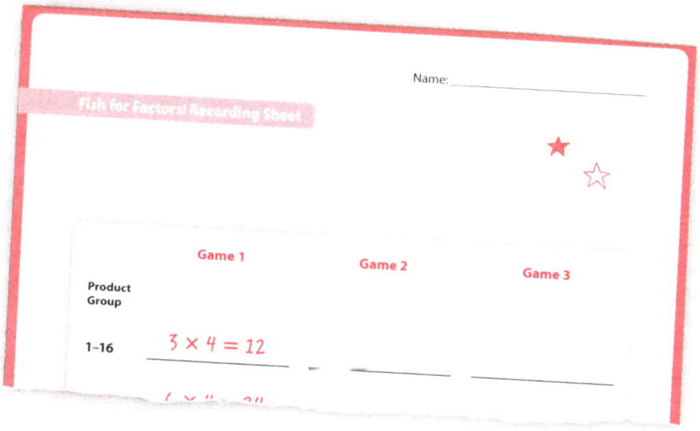

Name: ______________________________

Fish for Factors! Recording Sheet

Product Group	Game 1	Game 2	Game 3
1–16	________	________	________
17–32	________	________	________
33–48	________	________	________
49–64	________	________	________
65–81	________	________	________

Number Cards 3–9

3	4	5	6	7
8	9			
3	4	5	6	7
8	9			

Number Cards 3–9

3	4	5	6	7
8	9			
3	4	5	6	7
8	9			

Unit 1 Practice

Name: ____________________

Operations and Algebraic Thinking, Part 1

In this unit you learned to:	Lesson
explain multiplication using equal groups and arrays.	1, 2
use order and grouping to make multiplying easier, for example: $6 \times 2 \times 5$ is equal to $6 \times (2 \times 5)$.	2
break apart numbers to make multiplying easier, for example: 3×8 is equal to $(3 \times 4) + (3 \times 4)$.	3
understand division as a multiplication problem, for example: $10 \div 2$ can be shown as $2 \times \square = 10$.	4, 5
use the multiplication and division facts up through 10s.	6
find the rule for a pattern and explain why the pattern works.	7

Use these skills to solve problems 1–6. Fill in the blanks below to write a multiplication or division sentence for each picture in problems 1 and 2.

1

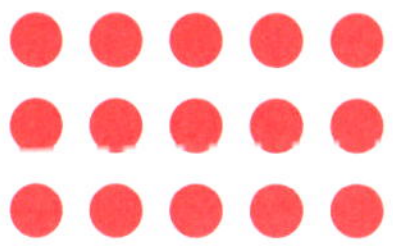

Solution: _____ × _____ = _____

2

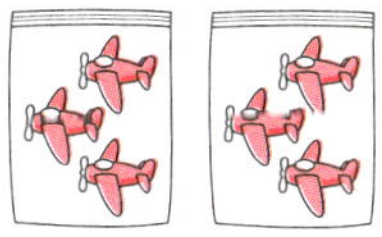

Solution: _____ ÷ _____ = _____

3 The classroom has 8 boxes of crayons. There are 7 crayons in each box. Which shows one way to break apart the numbers to find the total number of crayons? Circle the letter of the correct answer.

A $(4 \times 5) + (4 \times 2)$

B $(8 \times 1) + (8 \times 7)$

C $(8 + 5) \times (8 + 2)$

D $(8 \times 5) + (8 \times 2)$

Solve.

4 Choose *True* or *False* for each number sentence.

a. $4 \times 3 \times 5 = 5 \times 4 \times 3$ ☐ True ☐ False

b. $4 \times 3 \times 5 = 4 \times 15$ ☐ True ☐ False

c. $4 \times 3 \times 5 = 4 + 15$ ☐ True ☐ False

d. $4 \times 3 \times 5 = 12 \times 15$ ☐ True ☐ False

5 Jaime has 35 baseball cards. He wants to give each of his 5 friends an equal number of cards. Which facts can be used to find the number of cards he can give each of his friends? Circle the letter for all that apply.

A $35 \div 5 = 7$

B $35 - 5 = 30$

C $5 + 30 = 35$

D $5 \times 7 = 35$

E $35 \div 7 = 5$

6 **Part A**

Mateo wrote two facts of a fact family . Then he erased some of the numbers. Fill in the missing numbers below.

______ $\times 8 = 16$

$16 \div$ ______ $= 2$

Part B

If you know only one of the facts above, can you still fill in the rest of the fact family? Explain why or why not.

____

____

Unit 1 Performance Task

Name: ______________________

Answer the questions and show all your work on separate paper.

Principal Evans has 24 baby chickens.

- She shares the chicks among 5 classrooms.
- Each class gets at least 4 chicks.
- There can be no more than 3 chicks in one cage.

Make a plan for sharing the chicks.
Tell how many chicks each class room gets. Also tell how many cages each classroom needs and how many chicks to put in each cage.

Checklist

Did you . . .

- ☐ organize your information?
- ☐ check that your plan fits the rules?
- ☐ write a complete answer?

Reflect on Mathematical Practices

1 **Reason Mathematically** How did multiplication, division, addition, or subtraction help you create your plan?

2 **Model with Mathematics** What drawings or models did you use? How did these help you understand the problem?

Performance Task Tips

Word Bank Here are some words that you might use in your answer.

each	multiply	total	left over
product	as many	share	divide

Models Here are some models that you might use to find the solution.

Sentence Starters Here are some sentence starters that might help explain your work.

If each classroom gets ______________________________

For every cage ____________________________________

The rest of the chicks ______________________________

Unit 1 Vocabulary

Name: ______________________

My Examples

array

a set of objects arranged in equal rows and equal columns

factor

a number that is multiplied

multiplication

an operation used to find the total number of items when you have equal-sized groups

multiply

combine equal groups

My Examples

product

the result of multiplication

times

how you say a multiplication sign when you are reading a number sentence

division

an operation used to separate a number of items into equal-sized groups

divide

separate into equal groups

My Examples

fact family

a group of related number sentences that use the same numbers, but in a different order

dividend

the number you divide in a division problem

divisor

the number you divide by in a division problem

quotient

the result of division

My Examples

pattern

a list of numbers or shapes that follow a rule, so you can predict what comes next in the list

rule

a procedure that is followed to go from one number or shape to the next in a pattern

even number

a number that can be divided into 2 equal groups

odd number

a number that cannot be divided into 2 equal groups

Dear Family,

This week your child is learning to use place value to round numbers.

rounding: to find the nearest ten or nearest hundred, for example

Rounding is useful to give you an idea of the size of a number when you don't have to be exact. For example, when you buy several items you might round each price to the nearest ten dollars before adding them all in your head.

These blocks show the number 217. How do you round 217 to the nearest hundred?

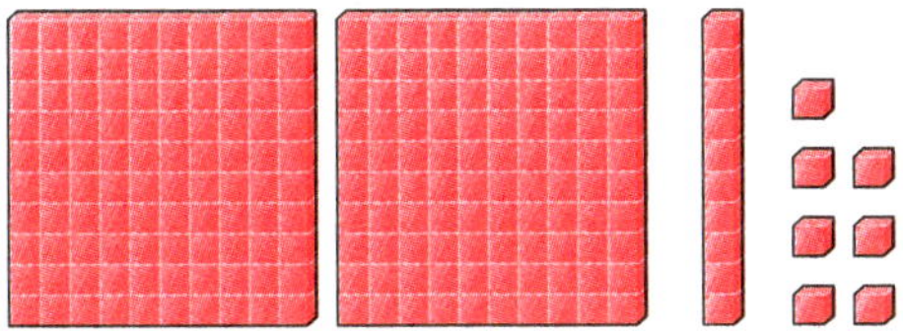

217 is:
2 hundreds + 1 ten + 7 ones

You need to decide whether 217 is *more* or *less* than halfway between 200 and 300.

Five tens is exactly half of one hundred. So, if there are fewer than 5 tens in the number, it's less than halfway between 200 and 300. If there are 5 or more tens, the number is closer to 300.

Since 217 has only 1 ten, 217 rounded to the nearest **hundred** is 200. We say it *rounds down* to 200.

To round 217 to the nearest **ten**, look at the ones. The number is between 210 and 220. If there are fewer than 5 ones, it's closer to 210. If there are 5 or more ones, it's closer to 220.

Since 217 has 7 ones, 217 *rounds up* to 220.

Invite your child to share what he or she knows about using place value to round numbers by doing the following activity together.

NEXT

Rounding Numbers Activity

Materials: 0–8 digit cards, bag, game board, and recording chart below

Play this game with your child to practice rounding.

- Cut out digit cards and place them in a bag.
- Draw 3 digit cards and record them in any order.
  Example: 2, 7, 4
- Write a 3-digit number using the numbers drawn.
  Example: 472
- Round the number to the nearest hundred. *Example: 500*
- Shade in the hundred number on your game board.
- The first player with 5 numbers shaded wins.

Player 1	100	200	300	400	500	600	700	800	900
Player 2	100	200	300	400	500	600	700	800	900

Player 1:

Digits	3-digit number	Rounded to nearest hundred

Player 2:

Digits	3-digit number	Rounded to nearest hundred

0	1	2	3	4
5	6	7	8	

Use Place Value to Round Numbers

Name: ____________________

Prerequisite: Use Place Value to Break Apart Numbers

Study the example showing the value of a three-digit number. Then solve problems 1–7.

Example

A digit's place in a number tells its value.

To show the value of each digit in the number 485, you can use a chart.

Hundreds	Tens	Ones
4	8	5

485 = 400 + 80 + 5

Fill in the blanks.

1 732 = 700 + 30 + 2

732 = _____ hundreds + _____ tens + _____ ones

2 201 = 200 + 1

201 = _____ hundreds + _____ ones

3 Complete the chart. The first row is done for you.

	Hundreds	Tens	Ones
105	1	0	5
_____	9	1	3
_____	7	9	0
358	_____	_____	_____

Solve.

4 Complete the chart.

	Hundreds	Tens	Ones
322	______	______	______
565	______	______	______
300	______	______	______

5 Can you solve this number riddle? Here are the clues.

- The number has 6 hundreds.
- The tens digit has a value of 50.
- The ones digit is the difference between the digits in the hundreds place and tens place.

What is the number? Circle the correct answer.

506 651 615 561

6 Use the three digits shown on the cards to make the greatest number you can. Use each digit once.

greatest number ______

7 Use the same three digits to make the least number you can. Use each digit once.

least number ______

Name: ____________________

Round to the Nearest Ten

Study the example about rounding to the nearest ten. Then solve problems 1–8.

Example

Robert always tells his friend how many points he earns on his video game. He rounds the number to the nearest ten. On Saturday, Robert earned 63 points. How many points did he tell his friend that he earned?

60 61 62 **63** 64 65 66 67 68 69 **70**

63 is between the tens 60 and 70. Since 63 is closer to 60, Robert tells his friend that he earned 60 points.

1 Later that afternoon, Robert spent more time playing the video game. He earned 88 points. How many points did he tell his friend that he earned?

______

2 The number 157 is between which two tens? Circle the two tens on the number line.

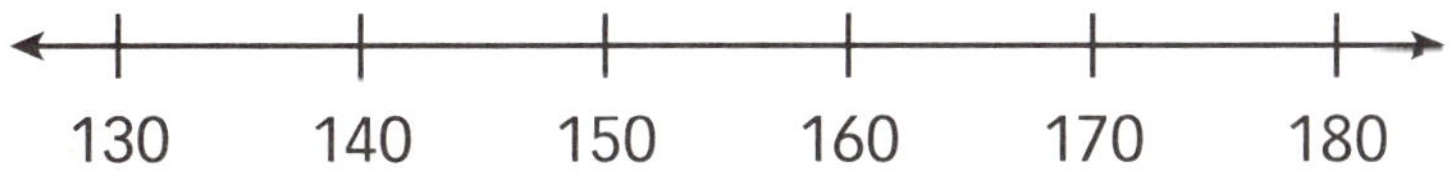

3 What is 157 rounded to the nearest ten? ______

Vocabulary

round (a whole number) find the nearest ten, hundred, or other place value. For example, 28 rounds to 30, and 21 rounds to 20.

Solve.

4 To earn money, you brush dogs. You are so busy that you hire your friends to help. You pay your friends $1 for each dog they brush. You only have $10 bills to pay them with. You must round each payment to the nearest ten. Show how much each friend gets paid.

Friend	Number of Dogs Brushed	Payment to the Nearest $10
Jessica	12	$ _______
Sophie	18	$ _______
Mia	22	$ _______

5 **a.** The number 767 is between what two tens?

_______ and _______

b. What number is halfway between these two tens? _______

c. Is 767 less than or greater than the halfway number? _______________________________

d. Will it round up or down? _______

e. What is 767 rounded to the nearest ten? _______

6 **a.** The number 342 is between what two tens?

_______ and _______

b. Will it round up or down? ____________________

c. What is 342 rounded to the nearest ten? _______

7 What is a number less than 930 that rounds to 930?

____

8 What is a number greater than 930 that rounds to 930? _______

Name: ___________________________

Round to the Nearest Hundred

Study the example about rounding to the nearest hundred. Then solve problems 1–10.

Example

There are 127 crayons in a bin. What is 127 rounded to the nearest hundred?

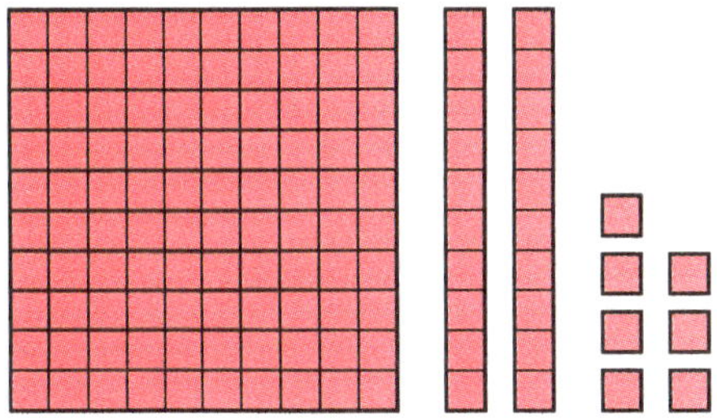

In the drawing, you can see that 127 is 1 hundred + 2 tens + 7 ones.

The number 127 is between 100 and 200. The halfway number between 100 and 200 is 150. The number 127 is less than the halfway number.

So, 127 is nearer to 100 than to 200. 100 is the nearest hundred to 127.

1. The number 684 is between which two hundreds? Circle the two hundreds on the number line.

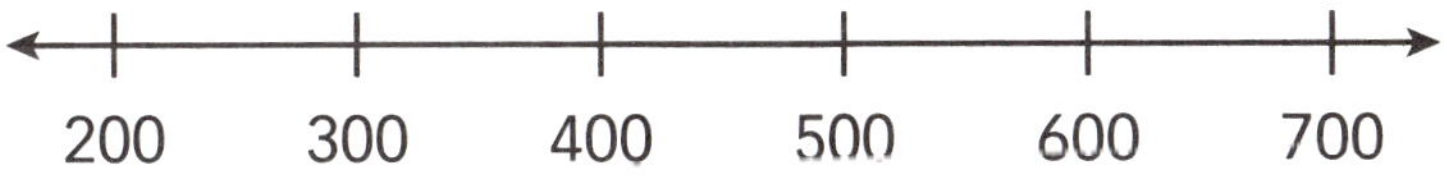

2. What is the halfway number between the two hundreds you circled? ______

3. What is 684 rounded to the nearest hundred? ______

4. What is 694 rounded to the nearest hundred? ______

5. What is 674 rounded to the nearest hundred? ______

6. What is 624 rounded to the nearest hundred? ______

Solve.

7 Answer the questions below to round 377 to the nearest hundred.

a. The number 377 is between what two hundreds? ______ and ______

b. What number is halfway between these two hundreds? ______

c. Is 377 less than or greater than the halfway number? ________________________________

d. Will you round up or down? ______

e. What is 377 rounded to the nearest hundred? ______

8 The chart below shows the miles between U.S. cities. Round each distance to the nearest hundred miles.

Cities	Distance in Miles	Distance to the Nearest Hundred Miles
Phoenix and Las Vegas	292	________
Los Angeles and San Francisco	386	________

9 Can you solve this riddle about a number? Here are the clues.

- The number is between the two hundreds, 500 and 600.
- The number is greater than the halfway number.
- You will round up to round this number to the nearest hundred.

What is the number? Circle the correct answer.

525 575 501 650

10 What is 999 rounded to the nearest hundred? _______

Name: ____________________

Use Place Value to Round Numbers

Solve the problems.

1 A science museum has 73 exhibits. What is 73 rounded to the nearest hundred?

____

2 Which two numbers, rounded to the nearest hundred, both round to 400?

A 349 and 350

B 449 and 450

C 350 and 351

D 450 and 451

Hans chose **A** as the correct answer. How could he get that answer?

____

____

____

3 Decide if the following numbers will round to 300. Circle *Yes* or *No*.

286 rounded to the nearest hundred	Yes or No
342 rounded to the nearest hundred	Yes or No
297 rounded to the nearest ten	Yes or No

Solve.

4 Which numbers, when rounded to the nearest hundred, round to 100? Circle all that are correct.

A 149

B 49

C 75

D 162

What is the least number that rounds to 100 as the nearest hundred? What is the greatest?

5 According to one science museum, the world's tallest man was 8 feet 11 inches tall. That is 107 inches. His weight was 490 pounds.

What is 107 rounded to the nearest hundred?

____

What is 490 rounded to the nearest hundred?

____

Which two hundreds is 490 between?

6 Cameron read that the average American eats about 130 pounds of potatoes each year.

a. What is a number less than 130 that rounds to 130 when rounding to the nearest ten? ________

b. What is a number greater than 130 that rounds to 130 when rounding to the nearest ten? ______

c. What is 130 rounded to the nearest hundred?

____

What numbers do you say when you count by tens from 100 to 150?

Dear Family,

This week your child is using place value to add and subtract.

For example, one way to use place value to add 153 + 260 is shown below.

You can add the ones first, then add the tens, then add the hundreds, writing each sum on a line by itself. Then you add the three **partial sums** to get the total.

```
  153
+ 260
-----
    3 → ones
  110 → 5 tens + 6 tens = 11 tens, or 1 hundred + 1 ten, or 110
  300 → 1 hundred + 2 hundreds = 3 hundreds, or 300
-----
  413
```

The subtraction problem below shows another way to use place value.

To subtract 260 − 153, you can use a number line to show the related addition equation, 153 + ? = 260.

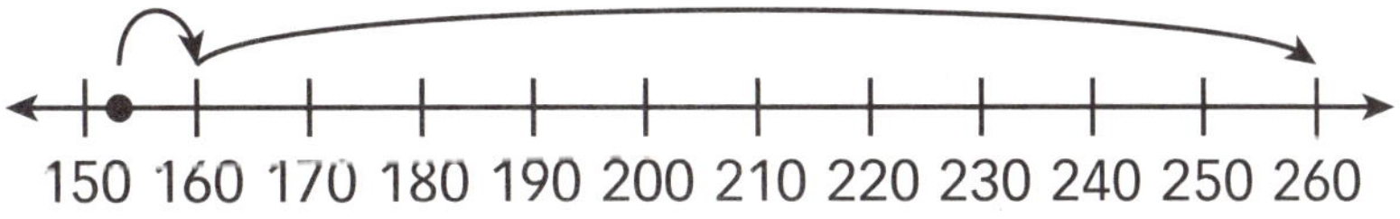

153 + 7 = 160 → Add some ones to get the next ten.

160 + 100 = 260 → Add some hundreds to get to the hundred you are looking for.

7 + 100 = 107

153 + 107 = 260, so 260 − 153 = 107

Invite your child to share what he or she knows about using place value to add and subtract by doing the following activity together.

NEXT

Use Place Value to Add and Subtract Activity

Materials: 3 number cubes, pencil and paper

Play this adding game with your child to practice adding three-digit numbers. The goal of this game is to get a sum greater than 500 by adding a three-digit number to 250.

- Have your child roll three number cubes.
- Ask your child to form a three-digit number from the number cubes. (If the rolls are 2, 6, and 1, the possible numbers are 126, 162, 216, 261, 612, and 621.) Write down the chosen number.
- Your child adds 250 to the number, using any addition strategy.
- If the sum is greater than 500, then he or she wins the round. If not, you win the round.
- Switch roles. Play 5 rounds for best out of 5.
- Ask your child questions during the game such as
  - Does it matter which number I form out of the three number cubes? How will it change the sum?
  - How can I pick my number to make sure my sum is as large as possible?
- **Variation:** As an alternative, play a subtraction game to practice subtraction strategies. Both players roll the 3 number cubes and make a 3-digit number. Subtract your numbers from 800. The player with the smallest difference is the winner of the round.

Use Place Value to Add and Subtract

Name: ______________________

Prerequisite: Add and Subtract by Breaking Apart Numbers

Study the example showing two ways to break apart numbers to subtract them. Then solve problems 1–8.

Example

$$\begin{array}{r} 369 \\ -\ 154 \\ \hline \end{array} \longrightarrow \begin{array}{r} 300 + 60 + 9 \\ 100 + 50 + 4 \\ \hline \end{array}$$

9 ones − 4 ones = 5 ones ⟶ 5

6 tens − 5 tens = 1 ten ⟶ 10

3 hundreds − 1 hundred = 2 hundreds ⟶ + 200

$$\begin{array}{r} 5 \\ 10 \\ +\ 200 \\ \hline 215 \end{array}$$

369 − 154 = 215

Break apart the numbers. Show the hundreds, tens, and ones.

1 324 = ______ + ______ + ______

2 497 = ______ + ______ + ______

Write the numbers.

3 2 hundreds + 5 tens + 6 ones = ______

4 8 hundreds + 0 tens + 4 ones = ______

Solve.

5

$$\begin{array}{r} 133 \\ +\ 214 \\ \hline \end{array} \longrightarrow \begin{array}{r} 100 + 30 + 3 \\ 200 + 10 + 4 \\ \hline \end{array}$$

Add the ones. ______

Add the tens. ______

Add the hundreds. ______

Result: ______

133 + 214 = ______

6

$$\begin{array}{r} 789 \\ -\ 506 \\ \hline \end{array} \longrightarrow \begin{array}{r} 700 + 80 + 9 \\ 500 + \ \ 0 + 6 \\ \hline \end{array}$$

Subtract the ones. ______

Subtract the tens. ______

Subtract the hundreds. ______

Result: ______

789 − 506 = ______

7

$$\begin{array}{r} 517 \\ +\ 321 \\ \hline \end{array}$$

8

$$\begin{array}{r} 845 \\ -\ 243 \\ \hline \end{array}$$

Name: ______________________

Use Place Value to Add

Study the example problem showing how regrouping can help you add three-digit numbers. Then solve problems 1–8.

Example

On the weekend, 172 adults and 253 children went to the fair. How many people went to the fair on the weekend?

```
  172
+ 253
-----
    5  ──────→ 2 ones + 3 ones
  120  ──────→ 7 tens + 5 tens
  300  ──────→ 1 hundred + 2 hundreds
-----
  425
```

	1		
	1	7	2
+	2	5	3
	4	**2**	**5**

Regroup 10 tens

Fill in the blanks to add.

1

```
  124
+ 253
-----
 ____  ──────→ 4 ones + 3 ones = 7 ones
 ____  ──────→ 2 tens + 5 tens = 7 tens
 ____  ──────→ 1 hundred + 2 hundreds = 3 hundreds
  377
```

2

	1		
	4	5	9
+	2	6	0
		1	

Solve. Fill in the blanks to add.

3

631	→	600	+	____	+	1		
+ 368	→	____	+	60	+	8		
		900	+	90	+	____	=	____

4

167	→	____	+	____	+	7		
+ 208	→	____	+	0	+	____		
		____	+	____	+	____	=	____

5

	2	2	8
+	1	3	6

7

  151
+ 154

6

	2	5	1
+	2	5	4
			5
	1	0	0
	4	0	0

8

  368
+ 245

300 + ____ + 8
____ + 40 + 5

500 + 100 + ____ = ____

Name: ______________________

Use Place Value to Subtract

Study the example showing how place value can help you subtract three-digit numbers. Then solve problems 1–6.

Example

The balloon artist at the fair sold 253 balloons. Of those, 129 were monster heads. How many balloons were not monster heads?

$$\begin{array}{r} 253 \\ -\ 129 \\ \hline \end{array}$$

253 = 2 hundreds + 5 tens + 3 ones
or 2 hundreds + 4 tens + 13 ones
129 = 1 hundred + 2 tens + 9 ones
253 − 129 = 1 hundred + 2 tens + 4 ones

124 balloons were not monster heads.

Fill in the blanks to add.

1

$$\begin{array}{r} 352 \\ -\ 147 \\ \hline \end{array}$$

352 = ______ hundreds + ______ tens + 2 ones
or ______ **hundreds** + **4 tens** + ______ **ones**
147 = ______ **hundred** + **4 tens** + ______ **ones**

Subtract hundreds: ______ hundreds
Subtract tens: 0 tens
Subtract ones: ______ ones
352 − 147 = ______

2

$$\begin{array}{r} 459 \\ -\ 260 \\ \hline \end{array}$$

459 = ______ hundreds + ______ tens + 9 ones
or 3 **hundreds** + **15 tens** + ______ **ones**
260 = ______ **hundreds** + ______ **tens** + ______ **ones**

Subtract hundreds: ______ hundred
Subtract tens: ______ tens
Subtract ones: ______ ones
459 − 260 = ______

Solve.

3 621 − 570

621 = ______ hundreds + ______ tens + ______ one
or 5 **hundreds** + **12 tens** + ______ **one**
570 = ______ **hundreds** + ______ **tens** + ______ **ones**

Subtract hundreds: ______ hundreds
Subtract tens: ______ tens
Subtract ones: ______ one
621 − 570 = ______

4 905 − 425

905 = ______ hundreds + ______ tens + ______ ones
or ______ **hundreds** + **10 tens** + ______ **ones**
425 = ______ **hundreds** + ______ **tens** + ______ **ones**

Subtract hundreds: ______ hundreds
Subtract tens: ______ tens
Subtract ones: ______ ones
905 − 425 = ______

Subtract. Regroup if needed.

5 252 − 136

6 636 − 158

Name: ______________________

Add On to Subtract

Study the example showing how to subtract by adding on. Then solve problems 1–8.

Example

310 students went to the art museum. 195 students left at 9 A.M. The others left at 9:30 A.M. How many students left for the museum at 9:30 A.M.?

310 − 195 = ☐, or 195 + ☐ = 310

Add on to 195 to get to 310.

Add 5: 195 + 5 = 200

Add 100: 200 + 100 = 300

Add 10: 300 + 10 = 310

5 + 100 + 10 = 115

195 + 115 = 310 310 − 195 = 115

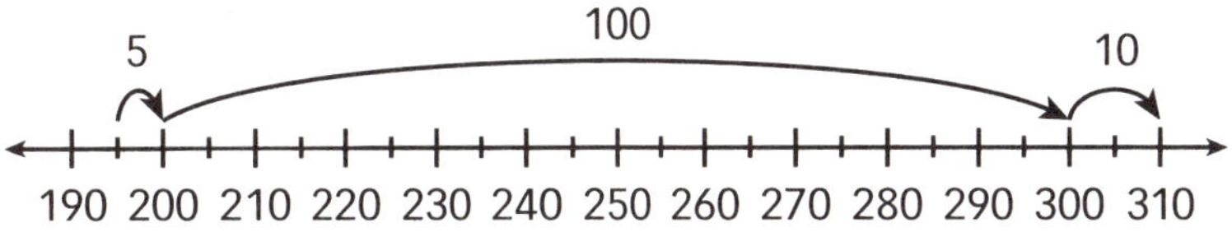

So, 115 students left at 9:30.

Fill in the blanks to show adding on to subtract.

1. 75 + 5 + ______ = 100, so 100 − 75 = ______

2. 114 + 6 + ______ + ______ = 132, so 132 − 114 = ______

3. 162 + 8 + ______ + 1 = 201, so 201 − 162 = ______

Solve.

4. 501 − 470 = ______

   Explain how you can start with 470 and add on to solve.

   ____

   ____

   ____

Solve.

5 $100 - 78 =$ ______

Explain how you can start with 78 and add on to solve.

____

____

____

6 $200 - 96 =$ ______

Explain how you can start with 96 and add on to solve.

____

____

____

7 $305 - 296 =$ ______

Explain how you can start with 296 and add on to solve.

____

____

____

8 $303 - 196 =$ ______

Explain how you can start with 196 and add on to solve.

____

____

____

____

Name: ______________________

Use Place Value to Add and Subtract

Solve the problems.

1 For the recycling project, Ben's class collected 192 glass bottles and 340 plastic bottles. How many bottles did they collect in all? Which two number sentences could you use to solve the problem.

A (100 + 90 + 2) + (300 + 40) = ☐

B (300 + 4) + (100 + 9 + 2) = ☐

C (1 + 3) + (9 + 4) + (2 + 0) = ☐

D (100 + 300) + (90 + 40) + (2 + 0) = ☐

2 For the recycling project, Karen's class collected 234 cans and 120 cardboard boxes. How many more cans than boxes did they collect? Which two number sentences could you use to solve the problem.

A 234 + ☐ = 120

B 120 + ☐ = 234

C ☐ + 234 = 120

D 234 − 120 = ☐

3 Students at Haley's school collected labels from cans. The third grade collected 278 labels and the fourth grade collected 219 labels. How many labels did they collect in all?

Show your work.

Solution: ______________________

Solve.

4 At the recycling fair, 193 glasses of orange juice and 270 glasses of lemonade were sold. How many more glasses of lemonade were sold than glasses of orange juice?

Show your work.

Solution: ______________________________

5 On the last day of the recycling fair, 257 children and 145 adults went to the concert. How many people went to the concert?

A 302

B 392

C 402

D 492

Cindy chose **A** as the correct answer. How could she get that answer? ______________________________

____

____

____

6 Look at problem 5. How many more children than adults went to the concert?

Show your work.

Solution: ______________________________

Dear Family,

This week your child is learning about using place value to multiply.

Place value can help us understand how to multiply a one-digit number, like 3, by a two-digit multiple of 10, like 40.

You can use base-ten blocks to understand this problem. These base-ten blocks show 3 groups of 40.

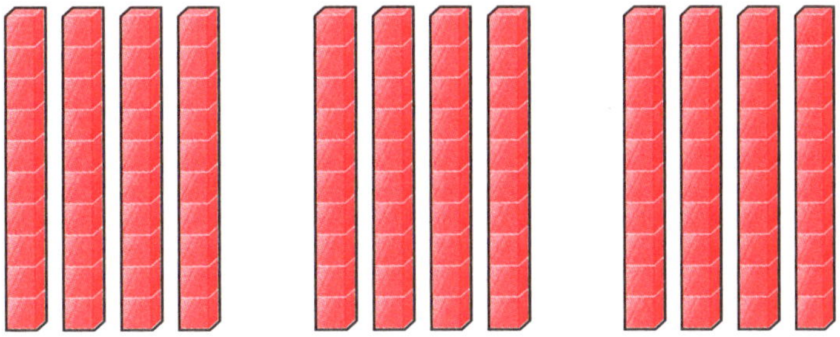

3 groups of 4 tens is 3×4 tens, or 12 tens.
12 tens is the same as 120.

Another way to think about this problem, without the base-ten blocks, is to rewrite the problem. Think about 40 as 4×10. Then:

$$3 \times 10 = 3 \times (4 \times 10)$$

When you multiply you can change the grouping without changing the answer:

$3 \times (4 \times 10)$ is the same as $(3 \times 4) \times 10$.
3×4 is 12, and 12×10 is 120.
So, again, $3 \times 40 = 120$.

Invite your child to share what he or she knows about using place value to multiply by doing the following activity together.

NEXT

Using Place Value to Multiply Activity

Materials: 2 number cubes

Play a game with your child to practice multiplying by a multiple of 10. The winner of each round is the player with the greater product.

- Each player rolls one number cube. The first roll gives you each your first factor.

  For example, if the cube rolled is a 5, the first factor is 5.

- Roll again and multiply the number on the cube by 10. This is your second factor.

  For example, if the cube rolled is a 3, the second factor is 30.

- Find the product of your two factors.

  For example, to find 5 × 30:
  5 × (3 × 10)
  (5 × 3) × 10
  15 × 10 is 15 tens, which equals 150.

- The player with the greater product wins the round.
- Play 5 rounds for best out of 5.

Use Place Value to Multiply

Name: ______________________

Prerequisite: Break Apart Numbers to Multiply

Study the example showing how to break apart numbers to multiply them. Then solve problems 1–14.

Example

Jojo is learning his multiplication facts. He needs to know 8×4. He already knows $5 \times 4 = 20$ and he knows $3 \times 4 = 12$. Since $5 + 3 = 8$, he can add $20 + 12$ to find 8×4.

$20 + 12 = 32$

$8 \times 4 = 32$

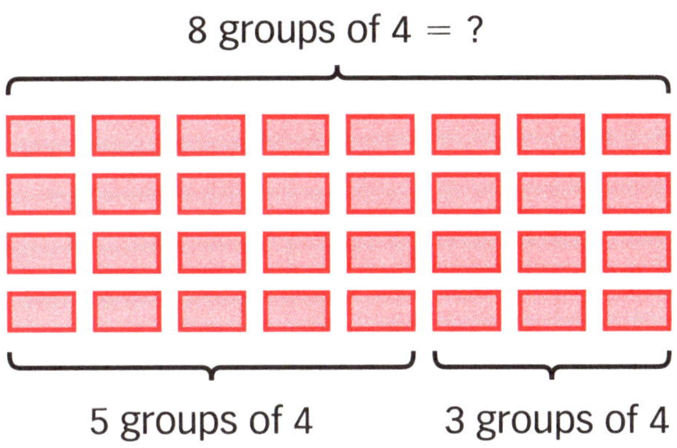

1 Jordan solved 6×5 by breaking apart the 6 into $5 + 1$. Which of the following correctly shows the next step to find the solution? Circle the letter of the correct answer.

A $(5 \times 6) + (1 \times 6)$

B $(5 + 6) + (1 + 6)$

C $(6 \times 5) + (1 \times 5)$

D $(5 \times 5) + (1 \times 5)$

Fill in the blanks to complete the number sentences.

2 $8 \times 5 = (4 \times 5) + ($ _______ $\times 5)$

$8 \times 5 = 20 +$ _______

$8 \times 5 =$ _______

3 $7 \times 8 = ($ _______ $\times 8) + (5 \times 8)$

$7 \times 8 =$ _______ $+ 40$

$7 \times 8 =$ _______

Solve.

Jenna has 6 packs of 7 pencils. To find out how many pencils she has, she writes, $6 \times 7 = ?$ Fill in the blanks to show how Jenna could figure out 6×7 using other facts she may know.

4 $6 \times 7 = (3 \times 7) + (\_\_\_\_\_\_ \times 7)$

$6 \times 7 = \_\_\_\_\_\_ + \_\_\_\_\_\_$

$6 \times 7 = \_\_\_\_\_\_$

5 $6 \times 7 = (6 \times 5) + (6 \times \_\_\_\_\_\_)$

$6 \times 7 = \_\_\_\_\_\_ + \_\_\_\_\_\_$

$6 \times 7 = \_\_\_\_\_\_$

6 Use the array to show another way Jenna could break apart these numbers to find 6×7.

7 Complete the number sentence to show how you broke apart the array into two smaller arrays.

$6 \times 7 = (\_\_\_\_\_\_ \times \_\_\_\_\_\_) + (\_\_\_\_\_\_ \times \_\_\_\_\_\_)$

Fill in the blanks to write the numbers in a different way.

8 10 tens = ______

9 50 tens = ______

10 200 = ______ tens

11 210 = ______ tens

12 240 = ______ tens

13 25 tens = ______

14 63 tens = ______

Name: ______________________

Break Numbers into Tens and Ones to Multiply

Study the example showing how you can break a number into tens and ones to help you multiply. Then solve problems 1–8.

Example

Hobbit's Hobby Store has 4 shelves of glue. Each shelf has 30 bottles of glue. How many bottles of glue are on the shelves?

30 bottles on each shelf.

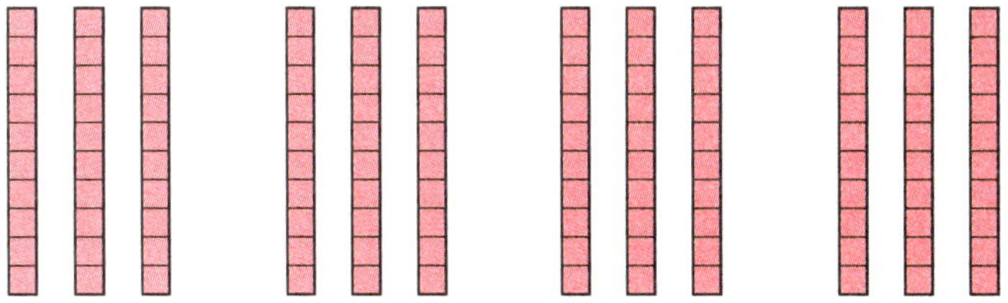

You can use factors and grouping.

4×30

$4 \times (3 \times 10)$

$(4 \times 3) \times 10$

$12 \times 10 = 120$

4 groups of 3 tens or 12 tens.
12 tens is 120.

There are 120 bottles of glue on the shelves.

The hobby store has 3 boxes of wheels.
There are 50 wheels in each box.
How many wheels does the hobby store have?

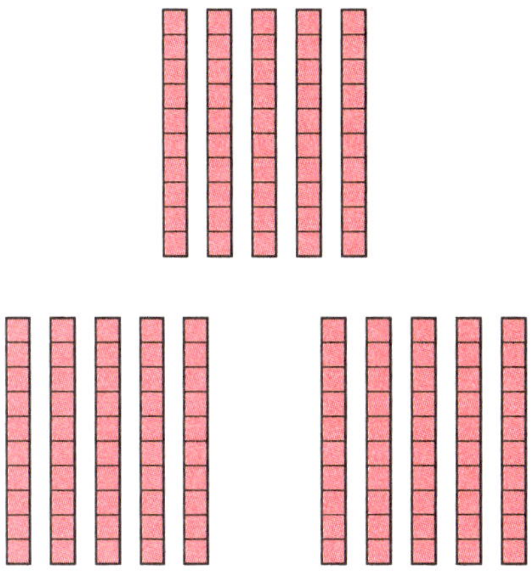

1 You can write 50 as _______ $\times$ 10.

2 $3 \times (5 \times 10)$ is one way to group the factors. Use parentheses to show another way to group the factors.

$3 \times 5 \times 10$

3 $3 \times 5 \times 10 =$ _______ $\times$ 10

4 The hobby store has _______ wheels.

Solve.

5 Draw a line to match each problem with another way to write it.

5×60	$(4 \times 3) \times 10$
6×40	$10 \times (5 \times 4)$
50×4	$(5 \times 6) \times 10$
6×30	$(6 \times 3) \times 10$
40×3	$(6 \times 4) \times 10$

6 Write the multiplication sentence that the base-ten models show.

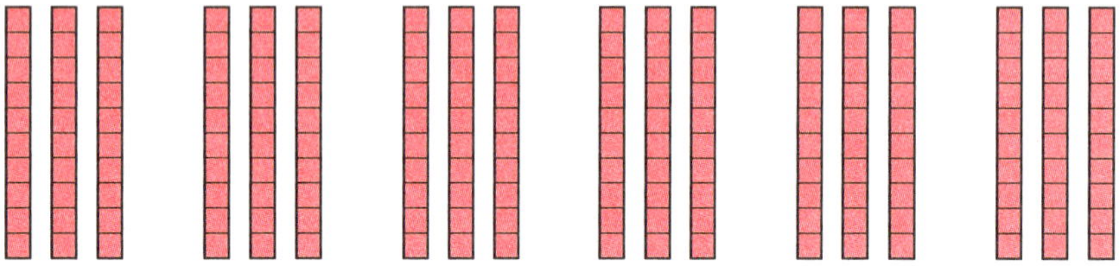

Multiplication sentence: ____________________________

7 Fill in the blanks to show how to find 4×70.

$4 \times 70 = 4 \times (\_\_\_\_\_\_ \times 10)$

$= (4 \times \_\_\_\_\_\_) \times 10$

$= 28 \times 10 = \_\_\_\_\_\_$

$4 \times 70 = \_\_\_\_\_\_$

8 $6 \times 20 = \_\_\_\_\_\_$

Show your work.

Solution: ______

Name: ______________________________

Use Place Value to Multiply

Solve the problems.

1 There are 6 rows of students at the play. Each row has 40 students. How many students are at the play?

Show your work.

Solution: ______ students are at the play.

2 Tyra bakes some cookies. Each cookie tray has 30 cookies. She uses 5 cookie trays. How many cookies does she bake?

Show your work.

Solution: She bakes ______ cookies.

3 Six buses of students visit Butterfly Wonderland. Each bus holds 30 students. How many students visit Butterfly Wonderland?

Show your work.

Solution: ______ students visit Butterfly Wonderland.

Solve.

4 The snack bar at the soccer field has 7 boxes of protein bars. There are 20 bars in each box. How many bars are there in all the boxes?

A 27 bars

B 13 bars

C 140 bars

D 280 bars

Simon chose **A** as the correct answer. How did he get that answer?

____

____

____

5 Lauren makes bracelets using small beads. She uses 60 beads for each bracelet. How many beads does Lauren need to make 7 bracelets?

A 42 beads

B 67 beads

C 420 beads

D 670 beads

6 Explain how you figured out the correct answer to problem 5.

____

____

____

____

____

____

Unit 2 Game

Name: ____________________

Tic-Tac-Times-Ten

What you need: Recording Sheet, Game Board, 2 number cubes (2–7 and 3–8), 30 two-color counters

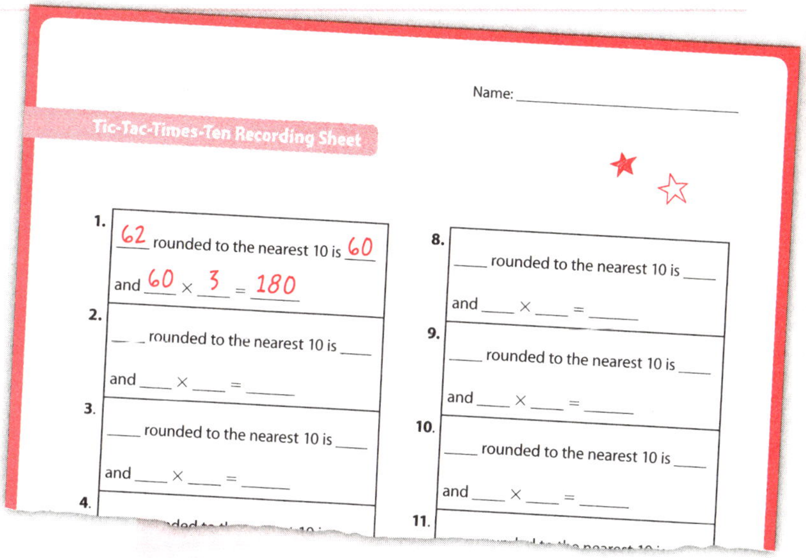
Name: ____________________

Tic-Tac-Times-Ten Recording Sheet

1. 62 rounded to the nearest 10 is 60
and 60 × 3 = 180

2. ____ rounded to the nearest 10 is ____
and ____ × ____ = ____

3. ____ rounded to the nearest 10 is ____
and ____ × ____ = ____

4.

8. ____ rounded to the nearest 10 is ____
and ____ × ____ = ____

9. ____ rounded to the nearest 10 is ____
and ____ × ____ = ____

10. ____ rounded to the nearest 10 is ____
and ____ × ____ = ____

11.

Directions

- Take turns. Roll the number cubes. Use the numbers to write a two-digit number on the Recording Sheet.
- Round the number to the nearest 10 and record that number on the Recording Sheet.
- Multiply your rounded number by a 1-digit number that you choose. Try to get a product that is on the Game Board.
- Record the number sentence on the Recording Sheet. If the product is on the Game Board and is not already covered, put a counter of your color in that space.
- The first player to cover 4 spaces in a row on the Game Board wins. If the Game Board is filled and no one has won, the player with the most spaces covered is the winner.

Name: ____________________

Tic-Tac-Times-Ten Recording Sheet

1. ____ rounded to the nearest 10 is ____
and ____ × ____ = ______

2. ____ rounded to the nearest 10 is ____
and ____ × ____ = ______

3. ____ rounded to the nearest 10 is ____
and ____ × ____ = ______

4. ____ rounded to the nearest 10 is ____
and ____ × ____ = ______

5. ____ rounded to the nearest 10 is ____
and ____ × ____ = ______

6. ____ rounded to the nearest 10 is ____
and ____ × ____ = ______

7. ____ rounded to the nearest 10 is ____
and ____ × ____ = ______

8. ____ rounded to the nearest 10 is ____
and ____ × ____ = ______

9. ____ rounded to the nearest 10 is ____
and ____ × ____ = ______

10. ____ rounded to the nearest 10 is ____
and ____ × ____ = ______

11. ____ rounded to the nearest 10 is ____
and ____ × ____ = ______

12. ____ rounded to the nearest 10 is ____
and ____ × ____ = ______

13. ____ rounded to the nearest 10 is ____
and ____ × ____ = ______

14. ____ rounded to the nearest 10 is ____
and ____ × ____ = ______

Tic-Tac-Times-Ten Game Board

300	720	140	360	150	240
270	540	240	120	250	320
420	160	280	100	480	630
180	450	210	120	640	810
350	490	400	560	180	200

Four in a row wins!

Unit 2 Practice

Name: ___________________________

Number and Operations in Base Ten

In this unit you learned to:	Lesson
use place value to round numbers to the nearest 10 and to the nearest 100, for example: • 315 rounded to the nearest 10 is 320. • 826 rounded to the nearest 100 is 800.	8
use place value to add and subtract, for example: $29 + 48 = (20 + 40) + (9 + 8)$.	9
solve word problems by adding and subtracting using place value.	9
use place value to multiply, for example: $6 \times 40 = 6 \times (4 \times 10)$ $= (6 \times 4) \times 10$ $= 24 \times 10$ $= 240$.	10

Use these skills to solve problems 1–7.

1 163 rounded to the nearest ten is ________.

163 rounded to the nearest hundred is ________.

2 Which statements are true? Circle all that apply.

A $10 \times 25 = 250$

B $30 \times 4 = 120$

C $50 \times 4 = 20$

D $18 \times 10 = 108$

E $5 \times 60 = 300$

3 Which expressions are equivalent to 5×30? Circle all that apply.

A $3 \times 5 \times 10$

B 10×15

C 8×10

D 3×50

E $5 \times 10 \times 3 \times 10$

Solve.

4 What is the greatest number that rounds to 500 when rounded to the nearest hundred?

____

5 What is the greatest number that rounds to 500 when rounded to the nearest ten?

____

6 Third graders at South School have collected 108 boxes of pasta and 246 boxes of cereal for the food drive. How many boxes of pasta and cereal did they collect altogether?

Show your work.

Solution: They collected ______ boxes.

7 Third graders at South School have collected 412 cans of food for a food drive. They want to collect 500. How many more cans do they need?

Show your work.

Solution: They need to collect ______ more cans.

Unit 2 Performance Task

Name: ______________________

Answer the questions and show all your work on separate paper.

The school store has pencils in three colors: red, blue, and yellow.

- The store should have between 700 and 900 pencils.
- The store should have at least 200 of each color pencil.

Today, the store has 155 red pencils, 238 blue pencils, and 206 yellow pencils. It's time to order some pencils! The store can buy pencils in boxes of 72 (6 dozen) or 144 (12 dozen).

If you were buying the pencils, how many of each color would you buy? Make a plan. Tell why you decided to buy the number of pencils that you chose.

Checklist

Did you . . .

- ☐ make a chart?
- ☐ make sure your numbers meet the goal?
- ☐ check that the results make sense?

Reflect on Mathematical Practices

1 **Keep Working to Solve Problems** How did you start working on this problem? Did you get stuck while you were working? How did you decide what to do next?

2 **Reason Mathematically** If you rounded or estimated, explain how that helped you decide on a plan or check that your plan made sense.

Performance Task Tips

Word Bank Here are some words that you might use in your answer.

equal	sum	total
round	at least	compare
more	estimate	add
plus	enough	about

Models Here are some models that you might use to find the solution.

Red	Blue	Yellow	Total

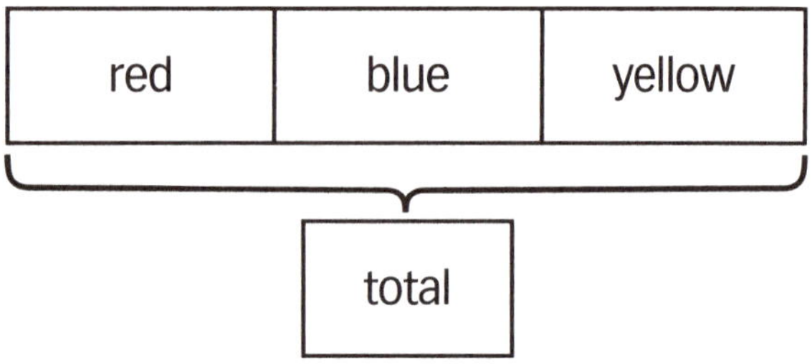

Sentence Starters Here are some sentence starters that might help explain your work.

To have 200 red pencils, ______________________________

The store needs to buy ______________________________

The total number of pencils ______________________________

Unit 2 Vocabulary

Name: ____________________

My Examples

round a whole number

find the nearest ten or nearest hundred, for example

My Words

My Words

My Examples

Dear Family,

This week your child is solving one-step word problems using multiplication or division.

For example, he or she might see a problem like this one.

> Tom created a patio using square tiles side-by-side with no gaps. He used 24 square tiles and made 6 rows. Tom used the same number of squares in each row. How many squares did he put in each row?

One way to make sense of a problem like this is to make a grid showing rows of tiles with the same number in each row. Draw one tile in each row, until all 24 tiles are used. Then count to see how many tiles are in each row.

Or, you can use multiplication or division sentences to find the number of squares in each row, since all the rows are equal groups.

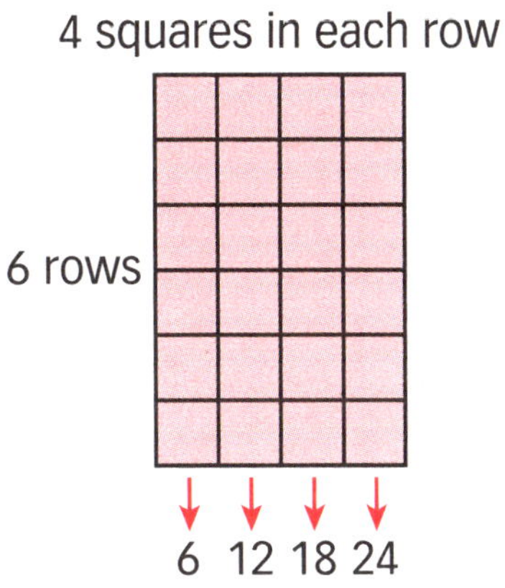

$6 \times ? = 24$ or $24 \div 6 = ?$

However you solve the problem, you find that Tom put 4 squares in each row.

Invite your child to share what he or she knows about solving one-step word problems using multiplication and division by doing the following activity together.

NEXT

One-Step Word Problems Activity

Materials: 40 small objects (pennies, buttons, paper clips)

Do this activity with your child to practice relating word problems to multiplication and division.

- Using some of the objects, ask your child to create an array.
- Take turns making up and solving word problems about your array.
- Each time, have your child say a number sentence to describe the problem.
- Ask your child to say whether he or she used multiplication or division to solve the problem.

Example:

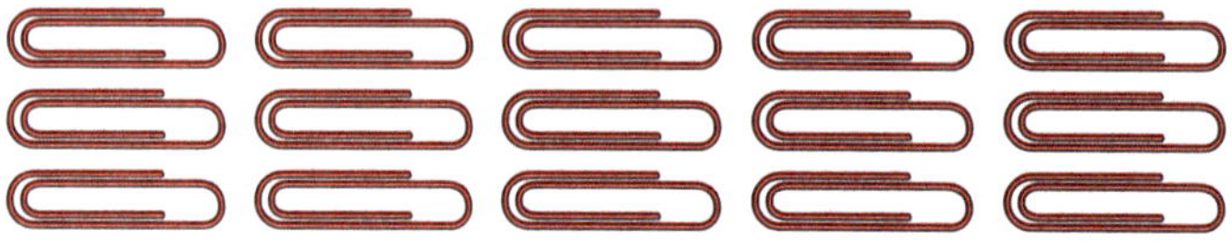

Paul pasted 15 stickers in his scrapbook. He put 5 in each row. How many rows of stickers did he make?

Number sentence:

$15 \div 5 = \mathbf{3}$ or $5 \times \mathbf{3} = 15$

Nigel has 15 cookies. He puts them in equal groups onto 3 plates. How many cookies are on each plate?

Number sentence:

$15 \div 3 = \mathbf{5}$ or $3 \times \mathbf{5} = 15$

Solve One-Step Word Problems Using Multiplication and Division

Name: ______________________

Prerequisite: Write Multiplication and Division Sentences

Study the example showing how to write multiplication and division sentences for equal groups. Then solve problems 1–12.

Jin has 3 rows of frog stickers with 5 stickers in each row.

Multiplication:
3 rows × 5 stickers in each row is 15 stickers
$3 \times 5 = 15$

Division:
15 stickers shared into 3 rows of 5
$15 \div 3 = 5$

1 How many rows of cat stickers are there? ________

2 How many cat stickers are in each row? ________

3 Write the multiplication sentence for the array of cat stickers.

____

4 How many dog stickers are there? ________

5 How many groups of dog stickers are there?

____

6 Write a division sentence that says the 10 stickers are shared into 2 groups of 5.

____

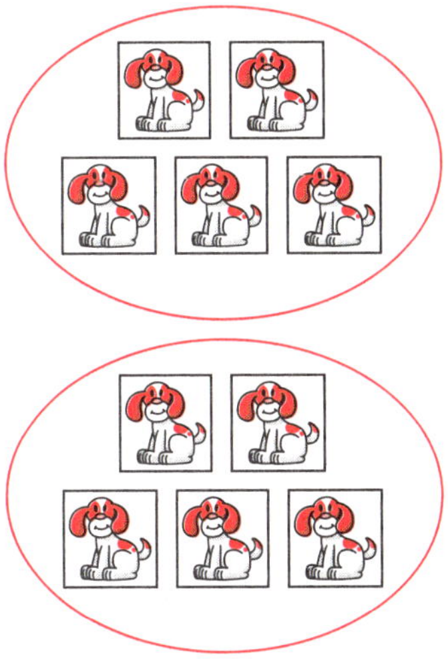

Solve.

7 Write a multiplication sentence to describe the equal groups of hexagon stickers on the right.

____

8 Write a division sentence to describe the equal groups of hexagon stickers.

____

There are 4 cards with 3 triangle stickers on each card.

9 Sketch the cards with the triangle stickers.

10 Write a multiplication sentence to describe the equal groups of triangle stickers.

____

11 Write a division sentence to describe the equal groups of triangle stickers.

____

There are 15 circle stickers. They are on 3 cards, in groups of 5.

12 Write a multiplication sentence and a division sentence to describe the equal groups of circle stickers.

____

____

Name: ______________________

Solve Problems About Equal Groups

Study the example that shows how a drawing can help you understand problems about equal groups. Then solve problems 1–8.

Example

24 students signed up for an Irish folk dancing class. There are 4 students in each group. How many groups are there?

Draw a picture.
24 students
4 in each group
N groups

Write a number sentence.
$24 \div 4 = N$
$N = 6$

There are 6 groups of students.

18 students take hula dance classes. There are 6 students in each class. How many classes are there?

1 Make a drawing for this problem. Use ☺ for each student. Make groups to show the classes.

2 Complete the multiplication and division sentences for this problem. Write the value of *N*.

$18 \div$ _____ $= N$ $N \times$ _____ $= 18$ $N =$ _____

3 How many hula dance classes are there? _______

Solve.

There are 2 classes for Mexican folk dance. There are 8 students in each class. How many students take Mexican folk dance class?

4 What is the unknown that you need to find out?

____

5 Write a number sentence for the problem. Use *N* to stand for the number you need to find out. Solve the problem.

Number Sentence: ______________________

Solution: ______ students take Mexican folk dance class.

15 students take modern dance lessons. There are 3 students in each group. How many groups of students are there?

6 Write a number sentence for the problem. Then solve.

Number Sentence: ______________________

Solution: There are ______________________

7 If 15 more students sign up for modern dance, how many groups would there be?

Number Sentence: ______________________

Solution: There are ______________________

8 How can you use the answer to problem 6 to find the answer to problem 7?

____

____

____

Name: ____________________

Solve Problems About Arrays

Study the example that shows how an array can help you solve multiplication and division problems. Then solve problems 1–6.

Example

The art teacher wants to hang 18 drawings on the hall wall. She will hang 6 drawings in each row. How many rows of drawings will there be?

18 drawings
6 in each row
N rows

$18 \div 6 = N$ and $6 \times N = 18$

$18 \div 6 = 3$ and $6 \times 3 = 18$

There will be 3 rows of drawings.

$$\begin{array}{r} 6 \\ 6 \\ +\ 6 \\ \hline 18 \end{array}$$

In the art room, there are 20 easels. The easels are arranged in 4 equal rows. How many easels are in each row?

1. Draw an array to show the 20 easels in 4 rows. Put the same number in each row. Use a ☐ to show each easel.

2. Complete the division sentence to solve the problem. *N* stands for the unknown.

   20 ÷ ______ = *N*, so *N* = ______

3. How many easels are in each row. ____________

Solve.

4 The art room has 5 shelves of paint jars. There are 9 paint jars on each shelf. How many paint jars are in the art room?

Show your work.

Solution: ________________________________

5 There are 54 frames on the wall in an art store. The frames are in 6 equal rows. How many frames are in each row?

Show your work.

Solution: ________________________________

6 The store has 3 shelves with the same number of drawing pads on each shelf. There are 30 drawing pads in all. How many drawing pads are on each shelf?

Show your work.

Solution: ________________________________

Name: ______________________________

Solve Problems About Tiling

Study the example that shows how to use drawings and number sentences to help you solve multiplication and division problems about tiling. Then solve problems 1–6.

Example

Mrs. Milton puts same-size square tiles on the patio floor. She uses 21 tiles and makes 3 rows of tiles. All rows have the same number of tiles. How many tiles are in each row?

21 tiles
3 rows
N tiles in each row

3 rows

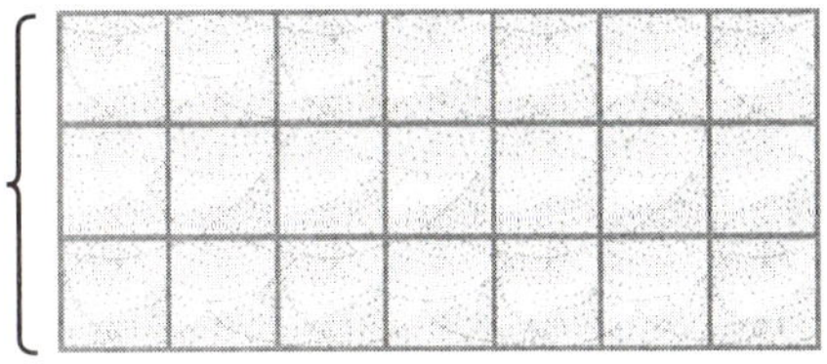

$$7 + 7 + 7 = 21$$

$21 \div 3 = N$ and $3 \times N = 21$

$21 \div 3 = 7$ and $3 \times 7 = 21$

There are 7 tiles in each row.

Mr. Salton paved the entrance to his house with stone tiles. He used 42 same-size square tiles. He put 7 tiles in each row. How many rows of tiles are there?

1 Make a drawing to show the rows of tiles.

2 Complete the division sentence to solve the problem. Use *N* to stand for the unknown number.

$42 \div$ ______ $= N$, so $N =$ ______

3 How many rows of stone tiles are there? ________

Solve.

4 Mrs. Ross made a quilt using same-size squares of fabric. She used 36 squares and put 9 squares in each row. How many rows are there?

Show your work.

Solution: ______________________________

5 There are 7 rows of squares on a game board. There are 9 squares in each row. How many squares are on the game board?

Show your work.

Solution: ______________________________

6 Each square on the game board in problem 5 has sides that are 2 inches long. How long and how wide is the section of squares?

Show your work.

Solution: The section of squares is

______ inches wide and ______ inches long.

Name: ______________________

Solve One-Step Word Problems

Solve the problems.

1 Dave tiles part of the kitchen wall. He makes 6 rows with 8 tiles in each row. How many tiles does he use?

Show your work:

Solution: ______________________

2 There are 36 paint brushes in 4 jars. Each jar has the same number of brushes. Which of these would you use to find the number of brushes in each jar? Circle the letter of all that apply.

A $36 + 4 = \square$

B $4 \times \square = 36$

C $36 \div 4 = \square$

D $36 - 4 = \square$

3 There are 2 racks and 14 paint aprons. There are the same number of aprons on each rack. How many aprons are on each rack?

Show your work.

Solution: ______________________

Solve.

4 There are 48 tubes of oil paint on trays. Each tray holds 6 tubes. How many trays of tubes are there?

Show your work.

Solution: ______________________________

5 There are 9 boxes of crayons with 8 crayons in each box. Which of these would you use to figure out the total number of crayons?

A $72 \div 8 = \square$

B $8 \times 9 = \square$

C $8 + 9 = \square$

D $72 \div \square = 9$

Renee chose **A** as the correct answer. Explain why that answer isn't correct.

____

____

6 The drawing shows the arrangement of bottles of glue in the art room. Write a multiplication equation and a division equation for this drawing.

Multiplication equation: ______________________________

Division equation: ______________________________

Dear Family,

This week your child is learning how to model two-step word problems using any mix of the four operations: multiplication, division, subtraction, or addition.

In a two-step problem, you might first have to add or subtract something before multiplying or dividing. Or you might have to multiply, and then multiply again.

Suppose you have 5 baskets of apples and each basket has 8 apples. And suppose you need 25 apples to make apple pies. There are two steps if you want to figure out how many apples will be left over.

One way to think about the problem is to make a diagram.

In this problem, the first step is to multiply to find out how many apples you have to start. 5 groups of 8 is a total of 40 apples.

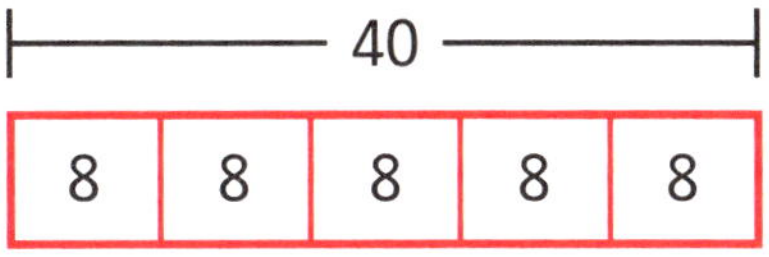

$5 \times 8 = 40$

The second step is to subtract to find out how many are left after you make pies. 25 apples will be used for pies.

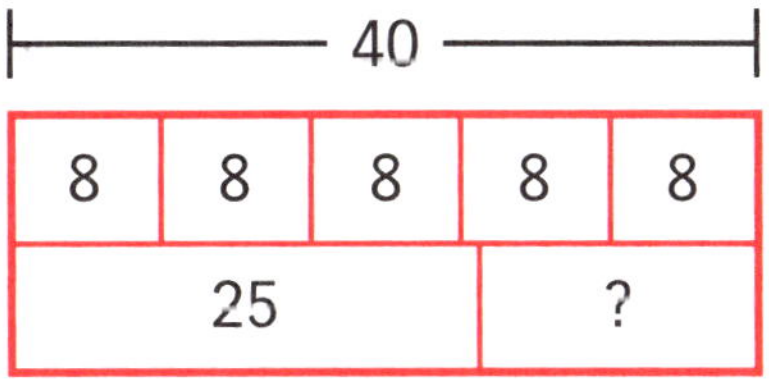

$40 - 25 = 15$

You'll have 15 apples left after you make pies.

Knowing how to use diagrams like this is particularly useful when problems involve larger numbers or more steps.

Invite your child to share what he or she knows about how to model two-step word problems using any of the four operations by doing the following activity together.

NEXT

Two-Step Word Problems Activity

Make up two-step word problems that use any of the four operations with numbers you encounter in your everyday life. Use ideas like these:

- Laurie has $25. If she buys 3 books for $7 each, how much will she have left?

- Mark sold 35 tins of popcorn for the school fundraiser on Monday. On Tuesday he sold 12 more tins of popcorn than he did on Monday. How many tins did he sell in all on Monday and Tuesday?
- Containers of yogurt are sold in packs of 4. A case holds 8 packs of yogurt. How many containers of yogurt are in 2 cases?

Have your child draw a picture, diagram, or number line to illustrate the word problem, then write and solve a number sentence.

Give your child several two-step problems to solve. Vary the operations needed to solve the problems. Be on the look-out for actual problem situations that may arise in your own family's life, too!

Lesson 12

Model Two-Step Word Problems Using the Four Operations

Name: ______________________

Prerequisite: Model One-Step Word Problems

Study the example showing how to model a one-step word problem. Then solve problems 1–10.

Example

Eight students in art class each made 3 paper flowers. How many paper flowers did the students make altogether?

3	3	3	3	3	3	3	3

$$8 \times 3 = ?$$

The students made 24 flowers.

32 students sat in equal groups at 8 lunch tables. How many students sat at each table?

1 Look at the model. Fill in the blank in the number sentence.

$$\_\_\_\_ \div 8 = ?$$

?	?	?	?	?	?	?	?

2 What is 32 ÷ 8? ______

3 How many students sat at each table? ______

Solve.

Art class has 27 students and music class has 34 students. How many more students are in music class than in art class?

4 Fill in the labels on the model for this problem.

5 Write a number sentence you could use to solve the problem.

____

6 How many more students are there in music class than in art class? ______

Students practiced 9 songs for the school concert. They practiced each song for 5 minutes. How many minutes did they practice?

7 Complete the model for this problem on the number line.

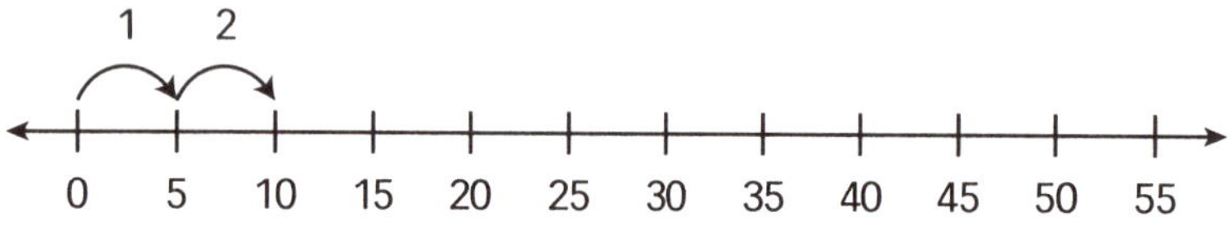

8 Write a number sentence you could use to solve the problem. _______________

9 How many minutes did the students practice? ______

10 Draw another model you could use to solve this problem.

____

____

____

Name: ______________________

Model Two-Step Problems with Multiplication

Study the example showing how to model two-step problems when one operation is multiplication. Then solve problems 1–8.

Example

Sally bought 6 bags of round beads to make bracelets. There are 4 round beads in each bag. She also bought 5 heart-shaped beads. How many beads did Sally buy?

Round beads:
6 groups of 4
6×4

All beads:
round beads + heart beads
$6 \times 4 + 5 = 29$

Sally bought 29 beads.

Jeff bought 3 cards of smile pins with 4 pins on each card. He gave one pin to his sister. How many smile pins did he have left?

1 Complete the number sentence for this problem.

$\square \times 4 - 1 = \square$

2 Jeff had _____ smile pins left.

Mary bought 4 boxes of markers and 2 extra markers. Each box had 5 markers. How many markers did she buy in all?

3 How many markers did Mary buy? _____

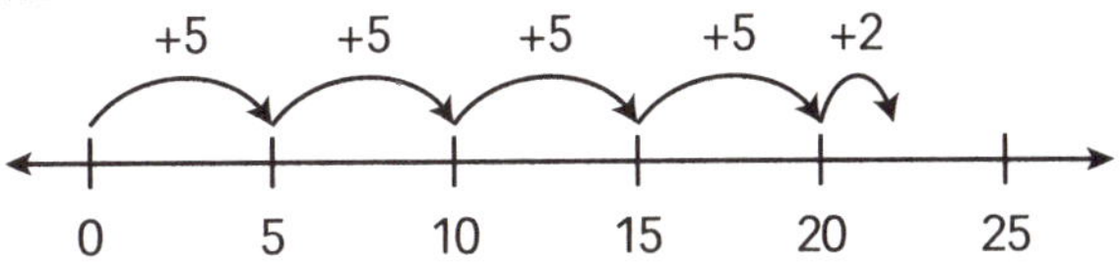

Solve.

The store had 4 baskets of apples with 8 apples in each basket. They sold 10 apples. How many apples were left?

4 Draw a model for the problem. Label the model.

5 Write a number sentence for the problem above.

____

____

6 How many apples were left? _____

7 Each package has 8 straws. Denise bought 8 packages. She used 61 straws to make a model of a house. How many straws did she have left?

Show your work.

Solution: She had _____ straws left.

8 The art teacher bought 6 boxes of colored pencils. Each box cost $8. She also bought a case for the pencils for $10. How much did she spend in all?

Show your work.

Solution: She spent ____________________________

Name: ______________________

Model Two-Step Problems with Division

Study the example showing how to model two-step problems when one operation is division. Then solve problems 1–11.

Example

For the food drive, third grade students collected 13 cans of vegetables and 14 cans of soup. They put the cans in bags with 3 cans in each bag. How many bags of cans did they have?

total number of cans
13 vegetables and 14 soups
$13 + 14 = 27$

in each bag
27 cans, 3 cans in each bag
$27 \div 3 = 9$
They had 9 bags of cans.

Students collected 12 red apples and 12 green apples. They put all the apples into bags, putting 6 apples in each bag. How many bags of apples did they have?

1. Write a number sentence that shows how many apples they collected. ______________________

2. They collected _____ apples.

3. Write a number sentence that shows how many bags of apples the students had. ______________

4. The students had _____ bags of apples.

5. Draw a model to check your work.

Solve.

The students collected 6 boxes with 6 grapefruit in each box. They put the grapefruit into bags. Each bag held 4 grapefruit. How many bags did they need?

6 Write a number sentence to show how many grapefruit the students collected. ______________

7 Write a number sentence to show how many bags they will need for the grapefruit. ______________

8 How many bags did the students need for the grapefruit? ______________________________

Students collect 7 boxes of potatoes with 8 potatoes in each box. Then they put all the potatoes into bags. There are 8 potatoes in each bag.

9 How many bags do the students need for the potatoes?

Show your work.

Solution: They need _____ bags.

10 Why might a student say this problem is "easy"?

____

____

____

11 Later the students collect 24 more potatoes. How many bags do they need for all the potatoes?

Show your work.

Solution: They need _____ bags.

Name: ______________________________

Solve Two-Step Word Problems

Solve the problems.

1 Susan bought 2 caps for \$9 each and an arm band for \$5. How much did she spend in all? Choose the answer that shows the correct two steps.

A $3 \times \$4 = \$12$
$\$7 + \$9 = \$16$

B $\$9 - \$5 = \$4$
$2 \times \$4 = \$8$

C $\$9 \times 2 = \$18$
$\$18 + \$5 = \$23$

D $\$9 - \$2 = \$7$
$7 \times \$5 = \$35$

Drawing a picture might help.

2 There were 9 students from grade 3 and 15 students from grade 4 in the game day event. The students were placed in teams of 6. How many teams were there?

Choose the answer that shows the correct two steps.

A $3 \times 4 = 12$
$12 \div 6 = 2$

B $9 + 15 = 24$
$24 \div 6 = 4$

C $24 \div 3 = 8$
$8 + 6 = 14$

D $15 - 9 = 6$
$6 \times 6 = 36$

What do the numbers 3 and 4 tell you?

3 Ann is on a running team. She ran 2 miles each day for 5 days. Over the weekend, she ran 4 more miles. How many miles did Ann run that week?

Show your work.

What are the two steps to solve this problem?

Solution: ______________________________

Solve.

4 There were 6 students sitting on each of the 4 benches at the race. Then 3 students left to get water. How many students were left on the benches?

Show your work.

Solution: ______________________________

5 The coach bought 9 packs of award ribbons with 4 ribbons in each pack. He gave all the ribbons to 6 teams. Each team got the same number of ribbons. How many ribbons did each team get?

Show your work.

Solution: ______________________________

6 Ken put 35 sports cards in 5 packs with the same number of cards in each pack. He gave 1 pack to his brother. How many cards did Ken have left? Circle the letter of the correct answer.

A 30 **C** 28

B 6 **D** 7

Brett chose **B** as the correct answer. How did he get that answer?

____

____

Dear Family,

This week your child is solving two-step word problems using any mix of the four operations, but this week the numbers are larger.

Here's a problem your child might see.

> Jenny has 152 peaches and she needs 8 peaches for each pie. If she first gives 72 peaches to her neighbor, how many pies can she make with the peaches she keeps for herself?

When the numbers are larger, it's particularly helpful to make a diagram.

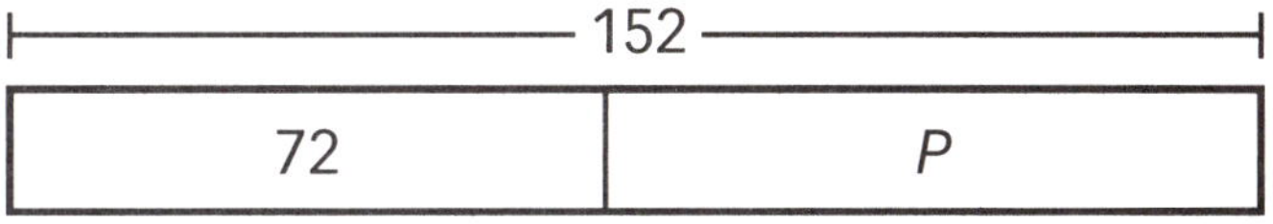

The diagram shows that Jenny started with 152 peaches, gave part to her neighbor, and kept P peaches for herself.

In this problem, the first step is to subtract to find out how many peaches Jenny kept. $152 - 72 = 80$, so Jenny kept 80 peaches.

The second step is to figure out how many groups of 8 peaches Jenny can make from her 80 peaches. Since there are equal groups, write a multiplication or division sentence to find how many equal groups (G).

$8 \times G = 80$ or $80 \div 8 = G$

$80 \div 8 = 10$, so Jenny can make 10 pies.

Invite your child to share what he or she knows about solving two-step word problems with greater numbers using the four operations by doing the following activity together.

NEXT

Word Problems Using the Four Operations Activity

Work with your child to make up a real-world problem this diagram could represent.

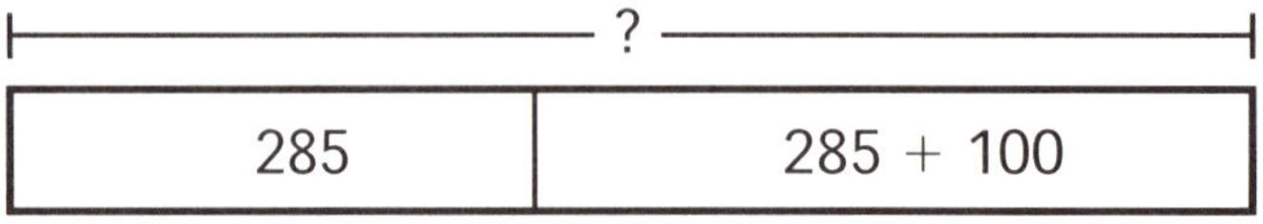

For example, you might make up a problem like the following.

> "We drove 285 miles on Saturday. On Sunday we drove 100 more miles than we drove on Saturday. How many miles did we drive in all over the weekend?"

Now, work with your child to write an equation for the problem. One equation could be:

$M = 285 + (285 + 100)$

$M = 285 + 385$

$M = 670$

The answer to the problem is, "We drove 670 miles."

Change the numbers and try creating a new problem to match the new numbers.

Solve Two-Step Word Problems Using the Four Operations

Name: ____________________

Prerequisite: Model Two-Step Word Problems

Study the example problem showing how to model a two-step word problem. Then solve problems 1–5.

Example

The art shop was almost out of rolls of tape. There were only 3 rolls left. The owner ordered 5 boxes with 6 rolls in each box. How many rolls of tape are there now?

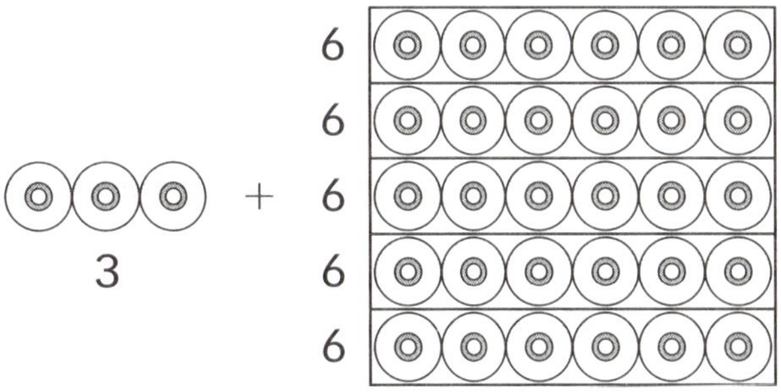

$5 \times 6 = 30$

$30 + 3 = 33$

There are 33 rolls of tape now.

1 Each box of party invitations costs $6. Jenny bought 3 boxes of invitations. She paid with a $20 bill. Complete the number sentences to find how much change Jenny got.

3 × $______ = $______

$20 − $______ = $______

Jenny got $______ in change.

2 There are 2 baskets, each holding 4 bags of bows. Each bag costs $3. Mr. Holms bought all of the bags. Complete the number sentences to find out how much he spent on bows.

2 × ______ = ______

______ × $3 = $______

He spent $______ on bows.

Solve.

3 Packages of party napkins are $4 each. Bags of party cups are $6 each. Mrs. Laurey bought 2 packages of party napkins and 1 package of party cups. How much did she spend in all?

Write number sentences, then write the solution.

Number sentences: ______________________________

Solution: She spent $ ______.

4 The gift shop sells red and white paper plates. They have 20 packs of red plates and 28 packs of white plates. All packs of plates are on 6 shelves with the same number of packs on each shelf. How many packs of plates are on each shelf?

Show your work.

Solution: There are ______ packs on each shelf.

5 Large tablecloths are $12 each. Small ones are $8 each. How many small tablecloths can you buy for the same price as two large tablecloths?

Show your work.

Solution: You can buy ______ small tablecloths.

Name: ______________________

Solve Two-Step Problems

Study the example problem showing how to solve a two-step word problem. Then solve problems 1–5.

Example

Students in the science club raised $210 for lab equipment. They bought 7 packs of batteries for $9 each. How much money did they have left?

X is how much money was left.

$7 \times 9 + X = 210$

$63 + X = 210$

$210 - 63 = X$

$210 - 63 = 147$

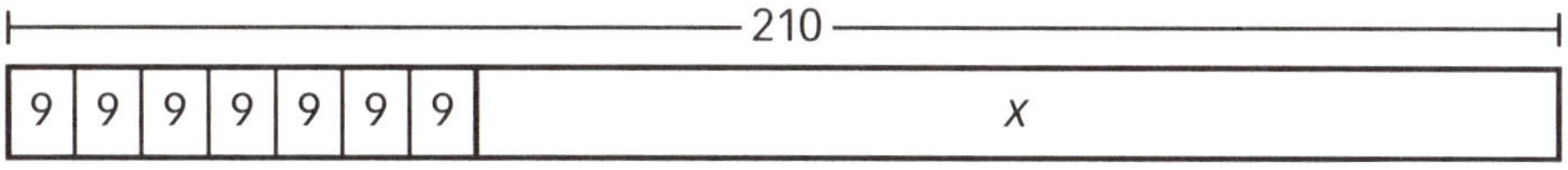

They have $147 left.

1 Mrs. Horn needs 50 rulers for the art room. She has 7 packs with 4 rulers in each pack. How many more rulers does she need? Complete the number sentences to solve the problem.

X is how many more rulers she needs.

$7 \times \square + X = 50$

$\square + X = 50$

$\square - \square = X$, and $X = \square$

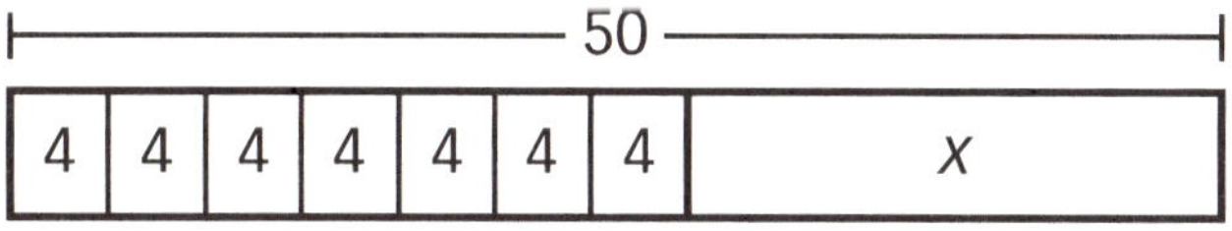

Solution: Mrs. Horn needs ______ more rulers.

2 The principal wants to buy a banner that costs $95. Five parents each donate $6 for the banner. How much more money is needed? Complete the number sentences to solve the problem.

$\square \times \square + X = 95$

$\square + X = 95$

$X = \square$

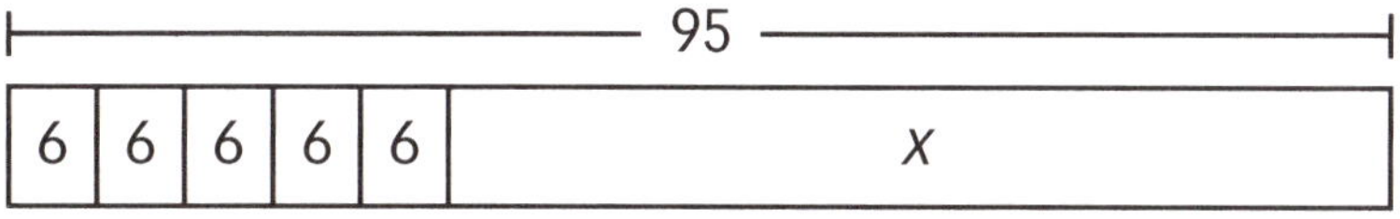

Solution: They need ______ more.

Solve.

3 A camp needs 100 students to help with the 4-year old campers. Eight students from 4 different classes have agreed to help. How many more students are needed?

Show your work.

Solution: ______________________________

4 The music teacher had \$75. He bought 4 folk song books for \$9 each. Does he have enough money to buy a music stand for \$49? If not, how much more money does he need?

Show your work.

Solution: ______________________________

5 Mr. Berg bought 5 number puzzles and 3 word puzzles for his students. The puzzles were \$7 each. Mr. Berg used a \$60 gift card to pay for the puzzles. How much change did he get?

Show your work.

Solution: ______________________________

Name: ______________________

Estimate Solutions to Two-Step Word Problems

Study the example showing how to estimate the solution to a two-step word problem. Then solve problems 1–4.

Example

The city garden has red and pink rose bushes. There are 119 red rose bushes. There are 17 fewer pink rose bushes than red rose bushes. About how many rose bushes are in the city garden?

Round to the nearest 10 and solve.
119 rounds to 120 and 17 rounds to 20.
I know 120 – 20 is 100,
so I *estimate* 100 pink rose bushes.
I know 120 + 100 = 220,
so I *estimate* 220 rose bushes.

Rose Bushes

Red	Pink
119	119 − 17
(about 120)	(about 120 − 20, or 100)

$119 + (119 - 17) = X$
$119 + 102 = X$ and $X = 221$

The actual number of rose bushes in the garden is 221. That's close to 220, so 221 is reasonable.

For the concert, 109 adult tickets were sold. 67 more student tickets were sold than adult tickets. How many tickets were sold in all?

1 Complete the chart to show the information in the problem. Round to the nearest hundred.

Tickets Sold

Adults	Students
(about ______)	(about ______ + ______)

2 Write a number sentence to estimate the total number of tickets sold. Then find the actual total.

______________________ = *X*

________ = *X*

Solution: About ______ tickets were sold.

Really, ______ tickets were sold.

Solve.

3 In the school parking lot there were 113 fewer bikes than cars. There were 185 cars. How many cars and bikes were in the parking lot?

Round to the nearest ten to estimate. Then complete the chart.

Cars	Bikes
185	185 − 113
(about 190)	(about 190 − ______, or ______)

______ + ______ − ______ = X

X = ______

Estimate: There were about ______ cars and bikes.

Actual: ______ + ______ − ______ = X

X = ______

Solution: There were ______ cars and bikes in all.

4 Sarah read 215 pages of her book during the first week of vacation. During the second week she read 62 more pages than in the first week. How many pages did she read in the two weeks? Round to the nearest ten to estimate, then solve.

Show your work.

Estimate: She read about ______ pages during the two weeks.

Actual: ____

____

Solution: Sarah read ______ pages.

Name: ______________________

Estimate and Solve Two-Step Word Problems

Solve the problems.

1 Students collected cans to make robots. They collected 127 small cans. They collected 47 fewer large cans than small cans.

Which number sentence could you use to figure out the total number of cans? X is the unknown number of cans.

A $127 - 47 = X$

B $127 + 127 + 47 = X$

C $89 + 80 = X$

D $127 + 127 - 47 = X$

2 Jen has to put 180 cards into boxes of 6 cards each. She puts 150 cards into boxes.

Which number sentence could you use to figure out how many more boxes Jen needs? B stands for the unknown number of boxes.

A $180 = 6 \times B$

B $150 + 6 \times B = 180$

C $6 \times B + 180 = 150$

D $180 + 150 = 6 \times B$

3 An oil paint set costs $45 more than an easel. An easel costs $129. What is the total cost of the oil paint set and the easel?

Show your work.

Solution: ______________________

Solve.

4 Sam has 223 postcards from all around the world. He has 9 sets of 8 cards from countries in Africa. How many of Sam's cards are not from Africa?

Show your work.

Solution: ______________________________

5 A group of people walked 62 miles in Week 1 and 58 miles in Week 2. In Week 3, they walked 14 miles less than during Week 2. How many miles did the group walk in 3 weeks?

Show your work.

Solution: ______________________________

6 Donna used 30 buttons of different colors and sizes to make a design. She used 12 large blue buttons. The rest were small and yellow or small and green. There were the same number of yellow and green buttons. How many buttons were small and yellow?

A 9

B 22

C 18

D 42

Javy chose **C** as the correct answer. How did he get that answer?

____

____

____

Unit 3 Game

Name: ______________________

Two-Step Problems

What you need: Recording Sheet, 3 number cube (1–6)

Directions

- Take turns. On your turn, roll 3 number cubes.
- Use those 3 numbers to make up a word problem. The problem must have 2 steps and it must use multiplication.
- The goal is to make up a word problem with an answer for any Answer Target on the Recording Sheet.
- Draw a model and write a number sentence for your word problem on the Recording Sheet.
- If you can't make up a problem to fit an unused target, your turn ends.
- The first player to complete all 5 targets is the winner.

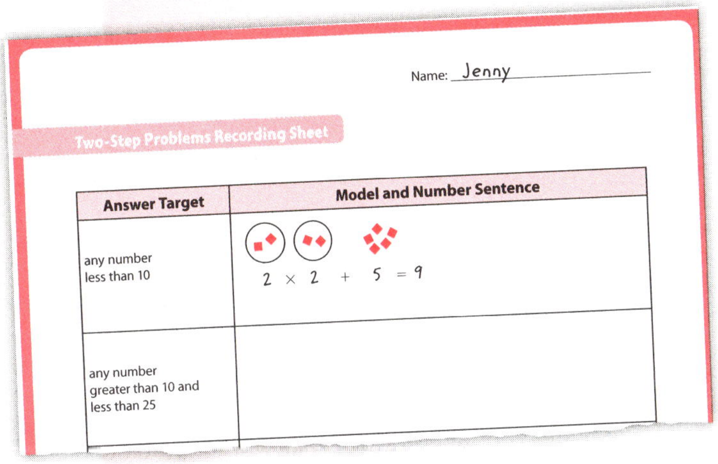
Name: Jenny

Two-Step Problems Recording Sheet

Answer Target	Model and Number Sentence
any number less than 10	2 × 2 + 5 = 9
any number greater than 10 and less than 25	

Name: ____________________

Two-Step Problems Recording Sheet

Answer Target	Model and Number Sentence
any number less than 10	
any number greater than 10 and less than 25	
any number greater than 25	
any even number	
any odd number	

Unit 3 Practice

Name: ____________________

Operations and Algebraic Thinking, Part 2

In this unit you learned to:	Lesson
solve one-step word problems using multiplication or division.	11
model two-step word problems using the four operations.	12
solve two-step word problems using the four operations.	13

Use these skills to solve problems 1–5.

1 There are 48 envelopes in 8 boxes. Each box has the same number of envelopes. Which of these can you use to figure out the number of envelopes in each box? Circle the letter of all that apply.

A $8 \times N = 48$

B $48 + 8 = N$

C $48 - N = 8$

D $48 \div 8 = N$

2 Martha made 3 fruit pies. She used 3 green apples and 15 red apples divided evenly among all the pies. How many apples were in each pie?

Show your work.

Solution: Each pie had ______ apples.

Solve.

3 Bob painted the room in his basement from 5:00 P.M. to 7:00 P.M. each night for 5 nights. On the weekend, he painted 4 more hours to finish the job. How many hours did it take Bob to paint the basement?

Show your work.

Solution: It took Bob _____ hours to paint the basement.

4 Fifty students went on a field trip. The school bus holds 32 students. Each school van has 3 rows of seats with 3 seats in each row. After the school bus is filled, how many vans are needed for the rest of the students?

Show your work.

Solution: They will need ______ vans.

5 The toy store had 3 cartons of dragon kites and 4 cartons of fish kites. There were 8 kites in each carton. By the end of the week, the store only had 2 kites left. How many kites did the toy store sell?

Let X stand for the number of kites sold. Complete the number sentence. Then write the answer.

$(4 + \_\_\_\_\_) \times 8 - \_\_\_\_\_ = X$

Solution: The store sold _____ kites.

Unit 3 Performance Task

Name: ____________________

Answer the questions and show all your work on separate paper.

Serena is in charge of ordering juice boxes for the class picnic. The class made these decisions:

- They need at least 50 juice boxes, but 80 is too many.
- They want 4 flavors.
- They want the same number of boxes of apple juice, orange juice, and pineapple juice.
- They want twice as many grape juice boxes as all the other flavors combined.

Make a chart to show how many boxes of each kind of juice Serena should order. Write a number sentence to show that the total number of juice boxes is between 50 and 80. Explain why you chose the numbers you did.

Checklist

Did you . . .

- ☐ make a chart?
- ☐ write a number sentence and show your work?
- ☐ explain why you chose your numbers?

Reflect on Mathematical Practices

1. **Make Sense of the Problem** How did you make sure that the total number of juice boxes is between 50 and 80? Explain any changes that you had to make to meet the goal.

2. **Model with Mathematics** Why did you choose the kind of model that you used? What other models could you have used?

Performance Task Tips

Word Bank Here are some words that you might use in your answer.

each	multiply	total
share	product	as many
less than	divide	more than
equal to		

Models Here are some models that you might use to find the solution.

Flavor	Boxes

O	A	P
G		
G		

Sentence Starters Here are some sentence starters that might help explain your work.

First I tried ______________________________

The total number of ______________________________

I think they should get ________ because ____________

Unit 3 Vocabulary

Name: ______________________

My Examples

multiplication

an operation used to find the total number of items when you have equal-sized groups

division

an operation used to separate a number of items into equal-sized groups

My Words

____

____

____

____

____

____

____

____

My Words

My Examples

Dear Family,

This week your child is exploring what a fraction is.

Fractions are numbers that describe equal parts of a whole.

denominator: the bottom number in a fraction. It tells how many equal parts are in the whole.

numerator: the top number in a fraction. It tells how many parts you have.

$\frac{1}{3}$ of this rectangle has been shaded.

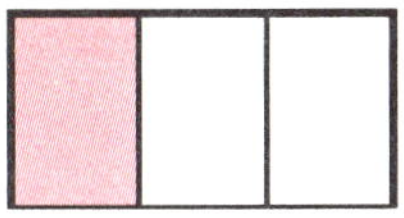

$$\frac{\text{1 part shaded}}{\text{3 equal parts in the whole}}$$

$\frac{1}{3}$ is a **unit fraction** because it names just one equal part of a whole.

$\frac{1}{4}$ is another example of a unit fraction.

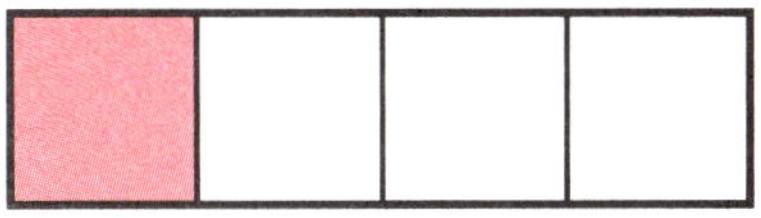

Three $\frac{1}{4}$ s of this rectangle have been shaded. So we write that $\frac{3}{4}$ is shaded.

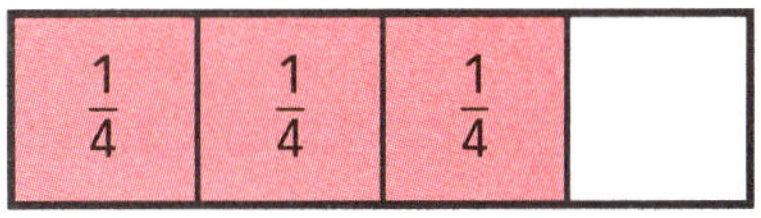

Invite your child to share what he or she knows about what a fraction is by doing the following activity together.

NEXT

Fraction Activity

Materials: pencil and paper, assorted items to divide, scissors or knife

Help your child become familiar with writing fractions by doing this activity together.

- Find at least three "whole" items in your house that can be divided into equal parts. Some examples are a sandwich, an apple, or a sheet of paper.
- Work together to show equal parts. For example, cut a sandwich into 4 parts that are the same size, or divide the paper into 8 equal parts.
- Then take turns saying and writing a fraction and then showing that fraction of the object. If the first person writes "one fourth" and writes "$\frac{1}{4}$," the other person points to 1 part of the sandwich. If the first person says "three eighths" and writes "$\frac{3}{8}$," the other person points to 3 parts of an object that has 8 equal parts.
- Use fractions with denominators of 2, 3, 4, 6, and 8.

Understand What a Fraction Is

Name: ______________________

Prerequisite: How can you find equal parts of a shape?

Study the example showing shapes divided into equal parts. Then solve problems 1–6.

Example

The circles are divided into equal parts. You use the number of equal parts to name the parts.

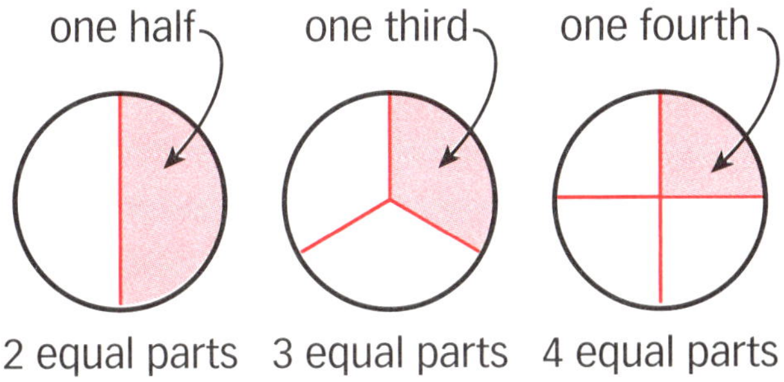

1 Which of these shows equal parts? Circle the letter for all that apply.

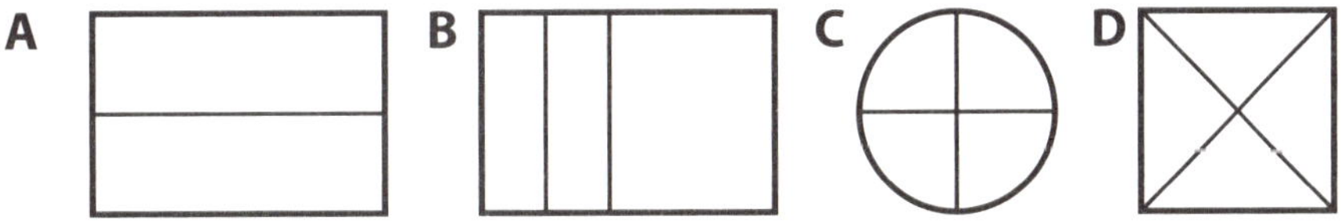

Fill in the blanks.

2 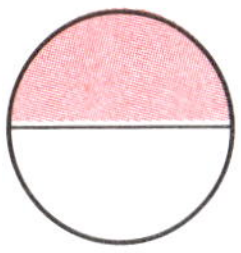

______ equal parts

Each part is one ______.

3 

______ equal parts

Each part is one ______.

Solve.

4 Divide the rectangles to make 4 equal parts in each one. Show a different way in each rectangle.

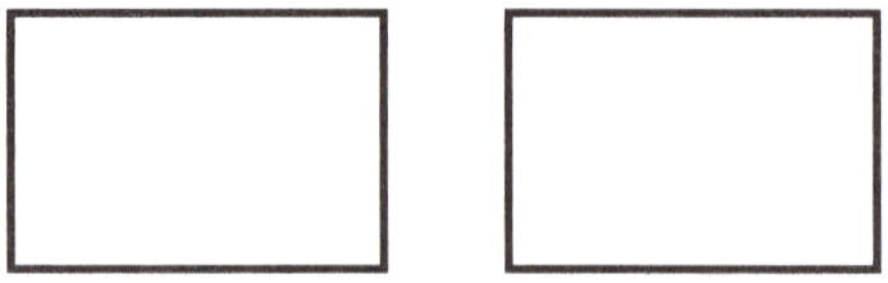

5 Which triangle is divided into thirds?

Explain your answer. ______________________________

____

____

____

____

____

Triangle A   Triangle B

6 Each pizza is cut into fourths. There are 8 people sharing the pizzas shown below. If each person takes one slice, will everyone get the same amount of pizza? Explain your answer.

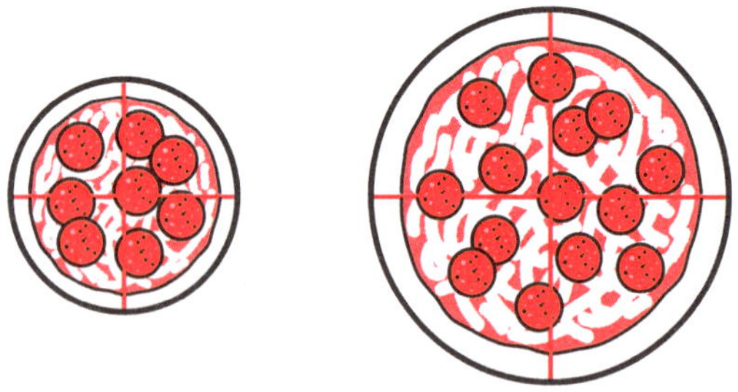

____

____

____

____

____

Name: ______________________

Describe Parts of a Whole with Fractions

Study the example that shows how to write a fraction for parts of a whole. Then solve problems 1–8.

Example

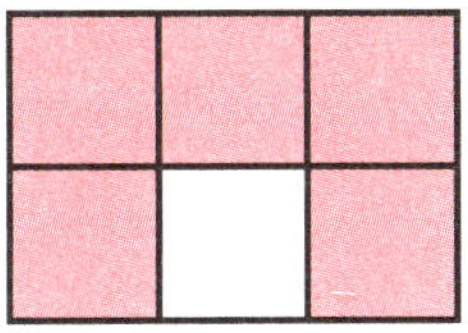

- There are 6 equal parts.
- Each part is one sixth.
- 5 parts are shaded.
- 5 sixths of the whole is shaded.
- This shows the fraction $\frac{5}{6}$.

Fill in the blanks.

1 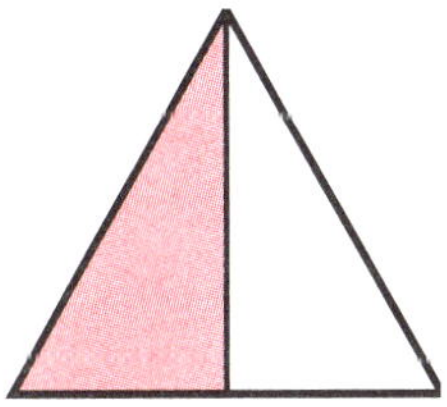

_______ shaded parts

_______ equal parts

_______ fraction

2 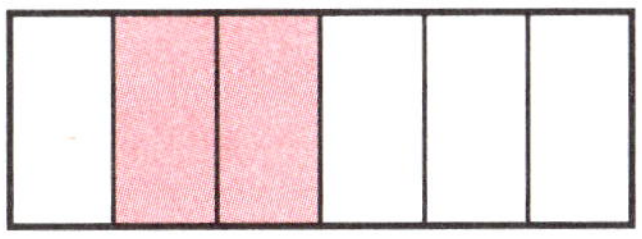

_______ shaded parts

_______ equal parts

_______ fraction

Vocabulary

fraction a number that names part of a whole.

Solve.

3 Shade this shape to show $\frac{3}{4}$.

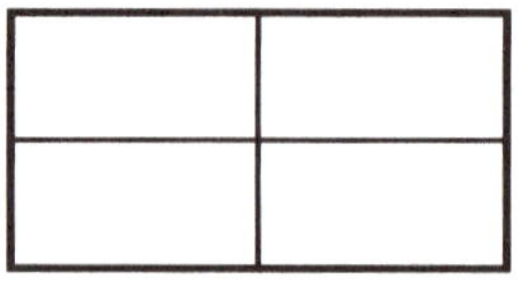

4 Shade this shape to show $\frac{2}{6}$.

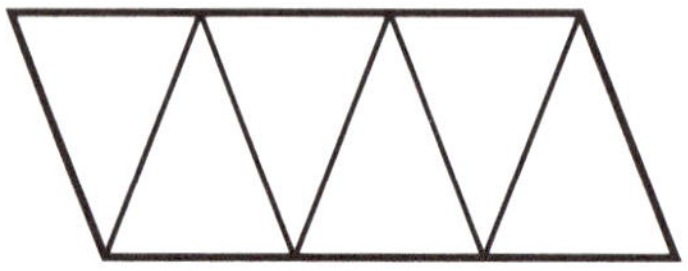

5 Shade 3 parts.

What fraction is shaded? ______

6 Shade 7 parts.

What fraction is shaded? ______

7  is $\frac{1}{4}$ of a rectangle.

Draw the rectangle. Show the parts.

8  is $\frac{1}{4}$ of a rectangle.

Draw the rectangle. Show the parts.

Then shade $\frac{2}{4}$ of your rectangle.

Name: ______________________

Reason and Write

Study the example. Underline two parts that you think make it a particularly good answer and a helpful example.

Example

Draw a rectangle with $\frac{4}{6}$ of it shaded.

Explain how you decided what to draw.

Show your work. Use pictures, words, or numbers to explain how you decided what to draw.

First I thought about how many equal parts are in $\frac{4}{6}$. There are 6 equal parts, so I drew 6 rectangles in a row to make one big rectangle with 6 equal parts.

Then I looked at the numerator. The 4 tells me that I should shade 4 parts. Since they are all the same, I can shade any 4. Here is the same rectangle with 4 parts shaded.

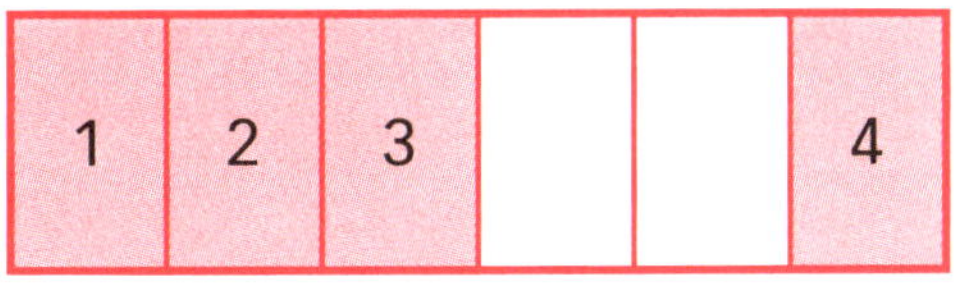

This rectangle has 4 out of 6 equal parts shaded, so $\frac{4}{6}$ of the rectangle is shaded.

Where does the example . . .
- use a picture to explain?
- use numbers to explain?
- use words to explain?
- give details?

Solve the problem. Use what you learned from the model.

Draw a rectangle with $\frac{3}{8}$ of it shaded.

Explain how you decided what to draw.

Show your work. Use pictures, words, or numbers to explain how you decided what to draw.

Did you . . .

- use a picture to explain?
- use numbers to explain?
- use words to explain?
- give details?

Dear Family,

This week your child is exploring fractions on a number line.

You can count fractions on a number line just like you can count whole numbers.

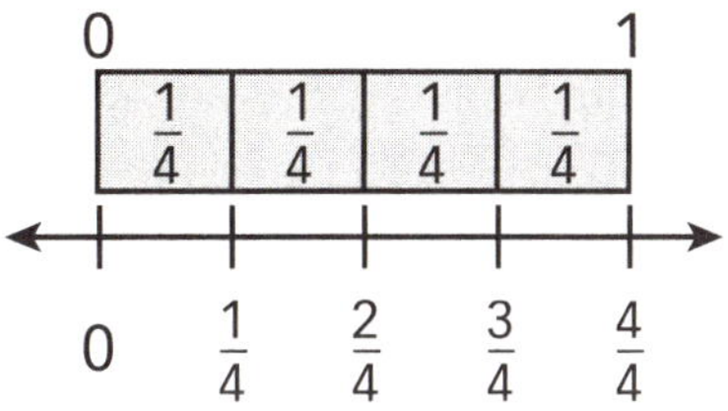

Number lines can also show fractions greater than 1. Each section between a pair of whole numbers (like 0 and 1 or 1 and 2) can be cut into the same number of equal parts.

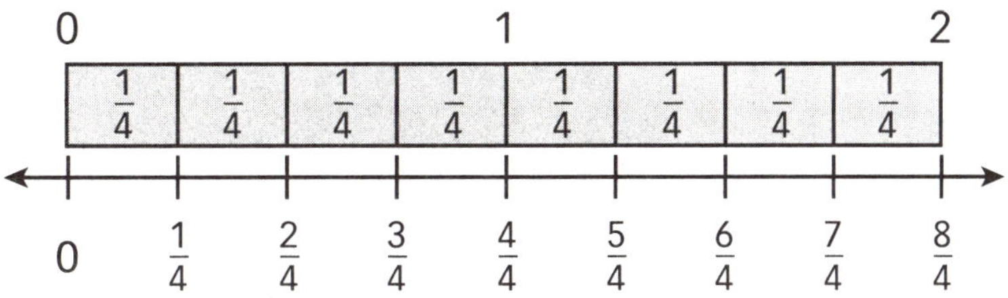

Then just keep counting the fractions. The number line above shows that 1 whole is the same as $\frac{4}{4}$, and 2 wholes is the same as $\frac{8}{4}$.

On the number line below, the fraction that names point B is $\frac{7}{3}$. You can tell because each whole has been cut into thirds. Counting up by thirds, 1 whole is 3 thirds, and 2 wholes is 6 thirds. B marks the seventh third, which we write as $\frac{7}{3}$.

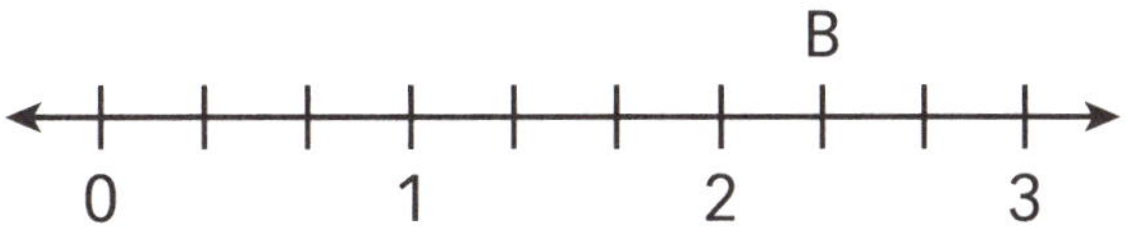

Invite your child to share what he or she knows about fractions on a number line by doing the following activity together.

Fractions on a Number Line Activity

Materials: 2 number cubes with numbers 1–6, blank number lines below, pencils

Give your child practice finding fractions on a number line with this activity.

- Take turns rolling the number cubes. The sum of the two numbers on the cubes tells the numerator of your fraction. The denominator in this activity will always be 8. The number lines below are already marked in eighths for you.
- On your turn, write the fraction on the number line and say the name of the fraction.

  For example, if the cubes rolled show 5 and 4, add 5 and 4 to get your numerator of 9. Then find and mark $\frac{9}{8}$ on the number line and say aloud, "My fraction is nine eighths."

- If you get the same numerator again on another turn, you skip your turn.
- The first player to label 5 different fractions wins.

Player 1

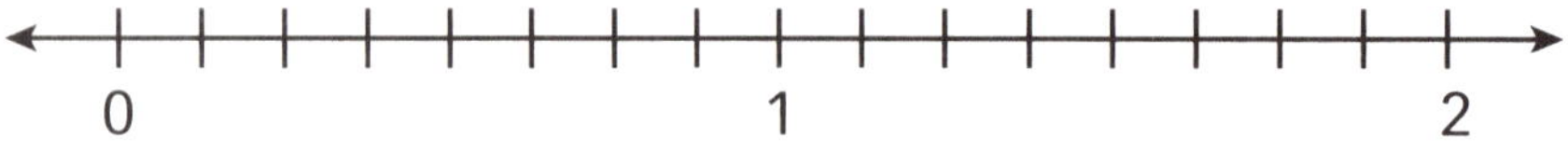

Player 2

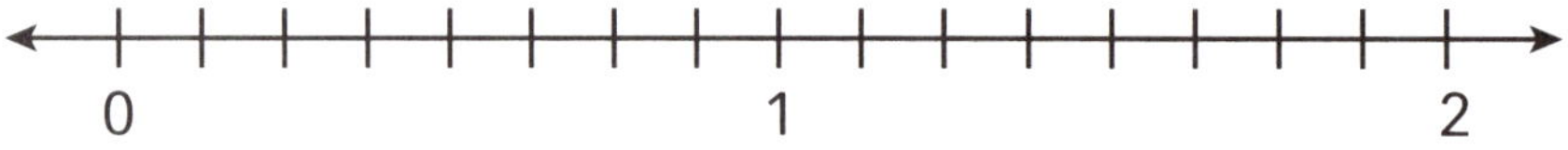

Understand Fractions on a Number Line

Name: ______________________________

Prerequisite: How can you place whole numbers on a number line?

Study the example showing points and sections on a number line. Then solve problems 1–6.

Example

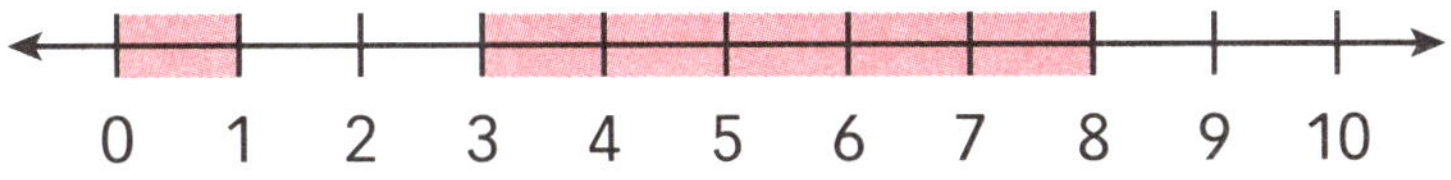

The part of the number line between 0 and 1 shows one whole.

The part of the number line between 3 and 8 shows 5 wholes.

Label the number lines with the missing numbers.

1

2

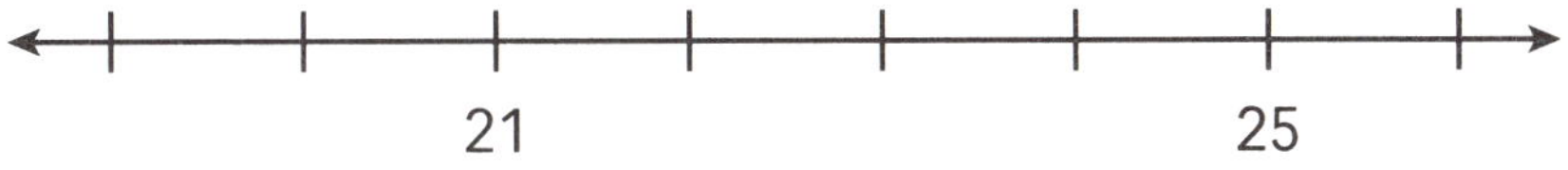

Remember, the numbers on a number line are greater as you move from left to right.

Solve.

3 This number line counts by ones. Write the numbers for the star and the heart.

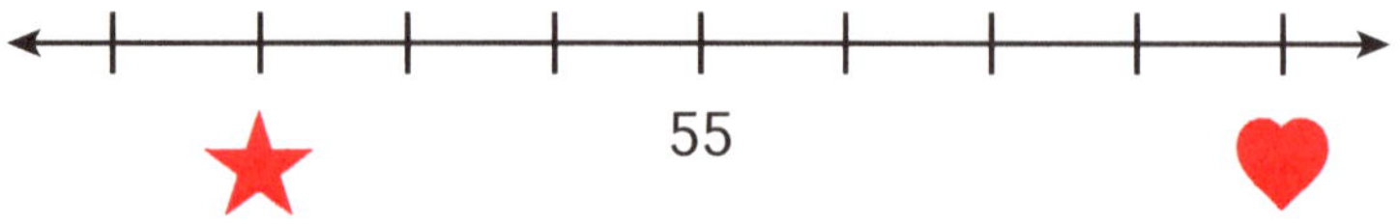

Star _______

Heart _______

4 This number line counts by ones. Write the numbers for the circle and the square.

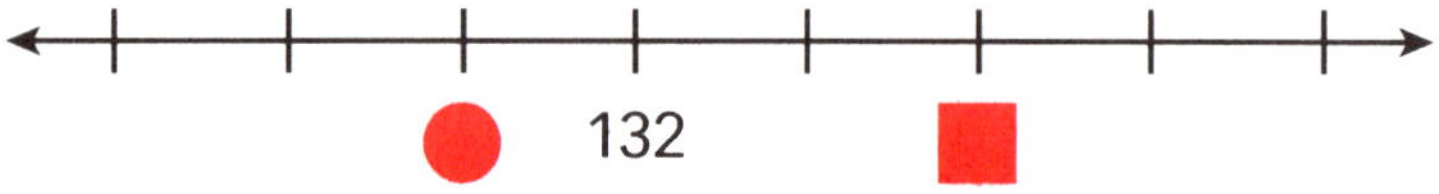

Circle _______

Square _______

Some marks are hidden on these number lines. Estimate. Choose the number marked by the star.

5

A 1 **C** 8

B 5 **D** 2

6

A 2 **C** 5

B 4 **D** 6

Name: ______________________

Use Equal Groups on a Number Line to Think About Fractions

Study how the example shows fractions on a number line. Then solve problems 1–12.

Example

The number line shows just the section from 0 to 1.

That is one whole.

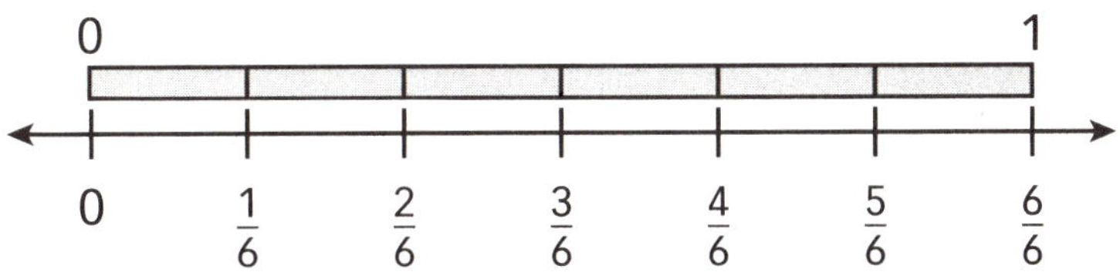

There are 6 equal parts in this section.

Each part is $\frac{1}{6}$ of the whole.

To label the marks, count like you do with whole numbers.

Use this number line to answer problems 1–4.

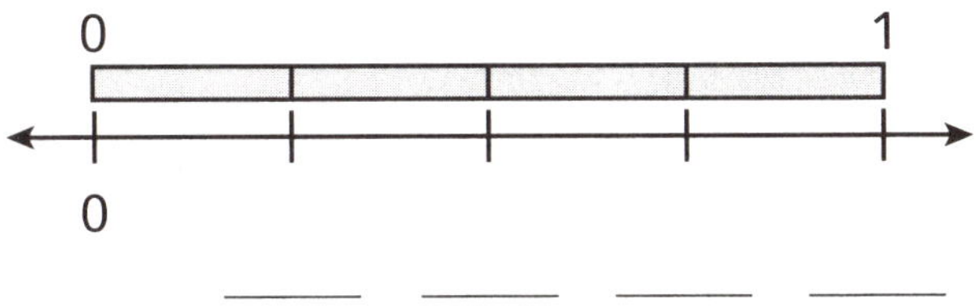

1. How many equal parts are there in this whole? _____

2. What fraction does each part show? _____

3. Label the marks on the number line.

4. What is another name for 1? _____

Vocabulary

fraction a number that names part of a whole..

Use this number line to answer problems 5–8.

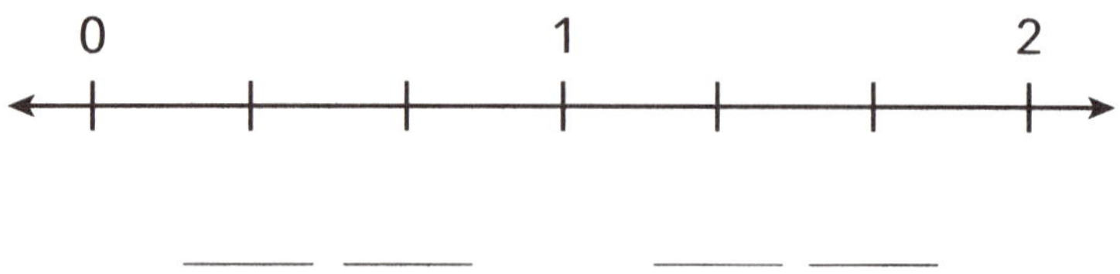

5 How many equal parts are between 0 and 1? ______

6 How many equal parts are between 1 and 2? ______

7 What fraction does each part show? ______

8 Write fractions to label the marks.

Use this number line to answer problems 9–11.

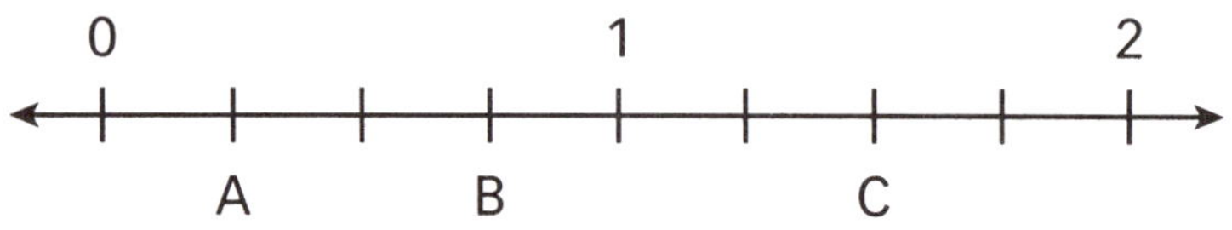

9 ***A*** is ______.

10 ***B*** is ______.

11 ***C*** is ______.

12 Write the fraction $\frac{3}{2}$ where it belongs on this number line.

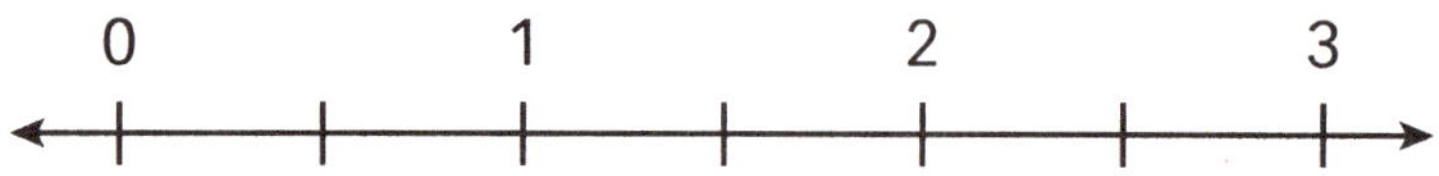

Explain how you knew where to put $\frac{3}{2}$.

____

____

Name: ______________________

Reason and Write

Study the example problem. Underline two parts that you think make it a particularly good answer and a helpful example.

Example

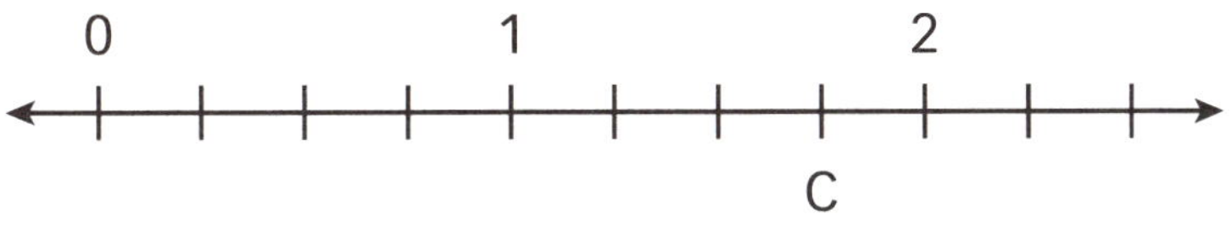

Peter said, "The fraction for point **C** is $\frac{3}{4}$."

Steve said, "The fraction for point **C** is $\frac{7}{4}$."
Who is right? How did you decide?
Who is wrong? What is the mistake?

Show your work. Use pictures, words, or numbers to explain how you decided what to draw.

Peter's answer is wrong. Peter saw that each whole is separated into 4 equal parts. So he knows that the denominator of the fractions is 4 and he has to count fourths.

Peter's mistake was he started counting fourths at 1 instead of at 0. The point for $\frac{3}{4}$ is closer to 0, where I drew it below.

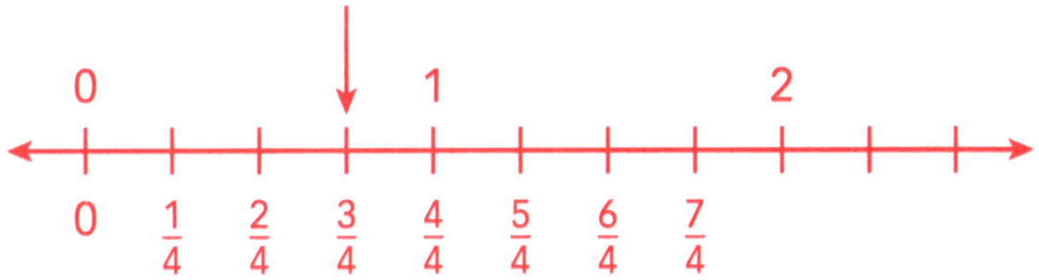

Steve was right. He knew that the denominator is 4 and he has to count fourths. He started counting with 0. From 0 to C there are 7 fourths. The fraction for point C is $\frac{7}{4}$.

Where does the example . . .

- use a picture to explain?
- use numbers to explain?
- use words to explain?
- give details?

Solve the problem. Use what you learned from the example.

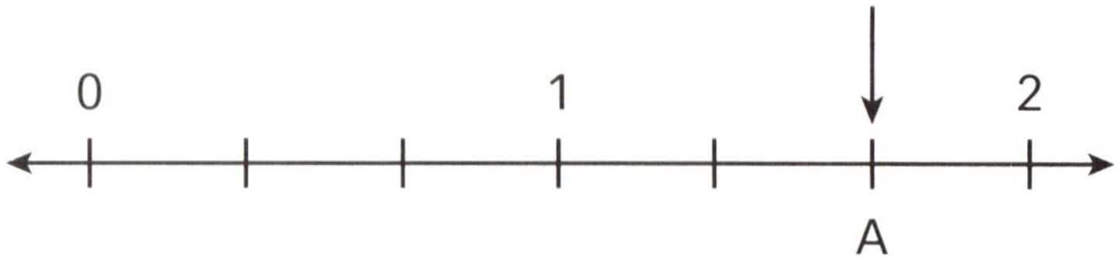

Jackie said that the fraction for point ***A*** is $\frac{5}{6}$.

Ann said that the fraction for point ***A*** is $\frac{5}{3}$.

Who is right? Tell how you know.

Who is wrong? What is the mistake?

Show your work. Use pictures, words, or numbers to explain how you decided what to draw.

Dear Family,

This week your child is exploring equivalent fractions.

Equivalent fractions show the same amount of the whole and name the same number, but they represent wholes that are cut into different numbers of equal-size pieces.

To cover the same amount as $\frac{1}{2}$ of a whole, you need two $\frac{1}{4}$s or three $\frac{1}{6}$s or four $\frac{1}{8}$s.

The diagram shows that:

$\frac{1}{2}$ and $\frac{2}{4}$ are equivalent fractions.

$\frac{1}{2}$ and $\frac{3}{6}$ are equivalent fractions.

$\frac{2}{4}$ and $\frac{4}{8}$ are equivalent fractions.

You can also show equivalent fractions using number lines. $\frac{1}{2}$ and $\frac{2}{4}$ are located at the same point on the number line, so they are equivalent.

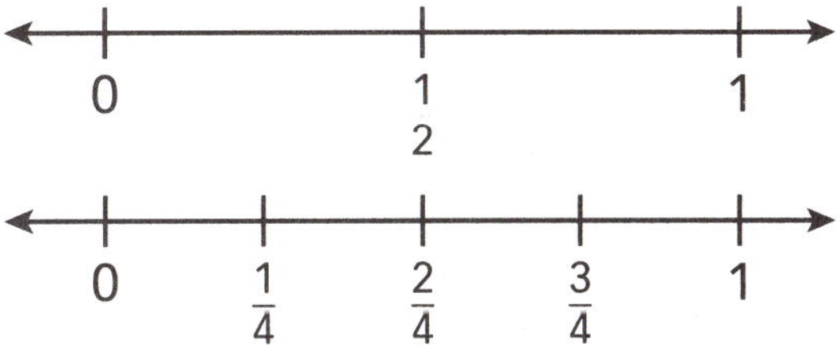

Notice that whenever we talk about equivalent fractions, we are always referring to the same-size whole. These rectangles are NOT the same size. They show that $\frac{1}{2}$ of a small rectangle is NOT equivalent to $\frac{2}{4}$ of a larger one.

Invite your child to share what he or she knows about equivalent fractions by doing the following activity together.

NEXT

Equivalent Fractions Activity

Materials: paper, pencil, scissors

Explore equivalent fractions with your child with home-made fraction strips.

- Work together with your child to cut a regular sheet of paper into 3 strips lengthwise, each about two inches wide.
- Fold one strip in half to make two parts that are the same size.
- Fold the second strip in half and then in half again to make 4 parts that are all the same size.
- Fold the last strip in half three times to make 8 equal parts.
- Unfold each strip. Draw lines on the fold lines, and then label the sections. The sections of first strip should be labeled $\frac{1}{2}$, and the second strip $\frac{1}{4}$, and the last strip $\frac{1}{8}$.
- Now, lay the strips next to each other, so the longest sides are touching. Use them to tell whether each of the following is true or false. Work together to circle True or False for each statement.

$\frac{1}{4} = \frac{2}{8}$ True False

$\frac{3}{4} = \frac{3}{8}$ True False

$\frac{1}{2} = \frac{4}{8}$ True False

$\frac{2}{2} = \frac{4}{4}$ True False

$\frac{2}{2} = \frac{2}{4}$ True False

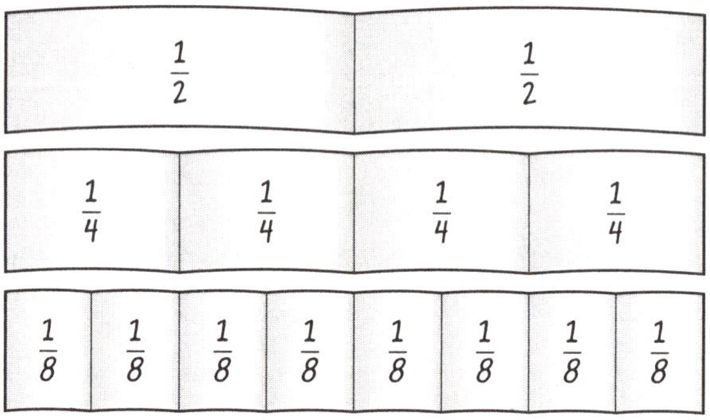

Understand Equivalent Fractions

Name: ____________________

Prerequisite: How can you model fractions?

Study the example showing a fraction with a number line and with a shaded shape. Then solve problems 1–6.

Example

Here are two models that show $\frac{3}{4}$.

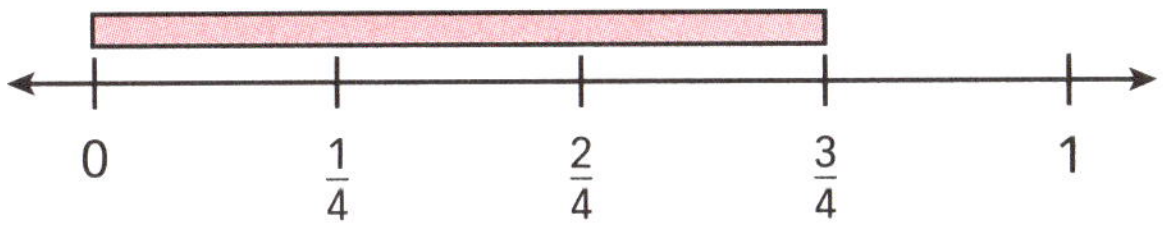

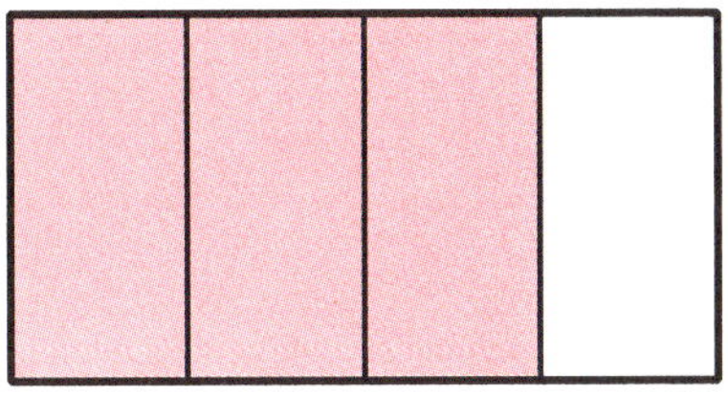

This section on the number line shows $\frac{3}{4}$.

3 parts shaded

4 equal parts in the whole

The fraction is $\frac{3}{4}$.

1 What fraction of the circle is shaded? ______

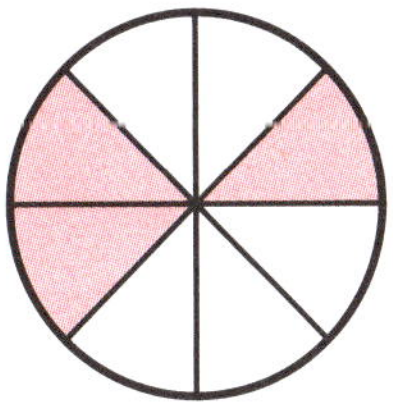

2 Label the marks on the number line with fractions. Draw a section to show $\frac{3}{6}$.

Solve.

3 What part of the whole shape is shaded?

Write the fraction. _______

4 Shade to show $\frac{7}{8}$ of the rectangle. Write the fraction for the part that is **not** shaded. _______

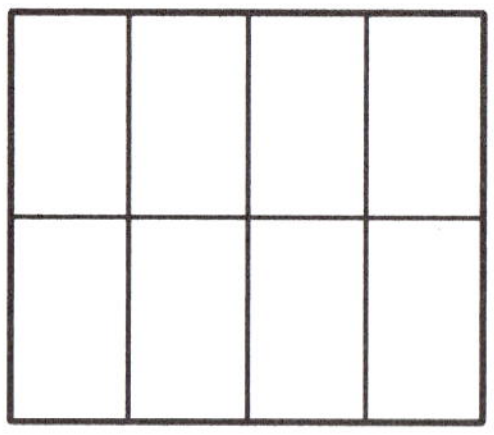

5 Tell whether each statement is correct. Choose *Yes* or *No*.

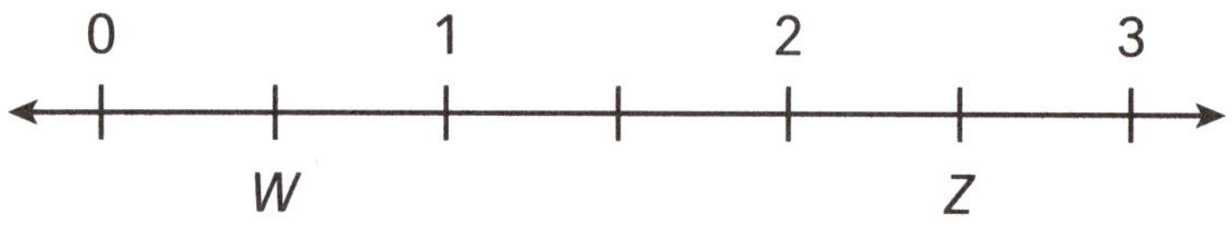

a. The fraction for point *W* is $\frac{1}{2}$. ☐ Yes ☐ No

b. The fraction for point *W* is 2. ☐ Yes ☐ No

c. The fraction for point *Z* is $\frac{6}{2}$. ☐ Yes ☐ No

d. The fraction for point *Z* is $\frac{5}{2}$. ☐ Yes ☐ No

6 Write the fraction for each letter on the number line. There may be more than one correct answer.

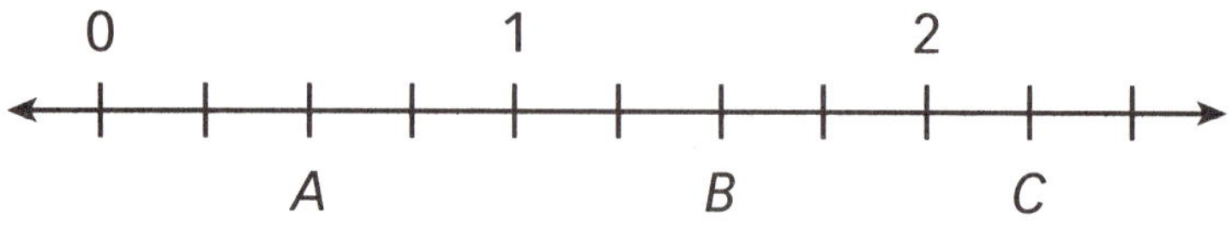

A ____________

B ____________

C ____________

Name: ____________________

Show Equivalent Fractions

Study how the example shows equivalent fractions with shaded shapes and number lines. Then solve problems 1–5.

Example

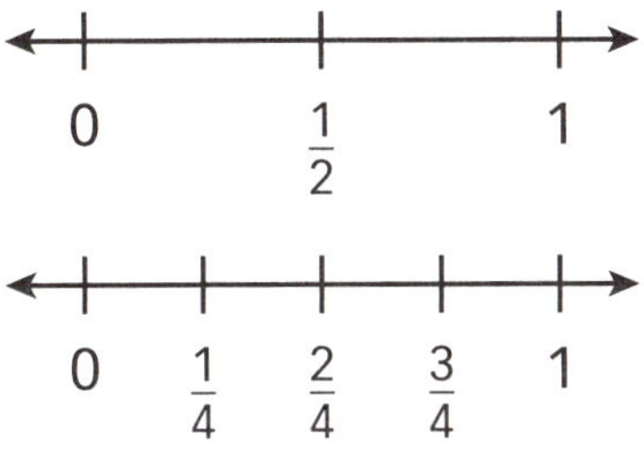

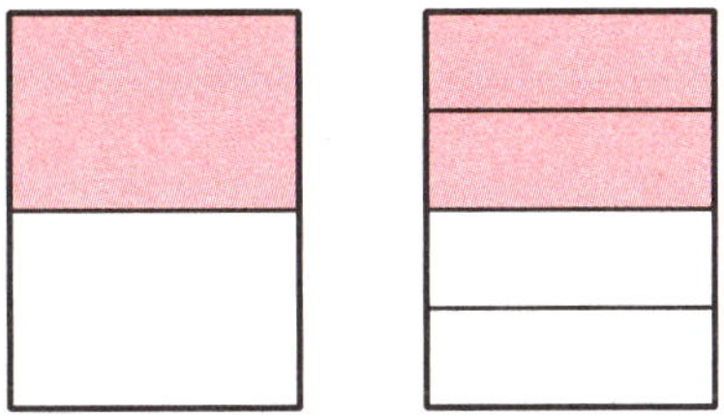

$\frac{1}{2}$ and $\frac{2}{4}$ are at the same place on the number lines.

$\frac{1}{2}$ is equivalent to $\frac{2}{4}$.

Both rectangles have the same amount of shading.

$\frac{1}{2}$ is equivalent to $\frac{2}{4}$.

1 Do these shapes show equivalent fractions? Circle *Yes* or *No*.

A.

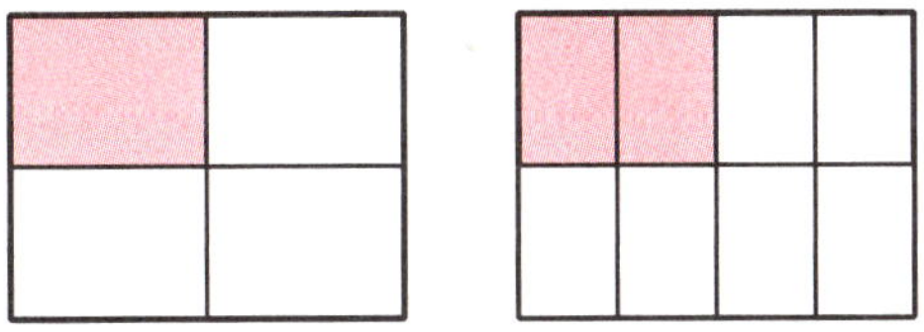

$\frac{1}{4}$ $\frac{2}{8}$

Yes No

B.

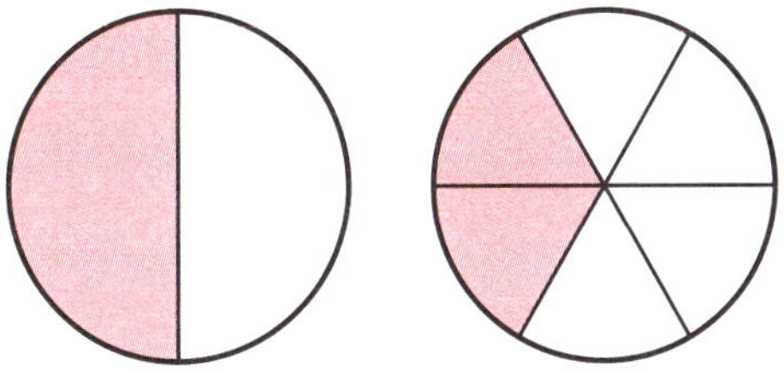

$\frac{1}{2}$ $\frac{2}{6}$

Yes No

Vocabulary

equivalent fractions fractions that name the same number.

$\frac{1}{2}$ and $\frac{2}{4}$ are equivalent.

Solve. Use the number lines to identify equivalent fractions in problems 2 and 3.

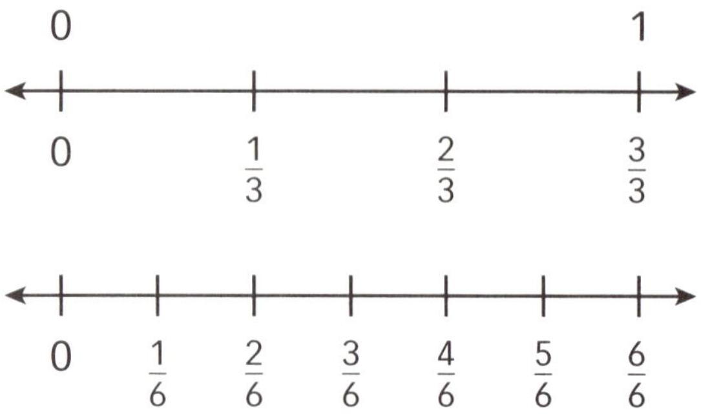

2 $\frac{2}{6} =$ ______

3 $\frac{2}{3} =$ ______

4 Look at the fractions shown by the shaded hexagons. Write equivalent fractions for the shaded parts.

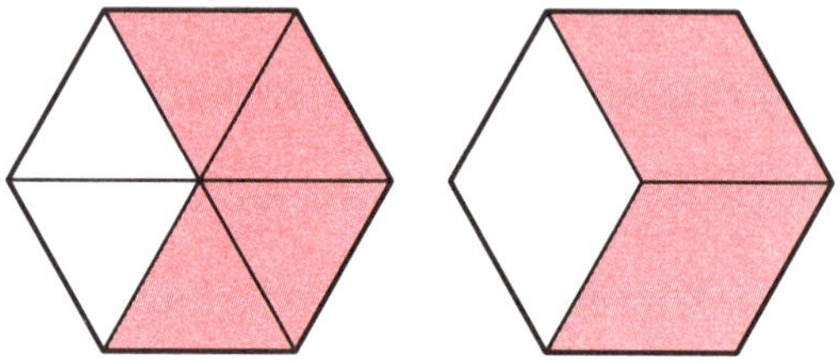

$\frac{\square}{\square} = \frac{\square}{\square}$

5 Shade $\frac{6}{8}$ of rectangle *A*.

A

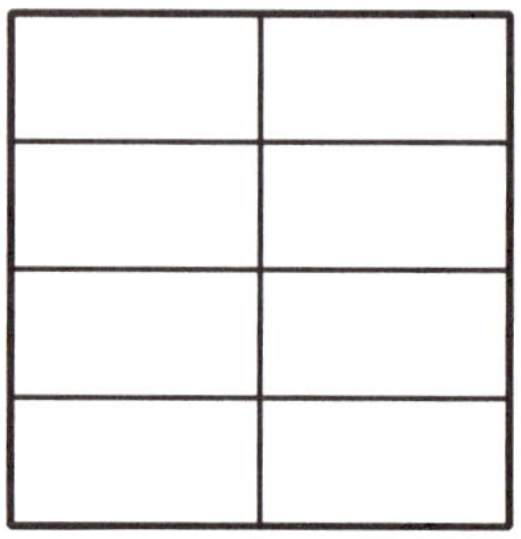

Shade rectangle *B* to show a fraction equivalent to $\frac{6}{8}$.

B

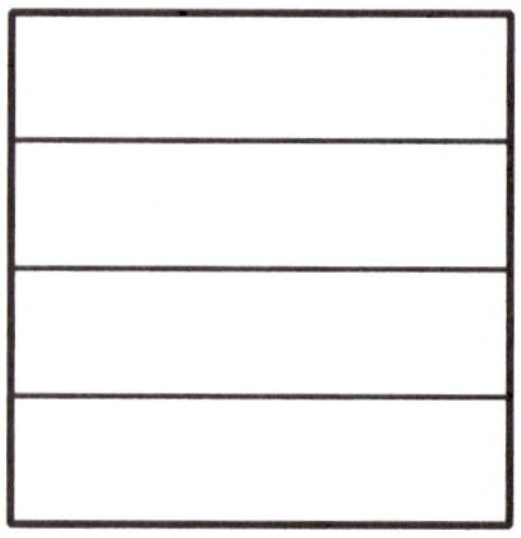

Write the equivalent fraction. ______

Name: ______________________

Reason and Write

Study the example problem. Underline two parts that you think make it a particularly good answer and a helpful example.

Example

Arlene drew circles *Y* and *Z*. She separated *Y* into fourths. She separated *Z* into eighths. She shaded 3 parts of *Y*. Then she shaded *Z* to show a fraction equivalent to the fraction for *Y*.

Y

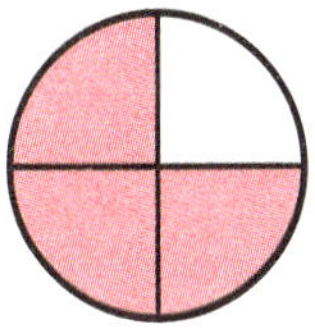

$\frac{3}{4}$

Arlene said, "Both circles have 3 parts that are shaded. That means that the fractions are equivalent: $\frac{3}{4} = \frac{3}{8}$."

Z

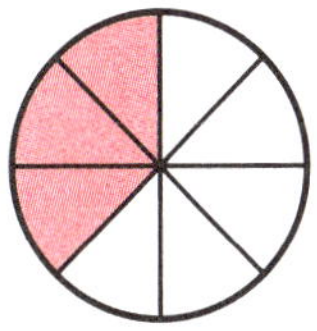

$\frac{3}{8}$

What did Arlene do right? What did she do wrong?

Show your work. Use pictures, words, or numbers to explain.

Arlene correctly made equal parts in both circles. She named the correct fractions for the parts she shaded.

Her mistake was shading only 3 parts of *Z*. The shading in both circles must cover the same amount of the whole to show equivalent fractions. Arlene should have shaded 6 parts of *Z* to show that $\frac{6}{8}$ is equivalent to $\frac{3}{4}$.

Y

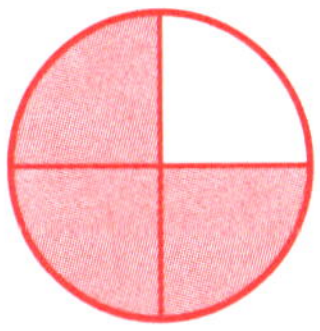

$\frac{3}{4}$

Z

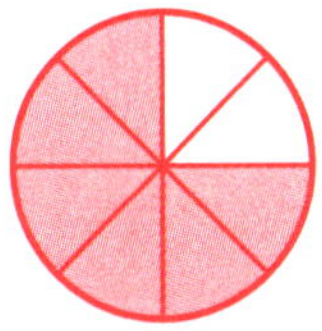

$\frac{6}{8}$

Where does the example . . .

- use a picture to explain?
- use numbers to explain?
- use words to explain?
- give details?

Solve the problem. Use what you learned from the example.

Shelley drew squares *A* and *B* to show equivalent fractions. She said, "I separated square *A* into 2 equal parts and square *B* into 8 equal parts. Then I shaded 2 parts of *A*. I shaded 4 parts of *B* to show an equivalent fraction. Since *B* has more equal parts, I doubled the number of shaded parts.

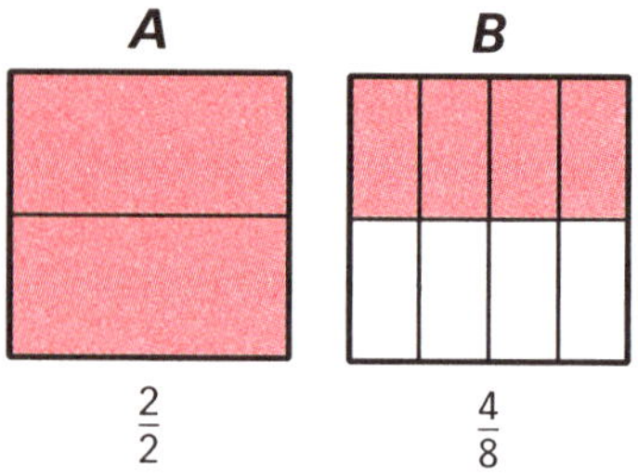

What did Shelley do right? What did she do wrong?

Show your work. Use pictures, words, or numbers to explain how you decided what to draw.

Did you . . .

- use a picture to explain?
- use numbers to explain?
- use words to explain?
- give details?

Dear Family,

This week your child is learning to find equivalent fractions.

Using a model, or diagram, to represent equivalent fractions helps make it clear why they are equivalent.

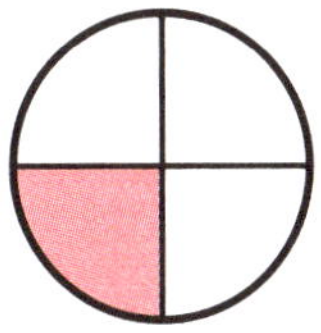

$\frac{1}{4}$

The diagrams to the right shows that $\frac{2}{8}$ and $\frac{1}{4}$ are equivalent because they cover the same amount of same-sized circles.

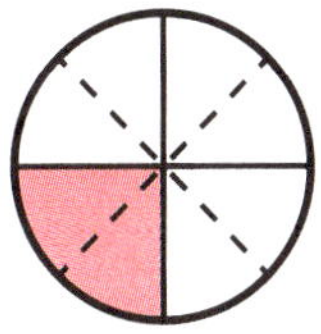

$\frac{2}{8}$

The circle showing $\frac{2}{8}$ has solid lines showing fourths, and dotted lines showing how each fourth was cut to make eighths. It helps you see that since eighths are smaller than fourths, you need more of them to cover the same amount.

A number line is another model that can show equivalent fractions.

This number line shows both fourths and eighths. Since $\frac{1}{4}$ and $\frac{2}{8}$ are at the same point, $\frac{1}{4}$ and $\frac{2}{8}$ are equivalent.

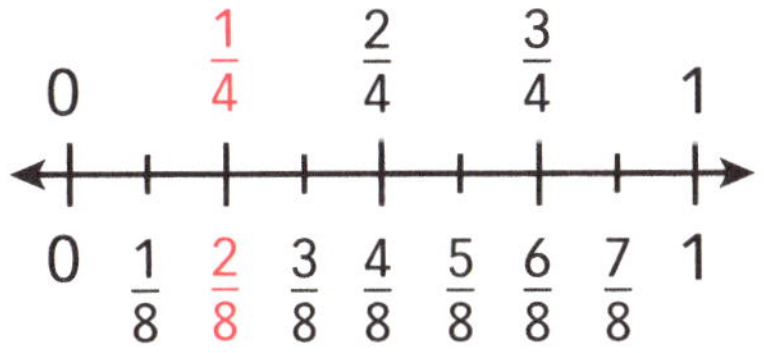

A whole number can be written as a fraction too, with a denominator of 1. A denominator of 1 means the whole has not been cut into parts. One whole can be written $\frac{1}{1}$, 2 wholes as $\frac{2}{1}$, and so forth.

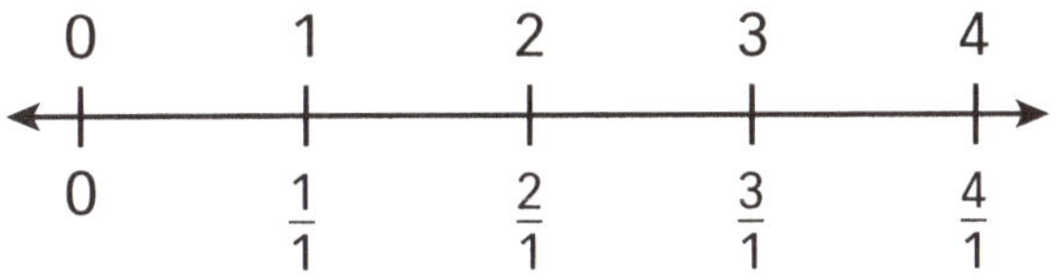

Invite your child to share what he or she knows about finding equivalent fractions by doing the following activity together.

NEXT

Equivalent Fraction Activity

Materials: Cards below, scissors

Play this matching game to practice recognizing equivalent fractions.

- Cut out the cards below and color the backs.
- Mix the cards and place them face down in two rows.
- Take turns.
- On your turn, flip 2 cards. Name the fractions.
- If the cards show equivalent fractions, keep them. If they are not equivalent, turn them back over in the same places as before.
- When all the equivalent fractions have been found, the player with the most cards is the winner.
- As you play, ask your child questions like:
    - If you keep the cards, how do you know the fractions are equivalent?
    - If you need to turn them back over, how do you know the fractions are not equivalent?

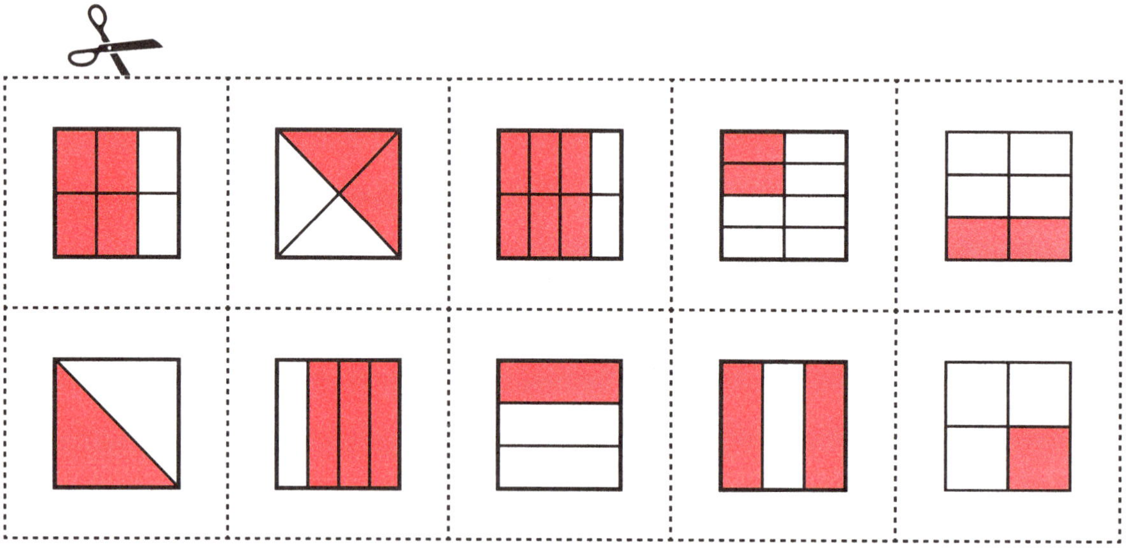

Find Equivalent Fractions

Name: ______________________________

Prerequisite: Identify Equivalent Fractions

Study the example showing how to decide if two fractions are equivalent. Then solve problems 1–7.

Example

The bars are the same size.

The parts are different sizes.

The same amount is shaded on each bar.

So, $\frac{1}{2} = \frac{3}{6}$.

$\frac{1}{2}$ and $\frac{3}{6}$ are equivalent fractions.

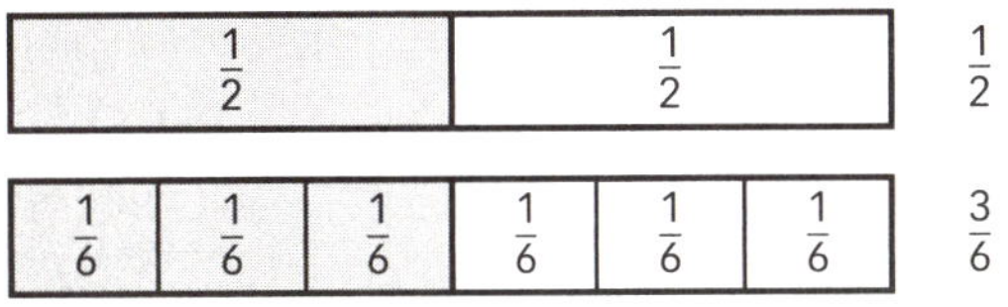

Shade the bars to show the equivalent fractions.

1

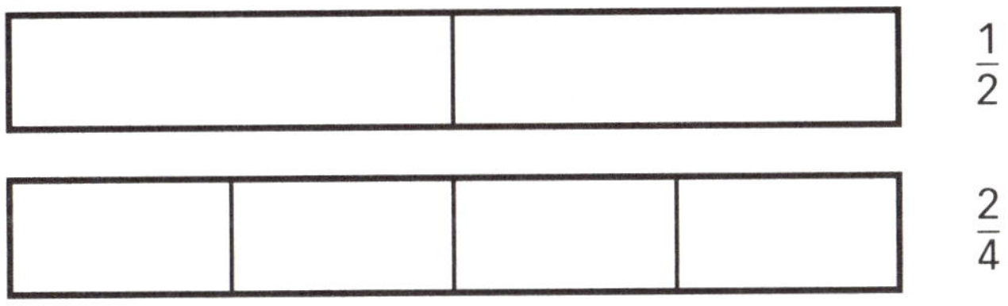

2

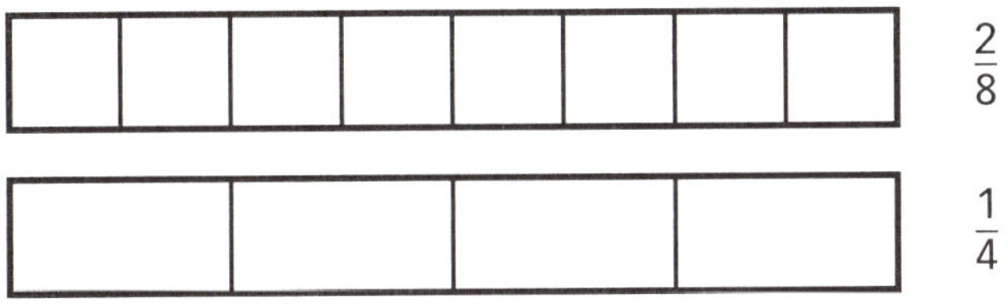

Write the equivalent fractions these bars show.

3

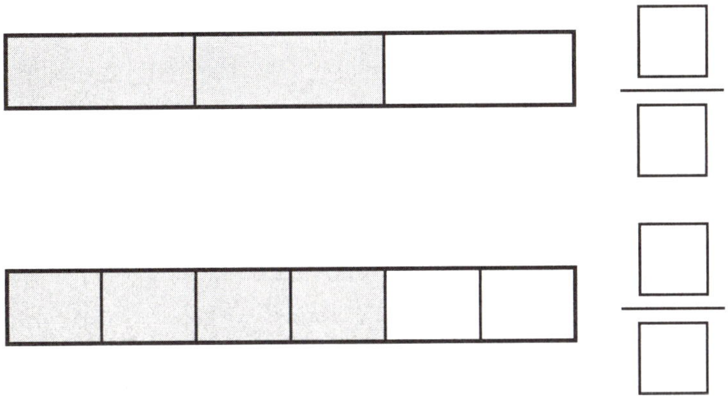

Vocabulary

equivalent fractions
fractions that name the same number.

$\frac{1}{2}$ and $\frac{2}{4}$ are equivalent.

Shade to show the fractions. Are the two fractions equivalent? Choose *Yes* or *No*.

4

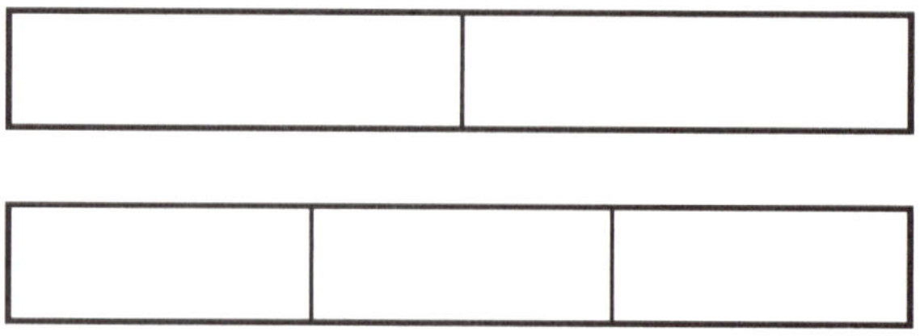

$\frac{1}{2}$

$\frac{1}{3}$

☐ Yes ☐ No

5

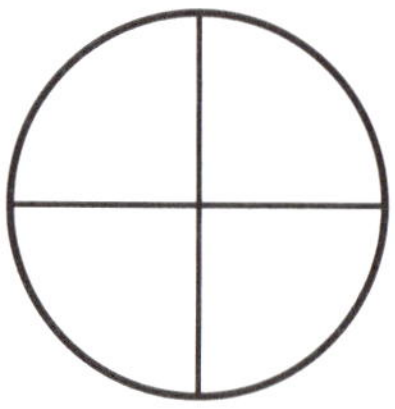

$\frac{3}{4}$

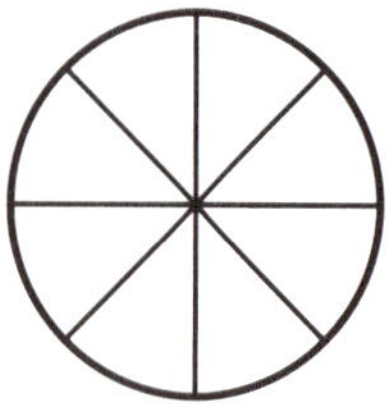

$\frac{6}{8}$

☐ Yes ☐ No

6

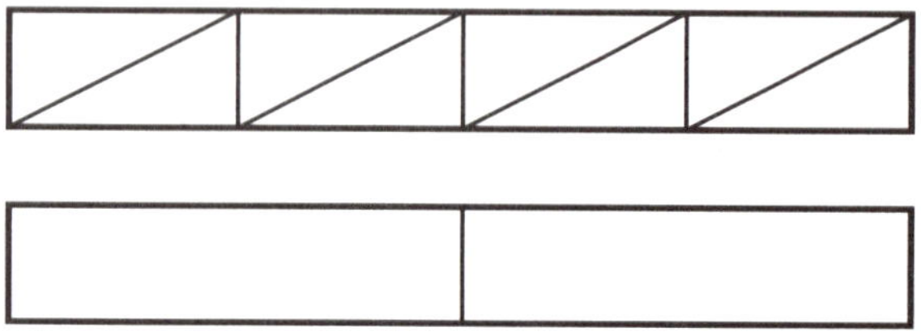

$\frac{4}{8}$

$\frac{1}{2}$

☐ Yes ☐ No

7 Use the bars to show that $\frac{2}{3}$ is **not** equivalent to $\frac{7}{8}$.

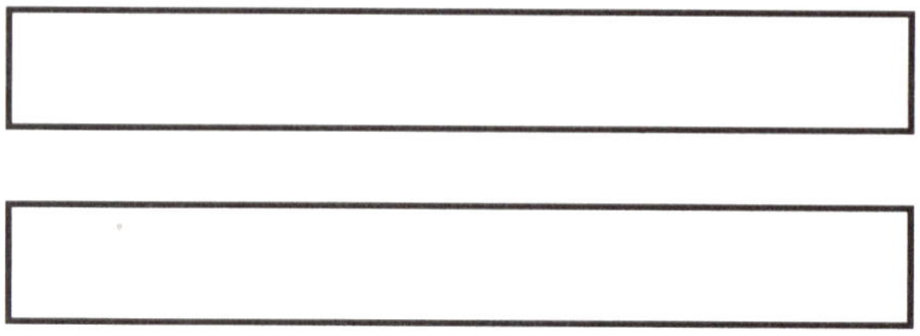

Explain how your drawing shows that $\frac{2}{3}$ and $\frac{7}{8}$ are not equivalent.

____

____

____

____

____

____

Name: ____________________

Find Equivalent Fractions

Study the example showing how to find equivalent fractions. Then solve problems 1–8.

Example

Maria colored $\frac{1}{3}$ of her art paper red. Erica colored $\frac{2}{6}$ of her art paper yellow. Did the two girls color the same amount of their art papers?

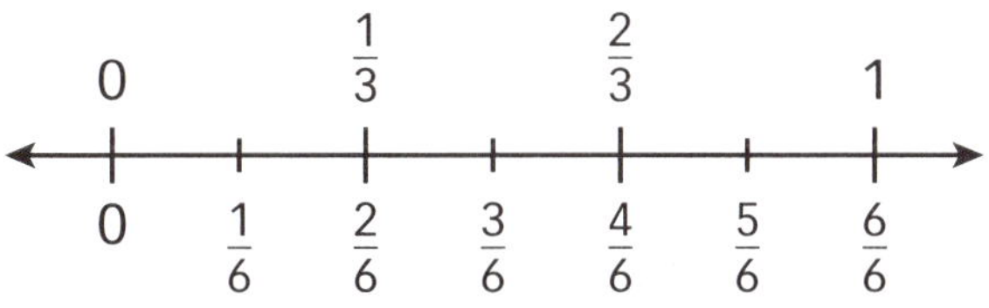

One third is equal to *two sixths*.

$$\frac{1}{3} = \frac{2}{6}$$

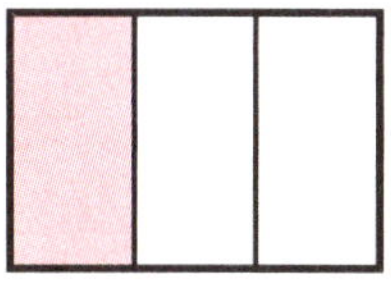

Maria colored $\frac{1}{3}$

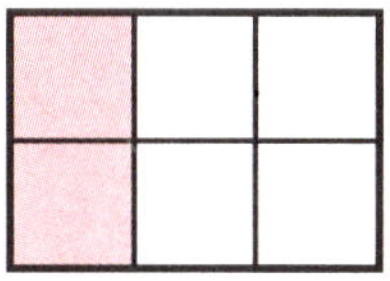

Erica colored $\frac{2}{6}$

Both girls colored the same amount of their art papers.

Use the number line to complete the equivalent fractions.

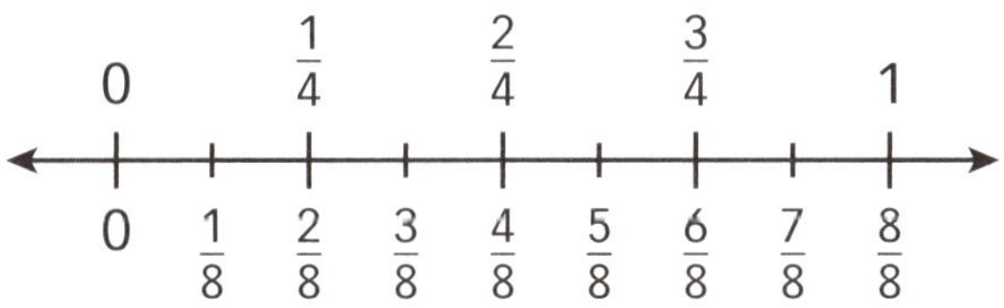

1 $\frac{1}{4} = \frac{\square}{8}$

2 $\frac{6}{8} = \frac{\square}{4}$

3 $\frac{2}{4} = \frac{\square}{\square}$

Vocabulary

equivalent fractions
fractions that name the same number.
$\frac{1}{2}$ and $\frac{2}{4}$ are equivalent.

Shade the bars to show equivalent fractions. Then fill in the blanks to write equivalent fractions.

4

$$\frac{1}{2} = \frac{\square}{8}$$

5

$$\frac{2}{3} = \frac{\square}{6}$$

Draw lines and shade to show equivalent fractions. Then fill in the blanks to write equivalent fractions.

6

$$\frac{1}{2} = \frac{\square}{4}$$

7

$$\frac{4}{6} = \frac{\square}{3}$$

8 What is a fraction equivalent to $\frac{4}{4}$? Explain how you know.

____

____

____

Name: ____________________

Write a Whole Number as a Fraction

Study the example showing different ways to write whole numbers as fractions. Then solve problems 1–13.

Example

Mrs. Clark cut 2 same-size pieces of colored paper into *sixths* to make strips for paper chains. How many strips did she make?

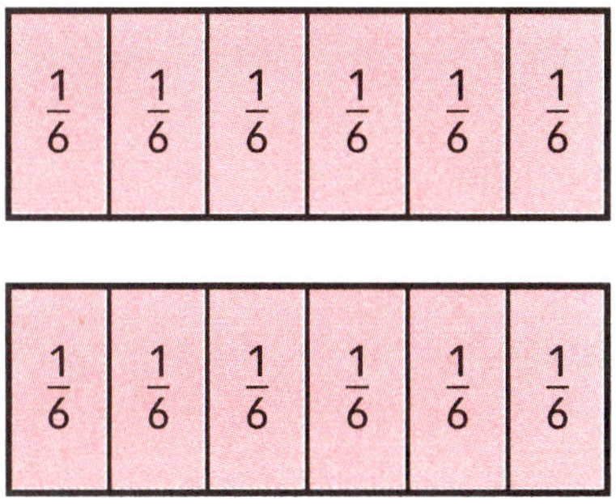

$$1 \text{ whole} = \text{six } \tfrac{1}{6}\text{s}$$

$$1 = \frac{6}{6}$$

$$2 \text{ wholes} = \text{twelve } \tfrac{1}{6}\text{s}$$

$$2 = \frac{12}{6}$$

Mrs. Clark made 12 strips. Each strip is $\frac{1}{6}$ of a whole piece of paper.

Write the whole numbers as fractions.

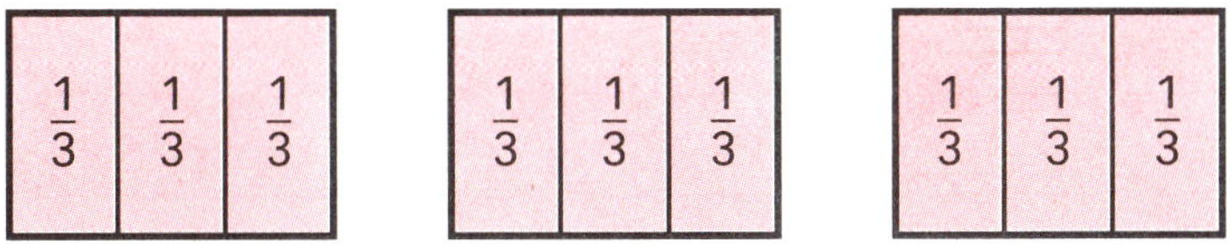

1 $1 = \frac{\square}{3}$

2 $2 = \frac{\square}{3}$

3 $3 = \frac{\square}{3}$

4 $4 = \frac{\square}{3}$

Use this number line to answer problems 5–8.

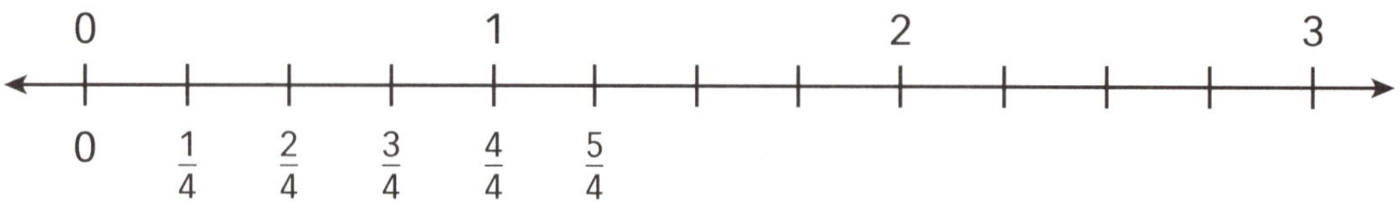

5 $1 = \frac{\square}{4}$

6 $2 = \frac{\square}{4}$

7 $3 = \frac{\square}{4}$

8 $0 = \frac{\square}{4}$

Use this number line to answer problems 9–11.

9 One whole is equal to ______ eighths.

10 16 eighths is equal to ______ wholes.

11 $3 = \frac{\square}{8}$

12 Use the model below to write a fraction equivalent to 3.

3 = ______

13 Draw a model to show $2 = \frac{8}{4}$.

Name: ______________________

Write a Whole Number as a Fraction with a Denominator of 1

Study the example showing different ways to write a whole number as a fraction with a denominator of 1. Then solve problems 1–14.

Example

The spaces between whole numbers on this number line are not divided into smaller parts. So, each whole has only 1 part.

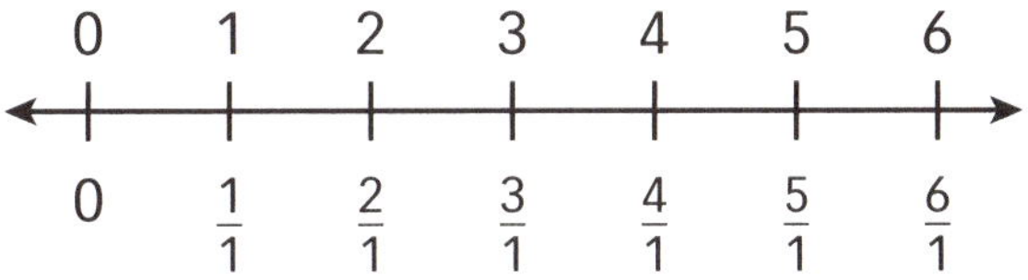

The number line shows that $\frac{3}{1}$ is equal to 3.

$\frac{3}{1}$ is a fraction name for 3.

Write the whole number for each fraction.

1 $\frac{4}{1} =$ ______

2 $\frac{2}{1} =$ ______

3 $\frac{5}{1} =$ ______

4 $\frac{8}{1} =$ ______

Write the fraction for each whole number.

5 $2 =$ ______

6 $5 =$ ______

7 $1 =$ ______

8 $7 =$ ______

Write the whole number for each fraction.

9 $\frac{9}{1}$ = ______

10 $\frac{10}{1}$ = ______

Write the fraction for each whole number.

11 12 = ______

12 18 = ______

13 Explain how to write a whole number as a fraction with a denominator of 1.

____

____

____

____

____

____

14 Bella says this model shows 3 wholes. She says it shows that if you write the whole number 3 as a fraction, you have to write $3 = \frac{12}{4}$.

How can you explain to Bella that there are other ways to write 3 as a fraction?

____

____

____

____

____

____

____

____

Vocabulary

numerator the number above the line in a fraction; it tells how many equal parts are described.

denominator the number below the line in a fraction; it tells how many equal parts are in the whole.

Name: ____________________

Find Equivalent Fractions

Solve the problems.

1 Use the number line.

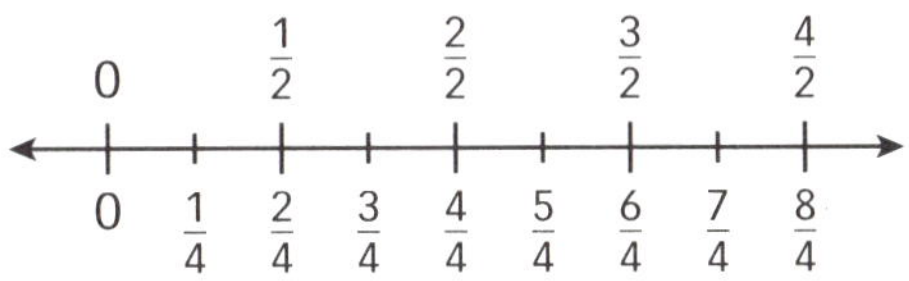

Which fraction is equivalent to $\frac{6}{4}$?

A $\frac{2}{3}$

B $\frac{4}{6}$

C $\frac{3}{2}$

D 2

2 Mrs. White is painting the fence in her yard. After painting $\frac{4}{6}$ of the fence she stops for lunch. Which fraction is equivalent to $\frac{4}{6}$?

A $\frac{1}{3}$

B $\frac{3}{2}$

C $\frac{2}{6}$

D $\frac{2}{3}$

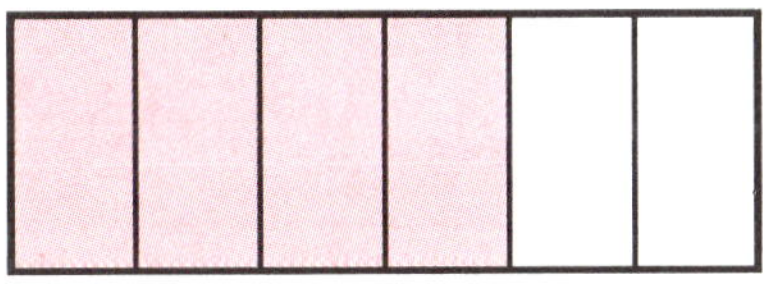

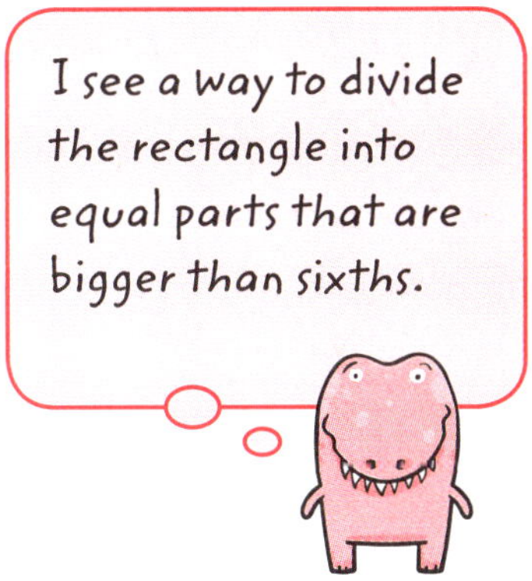

3 Draw a model to show that $3 = \frac{6}{2}$.

Explain your drawing.

____

____

____

Solve.

4 Jeff's pizza is cut into 8 equal pieces. He eats $\frac{1}{2}$ of it. What fraction of the pizza does he eat?

A $\frac{2}{8}$ **C** $\frac{4}{8}$

B $\frac{8}{8}$ **D** $\frac{3}{8}$

Samantha chose **A** as the correct answer. How did she get that answer?

____

____

____

How many eighths are equal to $\frac{1}{2}$? How many fourths?

5 Draw lines and shade rectangles *A* and *B* to show that $\frac{1}{4} = \frac{2}{8}$.

A ***B***

Explain your work.

____

____

____

How many equal parts will you show in A? In B?

6 Which statements are true? Circle the letter of all that apply.

A $\frac{4}{2} = 2$ **D** $\frac{2}{4} = \frac{1}{2}$

B $\frac{4}{1} = 4$ **E** $\frac{1}{2} = \frac{2}{1}$

C $\frac{1}{3} = 3$

Dear Family,

This week your child is exploring comparing fractions.

When two fractions have the same denominator, the numerator tells you which is more and which is less.

These fractions are built from the unit fraction $\frac{1}{6}$. So, the fraction with the most parts in the numerator is more.

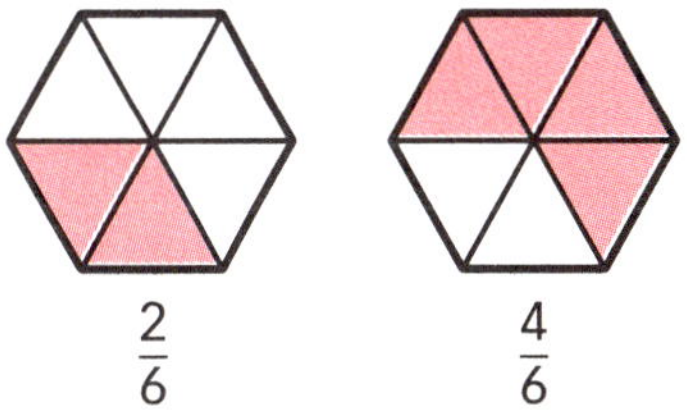

$\frac{4}{6}$ is more than $\frac{2}{6}$ because 4 parts is more than 2 parts when all the parts are equal to $\frac{1}{6}$ of the whole.

If two fractions have the same numerator, then the denominator can tell you which fraction is larger.

Compare the denominators of $\frac{1}{3}$ and $\frac{1}{8}$. When something is cut into 3 equal pieces, the pieces are larger than if the object is cut into 8 equal pieces. When there are fewer parts, each part is bigger.

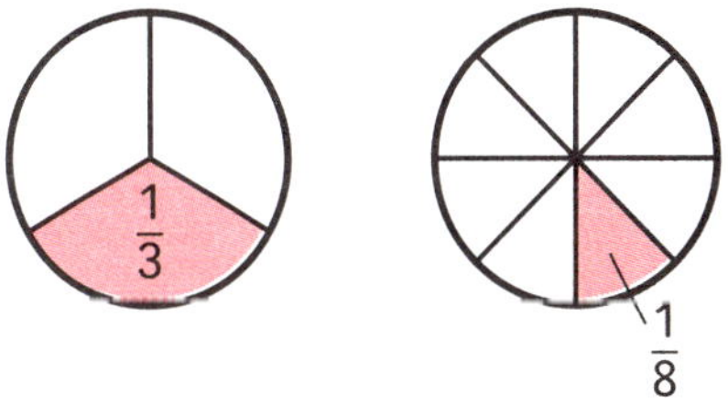

So, $\frac{1}{3}$ is greater than $\frac{1}{8}$.

This also shows that $\frac{2}{3}$ is greater than $\frac{2}{8}$, since 2 big pieces is more than 2 small pieces.

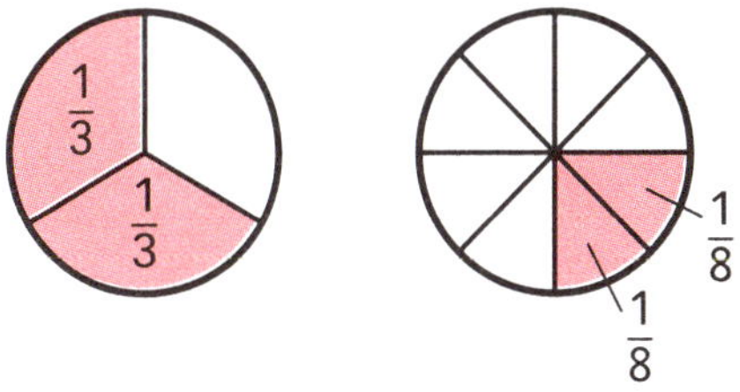

Invite your child to share what he or she knows about comparing fractions by doing the following activity together.

Comparing Fractions Activity

Materials: 2 small identical glasses or jars, measuring cups for $\frac{1}{4}$, $\frac{1}{3}$, and $\frac{1}{2}$, colored water

Use measured amounts of water to compare fractions. First experiment with fractions that have the same denominator, by using only the $\frac{1}{4}$-cup measure.

- Work with your child to pour $\frac{2}{4}$ cup colored water into one glass (call it Glass *A*) and $\frac{3}{4}$ cup into the other glass (call it Glass *B*). Place them side by side and compare. Which is more, $\frac{2}{4}$ or $\frac{3}{4}$?
- Repeat, to compare $\frac{2}{4}$ and $\frac{4}{4}$, $\frac{3}{4}$ and $\frac{4}{4}$, $\frac{2}{4}$ and $\frac{6}{4}$. Talk about how you can predict which will be more even before you measure the water into the glasses.

Now experiment with fractions that have different denominators but have the same numerator.

- Work with your child to pour $\frac{1}{3}$ cup of colored water into one glass (call it Glass *A*) and $\frac{1}{4}$ cup into the other glass (call this Glass *B*). Place them side by side and compare. Which is more, $\frac{1}{3}$ or $\frac{1}{4}$?
- Empty the glasses. Pour $\frac{2}{3}$ cup water into Glass *A* and $\frac{2}{4}$ cup into Glass *B*. Which is more, $\frac{2}{3}$ or $\frac{2}{4}$? Then compare $\frac{3}{3}$ and $\frac{3}{4}$.
- What pattern do you notice? How can you use that pattern to predict which is more, $\frac{7}{3}$ or $\frac{7}{4}$?
- Continue to experiment with other measurements. For example, use the measuring cups to compare $\frac{3}{2}$ to $\frac{3}{4}$, or compare $\frac{3}{2}$ to $\frac{1}{2}$. Have fun!

Understand Comparing Fractions

Name: ____________________

Prerequisite: How do you show equivalent fractions with shapes?

Study the example showing equivalent fractions. Then solve problems 1–8.

Example

Both circles are the same size. Both circles have the same amount of shading.

$\frac{1}{2}$ and $\frac{4}{8}$ are equivalent fractions.

$\frac{1}{2} = \frac{4}{8}$

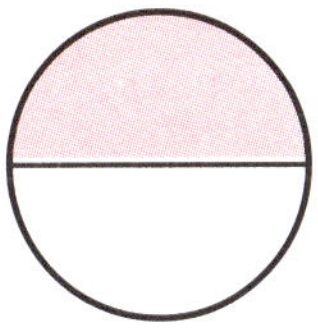

1 part shaded
2 equal parts in the whole
$\frac{1}{2}$

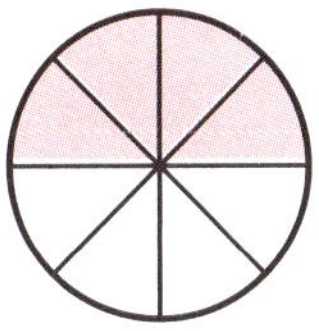

4 parts shaded
8 equal parts in the whole
$\frac{4}{8}$

Write equivalent fractions for the shaded parts.

1

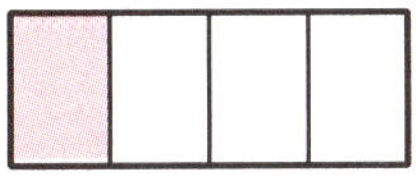

$\frac{1}{4} = \frac{\square}{8}$

2

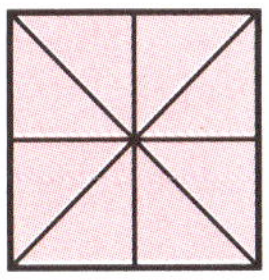

$\frac{4}{4} = \frac{\square}{\square}$

3

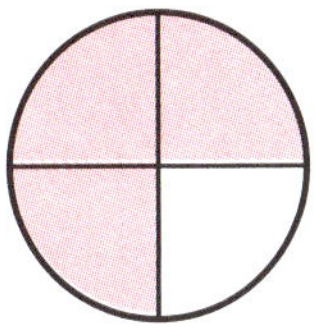

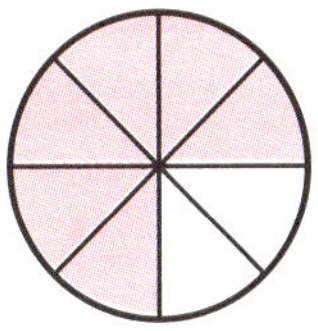

$\frac{3}{4} = \frac{\square}{\square}$

Vocabulary

equivalent fractions fractions that name the same number.

$\frac{1}{2}$ and $\frac{2}{4}$ are equivalent.

Shade the blank shape to show equivalent fractions. Then write the fractions.

4 

$\frac{\square}{\square} = \frac{\square}{6}$

5 

$\frac{\square}{\square} = \frac{\square}{3}$

6 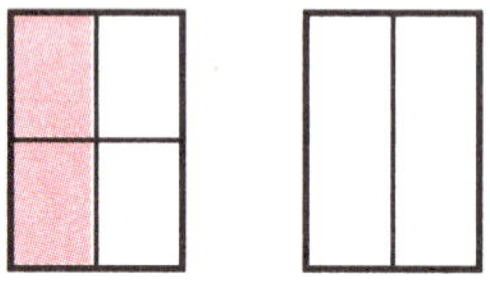

$\frac{\square}{\square} = \frac{\square}{\square}$

7 Write the fraction for each model.

a. 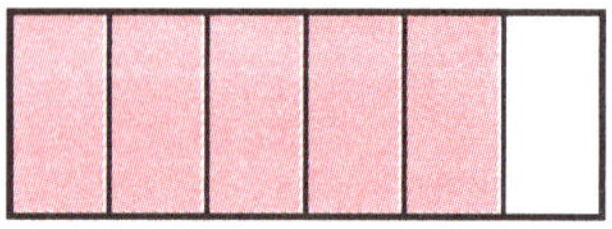

$\frac{\square}{\square}$

b. 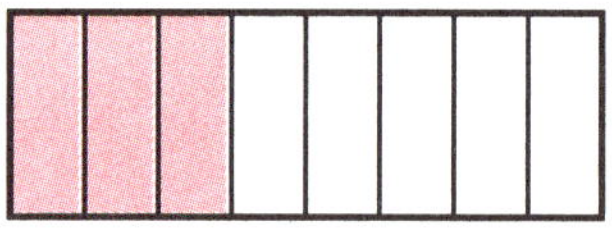

$\frac{\square}{\square}$

c. 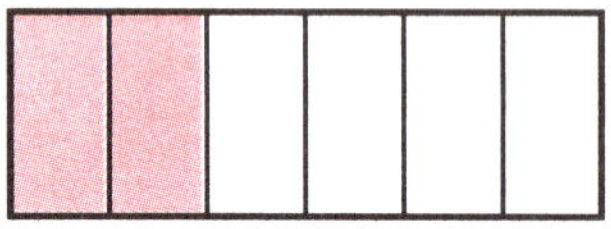

$\frac{\square}{\square}$

8 Which fraction in problem 7 is equivalent to $\frac{1}{3}$?

____

Name: ______________________

Use Models to Compare Fractions

Study how the example uses models to compare fractions. Then solve problems 1–8.

Example

Both rectangles are the same size.

If you make 8 equal parts, the parts are smaller than if you make 4 equal parts.

$\frac{1}{8}$ is less than $\frac{1}{4}$.

$\frac{1}{4}$ is greater than $\frac{1}{8}$.

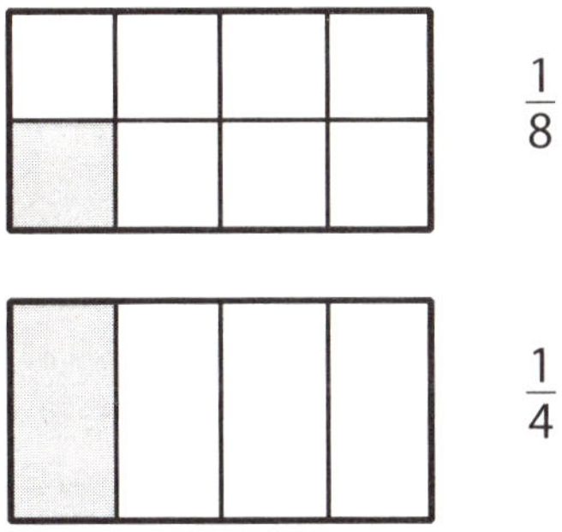

Write the fraction for the shaded parts. Circle the fraction that is *greater*.

1

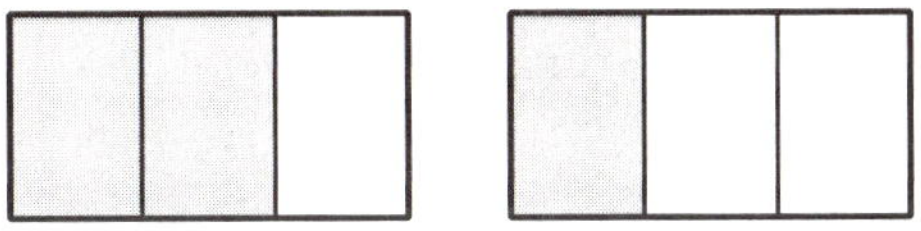

Fractions: ______ ______

2

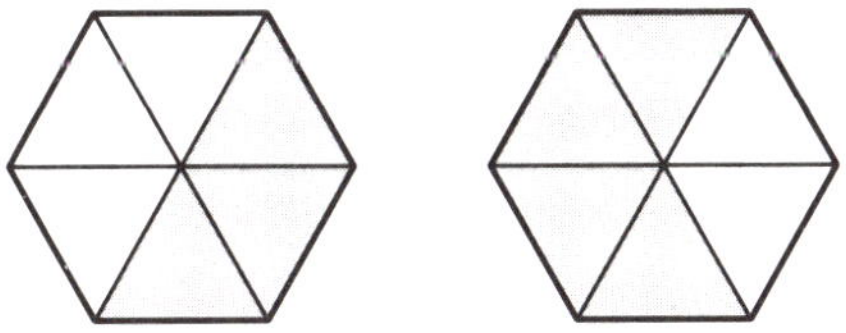

Fractions: ______ ______

3

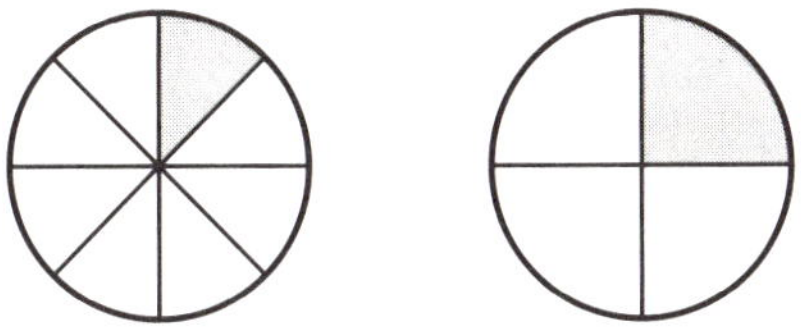

Fractions: ______ ______

Write the fraction for the shaded parts. Circle the fraction that is *less*.

4

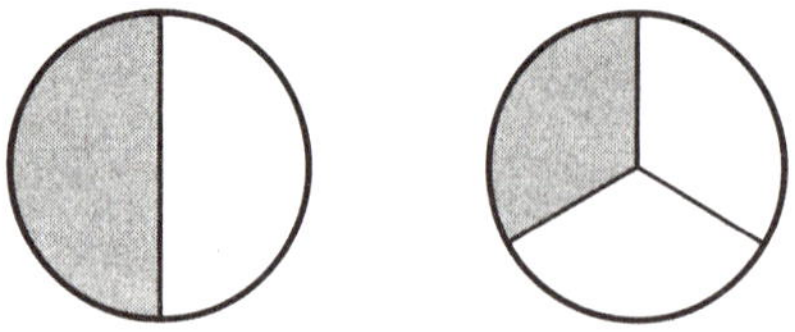

Fractions: ______ ______

5

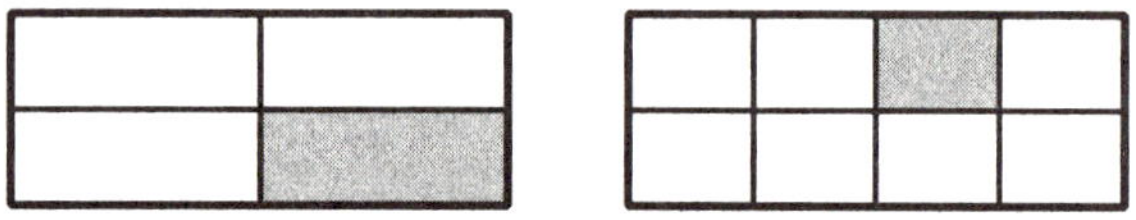

Fractions: ______ ______

6

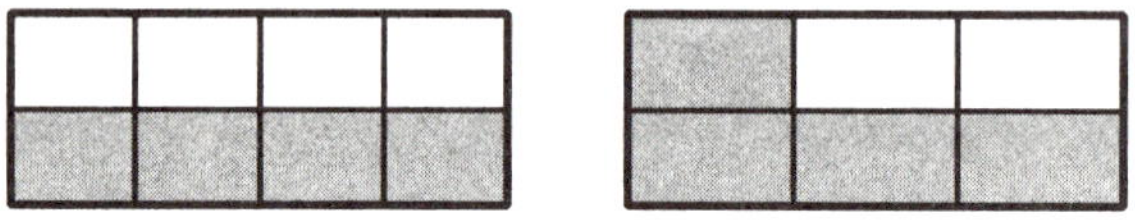

Fractions: ______ ______

Write the fraction for the shaded rectangle. Then shade the blank rectangle to show a fraction that is less. Write the fraction.

7

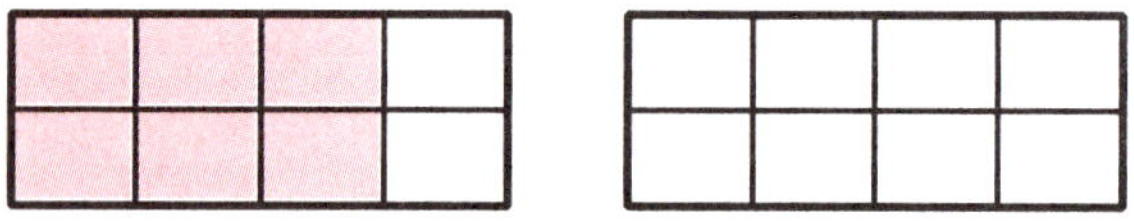

Fractions: ______ ______

8 Write a fraction less than $\frac{1}{4}$ that has a numerator of 1.

______

Name: ______________________

Reason and Write

Study the example problem. Underline two parts that you think make it a particularly good answer and a helpful example.

Example

Which fraction is greatest: $\frac{2}{3}$, $\frac{2}{4}$, or $\frac{2}{8}$?

Diane said, "$\frac{2}{8}$ is the greatest."

Sandra said, "$\frac{2}{3}$ is the greatest."

Who is right? Who is wrong? How did you decide? What was the mistake?

Show your work. Use pictures, words, or numbers to explain.

Sandra is right. She saw that 2 is the numerator in each fraction. She looked at the denominators to compare the fractions. I made a model to check the answer.

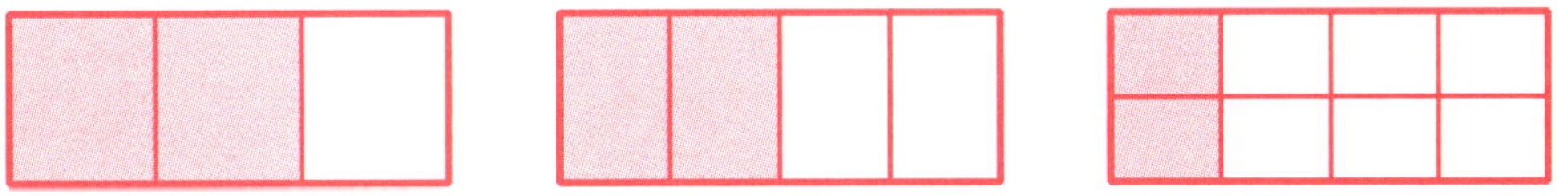

$\frac{2}{3}$ $\frac{2}{4}$ $\frac{2}{8}$

The model shows that thirds are bigger than fourths and thirds are bigger than eighths. So two thirds is bigger than two fourths.

Diane's answer is wrong. She may have compared the denominators of the fractions. She thought that $\frac{2}{8}$ is greatest because it has the greatest denominator. She may not have used a model or thought about the size of each of the equal parts.

Where does the example . . .
- use a picture to explain?
- use numbers to explain?
- use words to explain?
- give details?

Solve the problem. Use what you learned from the model.

Which fraction is the least: $\frac{3}{4}$, $\frac{3}{6}$, or $\frac{3}{8}$?

Eric said, "$\frac{3}{8}$ is the least."

Bob said, "$\frac{3}{4}$ is the least."

Who is right? Who is wrong? How did you decide?
What was the mistake?

Show your work. Use pictures, words, or numbers to explain how you decided what to draw.

Did you . . .

- use a picture to explain?
- use numbers to explain?
- use words to explain?
- give details?

Dear Family,

This week your child is learning about using symbols to compare fractions.

To compare fractions you can use the symbols <, > or =.

< means *is less than*. > means *is greater than*.

Which symbol would we use to compare $\frac{4}{8}$ and $\frac{4}{6}$?
It can help to use area models to compare fractions.

$\frac{4}{8}$

$\frac{4}{6}$

Or, you can use number lines to compare fractions.

The top number line is divided into eighths and shows $\frac{4}{8}$.

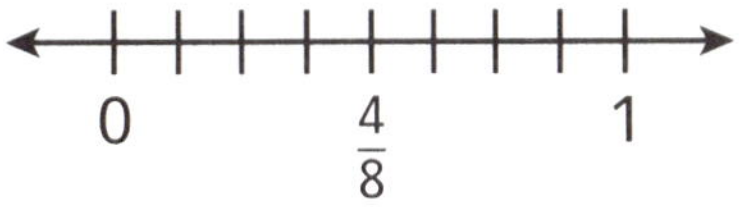

This bottom number line is divided into sixths and shows $\frac{4}{6}$.

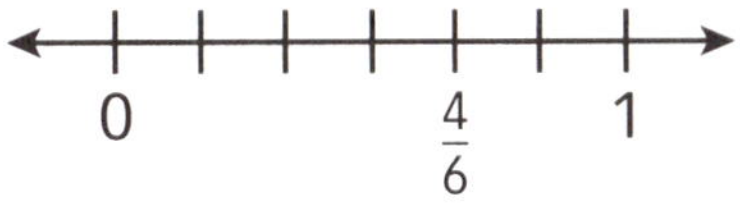

Both models show that $\frac{4}{8}$ is less than $\frac{4}{6}$. Of course that also means $\frac{4}{6}$ is greater than $\frac{4}{8}$. So, using symbols, we can write the comparison two different ways.

$\frac{4}{8} < \frac{4}{6}$ and $\frac{4}{6} > \frac{4}{8}$

Invite your child to share what he or she knows about using symbols to compare fractions by doing the following activity together.

NEXT

Comparing Fractions with Symbols Activity

Materials: number cards below, scissors, 2 bags, recording sheet below

Give your child practice comparing fractions with this activity.

- Cut out the cards below. Put the number cards in one bag and the Numerator/Denominator cards in the other bag. Players take turns.
- Player 1 draws a number from the bag and a Numerator or Denominator card from the other bag.
- Both players write a fraction based on the information. For example, if a 4 and the *Numerator* card are drawn, both players make up a fraction with 4 as the numerator.
- Discuss with your child, then record the correct symbol to compare the fractions. Remember: < *is less than* and > *is greater than*.
- Return both cards to the bags, and draw 2 more. Play a total of 5 rounds.

Player 1 Fraction	< or > or =	Player 2 Fraction

1	2	3	4	6	8
Numerator			Denominator		

Use Symbols to Compare Fractions

Name: ______________________________

Prerequisite: Compare Fractions

Study the example problem showing how to compare fractions shown with models. Then solve problems 1–9.

Example

Meg and Jay poured pink lemonade for themselves.

Meg's glass was $\frac{5}{8}$ full and

Jay's glass was $\frac{7}{8}$ full.

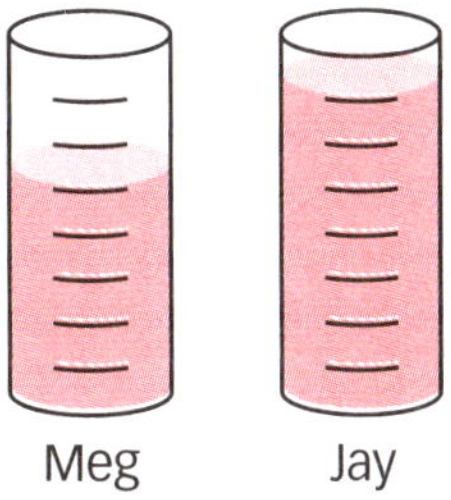

The fractions $\frac{5}{8}$ and $\frac{7}{8}$ have the same denominator. Compare the numerators.

Jay had more lemonade.

Label the model with the correct fractions. Then compare the fractions. Circle the *greater* fraction.

1 $\frac{2}{6}$ or $\frac{3}{6}$

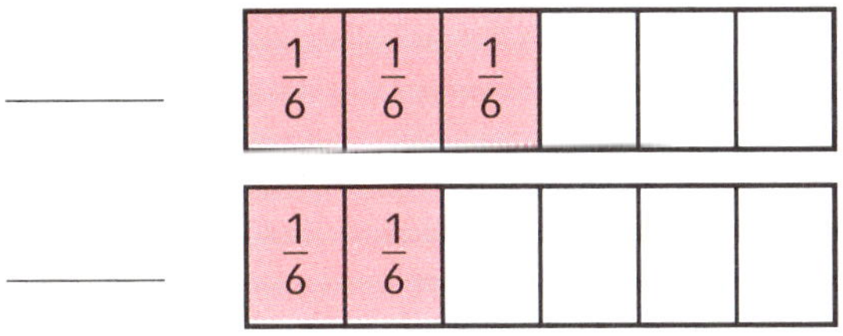

2 $\frac{3}{8}$ or $\frac{7}{8}$

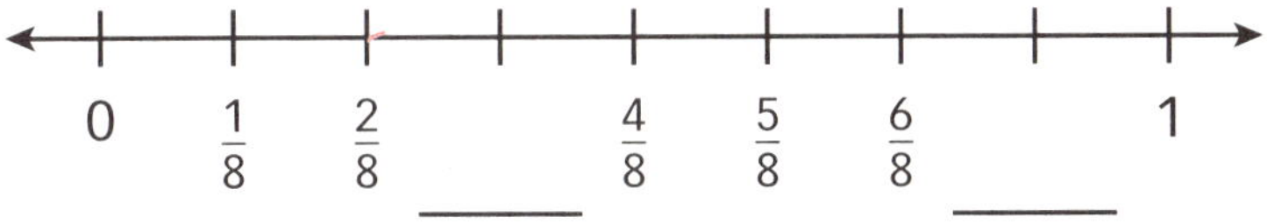

Compare each measuring cup with this one that is $\frac{3}{6}$ full. Write the correct fraction in each blank.

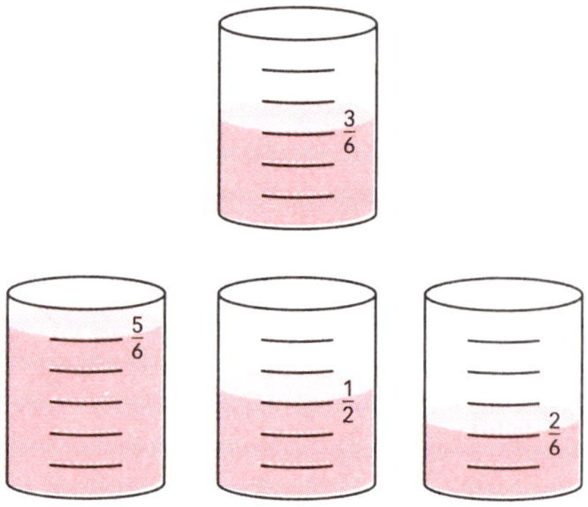

3 ______ is less than $\frac{3}{6}$.

4 ______ is equal to $\frac{3}{6}$.

5 ______ is greater than $\frac{3}{6}$.

Use the number line to compare fractions. Write the correct words in each blank.

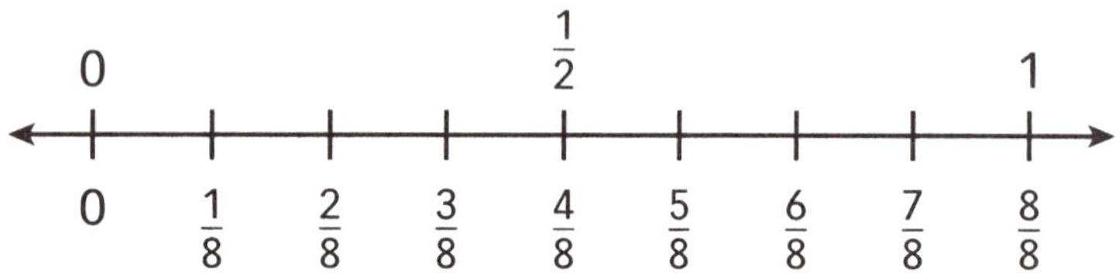

6 $\frac{5}{8}$ ____________________ $\frac{2}{8}$

7 $\frac{4}{8}$ ____________________ $\frac{1}{2}$

8 $\frac{1}{8}$ ____________________ $\frac{6}{8}$

9 $\frac{7}{8}$ ____________________ $\frac{5}{8}$

Word Bank

is less than

is greater than

is equal to

Name: ____________________

Compare Fractions Using Symbols

Study the example that shows how to use symbols to compare fractions. Then solve problems 1–16.

Example

Compare the fractions $\frac{3}{6}$ and $\frac{3}{8}$.

$\frac{3}{6}$ is greater than $\frac{3}{8}$.

$\frac{3}{6} > \frac{3}{8}$

$\frac{3}{8}$ is less than $\frac{3}{6}$.

$\frac{3}{8} < \frac{3}{6}$

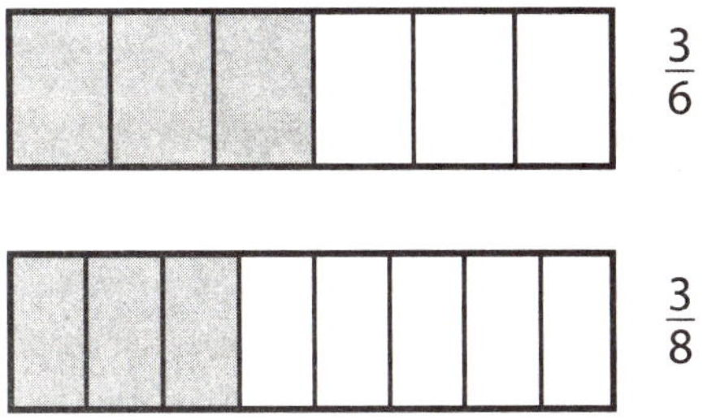

Use the models to compare the fractions in problems 1 and 2. Write <, >, or = .

1

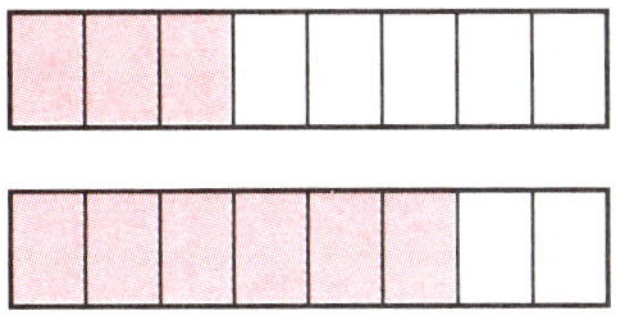

$\frac{3}{8}$ $\square$ $\frac{6}{8}$

2

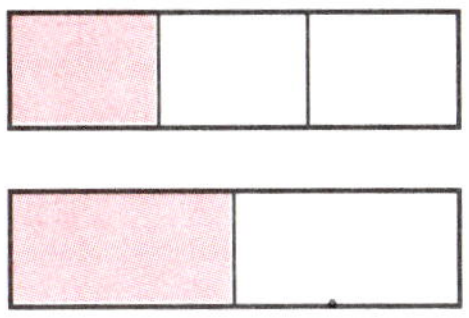

$\frac{1}{3}$ $\square$ $\frac{1}{2}$

Use the number lines to compare the fractions in problems 3–5. Write <, >, or = .

3 $\frac{3}{8}$ $\square$ $\frac{5}{8}$

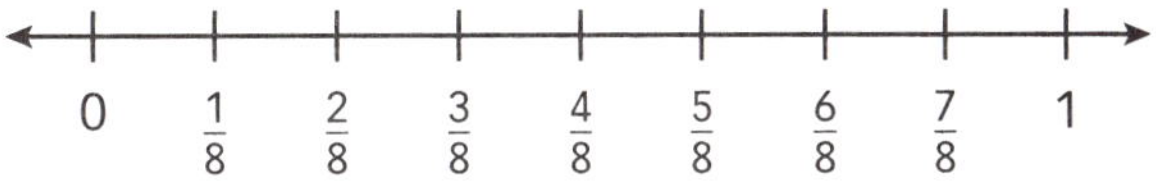

4 $\frac{4}{6}$ $\square$ $\frac{1}{6}$

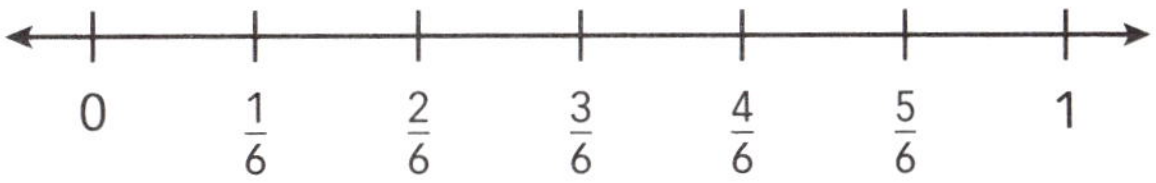

5 $\frac{5}{8}$ $\square$ $\frac{5}{6}$

Solve. Write the fraction shown in problems 6–10.

6  ______

7 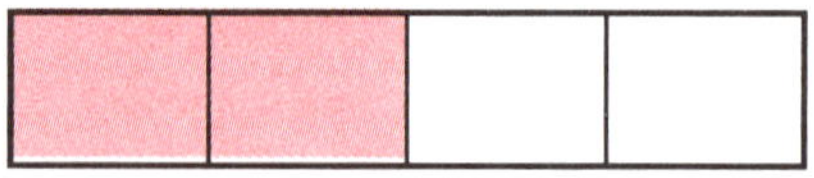 ______

8 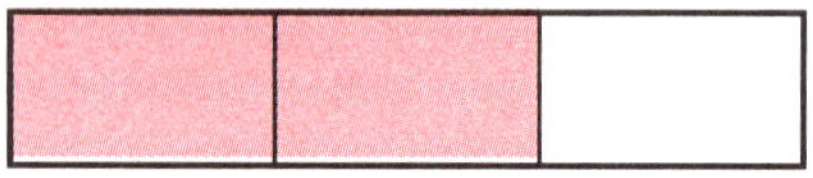 ______

9 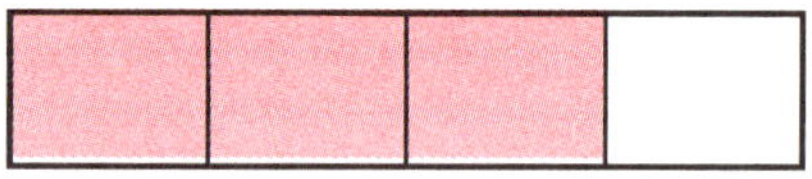 ______

10 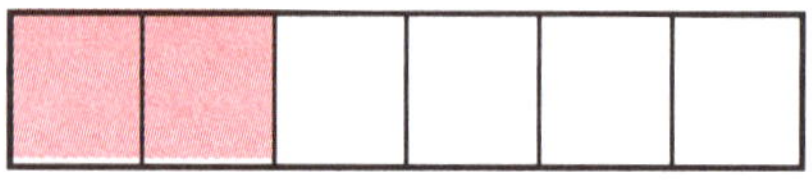 ______

Compare the fractions. You can use the models above to help you.

11 $\frac{2}{4}$ ☐ $\frac{2}{6}$

$\frac{2}{6}$ ☐ $\frac{2}{4}$

12 $\frac{2}{3}$ ☐ $\frac{2}{6}$

$\frac{2}{6}$ ☐ $\frac{2}{3}$

13 $\frac{3}{4}$ ☐ $\frac{3}{8}$

$\frac{3}{8}$ ☐ $\frac{3}{4}$

14 $\frac{2}{4}$ ☐ $\frac{3}{4}$

$\frac{3}{4}$ ☐ $\frac{2}{4}$

Write a fraction to make the statement true.

15 $\frac{6}{8} >$ ______

16 $\frac{1}{4} >$ ______

Name: ____________________

Solve One-Step Word Problems

Solve the problems.

1 Jan and Lee are playing a card game. Each player turns over one card. The player with the greater fraction wins both cards. Who wins the cards? Explain your thinking.

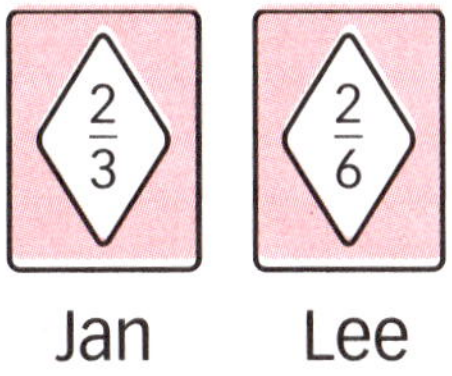

____

____

____

____

2 Dranny painted $\frac{1}{4}$ of her room in one day. Did she paint more or less than half of her room? Explain your answer.

____

____

____

3 Rob and Mike each have the same-size sandwich. Rob cut his sandwich into 3 equal parts and ate 2 parts. Mike cut his sandwich into 4 equal parts and ate 2 parts. Who ate more? Explain your answer.

____

____

____

Solve.

4 Kayla and Kevin have the same-size notebooks. Kayla covered $\frac{5}{6}$ of hers with stickers. Kevin covered $\frac{5}{8}$ of his with stickers. Who covered more of the notebook? Explain your answer.

5 Which statement is true?

A $\frac{1}{8} > \frac{3}{8}$

B $\frac{3}{8} > \frac{3}{4}$

C $\frac{3}{8} > \frac{1}{8}$

D $\frac{3}{4} > \frac{3}{2}$

Bella chose **D** as the correct answer. How did she get that answer?

6 Which fractions are less than $\frac{5}{6}$? Circle the letter of all that apply.

A $\frac{4}{6}$

B $\frac{5}{8}$

C $\frac{3}{6}$

D $\frac{6}{6}$

E $\frac{5}{4}$

Unit 4 Game

Name: ____________________

Equivalent Fraction Match

What you need:
Recording Sheet, Game Cards

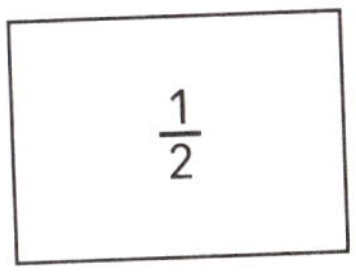

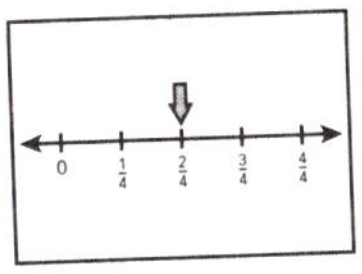

Directions

- Mix the Game Cards. Lay them face down in 3 rows of 6 cards each.
- Take turns. Flip over two cards.
- If the cards show equivalent fractions, keep the cards. Record the equivalent fractions on the Recording Sheet.
- If the cards do not show equivalent fractions, turn them back over.
- Keep playing until all the cards are matched or no more matches can be found. The player with the most matches is the winner.

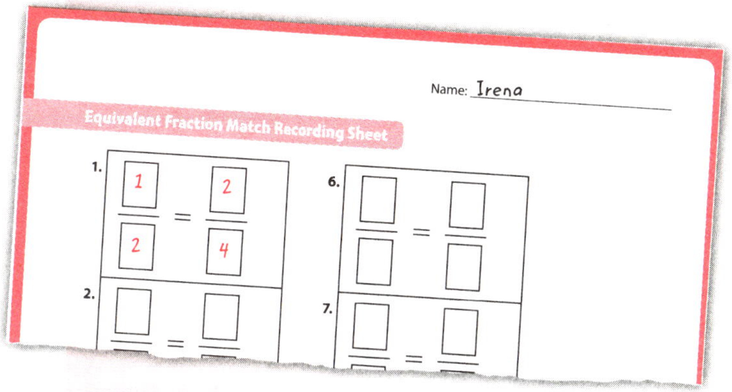

Name: ____________________

Equivalent Fraction Match Recording Sheet

1. $\frac{\square}{\square} = \frac{\square}{\square}$

2. $\frac{\square}{\square} = \frac{\square}{\square}$

3. $\frac{\square}{\square} = \frac{\square}{\square}$

4. $\frac{\square}{\square} = \frac{\square}{\square}$

5. $\frac{\square}{\square} = \frac{\square}{\square}$

6. $\frac{\square}{\square} = \frac{\square}{\square}$

7. $\frac{\square}{\square} = \frac{\square}{\square}$

8. $\frac{\square}{\square} = \frac{\square}{\square}$

9. $\frac{\square}{\square} = \frac{\square}{\square}$

Equivalent Fraction Match Cards

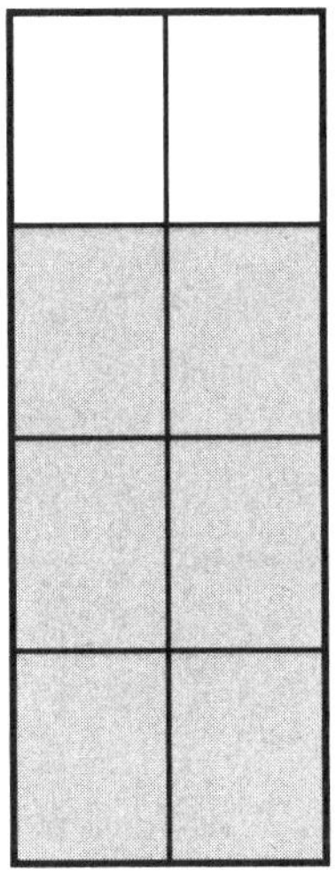

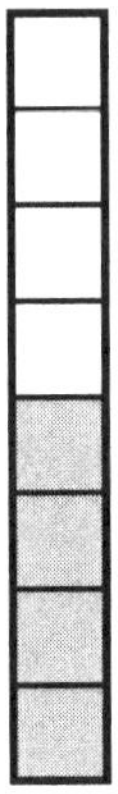

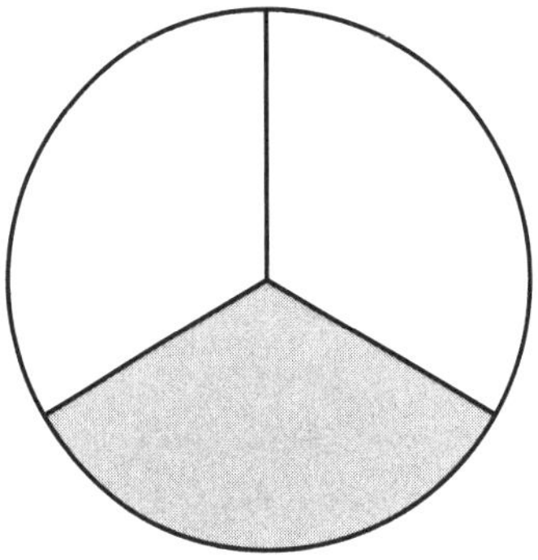

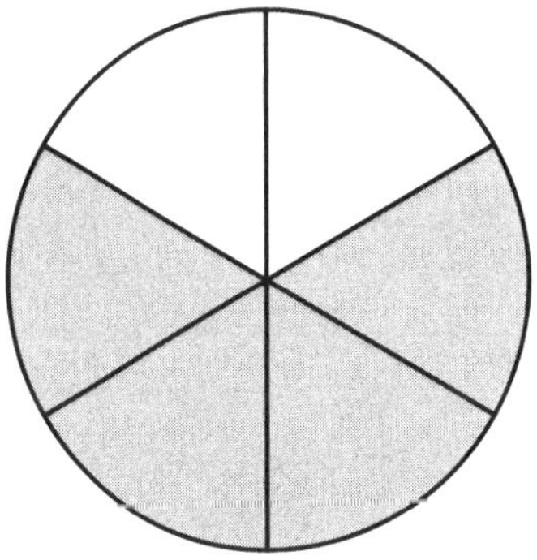

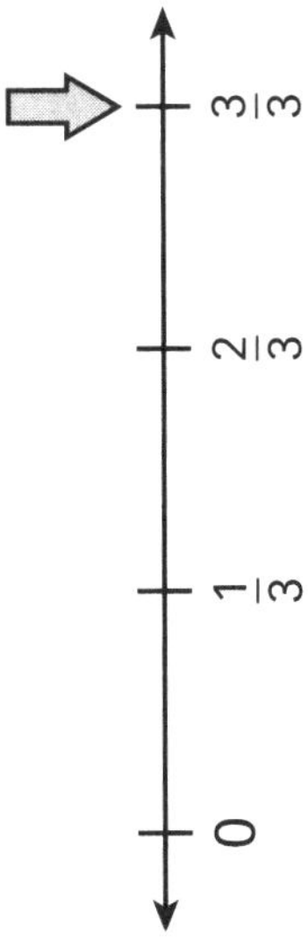

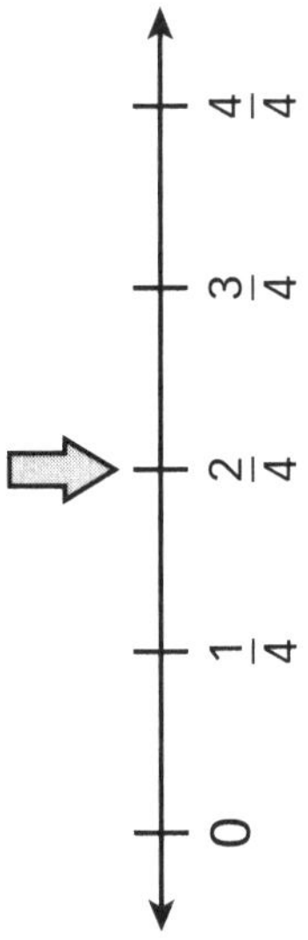

Equivalent Fraction Match Cards

$\frac{3}{4}$	$\frac{3}{6}$	$\frac{2}{6}$
$\frac{2}{8}$	$\frac{2}{2}$	$\frac{2}{3}$
$\frac{1}{8}$	$\frac{6}{6}$	$\frac{1}{2}$

Unit 4 Practice

Name: ____________________

Fractions

In this unit you learned to:	Lesson
use a fraction to show equal parts of a whole, for example: when a whole has 4 equal parts, each part is $\frac{1}{4}$ of the whole.	14
use a number line to show fractions and find a fraction on a number line.	15
understand equivalent fractions, for example: $\frac{1}{3} = \frac{2}{6}$ because they show the same amount.	16
find equivalent fractions, for example: fractions equivalent to $\frac{1}{2}$ include $\frac{2}{4}$, $\frac{3}{6}$, and $\frac{4}{8}$	17
write whole numbers as fractions, for example: $5 = \frac{5}{1}$ or $\frac{10}{2}$	17
compare fractions when they have same-sized wholes using $<$, $>$, and $=$, for example: $\frac{1}{3} > \frac{1}{8}$, $\frac{4}{6} < \frac{5}{6}$, and $\frac{2}{3} = \frac{4}{6}$	18 and 19

Use these skills to solve problems 1–5.

1 Which model shows $\frac{3}{4}$? Circle the letter for all that apply.

A

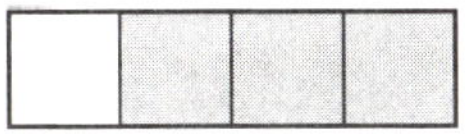

B

C

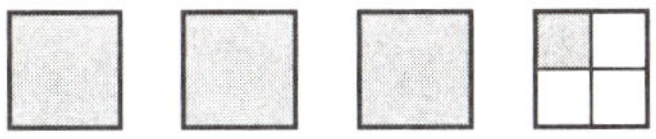

D

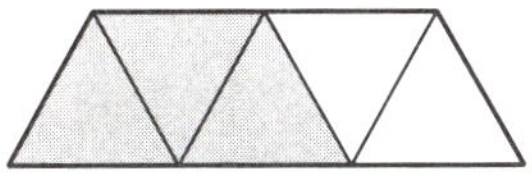

2 Anita cuts out a circle. Then she folds the circle into 8 equal parts. She colored 3 parts brown and 2 parts orange. What fraction of the total number of parts does she have left to color?

Show your work.

Solution: She had ________ of the circle left to color.

Solve.

3 Use the number line to write equivalent fractions.

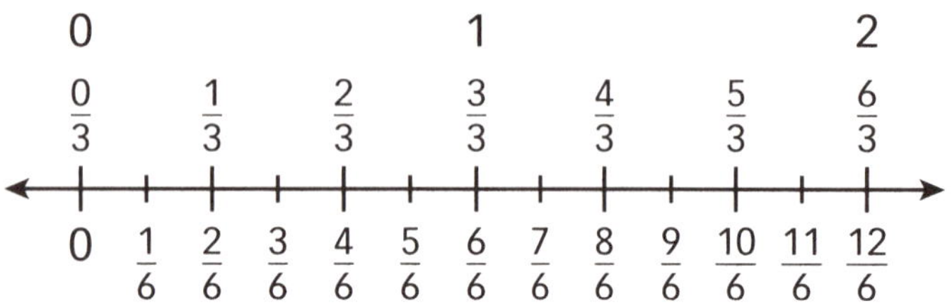

a. $\frac{4}{6} = \frac{\square}{\square}$

c. $1 = \frac{\square}{\square}$

b. $\frac{5}{3} = \frac{\square}{\square}$

4 Compare the fractions. Write *greater* or *less* in the blanks.

a. $\frac{2}{4}$ is ______________________________ than 1.

b. $\frac{3}{2}$ is ______________________________ than $\frac{3}{4}$.

c. $\frac{1}{2}$ is ______________________________ than $\frac{1}{4}$.

d. $\frac{7}{4}$ is ______________________________ than 2.

5 Anna, Dan, and Eric made scarves. All the scarves are the same size. The note on the right shows how much of each scarf is blue.

Anna's scarf is $\frac{3}{8}$ blue.

Dan's scarf is $\frac{3}{6}$ blue.

Eric's scarf is $\frac{3}{4}$ blue.

Who used the most blue? ________________

Who used the least blue? ________________

Explain how you got your answer. ____

____

____

Unit 4 Performance Task

Name: ____________________________

Answer the questions and show all your work on separate paper.

A kindergarten class needs help learning about "more" and "less." Your class will help them compare the amount of sand in same-size jars.

You have 3 pairs of jars that are all the same size. The two jars in each pair need to have a different amount of sand. Use these fractions to decide how full to make each jar.

$\frac{2}{2}$ $\frac{1}{2}$ $\frac{3}{8}$ $\frac{4}{8}$ $\frac{1}{8}$ $\frac{2}{8}$ $\frac{3}{4}$ $\frac{1}{4}$ $\frac{2}{6}$ $\frac{6}{6}$ $\frac{4}{6}$

For each pair of jars:

- Draw a picture of the jars.
- Label each jar with a fraction that tells how full it is.
- Compare the amount of sand in the jars. Write "more" or "less" under the picture of each jar.

Checklist

Did you . . .

- ☐ pair unequal fractions?
- ☐ draw a picture and label the amounts you drew?
- ☐ compare the amount of sand in the jars?

Reflect on Mathematical Practices

1 **Reason About Numbers** How did you decide which fractions to use for the pairs of jars?

2 **Make Models** How can you use models to compare fractions?

Performance Task Tips

Word Bank Here are some words that you might use in your answer.

more	less	compare
fraction	half	third
fourth	sixth	eighth

Models Here are some models that you might use to find a solution.

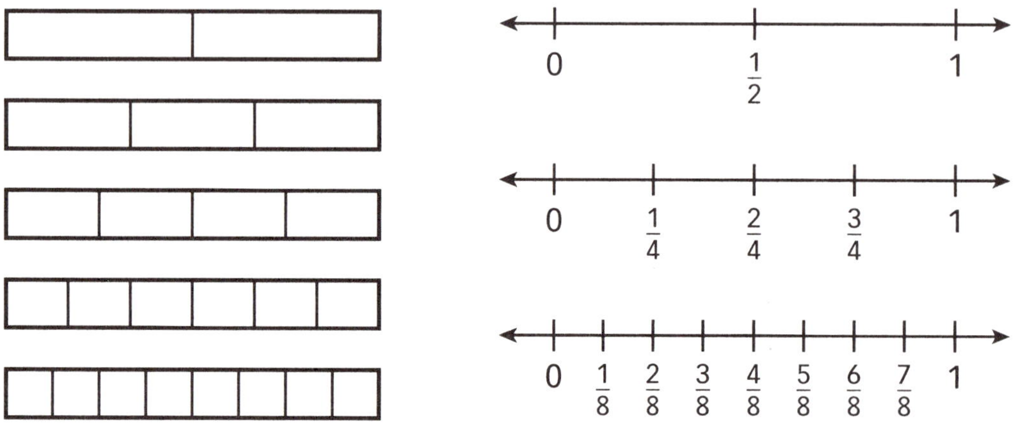

Sentence Starters Here are some sentence starters that might help explain your work.

I know that _____ is less than _____ because ____________

I know that _____ is more than _____ because ___________

Unit 4 Vocabulary

Name: ______________________

My Examples

fraction

a number that names part of a whole

denominator

the number below the line in a fraction. It tells how many equal parts are in the whole.

numerator

the number above the line in a fraction. It tells how many equal parts are described.

unit fraction

a fraction with a numerator of 1. Other fractions are built from unit fractions.

My Examples

equivalent fractions

fractions that name the same number

My Words

Dear Family,

This week your child is learning to read a clock to tell time to the nearest minute.

Children have learned that the short hand on a clock face shows the hour, and that it takes 1 hour for the short hand to move from one number to the next. They have learned that the long hand shows the minutes. This year they are learning to pay attention to and interpret the small marks that each show 1 minute.

They find the hour first: Because the short hand has gone past the 3 and isn't to the 4 yet, the *hour* on this clock is 3. (For children who don't often see analog clocks, reading the hour can be a little tricky.)

Then, to find the minutes past the hour, they learn to start at the 12 and count by 5s for each number (1, 2, 3, etc.) up to the number just before the minute hand (7). The number 7 marks 35 minutes past the hour. Then they count the 4 small marks past the 7 to the exact location of the minute hand, to get to 39. The time is 3:39.

Instead of counting by 5s to find the minutes, children can also practice using multiplication facts. They multiply 7 by 5 (because the space between each number is 5 minutes) and then add 4.

Sometimes it's more helpful to know how many minutes it is until the next hour. Your child is learning to count backward from the 12, first by fives and then by ones to read the time on this clock at 21 minutes *before* 4 o'clock.

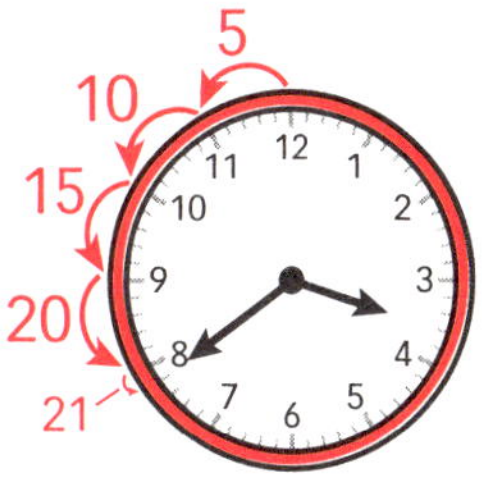

Invite your child to share what he or she knows about telling time to the minute by doing the following activity together.

NEXT

Telling and Writing Time Activity

Materials: two crayons of different lengths, pencil

Do this activity to help your child connect telling time to the minute with everyday events in your family life.

- Have family members take turns naming their favorite time of day, such as breakfast, bed time, or arriving home.
- Ask your child to place the crayons as hands on the clock to show the time of day that each activity happens. Help them record the time on the digital clocks. For example:
  - "I got home from work today at 5:43. Another way to say that time is 17 minutes before six o'clock."
  - "We got a phone message at 6:54 this morning. Another way to say that is 6 minutes before 7 o'clock."
- For more practice, place the hands on the clock, and ask your child to tell you the time.

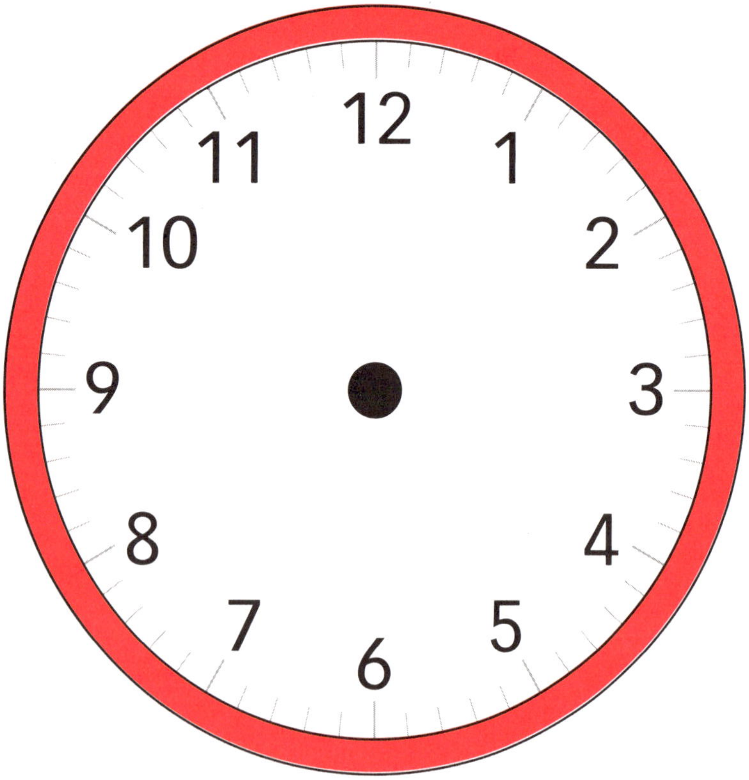

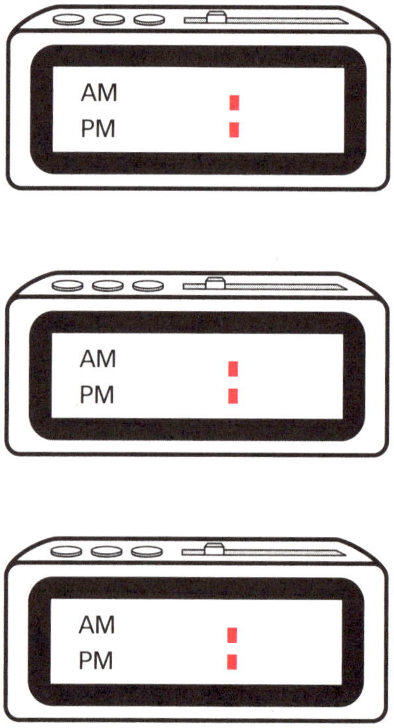

Tell and Write Time

Name: ___________________________

Prerequisite: Tell Time to 5-Minute Intervals

Study the example problem showing how to skip count to tell time. Then solve problems 1–6.

Example

The clock shows the time that Julian finished his guitar practice. What time did his practice end?

The hour hand is past the 4, but it isn't at the 5 yet. The minute hand points to the 7. Skip count by fives 7 times to find the minutes.

5, 10, 15, 20, 25, 30, 35

The clock shows 35 minutes after 4 o'clock.

Julian's guitar practice ended at 4:35.

Draw lines to match clocks that show the same time.

1

Write the time on the clocks so that each pair of clocks shows the same time.

2

3

4

Draw hour and minute hands so that each pair of clocks shows the same time.

5

6

Name: ______________________

Tell Time to the Minute

Study the example problem showing how to tell time to the minute. Then solve problems 1–9.

Example

What time does the clock show?

The hour hand shows that it is between 3 o'clock and 4 o'clock. It takes 5 minutes for the minute hand to move from one number to the next. It takes 1 minute for the minute hand to move from one mark to the next.

Count by fives from the 12 to the 7. Then count 2 more minutes.

The clock shows 37 minutes after 3, or 3:37.

1 Look at the red arrows on the clock. Count by fives and by ones to find the minutes before 4:00. Fill in the blanks.

5, 10, ______, ______, 21, ______, ______

______ minutes before ______

Write the time in two ways.

2 ______

______ minutes before ______

3 ______

______ minutes before ______

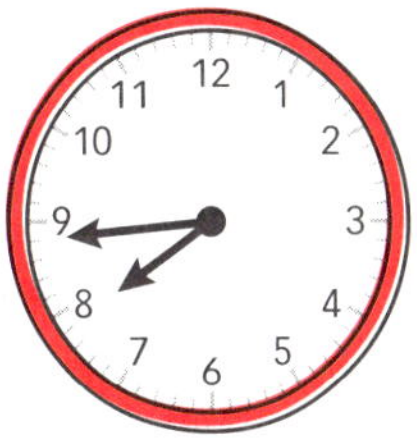

Write the time on the clock so that each pair of clocks shows the same time.

4

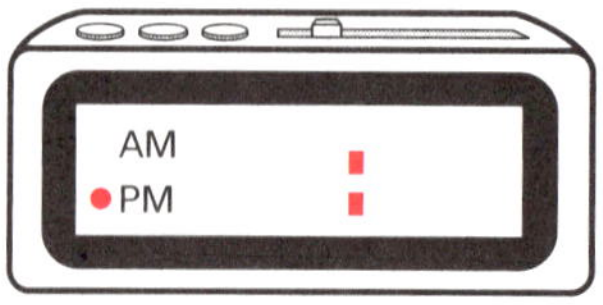

5

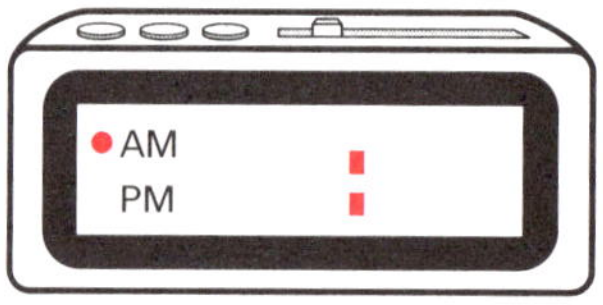

Draw the hands on the clock to show the time.

6 It is 13 minutes after 4.

M **7** It is 13 minutes before 7.

8 Write the time in three ways.

____

______ minutes after __________

______ minutes before __________

9 Look at the clock in problem 8.

What time will it be in 24 minutes?
Draw hands on the clock to show that time.

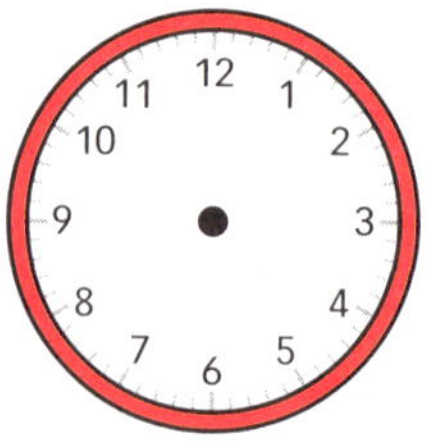

Name: ____________________

Tell and Write Time

Solve the problems.

1 Which phrases describe the time shown on the clock? Circle the letter for all that apply.

A 43 minutes after 7:00

B 43 minutes before 7:00

C 43 minutes before 8:00

D 17 minutes before 7:00

E 17 minutes before 8:00

F 17 minutes after 7:00

2 Carlotta got to the Toy Museum at 10:19. Circle the letter of the correct answer.

A 19 minutes before 10:00

B 19 minutes before 11:00

C 41 minutes before 10:00

D 41 minutes before 11:00

Josh chose **B** as the correct answer. How did he get that answer?

____

____

____

____

____

Solve.

3 Enrique left the science center at 12 minutes before 3:00. Draw hands on the clock to show this time.

4 Kamala got home from her jazz dance lesson at the time shown on the clock. Write the time in two ways.

____

_____ minutes before ________

5 Chen ate breakfast this morning at the time shown on the clock.

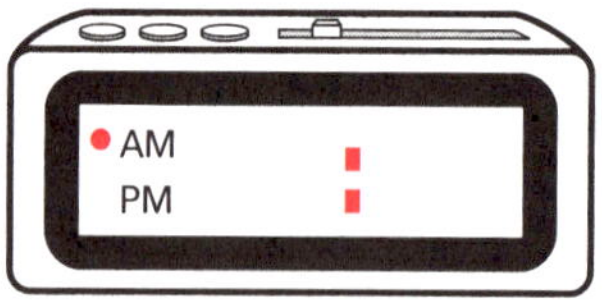

Write the time on the digital clock. Mark A.M. or P.M. Then tell the time before the hour.

_____ minutes before ________

Dear Family,

This week your child is learning to solve word problems involving elapsed time.

Elapsed time is the amount of time that has passed between a starting time and an ending time.

Your child might see a problem like this one, where you know the elapsed time and the starting time, and are asked to find the ending time.

> Paul started his homework at 3:30. He spent 10 minutes on math, 15 minutes on reading, and 22 minutes on science. What time was it after he did those three parts of his homework?

The first clock shows the time Paul started his homework, 3:30. The arrows show the movement of the minute hand as it moves through the 10 minutes he spent on math, then 15 minutes for reading, and then 22 minutes for science.

The minute hand ends up at 17 minutes past the hour. Since it moved past the 12, the hour changed from 3 to 4. Paul finished his homework at 4:17.

A number line is another way to show this.

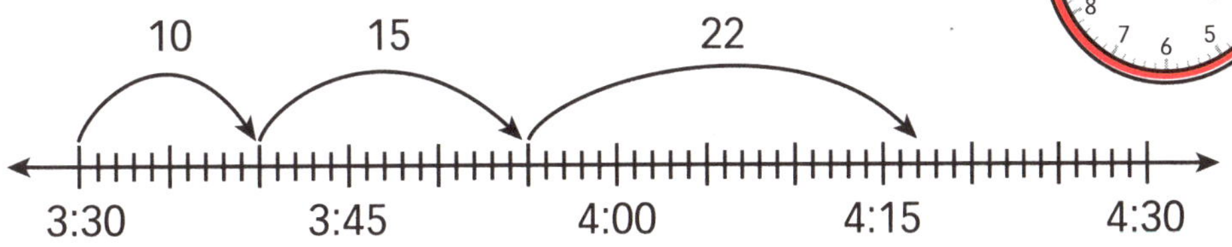

Starting at 3:30, the three jumps along the number line show how many minutes it took Paul to do the three parts of his homework. Where the last jump ends is the ending time, or the time that Paul finished his homework.

Invite your child to share what he or she knows about solving problems involving elapsed time by doing the following activity together.

NEXT

Solving Problems About Time Activity

Work with your child to solve real-life problems about elapsed time. Talk with your child about activities you enjoy doing together and how much time they take.

Then create stories in which you know the start time and how long activities take (the elapsed time). Talk about how to find the end time. Discuss how to use a clock or a number line (like the one shown) to help find the ending time.

For example: Donna started her swim lesson at 12:30. She warmed up for 5 minutes. For 10 minutes she practiced side breathing, and for 15 minutes she worked on her freestyle stroke. When did her lesson end?

Then, create stories where you know how long activities take (the elapsed time) and you know the end time, but need to find out the start time.

For example: Dinner needs to cook for 25 minutes, and then cool for 5 minutes. What time should dinner go in the oven if you want to eat at 6:30?

Finally, create stories where you know the start time and end time. Find how long the activity took (the elapsed time).

For example: You left work at 6:25 and got home at 7:05. How long did it take you to get home?

Best of all, recognize opportunities throughout the week when you yourself are actually solving problems about time. Share these problems with your child to provide *actual* real-world practice!

Solve Problems About Time

Name: ____________________

Prerequisite: Tell Time to the Minute

Study the example problem showing how to tell time to the minute. Then solve problems 1–7.

Example

Oscar took his pet hamster out of its cage to play. The clock shows what time it was. What time did Oscar take the hamster out of the cage?

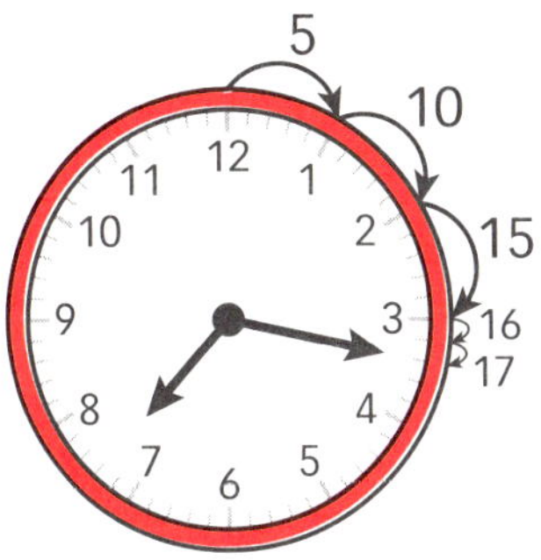

The hour hand shows that it is between 7 and 8 o'clock. It takes 5 minutes for the minute hand to move from one number to the next. It takes 1 minute for the minute hand to move from one mark to the next.

Count by fives from the 12 to the 3. Then count 2 more minutes.

The clock shows 17 minutes after 7, or 7:17.
Oscar took the hamster out of the cage at 7:17.

Draw lines to match clocks that show the same time.

1

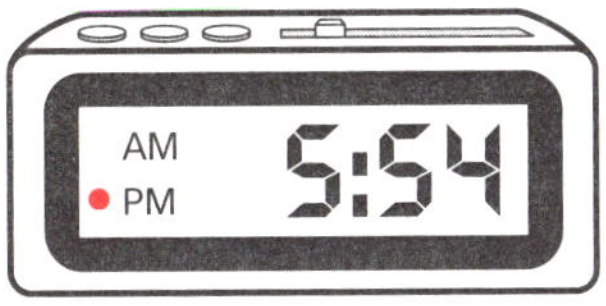

Solve.

2 Look at the arrows on the clock. Count by fives and by ones to find the minutes before the hour. Fill in the blanks.

5, ______, 11, ______, ______, ______

It is ______ minutes before __________.

Write the time in two ways.

3 __________

______ minutes before __________

4 __________

______ minutes before __________

Draw the hands on the clock to show the time.

5 It is 22 minutes before 4:00.

6 It is 9 minutes after 9:00.

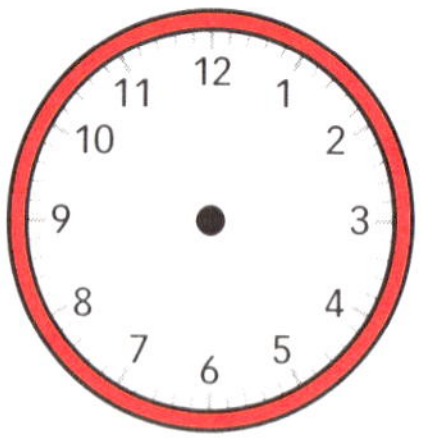

7 Write the times from problems 5 and 6 on the clocks below.

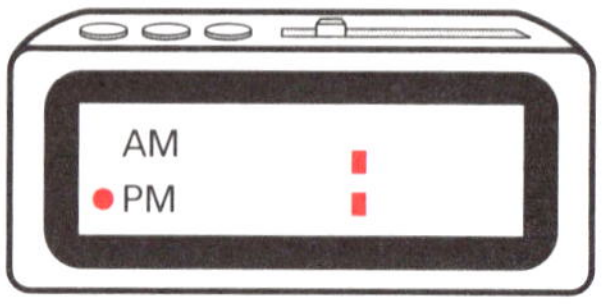

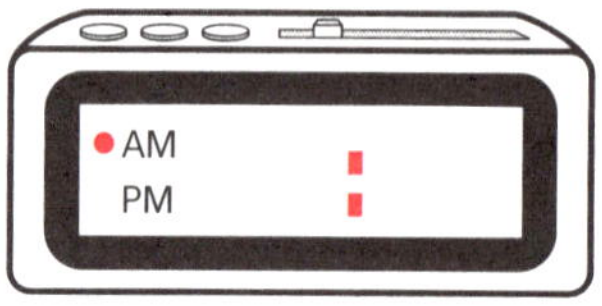

Name: ____________________

Find the End Time in Word Problems

Study the example problem showing how to find the end time when you know the start time and the elapsed time. Then solve problems 1–6.

Example

Anna started walking her dog, Pickles, at 2:40. She walked for 25 minutes. Then she played ball with Pickles for 15 minutes. What time did Anna finish?

Start at 2:40. Count 25 minutes for the walk. Then count 15 minutes for playing ball. The minute hand went past 12, so the hour moved ahead to the 3. The minute hand ended on the 4.

The second clock shows the end time, which is 3:20.

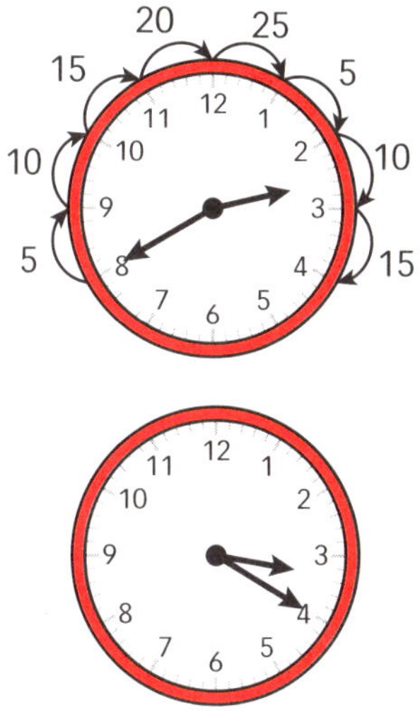

1 Alma got to the playground at 2:45. She spent 20 minutes on the swings and 10 minutes on the jungle gym. She played on the slide for 12 minutes. Then she went home. What time did Alma go home? Fill in the blanks.

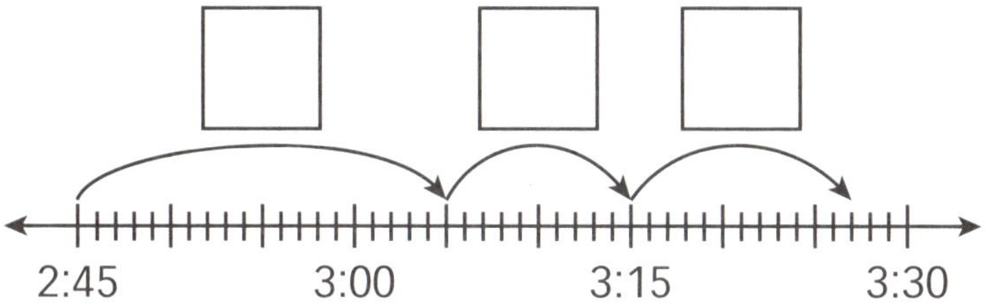

Alma went home at __________.

2 Juanita got in line for the Safari Ride at 11:55. She waited in line for 8 minutes. The ride lasted for 7 minutes. What time did she get off the ride?

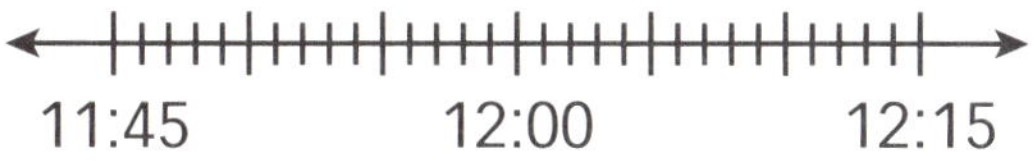

Solution: __________

Vocabulary

elapsed time the time between a start time and an end time.

Solve.

3 Jay went outside at 10:50 and spent 35 minutes looking for worms. Then he took 10 minutes to collect his gear. After that Jay went fishing. What time did Jay leave to go fishing? Draw hands on the clock to show the time. Write the time.

Jay left to go fishing at __________.

4 Kareem started climbing on the rock wall at 5:20. He climbed for 16 minutes. What time did Kareem finish climbing on the rock wall?

Solution: ______________________________

5 The Mendoza family left home at 10:30. They drove 25 minutes and stopped at the store. The family spent 20 minutes in the store. Then they drove another 13 minutes to get to the beach. What time did they get to the beach?

Show your work.

Solution: ______________________________

____

6 Sharna leaves school at 3:10. It takes 12 minutes for her to walk home from school. It takes 7 minutes for her to gather her soccer equipment and 10 more minutes to get to the soccer field. Soccer practice starts at 3:45. Sharna thinks she will be late. Do you agree? Explain.

____

____

____

Name: ______________________________

Find the Start Time in Word Problems

Study the example problem showing how to find the start time when you know the end time and the elapsed time. Then solve problems 1–5.

Example

Ming is riding her bike to Carmen's house. She wants to be there by 4:30. First she has to do homework for 30 minutes. The bike ride takes 15 minutes. What time should Ming start her homework?

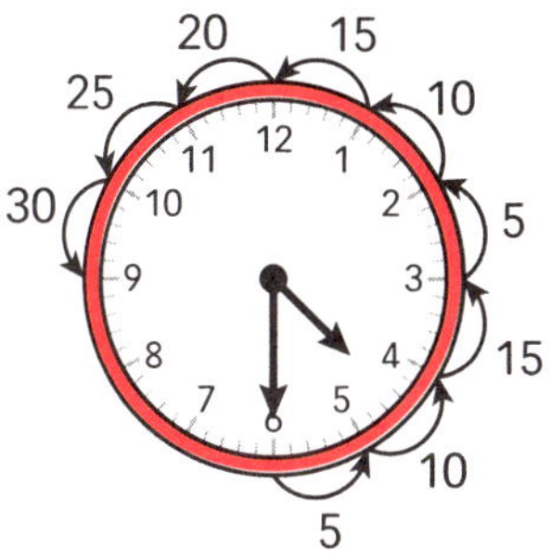

Start at 4:30. Count back 15 minutes for the bike ride. Then count back 30 minutes for homework. The minute hand went past 12, so the hour moved back to the 3. The minute hand ended on the 9.

The second clock shows the start time, which is 3:45. Ming should start her homework by 3:45.

1 Johanna and her mom want to get to the birthday party at 2:00. It is a 25-minute walk. On the way, they plan to stop for 15 minutes to get a card. What time should they leave? Show how to count backward on the number line.

Solution: ______________________________

____

2 If they drive, it takes 8 minutes to get to the party. Johanna and her mother still want to stop and get a card. What time should they leave if they drive to the party? Explain.

____

____

Solve.

3 A movie starts at 5:15. Rudy wants to get to the theater 25 minutes before the movie starts. It takes 10 minutes to drive to the theater. What time should Rudy leave home?

Show your work.

Solution: ______________________________

4 Carlos played on the playground for 12 minutes. Then he swam at the pool for 25 minutes. He finished at 12:00. What time did he start playing?

Show your work.

Solution: ______________________________

5 Allie was done with gymnastics practice at 7:30. At practice, she tumbled for 20 minutes. Then she worked on the balance beam for 10 minutes. Allie also practiced on the trampoline for 15 minutes. What time did she start practice?

Show your work.

Solution: ______________________________

Name: ____________________

Solve Problems About Time

Solve the problems.

1 The Soto family sat down at a table at a restaurant. Then they waited 10 minutes to order their food. They waited 20 minutes until the food arrived. They took 25 minutes to eat dinner and were done at 6:30. What time did they sit down at the table? Circle the letter of the correct answer.

A 5:25 **C** 5:45

B 5:35 **D** 7:25

Dana chose **D** as the correct answer. How did she get that answer?

____

____

____

2 Rashid made a stuffed bear at the toy store. He started at 4:40. He spent 25 minutes at the stuffing table and 21 minutes at the decorating table. Then he was done. What time did he finish?

Show your work.

Solution: ____________________

Solve.

3 Gino and his brothers, Brad and Tony, want to leave at 11:15 to go to the park. Choose *Yes* or *No* to tell whether each brother will be ready in time.

a. Gino starts at 10:50. He takes 15 minutes to shower and 8 minutes to get dressed. ☐ Yes ☐ No

b. Brad starts at 10:45. He takes 15 minutes to eat a sandwich and 10 minutes to wash up. ☐ Yes ☐ No

c. Tony starts at 11:05. He takes 9 minutes to get dressed and 3 minutes to brush his teeth. ☐ Yes ☐ No

4 How long is it from 7:06 to 7:32? Circle the letter of the correct answer.

A 16 minutes

B 24 minutes

C 26 minutes

D 38 minutes

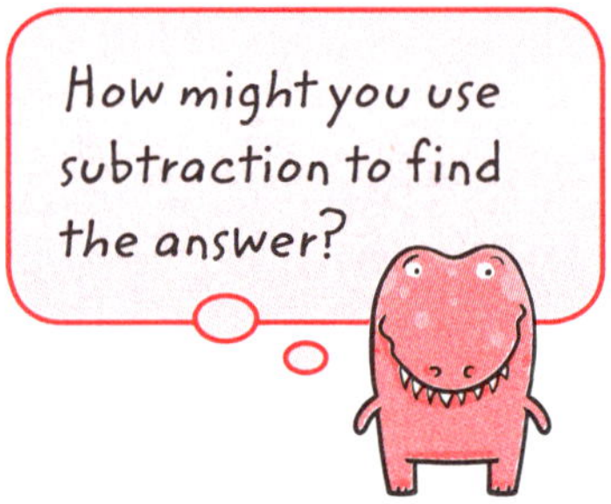

5 Nathan's family wants to be at Grandma's house by 10:45. They need to take a 50-minute bus ride. Then they have to walk for 12 minutes. They can take a bus that leaves at 9:45 or one that leaves at 9:30. Which bus should the family take? Explain.

Dear Family,

This week your child is learning about measuring liquid volume using liters.

Liquid volume is the amount of space a liquid takes up.

One standard unit used to measure liquid volume is called a liter. A **liter** is about the same amount as a quart. It is helpful to picture about how much a liter is. A liter is approximately:

the amount of water in a large water bottle

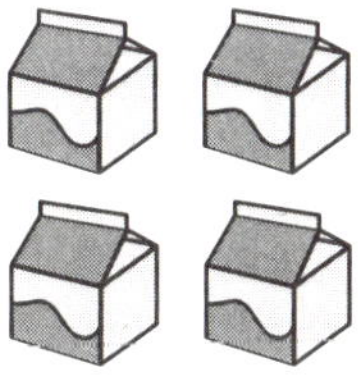

the amount of milk in 4 small milk cartons

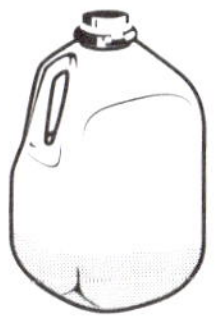

the amount of milk in $\frac{1}{4}$ of a gallon

Your child will use addition, subtraction, multiplication, and division to solve word problems related to liquid volume.

For example, the dotted lines on this water jug show sections that each hold 2 liters. There are 4 sections, so the container holds a total of 8 liters.

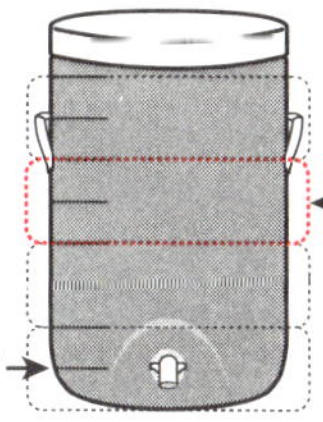

If this 8-liter container is filled with juice, and 4 teams want to share it equally, how many liters of juice will each team get?

Your child might write number sentences like these to solve this problem:

$8 \div 4 = ?$ or $4 \times ? = 8$

Invite your child to share what he or she knows about measuring liquid in liters by doing the following activity together.

NEXT

Liquid Volume Activity

Help your child develop familiarity with the size of a liter. Go on a scavenger hunt to find containers that hold *about one liter, less than one liter,* and *more than one liter.* Record the containers on the chart below. Remember, one liter is about

the amount of water in a large water bottle

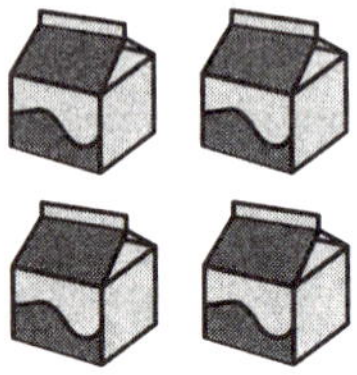

the amount of milk in 4 small milk cartons

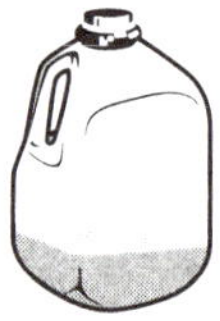

the amount of milk in $\frac{1}{4}$ of a gallon

Some containers you might find are a flower vase, a baby food jar, a garbage can, or a paper cup. Any of these can be a good start to your list.

About one liter	Less than one liter	More than one liter

If you have a 1-liter (or 1 quart) plastic beverage bottle or yogurt container, use it to check your thinking.

- Fill the liter bottle with water and then pour into each container to check whether the liter bottle holds more, less, or almost the same amount.
- Make the activity more challenging by estimating how many liters each of the larger objects holds, and then check your estimates!

Liquid Volume

Name: ______________________

Prerequisite: Use Measurement Tools

Study the example showing how to choose a tool to measure an object. Then solve problems 1–7.

Example

Which tool can you use to find out how much water the fish tank can hold?

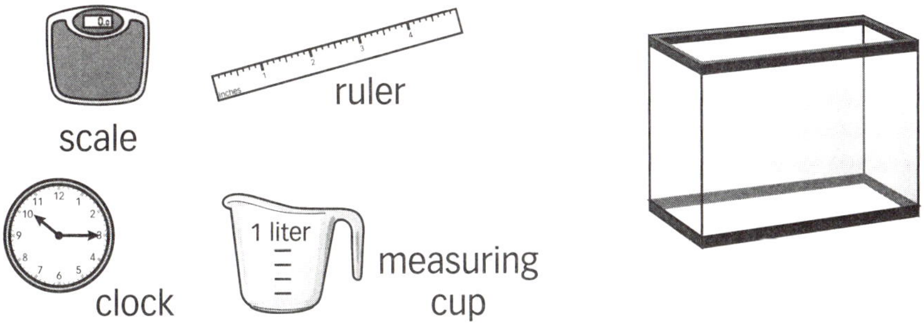

Use the measuring cup. Fill the one-liter measuring cup with water, and pour it into the fish tank. Count how many times you pour a full liter into the tank. Then you know how much water the fish tank can hold.

1 Which tool can you use to find out how long the fish tank is?

____

2 Which tool can you use to find out how tall the fish tank is?

____

3 Which tool can you use to find out how heavy the fish tank is?

____

Solve.

Chang emptied one full water bottle into a small bowl. The picture shows the result.

4 Which can hold more water, the bottle or the bowl? Explain your answer.

5 Do you think Chang could pour two full bottles of water into the bowl? Explain your answer.

6 Leo has a different-size bottle of water. He empties his bottle into a small bowl just like Chang's.

Will the bowl be full? Explain your answer.

7 Petra has some bottles of water exactly the same size as Chang's bottle. She empties 3 bottles of water into a different-size bowl. Do you think Chang's bowl or Petra's bowl is larger? Explain your thinking.

Name: ______________________

Estimate Liquid Volume

Study the example showing how to estimate liquid volume. Then solve problems 1–7.

Example

Jan is going to pour water into a picnic cooler. She is trying to estimate how many liters it can hold when it's full.

It looks like the cooler can hold about 12 bottles.

Since there would be space between the bottles, Jan estimates the cooler might hold about 15 liters of water.

1 The can of juice holds 1 liter. About how many liters could the pitcher hold? How did you decide?

____

____

____

____

____

2 Which of these items could hold about 1 liter of water? Circle the letter for all that apply.

A a trash can

B a bathtub

C a coffee pot

D a flower vase

3 A kitchen sink holds about 40 liters of water. What could hold more than 40 liters of water? Circle the letter of the correct answer.

A a bathtub

B a cooking pot

C a coffee cup

D a cereal bowl

Vocabulary

liter a unit of capacity, or liquid volume. Some water bottles hold one liter of water.

Solve.

4 This juice dispenser has 3 liters of juice in it. About how many liters does this juice dispenser hold when it is full? Circle the letter of the correct answer.

A 2 liters

B 3 liters

C 6 liters

D 10 liters

5 About how many liters of water can the large jug hold? Circle the letter of the correct answer.

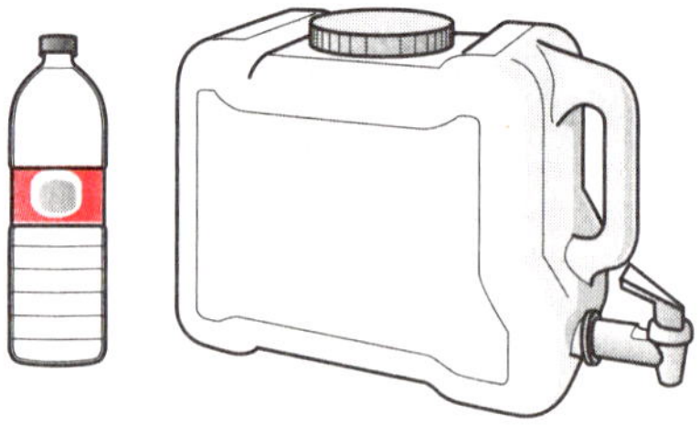

1 liter ? liters

A $\frac{1}{2}$ liter

B 1 liter

C 2 liters

D 8 liters

6 Explain how you estimated the answer to problem 5.

____

____

____

____

____

7 Look closely at the 1-liter water bottle and the large jug in problem 5. Explain how to estimate the fraction of the large jug that can be filled with 1 liter of water.

____

____

____

Name: ______________________

Solve Word Problems about Liquid Volume

Study the example showing how to solve a word problem about liquid volume. Then solve problems 1–8.

Example

Bridget fills 7 water coolers for the school picnic. Each cooler holds 9 liters of water. How many liters of water are in all the coolers?

Each cooler has the same amount of water, so you can multiply to find the total.

$7 \times 9 = 63$ liters

The coolers hold 63 liters of water.

1 Jose had a cooler with 25 liters of lemonade to take to school for his birthday party. Then he poured 1 liter from the cooler to keep at home. How many liters were left to take to school?

____

2 Ms. Lyon brought a cooler with 24 liters of lemonade to school to serve her students. The students are sitting at 8 different tables. She gives the same amount of lemonade to students at each table. How many liters does each table get?

____

3 Write a division sentence with an unknown to show how you solved problem 2.

____

Solve.

4 Samuel takes 5 coolers to his basketball game. Each cooler holds 9 liters of water. How many liters of water altogether did he take to the game?

Show your work.

Solution: ______________________________

5 Look at problem 4. If 3 coolers are completely empty after the game, how many liters of water are left?

Show your work.

Solution: ______________________________

6 The fuel tank in Janice's car holds 60 liters of gas. She has 20 liters of gas in her tank. How much more gas does she need to fill up the tank?

Show your work.

Solution: ______________________________

7 Bobby's aquarium holds 32 liters of water. He uses a 4-liter bucket to fill the tank. How many buckets of water are needed to fill the tank?

Show your work.

Solution: ______________________________

8 Terry has pitchers that hold 2 liters and 5 liters. How can he use these pitchers to measure out exactly 3 liters of water?

____

____

Name: ______________________

Solve Problems About Liquid Volume

Solve the problems.

1 Jeff brought 12 liters of orange juice to a party. The guests drank 7 liters of orange juice. How many liters of orange juice were left?

Show your work.

Solution: ______________________

2 Cathy fills a 10-liter bucket with pond water. She uses a 2-liter jar to scoop out water from the pond and pours it into her bucket. How many times does Cathy need to scoop water from the pond to fill the bucket?

Show your work.

Solution: ______________________

3 Maria is in charge of making punch for the party. She adds 2 liters of water to 1 liter of orange juice and 2 liters of soda. Then she adds 1 liter of crushed strawberry juice and 2 liters of pineapple juice to the mixture. How many liters of punch does Maria make?

Show your work.

Solution: ______________________

Solve.

4 Jessica has to fill a large aquarium with 48 liters of water. She owns a water jug that can hold 6 liters of water. How many times does she need to pour the water from the jug to fill the aquarium?

Show your work.

Solution: ______________________

5 Estimate whether each object holds less than, equal to, or more than a liter. Write *less, more,* or *equal.*

a.

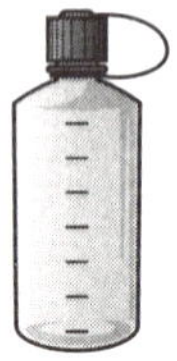

b.

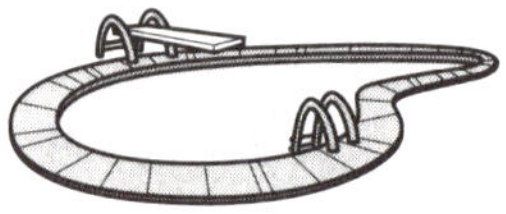

c.

a. __________ **b.** __________ **c.** __________

6 This jug has 2 liters of water in it. Which is the best estimate for how much water the jug could hold? Circle the letter of the correct answer.

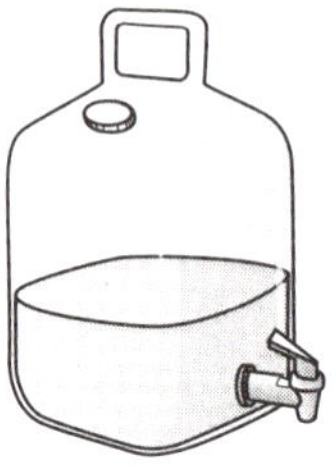

A 15 liters

B 10 liters

C 5 liters

D 2 liters

Alisha chose **A** as the correct answer.

Explain how you know she is wrong.

____

____

____

Dear Family,

This week your child is learning about measuring the mass of objects using units of grams or kilograms.

When we talk about measuring the mass of an object, we mean we are measuring how heavy it is.

Two units commonly used to measure mass are **grams** and **kilograms**.

- The mass of a paper clip is about 1 gram. 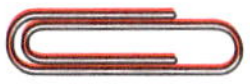
- The mass of a wooden baseball bat is about 1 kilogram. 

A kilogram is equal to 1,000 grams. So, it is also as heavy as 1,000 paper clips.

One way to find the actual mass of any object is to use a balance scale. In the picture, two 1-kilogram weights balance the bag of flour, showing that the mass of the flour is equal to 2 kilograms.

If you only want to estimate the approximate mass of something, one way to do that is to compare it to something else that you know the mass of. For example, if you lift these two books, they may seem to be about as heavy as the bag of flour. Since you know the bag of flour has a mass of 2 kilograms, you can estimate that the mass of the books is also about 2 kilograms. So, the mass of one book is about 1 kilogram.

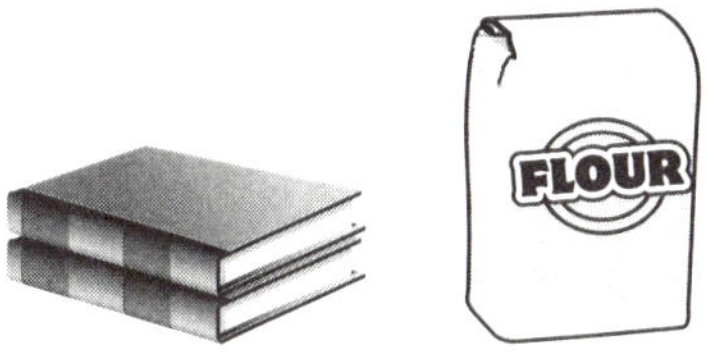

Invite your child to share what he or she knows about measuring mass by doing the following activity together.

NEXT

Mass Activity

Help your child develop familiarity with kilograms and grams. Go on a scavenger hunt to find objects that have a mass of about 1 gram and objects that have a mass of about 1 kilogram. Record the objects on the chart below.

Remember,

- 1 **gram** is about the mass of a paper clip.
- 1 **kilogram** is about the mass of a wooden baseball bat.

Some objects you might find are a rubber band, a library book, a dollar bill, a paper cup, a bag of rice. Any of these can be a good start to your list.

About 1 gram	More than 1 gram and less than 1 kilogram	About 1 kilogram

- If you have a full one-liter bottle of water, or a full quart-sized container of yogurt, those items are very close to 1 kilogram in mass. You may also have a 1-kilogram dumbbell. You can use any of those items to help you compare the mass of each object on your list to 1 kilogram.

Mass

Name: ____________________

Prerequisite: Use Measurement Tools

Study the example showing how to choose a tool to measure an object. Then solve problems 1–7.

Example

Which tool can you use to find out how heavy the fish tank is?

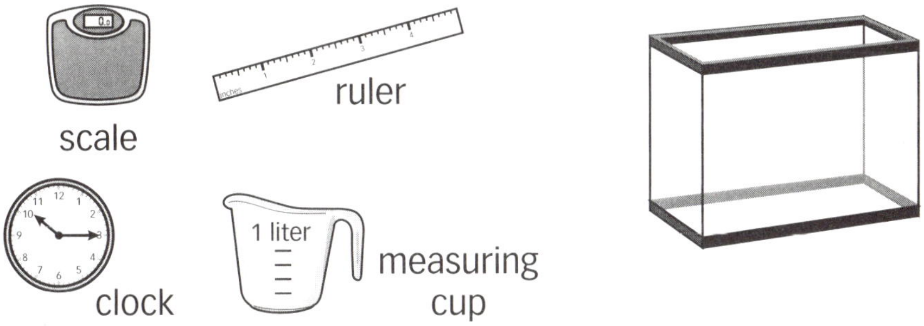

Use the scale. Put the fish tank on the scale and read the number of kilograms.

1. Which tool can you use to find out the amount of water the fish tank can hold?

   ____

   ____

2. Which tool can you use to find out how tall the fish tank is?

   ____

   ____

3. Which tool can you use to find out how heavy the measuring cup is?

   ____

   ____

Solve.

Anita placed an apple and a banana on a balance scale. She knows that the heavier side will be lower. Look at the picture.

4 Which has more mass, the apple or the banana? How do you know?

____

____

5 What would happen if you took the apple off the scale? Explain your answer.

____

____

In the picture, the mass of the water bottle is 1 kilogram.

6 Does one apple have a mass more or less than 1 kilogram? Explain.

____

____

In the picture, all the apples are exactly the same, and all the pears are exactly the same. The picture shows the result.

7 What do you think would happen if you put 1 apple on one side and 1 pear on the other side of the scale? Explain your answer.

____

____

Name: ______________________________

Estimate Mass

Study the example showing one way to estimate mass. Then solve problems 1–8.

Example

Dana wants to estimate how heavy her backpack is when she fills it with hardcover library books.

Each book has a mass of about 1 kilogram. She can fit 8 books in her backpack.

Dana estimates that her full backpack has a mass of about 9 kilograms, because the backpack has mass too.

1 Would you use grams or kilograms as the unit to measure the mass of a strawberry?

____

2 Would you use grams or kilograms as the unit to measure the mass of a puppy?

____

3 Would you use grams or kilograms as the unit to measure the mass of a pen?

____

4 A 1-liter bottle of water has a mass of about 1 kilogram. What could have a mass of more than 1 kilogram? Circle the letter for all that apply.

A a slice of bread

B a chair

C a watermelon

D a paper bag

Vocabulary

mass the amount of matter in an object. Objects with more mass are heavier.

kilogram a unit of mass. One liter of water has a mass of 1 kilogram.

gram a unit of mass. One paper clip has a mass of about 1 gram.

Solve.

5 A paper clip has a mass of 1 gram. Estimate the mass of a slice of bread and explain how you figured it out.

Estimated mass: ____________________

____

____

____

6 A bottle of water has a mass of 1 kilogram. Estimate the mass of a watermelon, and explain how you figured it out.

Estimated mass: ____________________

____

____

____

7 George says that his bicycle has a mass of 15 grams. Janet says the bicycle has a mass of 15 kilograms. Who do you think is correct? Why do you think so?

____

____

____

____

8 George took the front wheel off his bike and found its mass. What could the mass of the wheel be? Explain your reasoning.

____

____

____

Name: ______________________

Solve Word Problems about Mass

Study the example showing how to solve a word problem about mass. Then solve problems 1–7.

Example

A tree house is strong enough to hold up to 300 kilograms safely. Can 8 children who are all about 30 kilograms be in the tree house at once?

$$8 \times 30 = 8 \times 3 \times 10$$
$$= 24 \times 10$$
$$= 240$$

The 8 children have a total mass of 240 kilograms. 240 kilograms is less than 300 kilograms.

All 8 children can be in the tree house at once.

1 Jon has a bag of candy with a mass of 200 grams. Mark has a bag of candy with a mass of 215 grams. What is the mass of the two bags of candy combined?

Solution: The combined mass is ______________.

2 Brenda has 2 dogs. Their masses are 27 kilograms and 33 kilograms. What is the mass of the two dogs combined?

Solution: The combined mass is ______________.

3 Joe is shoveling snow. He estimates that he lifts 3 kilograms of snow with each full shovel. What is the total mass he lifts with 80 full shovels?

Solution: The total mass is about ______________.

Solve.

4 A houseplant has a mass of 15 kilograms. Barbara buys 3 houseplants of exactly the same mass. What is the mass of all the houseplants combined? Write a number sentence to solve the problem.

Solution: The combined mass is ________________.

5 Kara's filled lunchbox is 815 grams. Ben's filled lunchbox is 900 grams. How much lighter is Kara's lunchbox than Ben's lunchbox?

Solution: Kara's lunchbox is ______________ lighter.

6 Mark has 8 packs of pretzels in a paper bag. Each pack of pretzels is 90 grams. The bag is 85 grams. What is the mass of the paper bag with the pretzels in it?

Solution: The mass of the bag with the pretzels is

____.

7 Kathy's cloth grocery sack can hold 16 kilograms without ripping. She buys juice, soup, and rice at the store. The table shows the mass for 1 of each item. What is one way she can fill the sack with these items?

Item	Mass
juice	2 kilograms
soup	1 kilogram
bag of rice	5 kilograms

Show your work.

____

____

Name: ______________________

Mass

Solve the problems.

1 Bonnie's backpack has a mass 10 kilograms. She removes two large hardcover books that each have a mass of 2 kilograms. What is the mass of Bonnie's backpack now?

Show your work.

Solution: ______________________

Don't forget to label your answer. Are you finding the total mass in grams or kilograms?

2 Patricia buys 2 baskets of fruit. One has a mass of 13 kilograms. The other has a mass of 24 kilograms. What is the difference in mass between the 2 fruit baskets?

Show your work.

Solution: ______________________

What does it mean to find the difference between two numbers?

3 A basketball has a mass of 600 grams. What is a good estimate for the mass of a large balloon?

A 10 grams

B 60 grams

C 100 grams

D 600 grams

How is a basketball like a balloon, and how is it different?

Solve.

4 Erin had 900 grams of blueberries. She used 60 grams to make muffins and she ate 90 grams with her cereal. How many grams of blueberries did she have left?

Show your work.

Solution: ______________________________

5 A fruit salad recipe uses 150 grams of grapes, 250 grams of oranges, and 50 grams of strawberries. How many grams of fruit do you need to make two fruit salads?

Show your work.

Solution: ______________________________

6 Joanne bought 540 grams of strawberries. She was able to make 9 same-size smoothies with the berries. How many grams of strawberries did she use for each smoothie? Circle the letter of the correct answer.

A 10

B 50

C 54

D 60

Kayla chose **B** as the correct answer. How did she get that answer?

____

____

____

Dear Family,

This week your child is learning to solve problems about data in scaled graphs.

In a scaled pictograph, like the one to the right, each symbol represents more than one item.

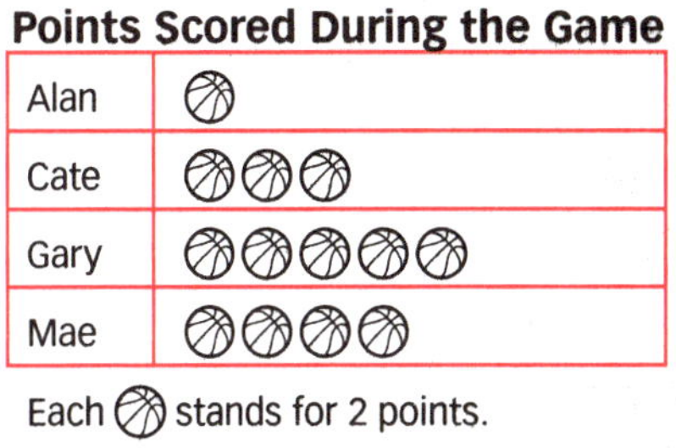

Using a scale of 2 or more allows more information to fit into a smaller space. Learning about scaled graphs gives your child a chance to apply the multiplication and division facts he or she has been practicing.

Pictograph: uses pictures or symbols to show data.
Key: tells what each symbol stands for.

In this pictograph, the key tells us that each stands for 2 points. You multiply the number of by 2 to find the total points each student scored. You can see that Cate scored 2 × 3, or 6 points.

Your child might see the same data on a scaled **bar graph**.

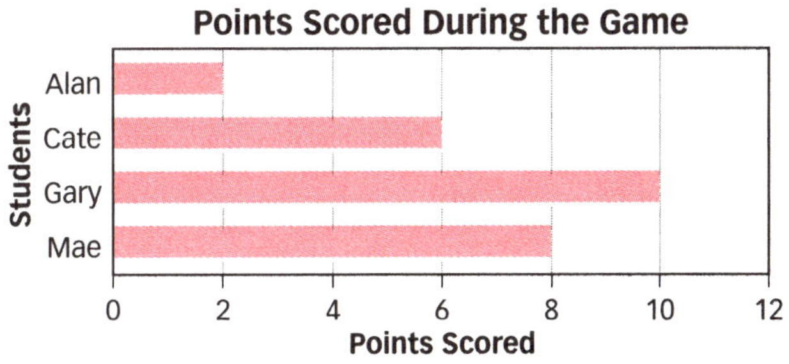

Your child will interpret the graph to answer questions like "How many points did Mae score?" or "How many more points did Mae score than Alan?".

Invite your child to share what he or she knows about solving problems using scaled graphs by doing the following activity together.

NEXT

Solving Problems Using a Scaled Graph Activity

Do this activity to support your child in learning to use multiplication and division facts to interpret scaled graphs.

Talk with your child about the data on this pictograph. Discuss questions such as:

- What does this graph show?
- How many teams are shown and what are their names?
- What does each soccer ball stand for?

Then ask each other questions that require using an operation such as addition, subtraction, multiplication, or division to solve. For example:

- How many more goals did the Eagles score than the Lions? (One number sentence used to solve this is $15 - 9 = 6$.)
- If 6 players on the Tigers' team each scored the same number of goals, how many did each score? (One number sentence used to solve this is $24 \div 6 = 4$.)

For real-world practice, keep an eye out for pictographs or bar graphs in magazines, online, or elsewhere. Utility bills can be a good source of bar graphs, for example. Share these examples with your child, and notice that they almost all use a scale of two or more to show the data.

Solve Problems Using Scaled Graphs

Name: ______________________________

Prerequisite: Read Pictographs and Bar Graphs

Study the example showing how to use a pictograph to answer a question. Then solve problems 1–8.

Example

Annie made a pictograph to show the types of books she read last summer. How many more mystery books than comedy books did Annie read?

Books Annie Read

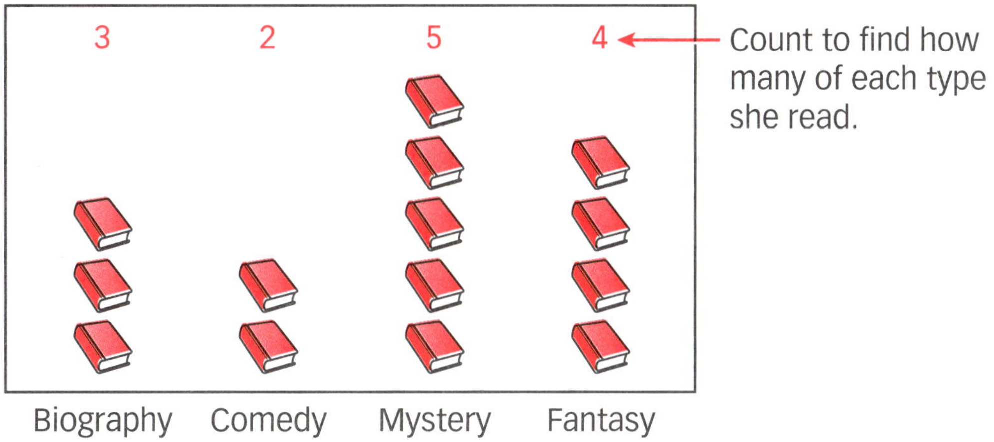

Write a number sentence to find the difference:

$5 - 2 = 3$

Annie read 3 more mystery books than comedy books.

Use the pictograph above to solve problems 1–3.

1. How many biography and fantasy books did Annie read in all? ______________________

2. How many fewer comedy books than biography books did Annie read? ______________________

3. How many books in all did Annie read last summer?

____

Vocabulary

pictograph a graph using pictures or symbols to show data.

data pieces of information.

The bar graph shows the number of each type of book Eddy read last summer.

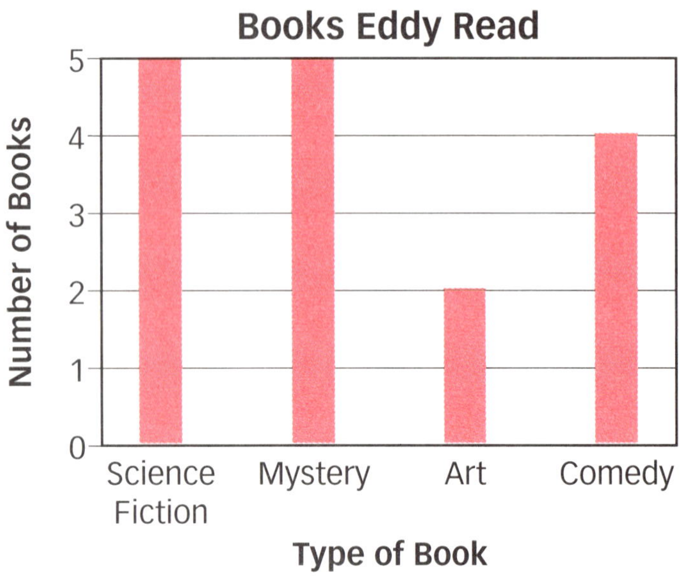

Use the bar graph to solve problems 4–8. Complete each sentence.

4. Eddy read the same number of __________________ and __________________ books.

5. Eddy read ____________ more comedy books than art books.

6. Eddy read ____________ mystery and art books.

7. Eddy read a total of ____________ books that were not science fiction.

8. Last summer Eddy read ____________ books altogether.

Vocabulary

bar graph a graph using bars to show data.

Name: ______________________

Read and Interpret Scaled Pictographs

Study the example showing how to read and interpret a scaled pictograph. Then solve problems 1–9.

Example

Some third graders went on a field trip to the zoo. They voted for their favorite animals. The pictograph shows their choices. How many students chose giraffes as their favorite?

The key shows that each picture stands for 4 students. The row for giraffes has 4 pictures.

You can add 4 four times:
$4 + 4 + 4 + 4 = 16$.
You can multiply 4 by 4: $4 \times 4 = 16$.
So, 16 students chose giraffes.

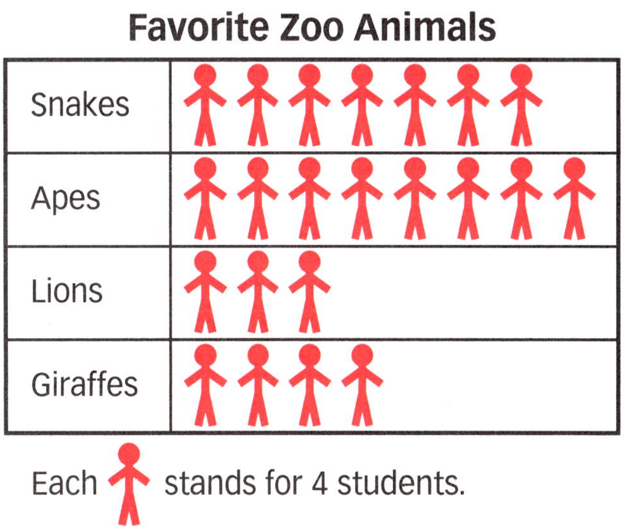

Use the pictograph to solve problems 1–4. Show your work.

1 How many students chose lions? __________

2 How many students chose snakes? __________

3 How many more students chose giraffes than lions? __________

4 How many fewer students chose lions than apes? __________

Vocabulary

key explanation of what each symbol represents in a pictograph.

scale the numbers that show the units used on a graph.

Use the pictograph to solve problems 5–9. Show your work.

Students voted for their favorite animal at the petting zoo. The pictograph shows the number of students who voted for each animal.

Favorite Zoo Animals

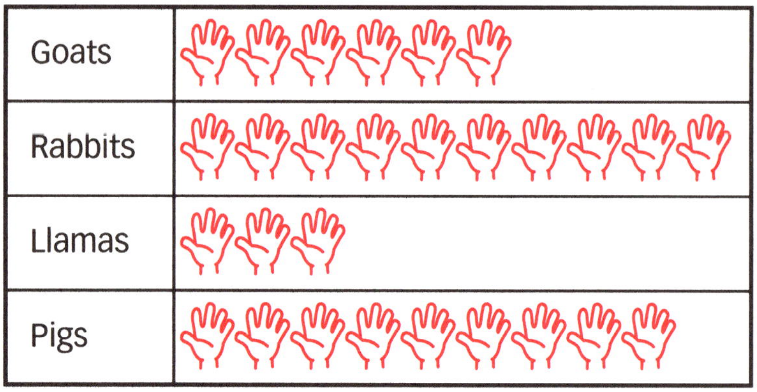

Each  stands for 6 students.

5 How many students voted for llamas? __________

6 How many fewer students chose goats than pigs? __________

7 How many votes did goats and rabbits get altogether? __________

8 How many more students chose rabbits than llamas? __________

9 Make your own statement about the data in the pictograph. Show how you know your statement is true.

____

____

____

____

Name: ____________________

Read and Interpret Bar Graphs

Study the example problem showing how to read and interpret a bar graph. Then solve problems 1–5.

Example

The bar graph shows the number of cartons of milk sold in one week. Were more cartons sold on Monday and Tuesday or on Wednesday and Thursday?

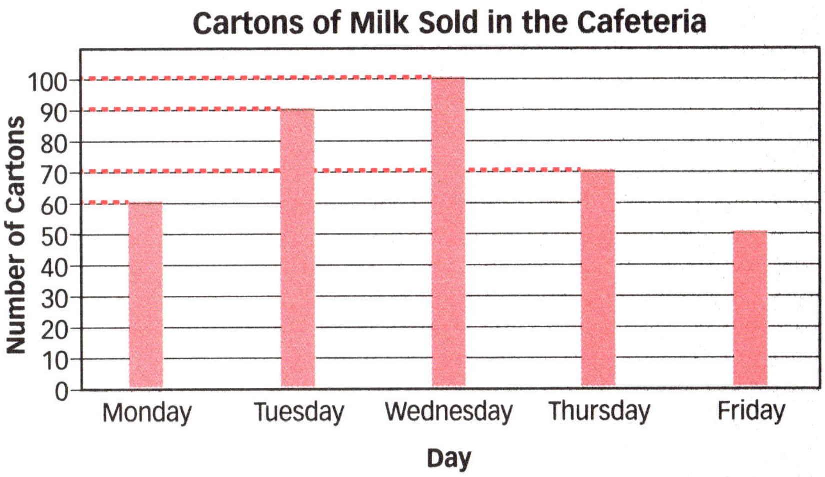

Look where the bars end. Read the scale on the left side of the graph:
Monday = 60, Tuesday = 90,
Wednesday = 100, Thursday = 70.

$60 + 90 = 150$ and $100 + 70 = 170$

More cartons of milk were sold on Wednesday and Thursday than on Monday and Tuesday.

Use the bar graph above to solve problems 1 and 2. Show your work.

1. How many cartons of milk were sold on the two days with the least number of cartons?

____

2. How many cartons of milk were sold in all that week?

____

Use the bar graph to solve problems 3–5. Fill in the blanks. Show your work.

The bar graph shows what students in Ms. Owens' class bought for lunch one day.

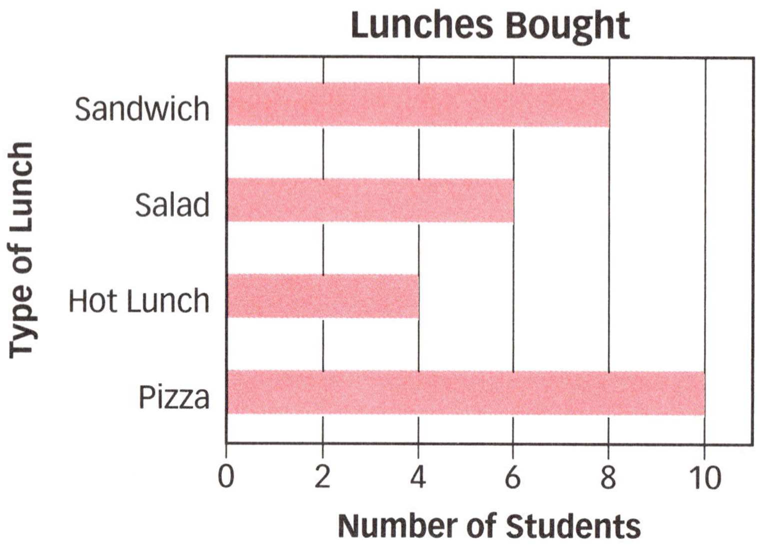

3 Students bought the same number of pizza lunches as ________________ and ________________ together.

4 The number of salads bought is 2 less than the number of ________________ bought.

5 Make your own statement about the data in the graph. Tell how you know your statement is true.

____

____

____

Name: ______________________

Solve Problems Using Scaled Graphs

Use the pictograph to solve the problems.

Mr. Green's science class does shadow experiments.
The pictograph shows the items they use.

Materials for Shadow Experiments

Masks	★★★★★★
Flashlights	★★★★
Blocks	★★★★★★★
Gloves	★★★
Rulers	★★★★

Each ★ stands for 10 items.

1 Which two items total 100? Circle the letter for all that apply.

A masks and rulers

B flashlights and blocks

C blocks and gloves

D masks and flashlights

2 How many gloves and rulers are used? Circle the letter of the correct answer.

A 7

B 10

C 40

D 70

Leo chose **A** as the correct answer. How did he get that answer?

____

____

Use the bar graph to solve the problems.

Ms. Duddy counted the jars of paint that are in the art room. She made a bar graph to show the data.

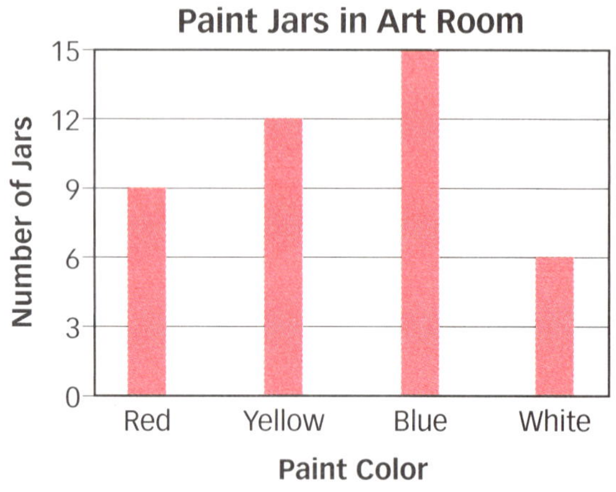

3 Tell whether each sentence is *True* or *False*.

a. There are as many jars of blue paint as jars of red and white paint combined. ☐ True ☐ False

b. There are more than 40 jars of paint in all. ☐ True ☐ False

c. There are fewer jars of yellow and red paint than blue and white paint. ☐ True ☐ False

4 What two colors of paint have at least 20 jars altogether? List two different pairs of colors.

____

____

____

____

Dear Family,

This week your child is learning to draw scaled graphs.

Suppose Mike collects data from his friends about their favorite bicycle color and records the data in this chart.

Favorite Bike Color

Color	Number
Blue	20
Green	10
Orange	5
Red	15

To display the data from the chart in a pictograph and in a bar graph, Mike needs to decide what scale to use. He could choose to just draw one symbol for each bike, but that seems like a lot of bikes. They would be hard to draw and harder to count accurately.

Since all the numbers in the chart are equal to 5 times something, a scale of 5 makes sense.

Favorite Bike Color

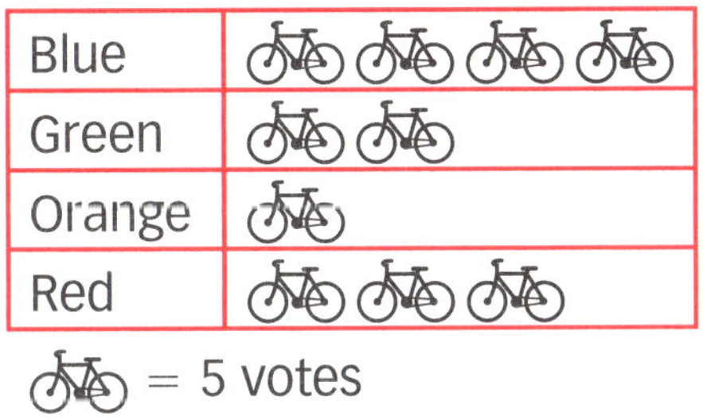

Favorite Bike Color

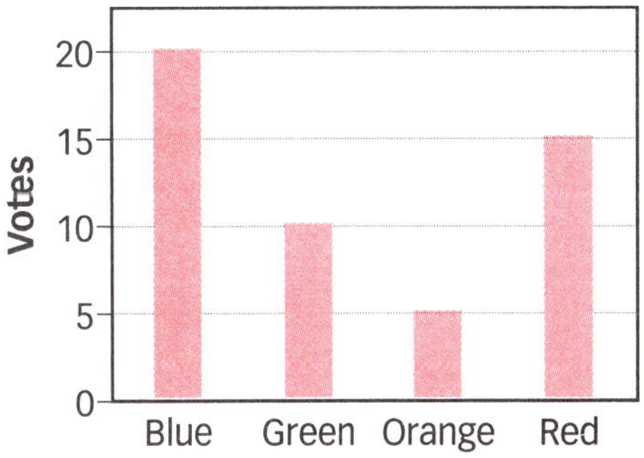

Invite your child to share what he or she knows about drawing scaled graphs by doing the following activity together.

NEXT

Draw Scaled Graph Activity

Materials: coins (or trail mix, blocks of different color or shapes, etc.), markers

Work with your child to create a scaled pictograph.

- Have your child collect a small number of coins.
- Have your child sort the pennies, nickels, dimes, and quarters, and count the number of each type of coin. Be sure there is an *even* number of each coin type (for example 2, 4, 6, 8, or 10 of each).
- Fill in the pictograph with the data. The key shows that each circle should stand for 2 coins.

Pennies	
Nickels	
Dimes	
Quarters	

Each ○ stands for 2 coins.

Ask each other questions about the graph such as:

- How many more pennies than nickels do we have?
- How many more quarters do we need to have as many quarters as nickels?
- How much are all the nickels worth altogether?
- If you and I shared the dimes equally, how many dimes would we each get?

Draw Scaled Graphs

Name: ____________________

Prerequisite: Interpret Scaled Graphs

Study the example problem showing how to interpret a pictograph. Then solve problems 1–8.

Example

The pictograph shows the number of students in each grade who helped with the school fair. How many helpers were from grade 2? Tell how you know.

School Fair Helpers

Grade 1	☺ ☺
Grade 2	☺ ☺ ☺
Grade 3	☺ ☺ ☺ ☺ ☺
Grade 4	☺ ☺ ☺ ☺ ☺ ☺ ☺ ☺ ☺ ☺
Grade 5	☺ ☺ ☺ ☺ ☺ ☺ ☺ ☺

Each ☺ stands for 5 students.

There are 3 faces in the row for grade 2.
$3 \times 5 = 15$
So, 15 helpers were from grade 2.

Use the pictograph above to solve problems 1 and 2.

1 Find the number of students from each grade who helped. Fill in the table.

Grade	Number of ☺	X	Each ☺ stands for	Number of Students
1		X		
2		X		
3		X		
4		X		
5		X		

2 How many students helped with the school fair altogether? Show your work.

____

Vocabulary

pictograph a graph using pictures or symbols to show data.

data pieces of information.

Solve.

3 Below is a key for a pictograph. How many circles would be used to show 24 people? Explain.

Key: Each ● stands for 4 people.

____

4 One row on a pictograph has 7 squares. Each square stands for 3 books. How many books does the row stand for? Explain.

____

5 Look at problem 4. How would you show 30 books on that pictograph? Explain.

____

____

6 Dana draws 4 triangles to stand for 32 trees. Fill in the blank to show the key she makes.

Each ▲ stands for ______ trees.

7 Look at problem 6. How many triangles would Dana use to show 48 trees? ______________________

8 Omar started this pictograph to show 60 baseballs. Complete the key, then draw circles to show 40 footballs.

Number of Balls

Baseballs	● ● ● ● ● ●
Footballs	

Each ● stands for ______ balls.

Name: ____________________

Draw a Scaled Pictograph

Study the example problem showing how to make a scaled pictograph. Then solve problems 1–8.

Example

Jess asked some students in her school which colors they like best. She recorded the data in a table first. How can she make a pictograph to show the data?

Blue	10
Green	5
Purple	20
Red	30
Yellow	15

$10 = 5 \times 2$

$5 = 5 \times 1$

$20 = 5 \times 4$

$30 = 5 \times 6$

$15 = 5 \times 3$

→

Blue	☺ ☺
Green	☺
Purple	☺ ☺ ☺ ☺
Red	☺ ☺ ☺ ☺ ☺ ☺
Yellow	☺ ☺ ☺

Each number has 5 as a factor. Use a scale of 5.

Each ☺ stands for 5 students.

1 Jess did not write a title for her graph. What is a good title?

____

2 Jess forgot that 15 students chose pink. She needs to add a row to the pictograph. Use words and pictures to show what the row should look like.

3 Could Jess use a scale of 1 for her pictograph? A scale of 4? Explain.

____

____

____

____

____

Vocabulary

scale the numbers that show the units used on a graph.

data pieces of information.

Use the table and pictograph to solve problems 4–8.

Pablo asked some students which sport they like best. He recorded the data in this table. Then he started to make a pictograph.

Sport	Number of Students
Baseball	14
Basketball	10
Biking	16
Skating	12
Soccer	18

____

Baseball	☺ ☺ ☺ ☺ ☺ ☺ ☺
Basketball	
Biking	
Skating	
Soccer	

Each ☺ stands for _____ students.

4 What scale is Pablo using for his graph? Tell how you know. Then fill in the key.

____

____

____

5 How many symbols do you need to show the number of students who like soccer? Why?

____

____

____

6 Which sport will have 5 symbols on the pictograph? Explain. ______________________

____

____

7 What is a good title for Pablo's graph? Write it above the graph.

8 Complete the pictograph.

Vocabulary

pictograph a graph using pictures or symbols to show data.

Name: ______________________

Draw a Scaled Bar Graph

Study the example problem showing how to make a scaled bar graph. Then solve problems 1–7.

Example

Zara painted faces at the fair. She kept track of the designs people chose. She recorded the data in the table. How can Zara make a bar graph?

Hearts	**40**
Monster	**80**
Lion	**30**
Ghost	**50**
Flower	**10**

Zara used a scale of 10. Count by 10s: **10**, 20, **30**, **40**, **50**, 60, 70, **80**. You use all the numbers in the table when you count by 10s.

Face Paint Designs

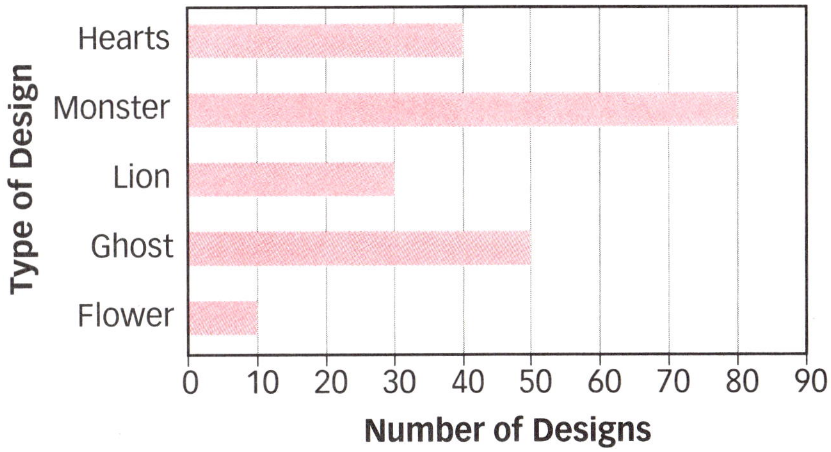

1 What is a good title for Zara's graph? Write it above the graph.

2 Could you use a scale of 2 or 5 to make the graph? Explain. ______________________

____

____

3 Why do you think Zara chose 10 as the scale instead of 2 or 5? ______________________

____

____

____

Vocabulary

bar graph a graph using bars to show data.

data pieces of information.

Use the table to solve problems 4–7.

The table shows the number of students who signed up for different games at the school fair.

Games at School Fair

Game	Number of Students
Balloon Toss	24
Relay Race	20
Sack Race	28
Softball Throw	12

4 Count by 3s. Write the numbers you say.

_____, _____, _____, _____, _____, _____,

_____, _____, _____, _____

5 Count by 4s. Write the numbers you say.

_____, _____, _____, _____, _____, _____,

_____, _____, _____, _____

6 You need to make a graph using the data in the table. Would you use a scale of 3 or 4? Explain.

____

____

____

7 Make a bar graph using the data in the table. Be sure to write a title, draw bars, and label all parts of the graph.

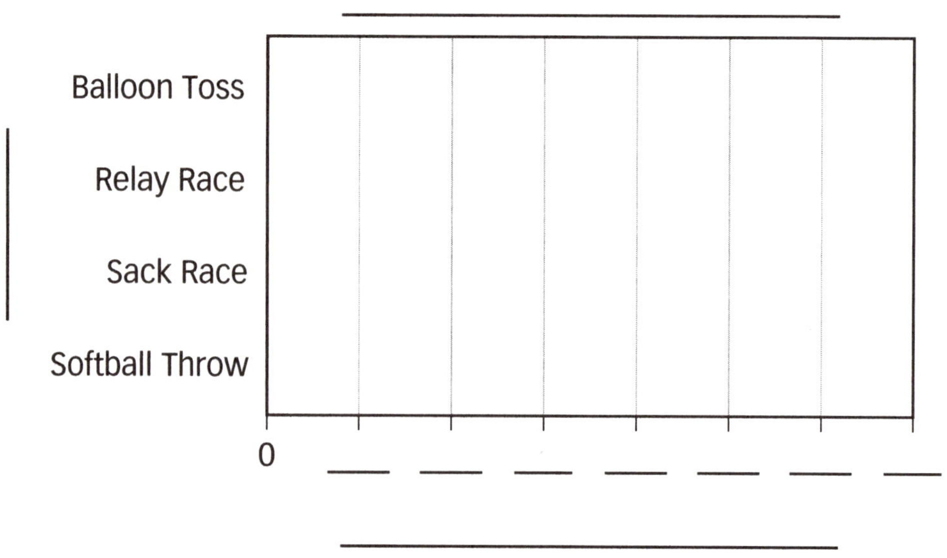

Name: ____________________

Draw Scaled Graphs

Erol asked students to name their favorite stickers. He recorded their answers in the table. Use the table to solve problems 1 and 2.

1 Erol makes a pictograph with a scale of 3. How many symbols does he use to show the number of students who chose butterflies? Circle the letter of the correct answer.

A 2

B 6

C 9

D 18

Favorite Stickers

Type of Sticker	Number of Students
Sports	15
Butterflies	6
Hearts	18
Stars	9
Cars	12

Carmen chose **D** as the correct answer. How did she get that answer?

____

____

____

Which is greater, the number of symbols or the actual number of students?

2 Erol uses a scale of 3 to make a pictograph of the sticker data. Tell whether each sentence is *True* or *False*.

a. The graph has 4 symbols in the row for car stickers. ☐ True ☐ False

b. The graph has 3 symbols in the row for star stickers. ☐ True ☐ False

c. The row for heart stickers has 3 more symbols than the row for butterfly stickers. ☐ True ☐ False

I would figure out and record the number of symbols needed for each kind of sticker.

Solve.

3 Ava asked students at her school to name their favorite rides at the amusement park. She recorded the results in the table. How can Ava decide what scale to use to make a graph?

Favorite Rides

Ride	Number of Students
Roller Coaster	15
Ferris Wheel	10
Flying Saucer	20
Haunted Train	30
River Falls	5

____

____

____

____

4 Label and draw a bar graph to show the data from the table above.

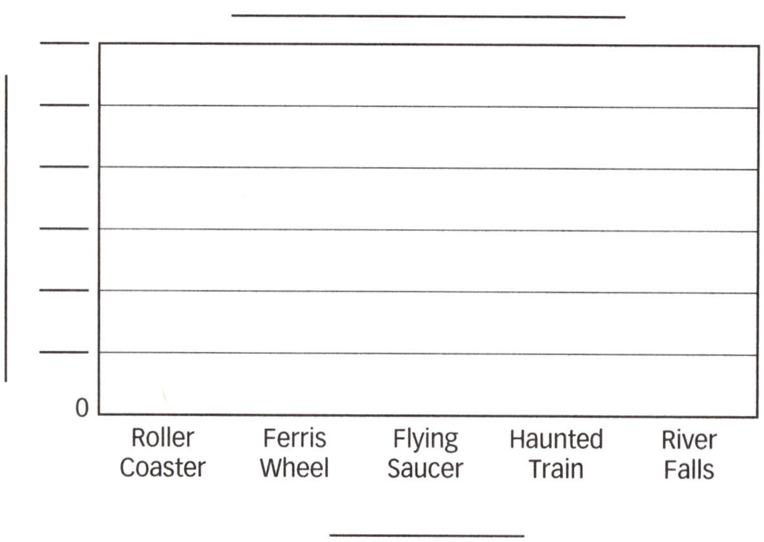

Dear Family,

This week your child is learning to measure length in fractions of an inch, and plot the data on line plots.

A **line plot** is a graph using marks along a number line to show how many objects are in different categories. In this lesson, using categories based on fractional measurements of length gives your child a chance to practice using a ruler, practice reading and writing mixed numbers like $2\frac{1}{2}$, and practice locating fractions on a number line.

Here is a table showing the lengths of some dragonfly wings. The wings have been measured to the nearest $\frac{1}{2}$ inch.

Lengths of Dragonfly Wings

Wing	A	B	C	D	E	F	G	H	I
Length	$\frac{3}{4}$	$\frac{1}{2}$	$1\frac{1}{4}$	$1\frac{1}{2}$	$1\frac{1}{4}$	$\frac{3}{4}$	1	$1\frac{1}{4}$	1

The data from the chart above is shown on the line plot below. There is an "X" for each wing length recorded. The line plot sorts the data for you, and makes it easy to see things like what wing length is most common.

Lengths of Dragonfly Wings

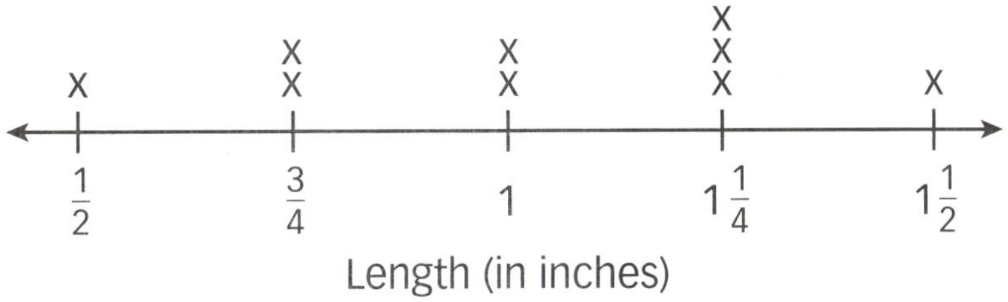

Invite your child to share what he or she knows about measuring length and plotting data on line plots by doing the following activity together.

NEXT

Line Plot Activity

Materials: 6 different writing tools such as pencils, pens, markers, or crayons, and an inch ruler

Work with your child to measure objects and create a line plot to show the data.

Measure each writing tool to the nearest $\frac{1}{2}$-inch and record the data in the table below.

Writing Tool Lengths

Writing tool	A	B	C	D	E	F
Length (to the nearest $\frac{1}{2}$ inch)						

Now work together to make a line plot.

- Use the shortest length to label the left end of the number line.
- Then label the rest of the number line. Label the longer marks with whole numbers. Let the shorter marks represent $\frac{1}{2}$-inch lengths.
- Mark one "X" to show the length of each writing tool.

Writing Tool Lengths

Discuss with your child questions such as:

- How would the line plot change if you had measured only crayons? Would the Xs likely be closer together or more spread out?
- What if you had measured only pencils?

You can check your thinking by trying it!

Measure Length and Plot Data on Line Plots

Name: ______________________

Prerequisite: Make Line Plots

Study the example problem showing how to make a line plot. Then solve problems 1–8.

Example

Kim picked some beans from the garden. She measured the length of each bean and made this table. Then she made a line plot.

Bean Length

Length (inches)	Number of Beans
2	1
3	3
4	5
5	4
7	1

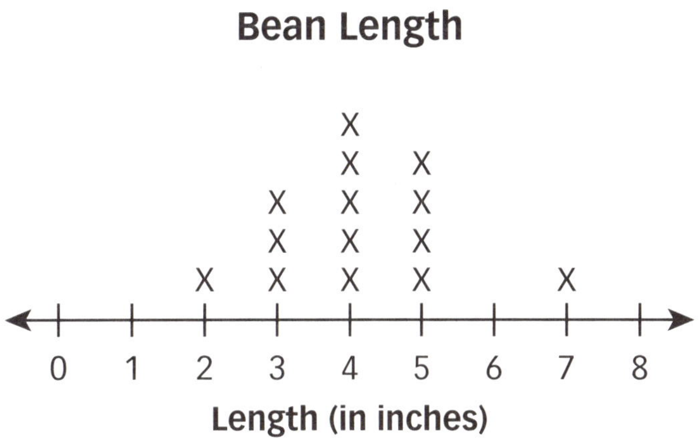

The bottom of the line plot lists bean lengths. Each X represents one bean. The number of Xs above a length is the number of beans of that length.

1 Which length has the greatest number of beans?

____

2 How many more beans are 4 inches than 3 inches?

____

3 How many beans are 5 inches or longer?

____

4 How many beans are shorter than 5 inches?

____

Vocabulary

line plot a graph using marks along a number line to show how many objects are in a set.

data a set of collected information.

Solve.

5 Complete the line plot using the data in the table.

Students' Shoe Length

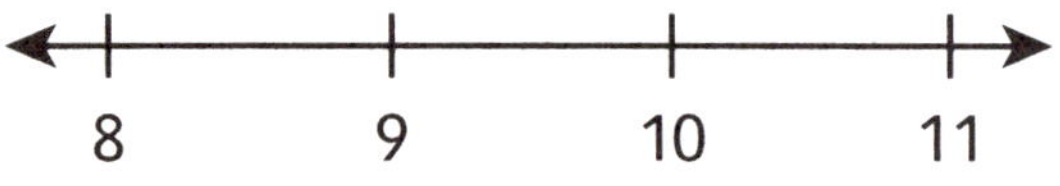

Length (in inches)

Students' Shoe Length

Shoe Length (inches)	Number of Students
8	6
9	5
10	5
11	4

6 Eve said that more students have shoes 10 inches or longer than 9 inches or shorter. Do you agree? Explain.

____

____

7 Han measured these 3 pieces of string. Write the lengths in the table.

String	**A**	**B**	**C**
Length (centimeters)			

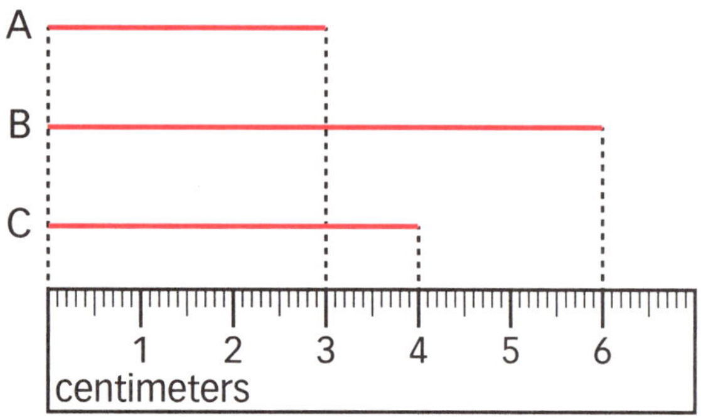

8 Han measured 4 more pieces of string. Two are 4 centimeters long and and two are 5 centimeters long. Make a line plot to show the lengths of all the pieces of string. Include a title for your line plot.

____

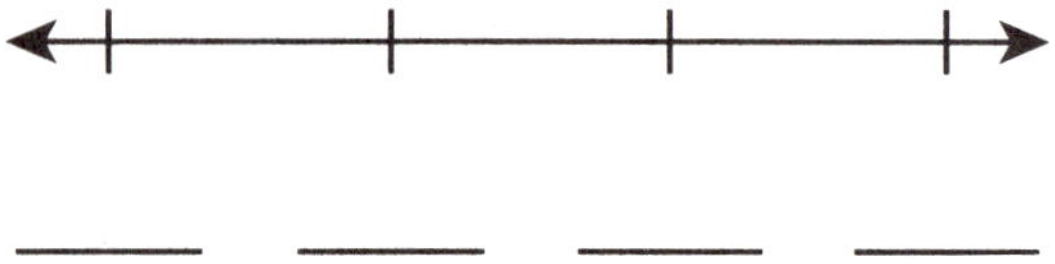

Length (in centimeters)

Name: ____________________

Measure Length to the Nearest $\frac{1}{2}$ and $\frac{1}{4}$ Inch

Study the example problem showing how to measure length to the nearest $\frac{1}{2}$ inch. Then solve problems 1–9.

Example

What is the length of the longest crayon?

Line up one end of the crayon with 0 on the ruler.

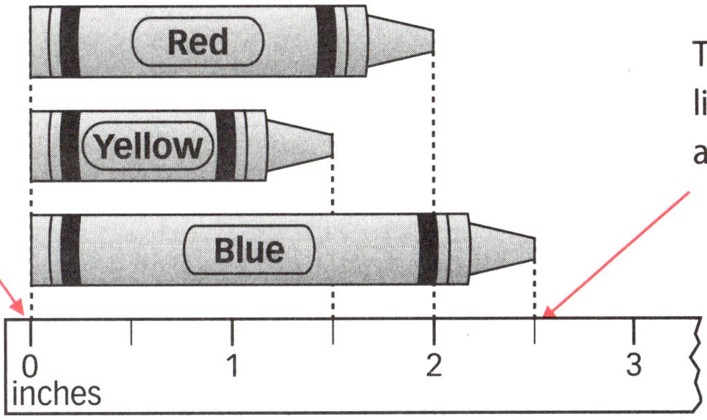

The other end lines up on a $\frac{1}{2}$-inch mark.

The tip of the longest crayon is halfway between 2 and 3 inches. It is $2\frac{1}{2}$ inches long.

1 The tip of the yellow crayon is between which two inches on the ruler? ____________________

2 To the nearest $\frac{1}{2}$ inch, how long is the yellow crayon?

____

3 What is the length of the red crayon? Tell how you know.

____

____

4 To the nearest $\frac{1}{2}$ inch, how long is this pink crayon? ____________________

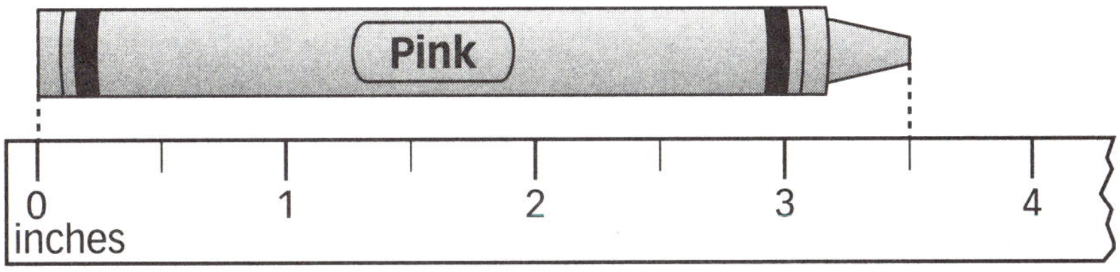

This ruler shows $\frac{1}{4}$-inch marks. Use the picture to solve problems 5–7.

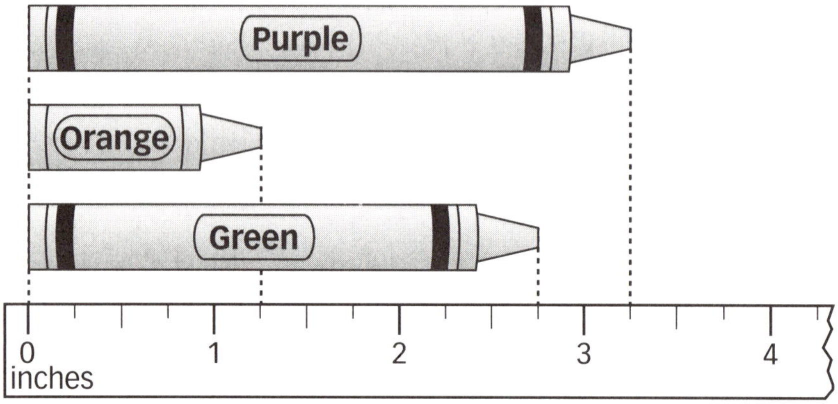

5 Which color crayon is $3\frac{1}{4}$ inches long?

____

6 How long is the green crayon? ______________

7 Write the length of the orange crayon. Explain how you found the length.

____

____

Use the picture to solve problems 8 and 9.

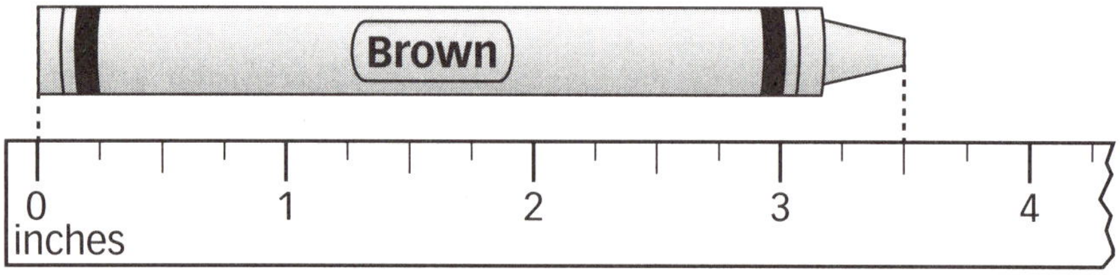

8 To the nearest $\frac{1}{2}$ inch, what is the length of the brown crayon? ______________

9 Can you also measure the brown crayon to the nearest $\frac{1}{4}$ inch? Explain.

____

____

Name: ______________________

Display Data in a Line Plot

Study the example that shows how to display data in a line plot. Then solve problems 1–3.

Example

Denise works in a candle shop. She measures and sorts the candles by length. How can Denise make a line plot for these candle lengths?

Candle	A	B	C	D	E	F	G	H
Length (inches)	$2\frac{1}{4}$	$2\frac{3}{4}$	$2\frac{3}{4}$	$3\frac{1}{2}$	$3\frac{1}{2}$	3	$2\frac{1}{4}$	$3\frac{1}{2}$

Make a number line and mark the candle lengths with Xs.

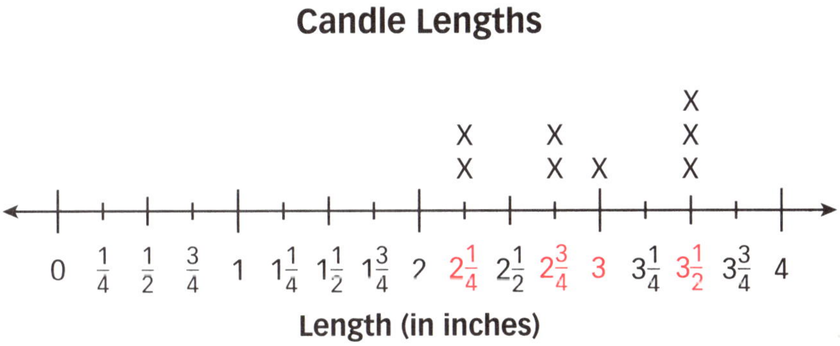

1 Denise measured more candles and recorded the lengths in this list. Make a line plot to display the data in the list. Use an X to stand for each candle.

____

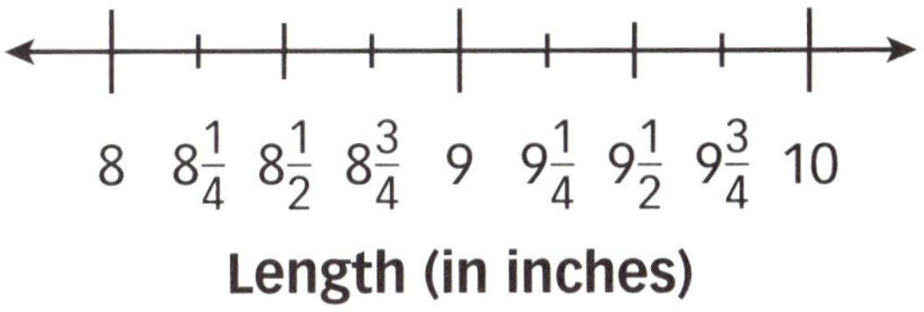

Candle Lengths (in inches)

$8\frac{1}{2}$	$9\frac{1}{2}$
$8\frac{3}{4}$	10
$9\frac{1}{2}$	$8\frac{1}{2}$
10	10
$8\frac{1}{2}$	$8\frac{3}{4}$
10	$8\frac{1}{2}$
$9\frac{1}{2}$	10

Solve.

2 Some students measured the length of each other's hair. They recorded the data in this list. Make a line plot to display the data.

Hair Length (inches)							
$5\frac{1}{2}$	$5\frac{1}{4}$	$6\frac{1}{2}$	$5\frac{3}{4}$	$6\frac{1}{2}$	$5\frac{3}{4}$	7	7
$7\frac{1}{2}$	$5\frac{1}{4}$	$6\frac{1}{4}$	$7\frac{1}{4}$	$5\frac{3}{4}$	$7\frac{1}{4}$	$6\frac{1}{2}$	$7\frac{3}{4}$

Hair length

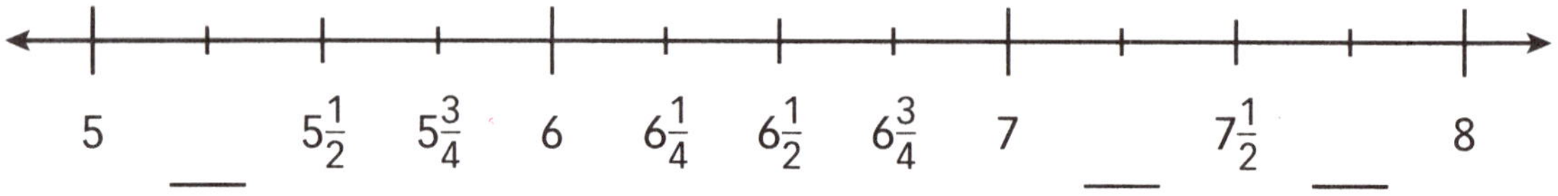

Length (in inches)

3 Jamal collected leaves for a science project. He recorded the lengths in this list. Make a line plot to display the data.

Lengths of Leaves (inches)							
$3\frac{1}{4}$	$5\frac{1}{4}$	$4\frac{1}{4}$	$5\frac{1}{4}$	$4\frac{1}{2}$	$5\frac{1}{2}$	$3\frac{1}{4}$	$3\frac{1}{2}$
$5\frac{3}{4}$	$5\frac{1}{2}$	$4\frac{3}{4}$	$5\frac{1}{2}$	$5\frac{3}{4}$	$3\frac{1}{2}$	$5\frac{1}{2}$	$3\frac{3}{4}$

____

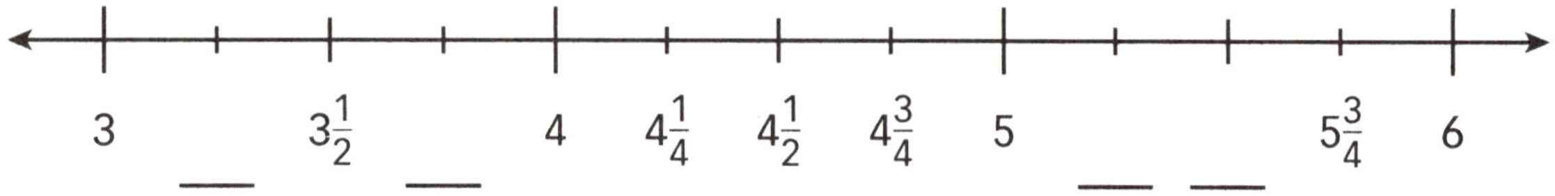

Length (in inches)

Name: ______________________

Measure Length and Plot Data on Line Plots

Solve the problems. Use these crayons to answer problems 1–3.

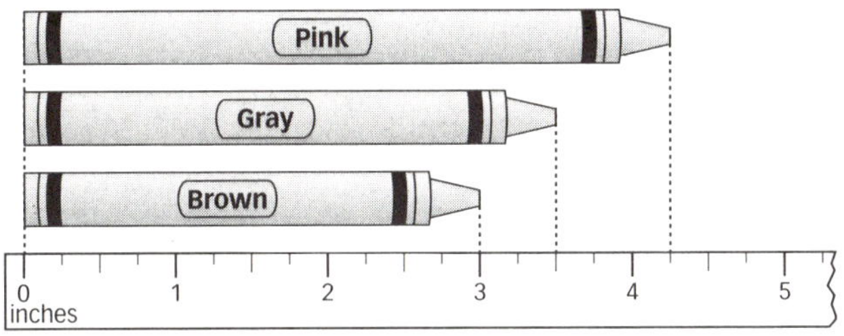

This ruler is not life-sized.

1 How long is the gray crayon? Circle the letter of the correct answer.

A 3 inches

B $3\frac{1}{4}$ inches

C $3\frac{1}{2}$ inches

D $4\frac{1}{4}$ inches

2 How long is the longest crayon? Circle the letter of the correct answer.

A 3 inches

B $3\frac{3}{4}$ inches

C $4\frac{1}{4}$ inches

D $4\frac{1}{2}$ inches

Jon chose **D** as the correct answer. How did he get that answer?

____

____

3 Another crayon is longer than the gray crayon and shorter than the pink crayon. What could the length of this crayon be?

Solution: ______________________________________

____

Use the line plot to solve problems 4 and 5.

Lengths of Toy Cars

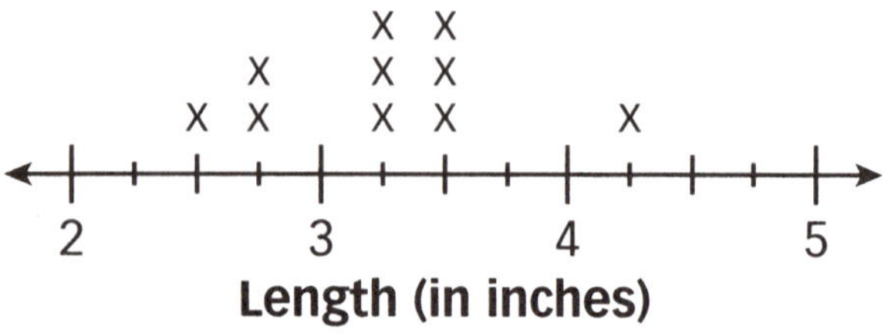

4 Which set of data was used to make the line plot?

How can you tell how many pieces of data there are by looking at the line plot?

A **Lengths of Toy Cars (inches)**

$2\frac{1}{2}$	$2\frac{3}{4}$	$3\frac{1}{4}$	$3\frac{1}{2}$	$4\frac{1}{4}$

B **Lengths of Toy Cars (inches)**

1	2	3	3	1

C **Lengths of Toy Cars (inches)**

$2\frac{1}{2}$	$2\frac{3}{4}$	$3\frac{1}{4}$	$3\frac{1}{2}$	$4\frac{1}{4}$
$3\frac{1}{4}$	$3\frac{1}{2}$	$3\frac{1}{2}$	$3\frac{1}{4}$	$2\frac{3}{4}$

D **Lengths of Toy Cars (inches)**

$2\frac{1}{2}$	$2\frac{3}{4}$	$3\frac{1}{4}$	$3\frac{1}{2}$	$4\frac{1}{4}$
1	2	3	3	2

5 How many toy cars are longer than 3 inches? Explain.

____

____

____

____

What does each X mean?

Dear Family,

This week your child is exploring the idea of measuring area.

Area is the amount of space a shape covers. In this lesson children learn that area is measured with **square units**.

They measure the area of a shape by covering the shape with square units, using these three rules:

- All of the square units must be the same size.
- There can be no gaps between the squares.
- The squares cannot overlap each other anywhere.

Then they count to find how many square units cover the shape.

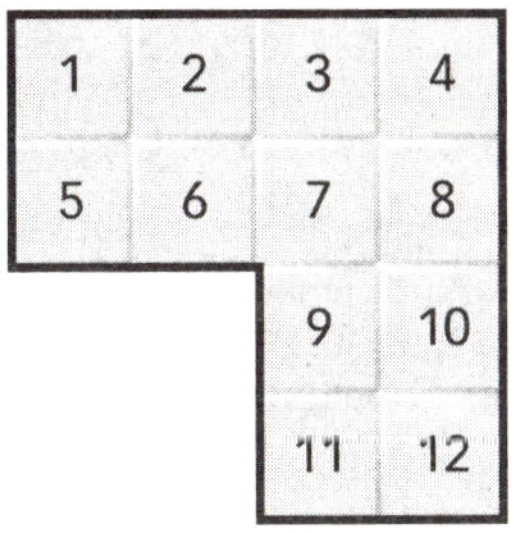

The area of this shape is 12 square units.

You can use smaller or larger square units to find the area of a shape. You just have to identify the size of the unit you're using.

Children will see that it takes fewer of the larger square units than the smaller square units to completely cover the shape.

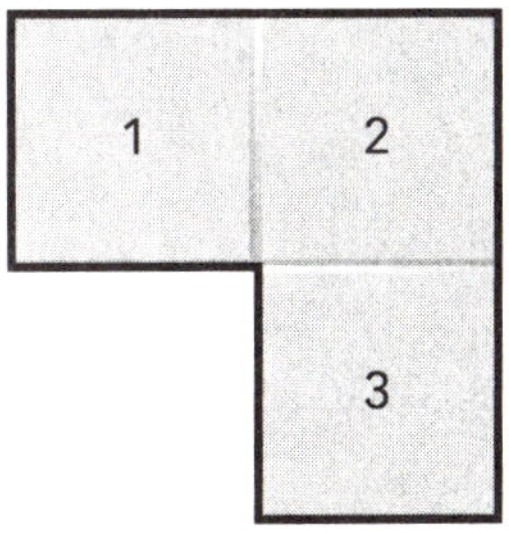

1 square unit

Invite your child to share what he or she knows about area by doing the following activity together.

NEXT

Area Activity

Work with your child to draw shapes that look like letters, and then find their areas.

For example, this shape looks like the letter C.

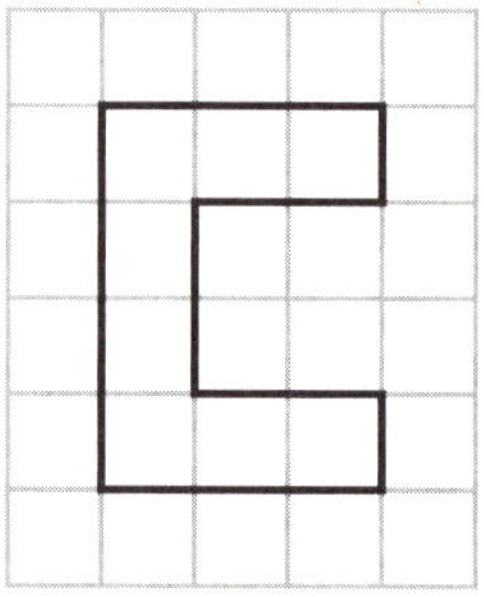

Use this style to draw the initial of your first name on the grid paper below.

- Find the area of the initial you drew by counting the square units.
- Now make your initial another way so that it has a different area.
- Can different initials have the same area? Draw an example.

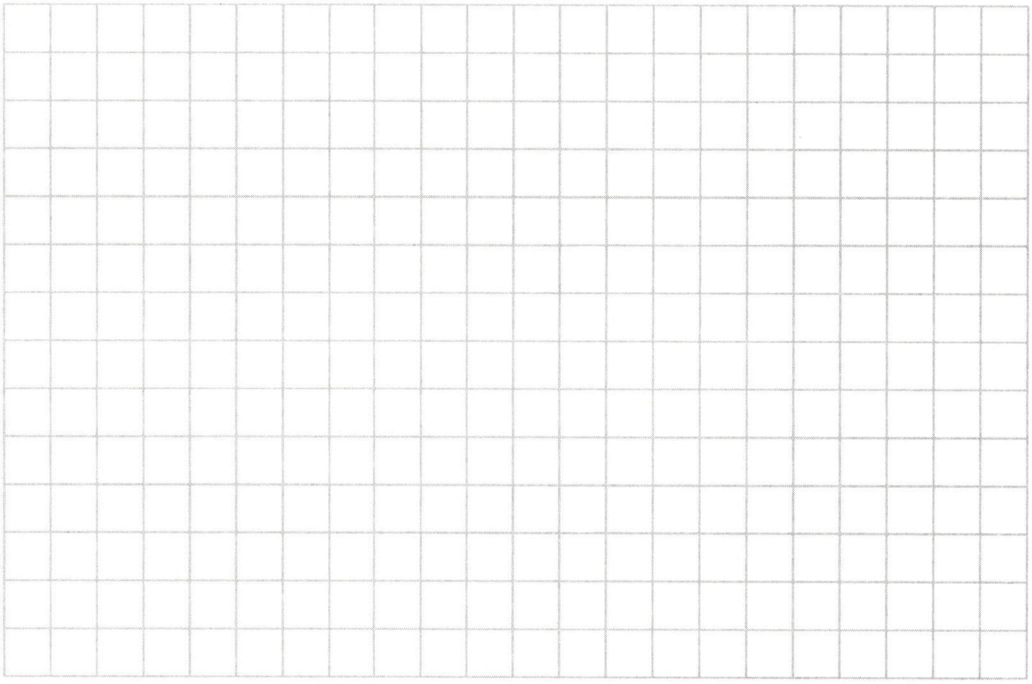

Lesson 27

Understand Area

Name: ______________________

Prerequisite: How can you break up a rectangle into squares of the same size?

Study the example showing how to break a rectangle into squares of the same size. Then solve problems 1–9.

Example

These rectangles are the same size. They are both broken into squares. Rectangle *A* is broken into bigger squares than Rectangle *B*.

Rectangle *A*

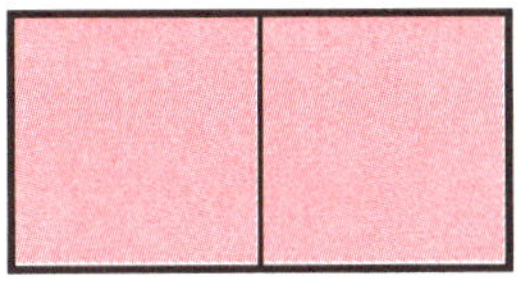

1 row of squares
2 squares in a row
2 squares in all

Rectangle *B*

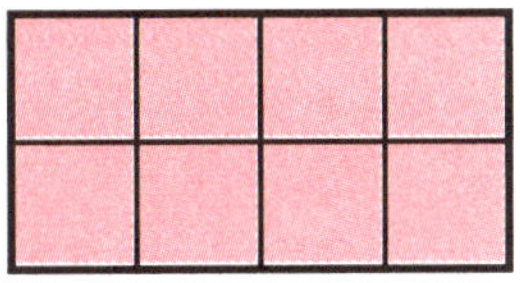

2 rows of squares
4 squares in a row
8 squares in all

1 Owen started drawing same-size squares in Rectangle *C*. Finish drawing the squares.

Rectangle *C*

2 How many rows of squares are there? How many squares are in each row?

____

3 How many squares are there in all? __________

4 Amelia started drawing same-size squares in Rectangle *D*. How many squares will there be altogether when she finishes? Tell how you know.

Rectangle *D*

____

____

____

Solve.

5 Draw lines to show how to fill the rectangle with the two different-size squares.

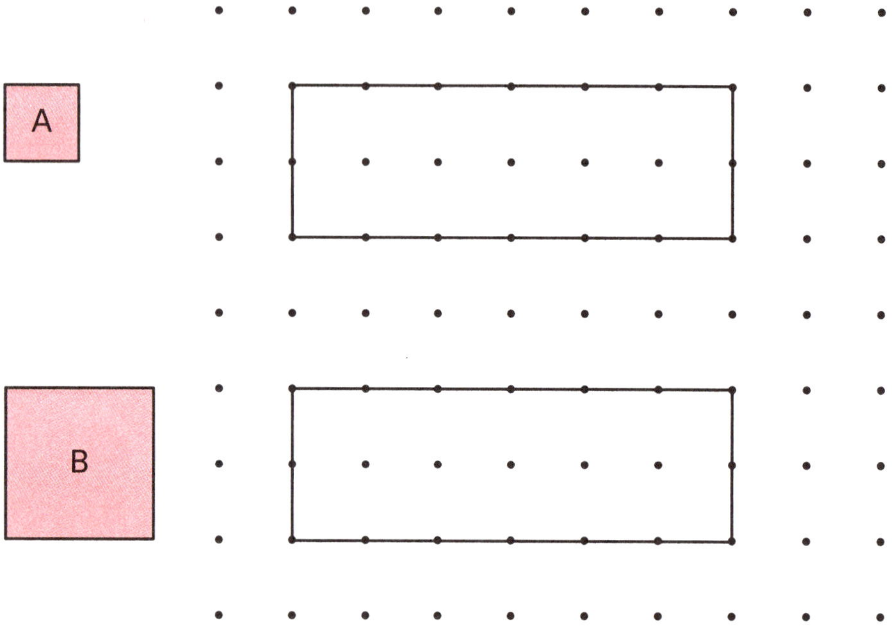

6 Look at square *A*. How many of these squares does it take to cover the rectangle? ____________

7 Look at square *B*. How many of these squares does it take to cover the rectangle? ____________

8 Explain why your answers to problems 6 and 7 are not the same.

____

____

____

9 Show how to cover the shape with squares of the same size. Use the fewest squares that you can. How many squares did you use?

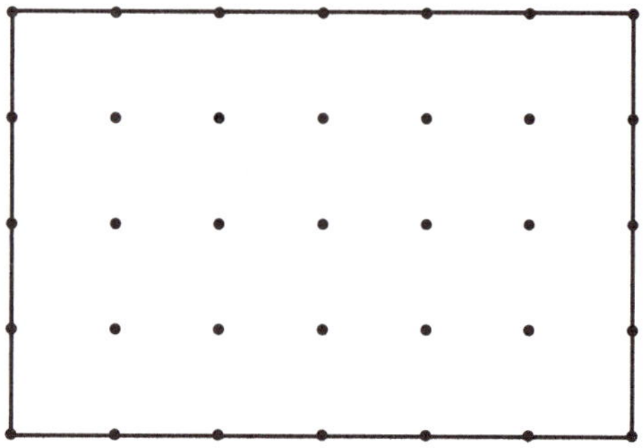

____

____

Name: ____________________

Find Area Using Different Square Units

Study the example showing how to count square units to find area. Then solve problems 1–7.

Example

The red shape is covered with squares the same size. What is the area of this shape?

Count the square units. The area of the shape is 12 square units. You must use same-size squares to find the area in square units.

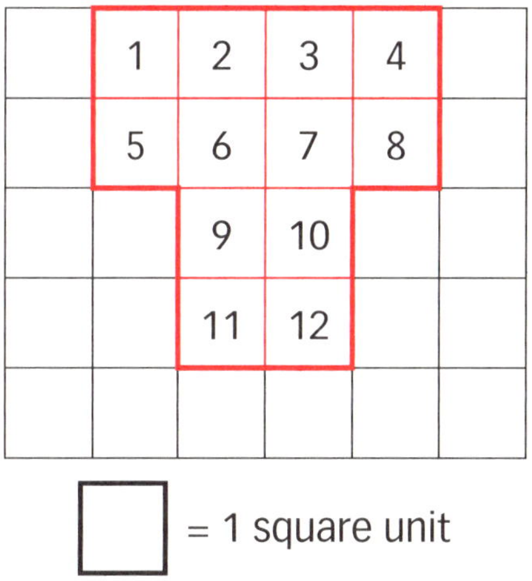

1 Count to find each area.

Area = ____ square units

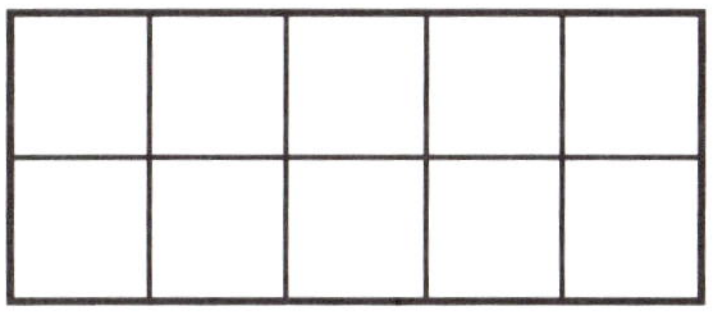

Area = ______ square units

2 What is the area?

1 square inch

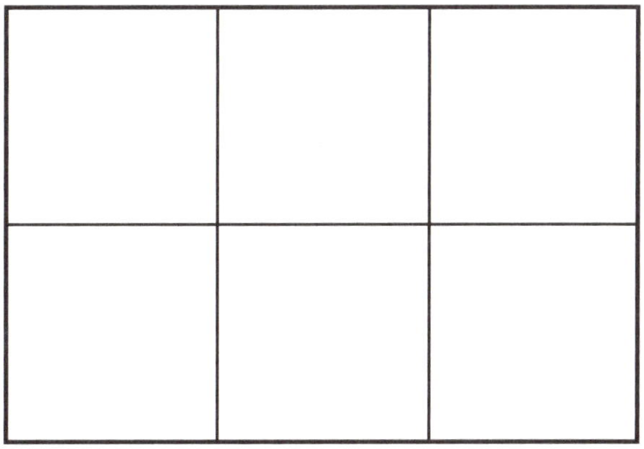

Area = ______ square inches

Vocabulary

area the amount of space a shape covers.

square unit a square with side lengths of 1 unit that is used to measure the area of a figure.

Solve.

3 What is the area of this rectangle?

 = 1 square centimeter

____

4 Ria says that the area of the Rectangle *A* is 9 square units. Do you agree? Explain.

____

____

____

Rectangle *A*

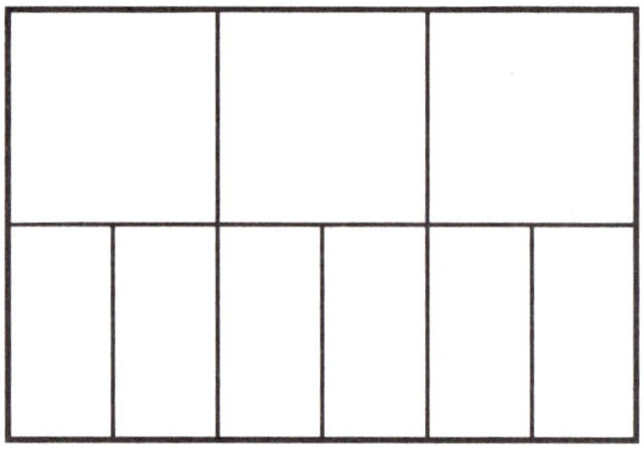

5 Fill in the blanks.

Rectangle *B* has __________ rows of squares.

There are __________ squares in each row.

6 How can you skip count to find the area of Rectangle *B*? Explain. Write the area.

____

____

____

____

Rectangle *B*

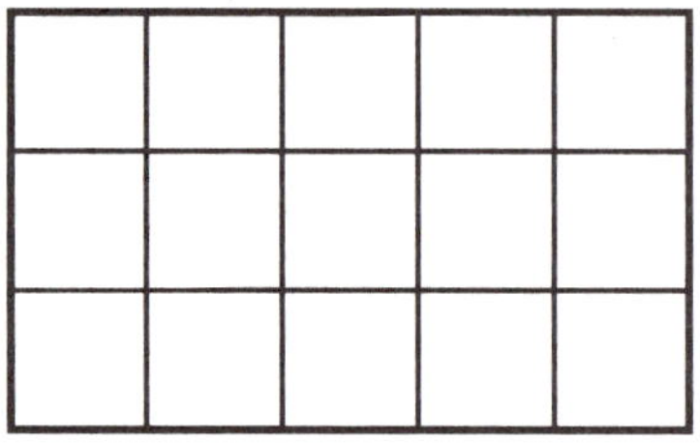

7 What is the area of Rectangle *C*? How does this compare to the area of Rectangle *B*? Are both rectangles the same size? Explain why or why not.

____

____

____

____

Rectangle *C*

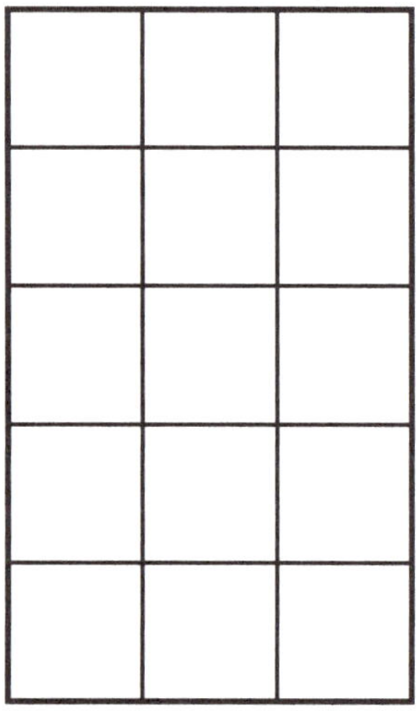

Name: ____________________

Reason and Write

Study the example. Underline two parts that you think make it a particularly good answer and a helpful example.

Example

Show and explain two different ways to find the area of the "C" shape below. Tell how you know that both ways work.

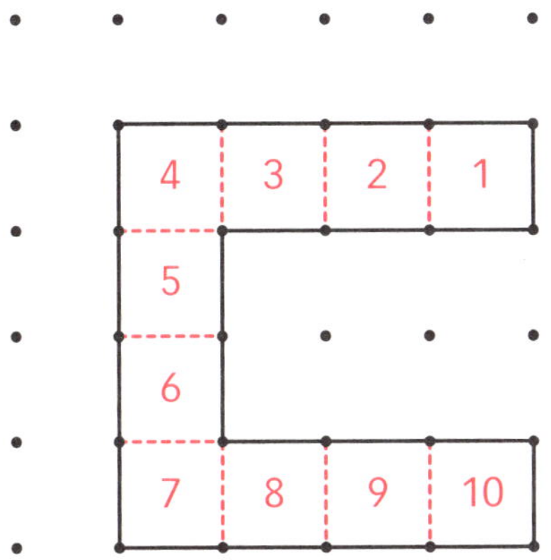

One Way

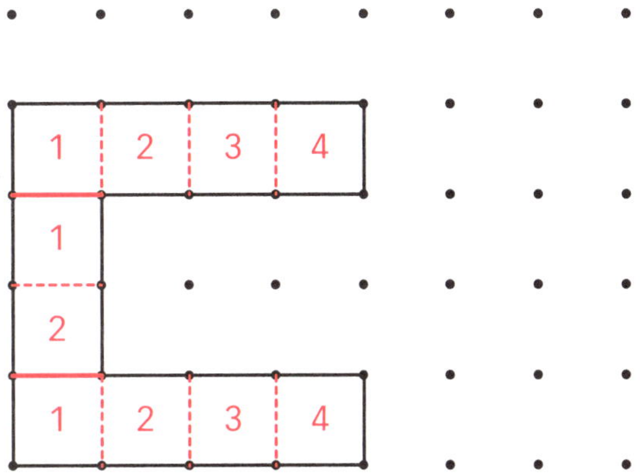

Another Way

Possible answer: One way I found the area is by counting each square unit in the shape. There are 10, so the area is 10 square units.

Another way I found the area is by dividing the shape into 3 different rectangles. I counted the square units in each rectangle to get 4, 2, and 4. Then I added 4 + 2 + 4 to get 10 square units.

In both ways, I counted each square unit exactly once. I got the same area using both ways.

Where does the example . . .

- show the two ways to find the area?
- explain how to find the area using each way?
- tell why both ways work?

Solve the problem. Use what you learned from the example.

Show and explain two different ways to find the area of the shape below. Tell how you know that both ways work.

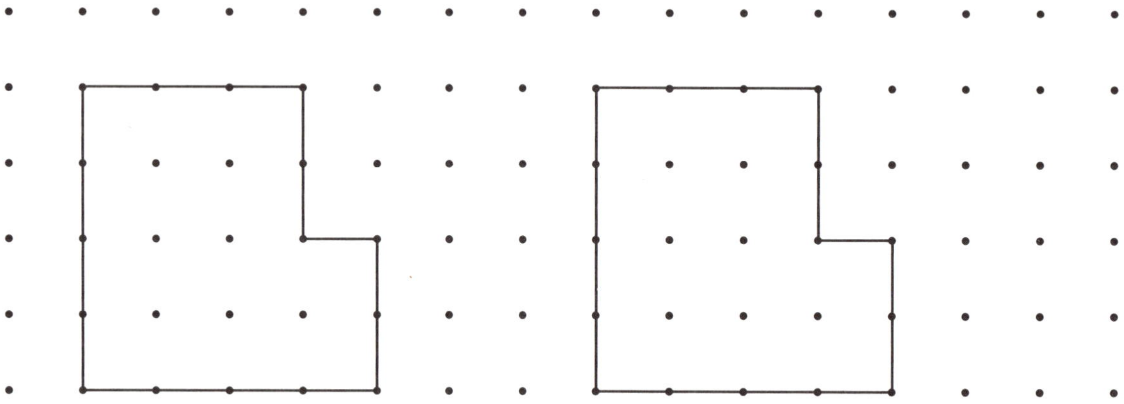

One Way   Another Way

Did you . . .

- show the two ways to find the area?
- explain how to find the area using each way?
- tell why both ways work?

Dear Family,

This week your child is learning to multiply to find the area of a rectangle.

Previously, your child learned that **area** is the number of square units that cover a shape, and then just counted the squares to find the area.

When the shape is a rectangle, you can use multiplication to find the number of square units that cover the shape.

In this rectangle, there are 5 rows each with 3 square units.

$5 \times 3 = 15$ tells how many square units in all.

There are 3 columns, each with 5 square units.

$3 \times 5 = 15$ tells how many square units in all.

The area of this rectangle is 15 square units.

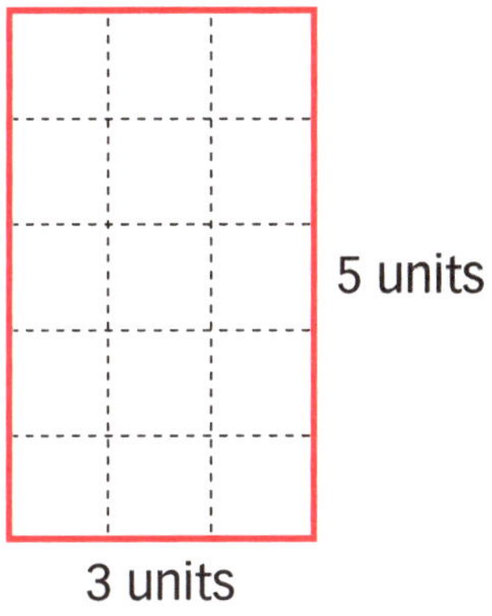

To find the area of *any* rectangle, multiply the length times the width (or the width times the length).

$4 \times 2 = 8$
$2 \times 4 = 8$

The area of this rectangle is 8 square centimeters.

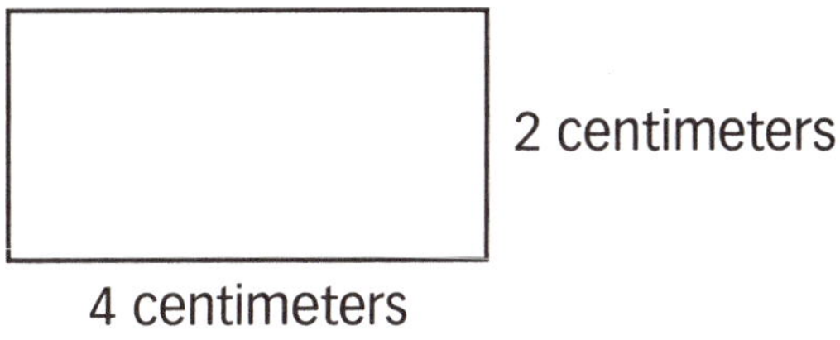

Invite your child to share what he or she knows about multiplying to find area by doing the following activity together.

NEXT

Multiplying to Find Area Activity

Materials: inch ruler or yardstick, calculator, pencil and paper

Practice using multiplication to find the area of different rectangular surfaces with your child.

Have a five-minute *Area Scavenger Hunt.*

Each player looks around the house for two rectangular objects. The goal is to find one with a "small" area and one with a "large" area.

Determine who found the larger rectangle.

- Measure the length and the width of the two "larger" rectangles.
- Use a calculator to multiply the length and width of each rectangle to calculate the area in square units (square inches, square feet, or square yards).
- Was the result what you expected?

Determine who found the smaller rectangle.

- Measure the length and the width of the two "smaller" rectangles.
- Use a calculator to multiply the length and width of each rectangle to calculate the area in square units (square inches, square feet, or square yards).
- Was the result what you expected?

Discuss with your child whether there could be another rectangle with the same area as yours, but with different length and width. For example, if you know a rectangle has an area of 24 square inches, what could the length and width be?

Multiply to Find Area

Name: ___________________________

Prerequisite: Count Square Units

Study the example showing how to count square units to find area. Then solve problems 1–6.

Example

What is the area of this rectangle?

There are 4 rows with 5 squares in each row.

You can skip count the rows by 5 to find how many squares there are: 5, 10, 15, 20. Or you can count each square.

Since there are 20 squares, the area is 20 square units.

1	2	3	4	5
6	7	8	9	10
11	12	13	14	15
16	17	18	19	20

1 Each square inside this rectangle is 1 square centimeter. What is the area? Tell how you know.

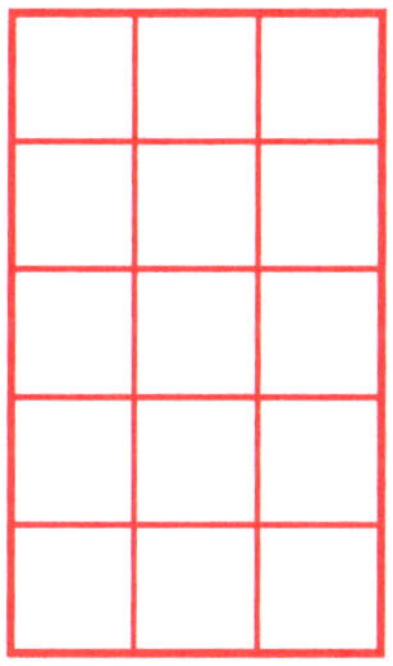

____

____

____

2 Find the area of each shape.

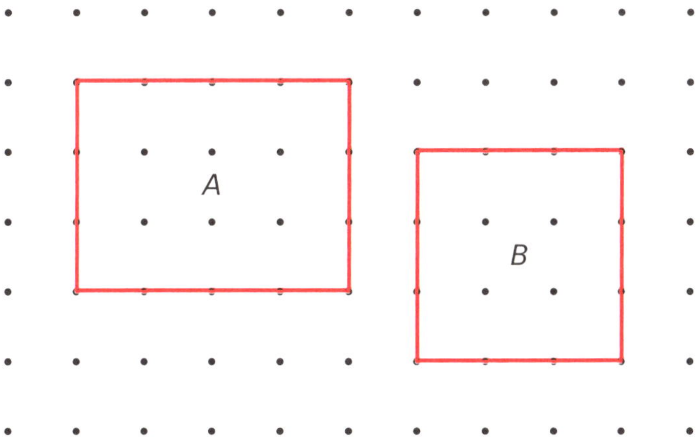

Rectangle *A*: Area = ______ square units

Rectangle *B*: Area = ______ square units

Vocabulary

area the amount of space a shape covers.

square unit a square with side lengths of 1 unit that is used to measure the area of a figure.

Solve.

3 Eva and Lin are gluing same-size squares onto pieces of paper. They each have the same size paper. Who will use fewer squares? Explain.

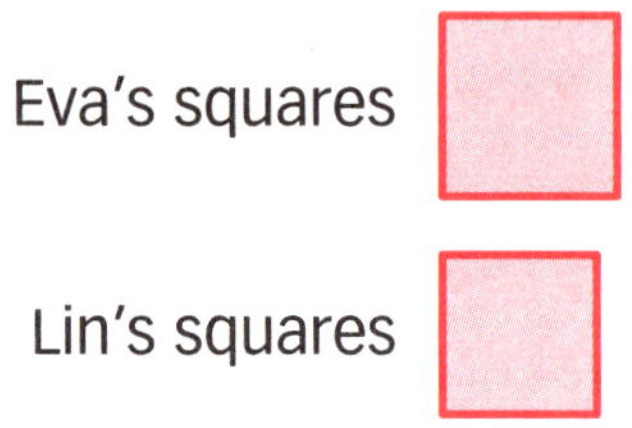

____

____

____

____

4 Shapes *A* and *B* are made of the same-size squares. Which shape has the greater area? Tell how you know.

A

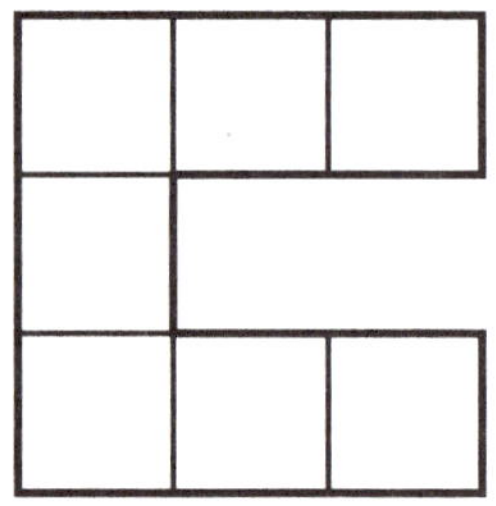

B

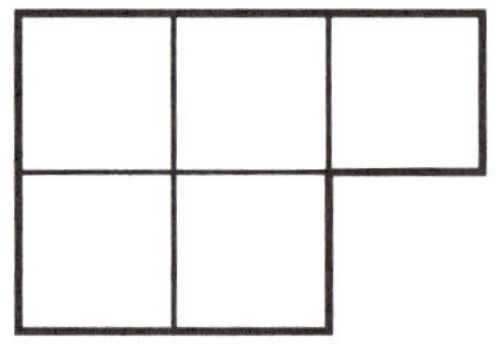

____

____

____

5 Draw a rectangle with an area of 10 square units. Draw another rectangle with an area of 11 square units. Label each shape with its area.

6 Can you make a rectangle that has two rows of squares with an area of 11 square units? Why or why not?

____

____

Name: ______________________________

Multiply to Find Area

Study the example showing how to multiply to find area. Then solve problems 1–9.

Example

A rectangle has a length of 4 centimeters and a width of 3 centimeters. What is the area?

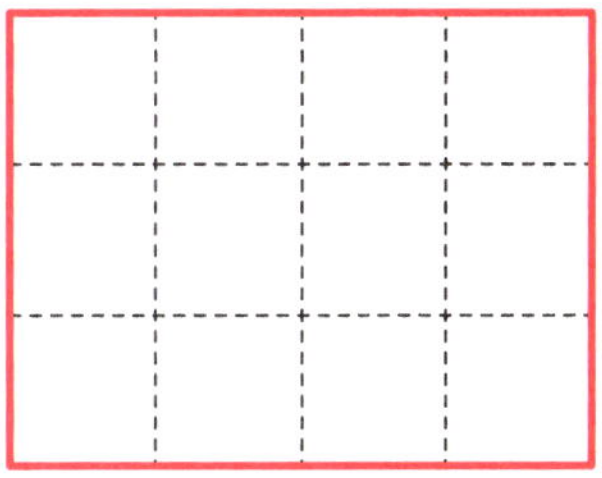

Fill the rectangle with 1-centimeter squares. There are 4 squares in a row and 3 rows.

You can multiply to find the total number of squares: $4 \times 3 = 12$.

The area is 12 square centimeters.

1 What is the area of this rectangle? Write a number sentence.

length	×	**width**	=	**area**
____ units	×	____ units	=	____ square units

2 A rectangle has a length of 8 inches and a width of 7 inches. What is the area of the rectangle?

____

____

____

3 A square has sides that are 4 centimeters long. What is the area? Write a number sentence.

____

____

____

Solve.

4 Write a number sentence to find the area of Rectangle *A*. Then write the area.

number sentence: ______________________________

area: ______________________________

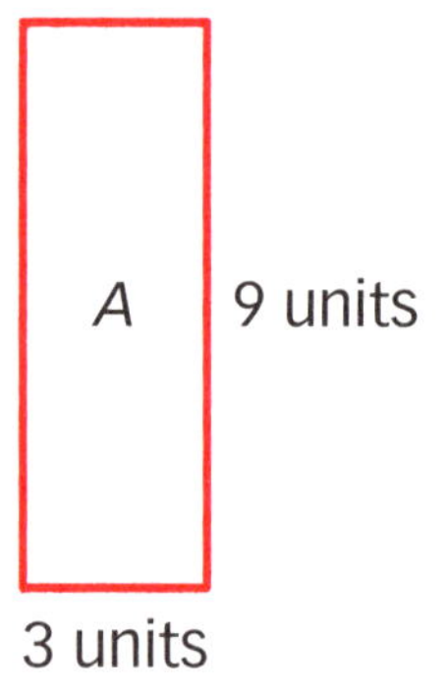

5 A rectangle has a length of 6 centimeters and a width of 5 centimeters. What is the area of the rectangle? Show your work.

____

____

6 What is the area of a square with sides that are 8 centimeters long? Show your work.

____

____

7 What is the area of Rectangle *B*? Show your work.

____

____

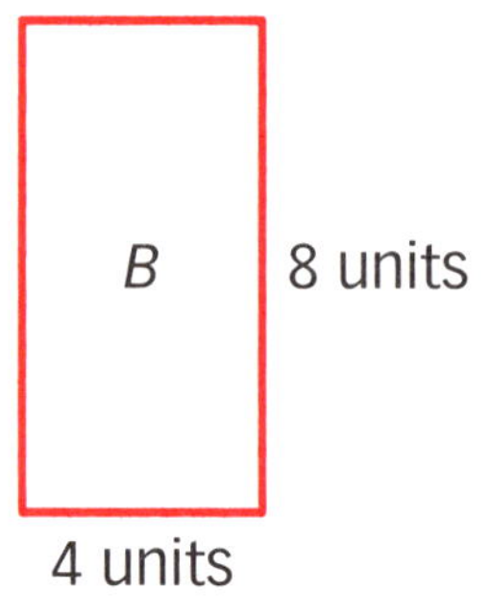

8 Lena draws a square with an area that is greater than the area of Rectangle *B*. What are two possible side lengths of Lena's square? Explain.

____

____

____

9 Pablo draws Rectangle *P*. He says that the area is greater than 50 square units. What could the missing side length be? Explain.

____

____

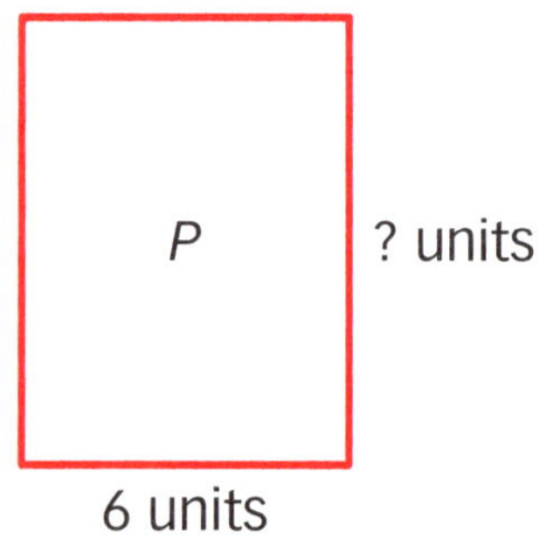

Name: ______________________

Solve Word Problems About Area

Study the example showing how to solve a word problem about area. Then solve problems 1–6.

Example

Ana's garden is 7 feet long and 7 feet wide. Noah's garden is 8 feet long and 6 feet wide. Which garden has a smaller area?

You can draw a model.
Then multiply length by width to find the area of each garden.

Ana's Garden

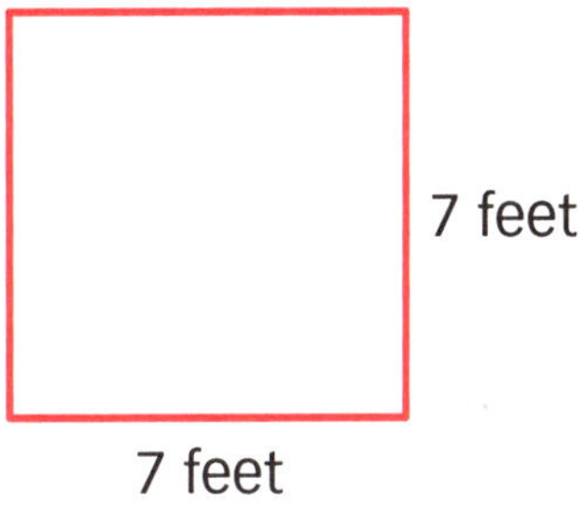

Noah's Garden

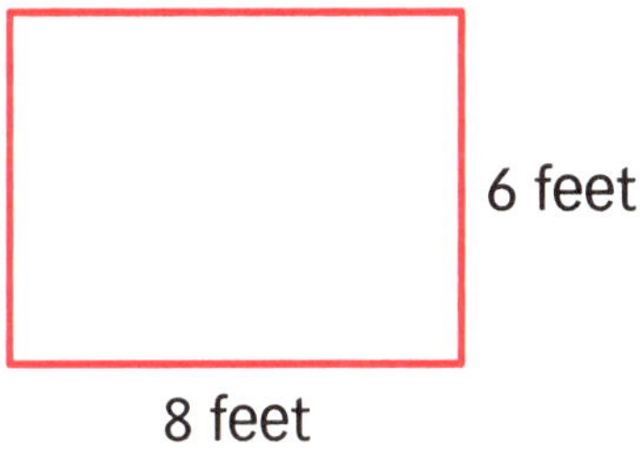

Ana: $7 \times 7 = 49$ square feet
Noah: $8 \times 6 = 48$ square feet

Noah's garden has a smaller area.

1 Roberto's desk is 4 feet long and 2 feet wide. What is the area of Roberto's desktop? Fill in the blanks.

length	×	width	=	area
____ feet	×	____ feet	=	____ square feet

2 Show how to find the area of this rug.

____

3 Vera buys a rug like the one in problem 2. Vera's rug is square. It has sides that are 4 feet long. Does Vera's rug cover more or less area than the rug in problem 2? Explain.

____

____

____

Solve.

4 Aiden prints a rectangular photo that is 4 units wide and 6 units long. Bella prints a square photo. It is 5 units on each side. Draw the photos and label the side lengths. Write the areas.

5 Draw and label a rectangle that has a smaller area than the area of a square that is 3 units on each side. Write the area of the rectangle.

____

____

6 Ron buys a rug for his room. The rug is 8 feet long and 5 feet wide. His room is 10 feet long and 10 feet wide. How much of the floor in Ron's room will not be covered by the rug?

Show your work.

Solution: _______________________________________

____

Name: ____________________

Multiply to Find Area

Solve the problems.

1 What is the area of the rectangle? Circle the letter of the correct answer.

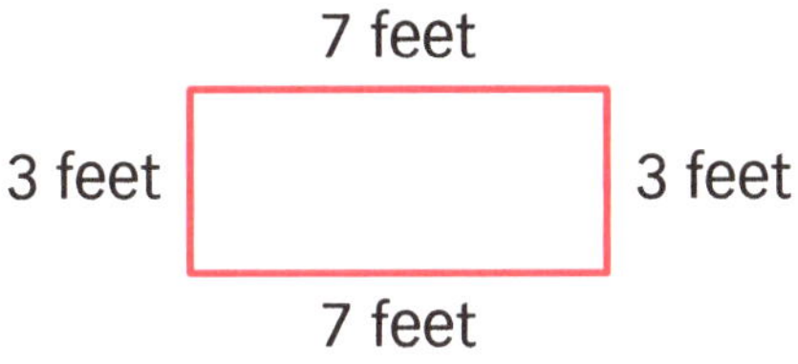

A 10 square feet

B 21 square feet

C 20 square feet

D 49 square feet

Diego chose **C** as the correct answer. How did he get that answer?

____

____

____

2 Which shapes have an area of 36 square units? Circle the letter for all that apply.

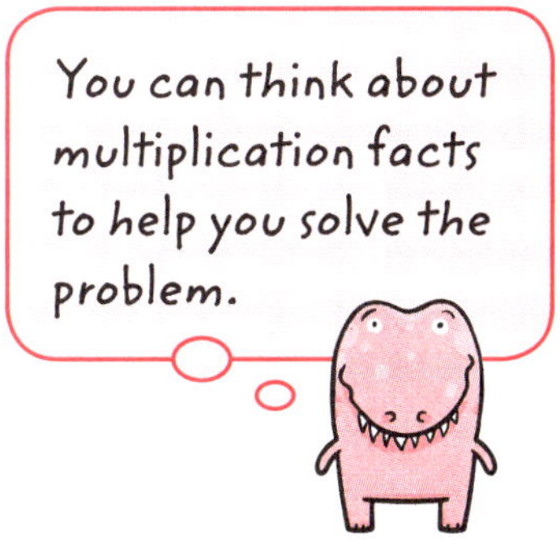

A a square with sides that are 18 units long

B a rectangle with a length of 9 units and a width of 4 units

C a square with sides that are 6 units long

D a rectangle with a length of 8 units and a width of 4 units

Solve.

3 Zach is helping his dad tile a shower wall. He has enough tiles to cover an area of 42 square feet. The shower wall is 8 feet high and 4 feet wide. Do they have enough tiles to cover the area?

Show your work.

Solution: ____________________

____

____

4 Mr. Diaz asks students to draw a shape with an area of 4 square units. Chad says that you can only draw a square. Do you agree? Explain.

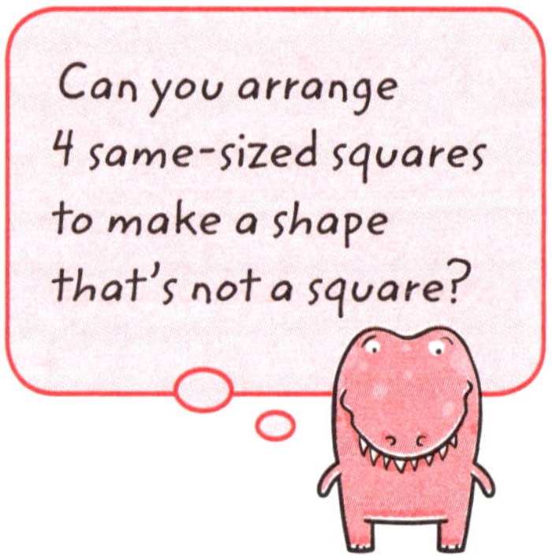

Solution: ____________________

____

____

____

5 A bulletin board is 8 feet long. It covers an area of 40 square feet. What is the width of the bulletin board?

Show your work.

Solution: ____________________

Dear Family,

This week your child is learning to find the area of a shape that is not a rectangle by adding up the areas of rectangles inside the shape.

There are several ways to find the area of this "T" shape.

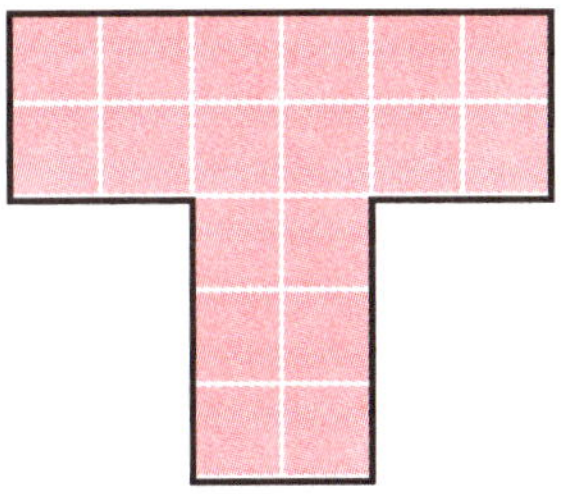

For example, you can add $(2 \times 6) + (3 \times 2)$:

$(2 \times 6) + (3 \times 2) =$
$12 + 6 = 18$

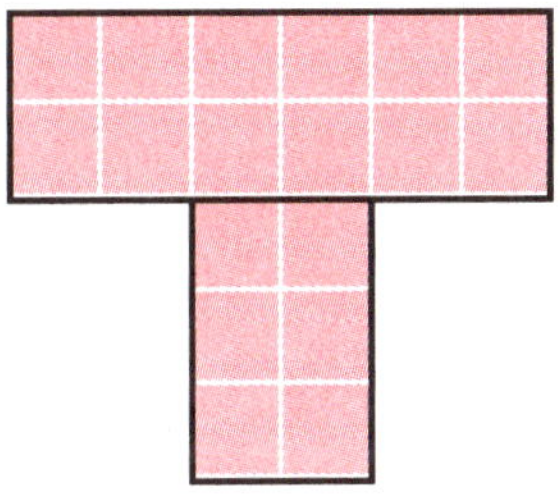

Or, you can add $(2 \times 2) + (2 \times 2) + (5 \times 2)$:

$(2 \times 2) + (2 \times 2) + (5 \times 2) =$
$4 + 4 + 10 = 18$

So, the area of the shape is 18 square units

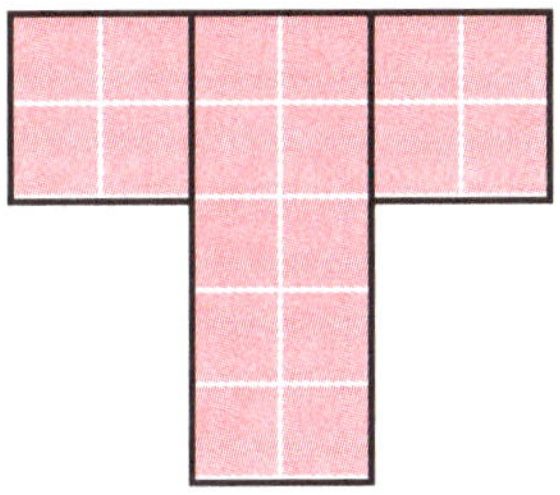

The more complicated the shape is, the more fun it is to find different ways to break it up into rectangles.

Invite your child to share what he or she knows about adding areas by doing the following activity together.

NEXT

Adding Areas Activity

Do this activity with your child to practice breaking apart a shape into rectangles to find its area.

First, invite your child to draw an interesting shape in the grid below. For example, the shape might look like this one, or it might be more complex.

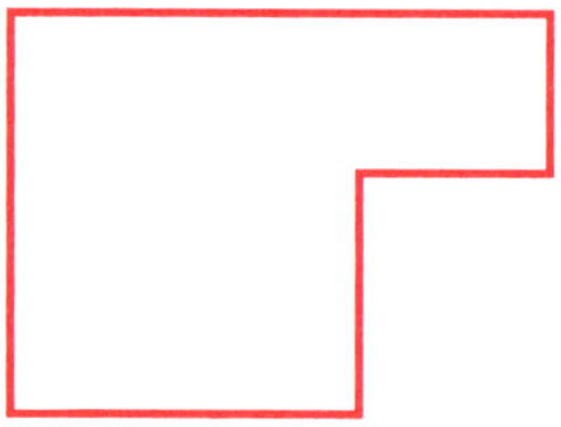

Then, work together to find the area of the shape by breaking the shape apart into 2 or more rectangles. Find the area of each rectangle, then add the areas.

Now, draw the same shape but break it apart in a different way.

Talk together about whether there other ways you can break apart your shape into rectangles. Will you always get the same area?

Add Areas

Name: ______________________

Prerequisite: Multiply to Find Area

Study the example problem showing how to find the area of a rectangle. Then solve problems 1–7.

Example

Riley glued 1-inch squares on paper to make this design. What is the area of the rectangle he made?

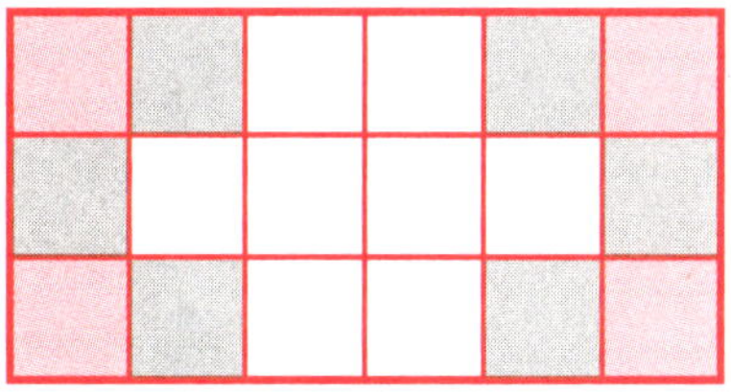

The rectangle has 3 rows of 6 squares. You can skip count to find the area: 3, 6, 9, 12, 15, 18.

You can multiply the length by the width to find the area: $6 \times 3 = 18$.

1 What are the length and width of this rectangle in square units? What is the area?

length: ______________ width: ______________

area: ______________

2 A rectangle has a length of 9 inches and a width of 8 inches. What is the area?

____

____

3 Write a number sentence for the area of this rectangle.

number sentence: ______________________________

area: ______________________________________

Vocabulary

area the amount of space a shape covers.

square unit a square with side lengths of 1 unit that is used to measure the area of a figure.

Solve.

4 This diagram shows the length and width of two greeting cards. Which card uses less paper?

Show your work.

Thank-You Card

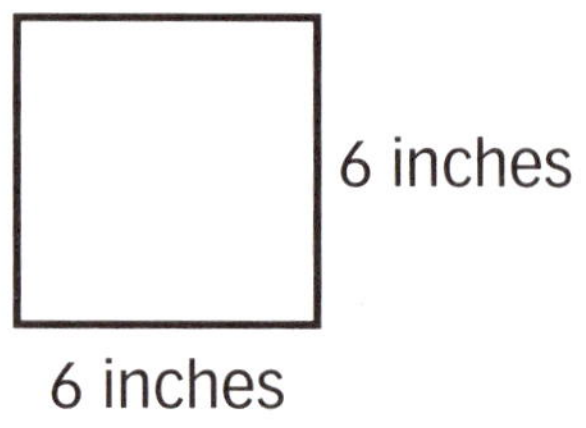

Birthday Card

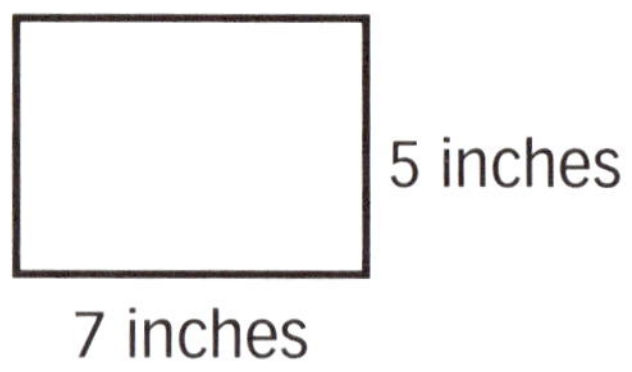

Solution: ______________________________

5 Write the length, width, and area of this shape.

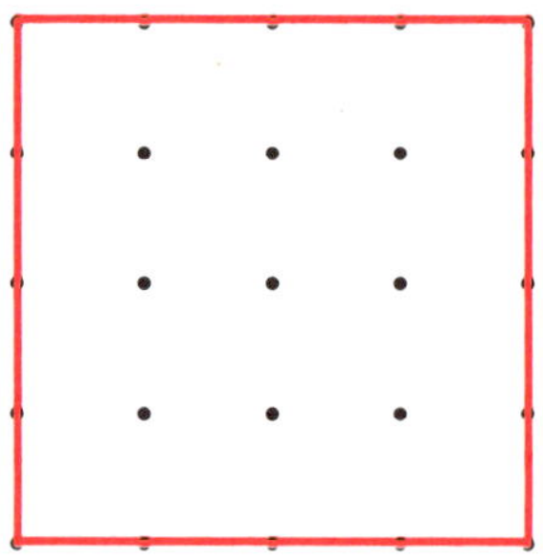

length: ______________________________

width: ______________________________

area: ______________________________

6 Lia wants to make a rectangular flower garden with an area of 24 square feet. Write two possible lengths and widths she could use.

____

____

7 A square has an area of 81 square centimeters. What is the length of each side of the square? Tell how you found your answer.

____

____

____

____

Name: ______________________

Area of Combined Rectangles

Study the example problem showing how to find the area of combined rectangles. Then solve problems 1–6.

Example

The diagram shows how Ms. Rigby covered her bulletin board with colored paper. What is the area of the whole bulletin board?

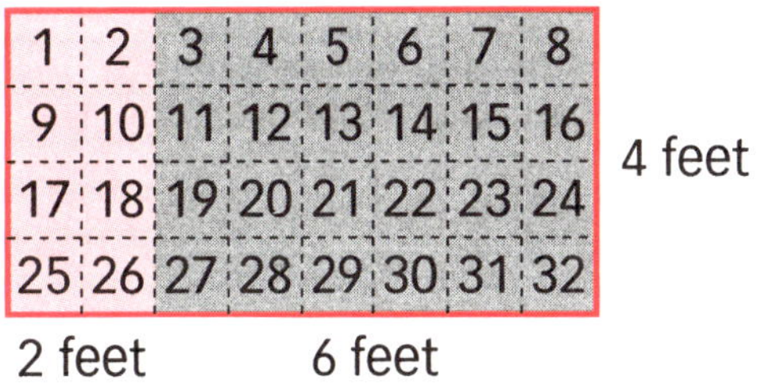

Area = 32 square feet

You can count the square units.
There are 32 squares.

You can multiply the length by the width.
Length = 2 feet + 6 feet, or 8 feet
Width = 4 feet
$8 \times 4 = 32$

1 Write a number sentence for the area of each section of the bulletin board.

left section: ______________________

right section: ______________________

2 Add the areas of the two sections. How does this area compare to the answer in the Example?

____

____

3 Baxter's dog run has a small covered section and a large open section. What is the total area of the dog run?

____

____

____

Baxter's Dog Run

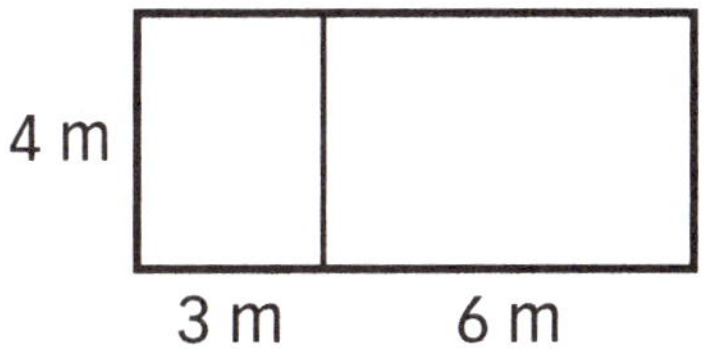

Solve.

4 Joaquin makes two paintings on small cards. The diagram shows how he hangs them together on the wall. Fill in the blanks.

a. The gray area is _______ square inches.

b. The red area is _______ square inches.

c. The total area is _______ square inches.

5 Show how to find the area of figure *A*.

____

____

____

____

____

____

6 Mila and her mom are tiling the playroom floor with two colors of tiles. They have 70 dark gray tiles and 30 light gray tiles. Each tile is 1 square foot. The diagram shows Mila's plan.

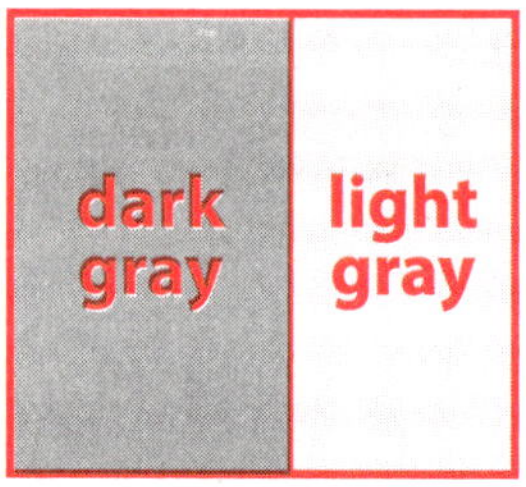

a. Show how to find the total area that they are tiling.

____

____

b. Will Mila's plan work with the tiles she has? Explain.

____

____

____

Name: ____________________

Area of Non-Rectangular Shapes

Study the example showing how to find the area of shapes that are not rectangles. Then solve problems 1–10.

Example

Mr. Carey made this shape with 1-inch tiles.
He asked his students to find the area.
Two students shared their work.

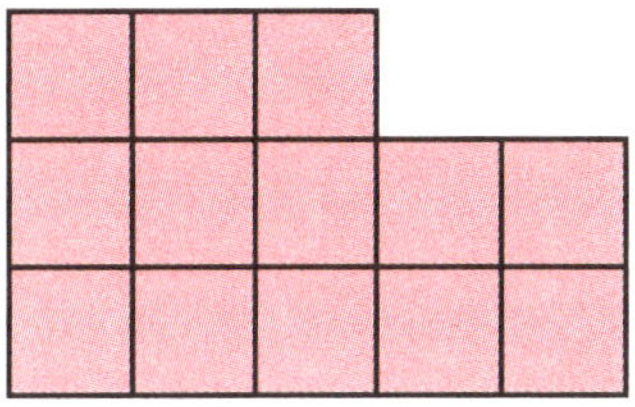

Renata's Way

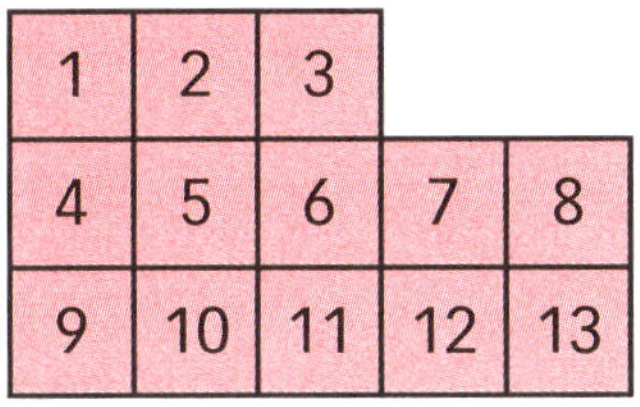

Marco's Way

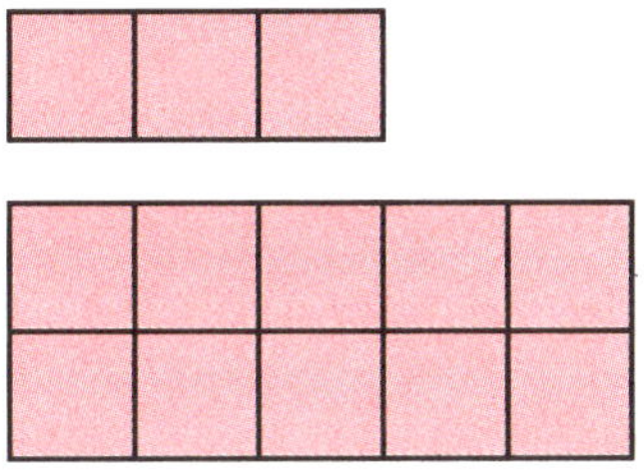

3 square inches

+

10 square inches

1 Marco broke the shape into two rectangles. Outline two rectangles to show Marco's way.

Marco's Way

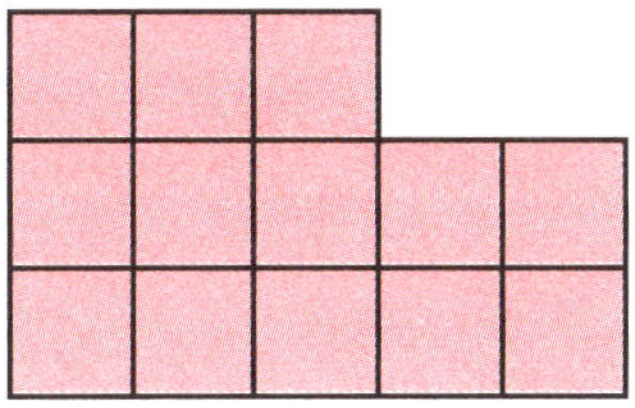

2 Write multiplication sentences to show the area of each rectangle you drew in problem 1.

____ inches × ____ inches = ____ square inches

____ inches × ____ inches = ____ square inches

3 Write an addition sentence to show the total area of the shape.

____ square inches + ____ square inches = ____ square inches

4 Sara broke the shape into two rectangles in a different way. Outline two rectangles to show Sara's way. Then show how to find the total area.

____

____

____

Sara's Way

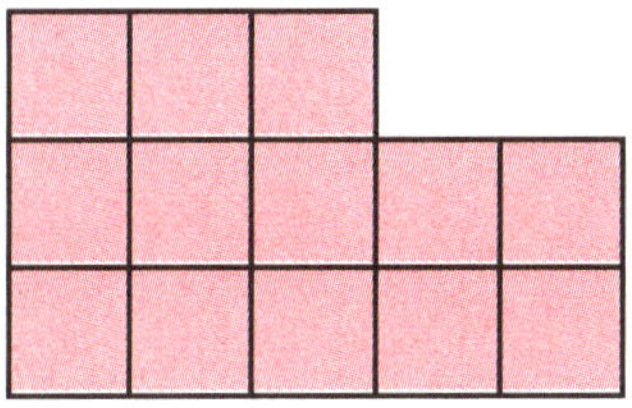

Solve.

5 Shade the rectangle in this shape that is 5 inches long and 2 inches wide. What is the area of this rectangle?

____

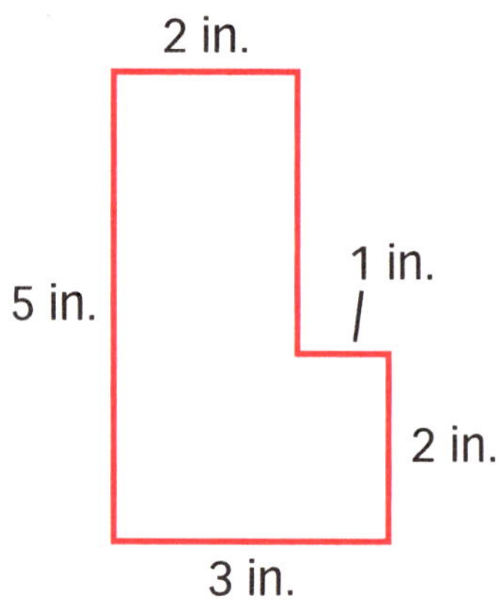

6 What is the area of the rectangle that is not shaded?

____

7 What is the total area of the shape?

____

8 Draw a line to break shape A into 2 rectangles. Then find the total area.

____

____

____

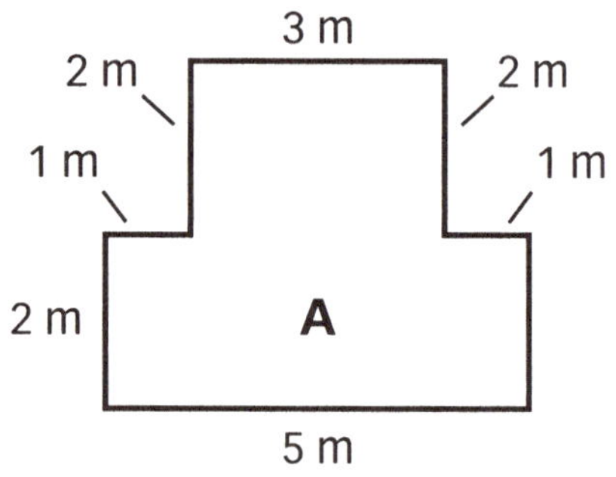

9 Draw lines to break shape B into 3 rectangles. Then find the total area.

____

____

____

____

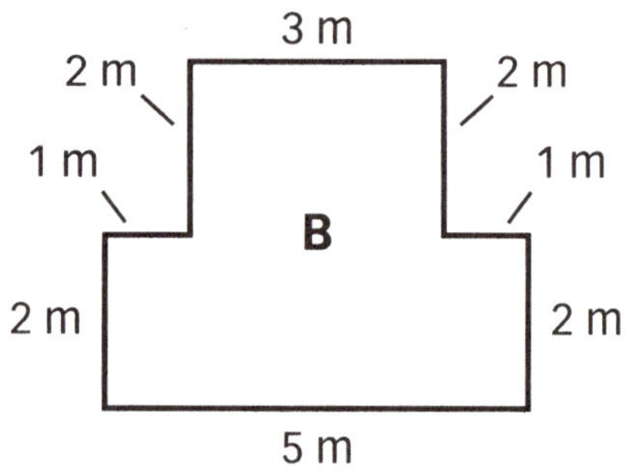

10 Draw lines to show two different ways to break this shape into rectangles. Then find the total area.

____

____

____

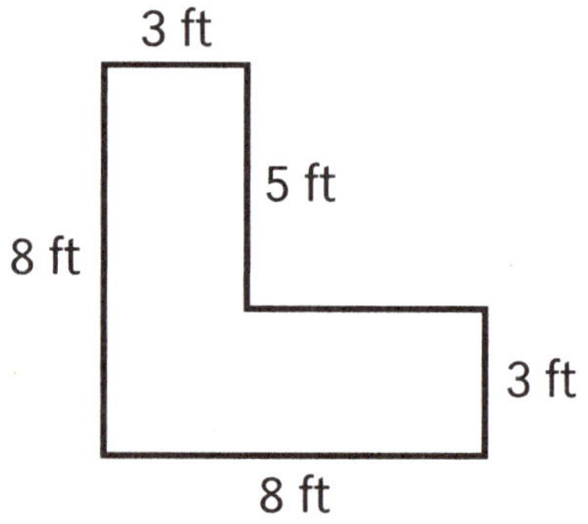

Name: ______________________

Solve Area Problems

Solve the problems.

1 Ross drew this diagram of his deck and flower garden. Which number sentences give the total area? Circle the letter for all that apply.

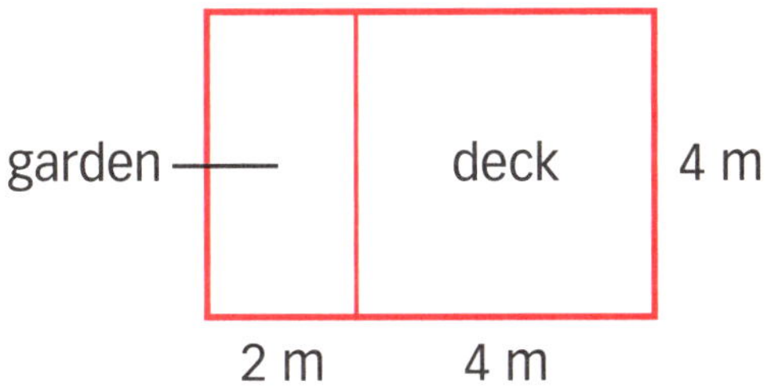

You can find the total length of the rectangle first. Or, you can break it into two rectangles.

A $4 + 4 = 8$ and $8 \times 2 = 16$

B $2 + 4 = 6$ and $6 \times 4 = 24$

C $4 \times 4 = 16$

D $2 \times 4 = 8$; $4 \times 4 = 16$; $16 + 8 = 24$

2 What is the area of this shape? Circle the letter of the correct answer.

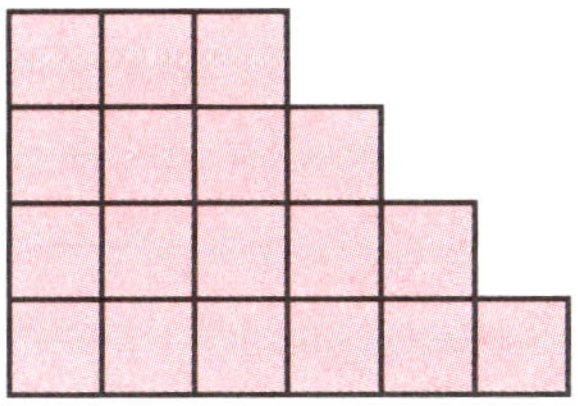

You can count or add to help solve the problem.

A 15 square units

B 18 square units

C 20 square units

D 24 square units

Rico chose **D** as the correct answer. How did he get that answer?

____

____

____

Solve.

3 The shaded squares in this diagram show Kyle's plan for tiling a floor. How many square feet of tile will he use?

Show your work.

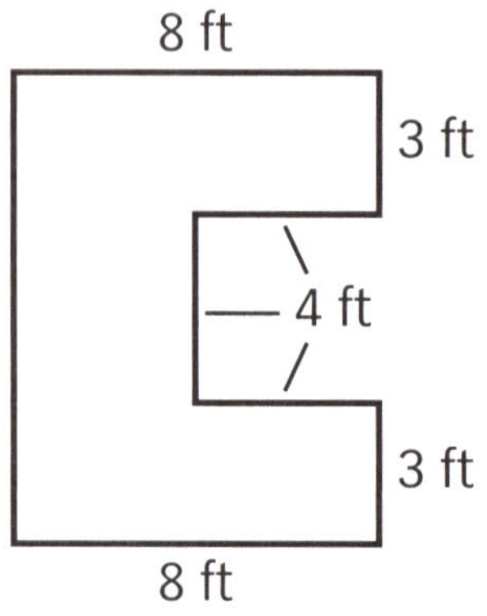

Solution: ______________________________

4 What is the area of this shape?

Show your work.

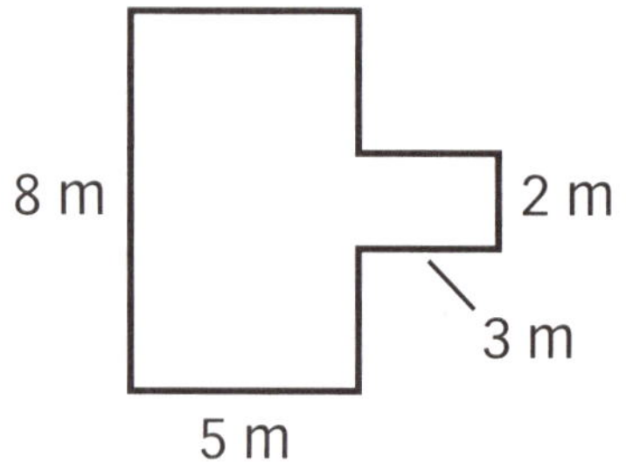

Solution: ______________________________

5 The diagram shows a tree house with a porch that Mr. Gates plans to build. What is the total area of the tree house and porch?

Show your work.

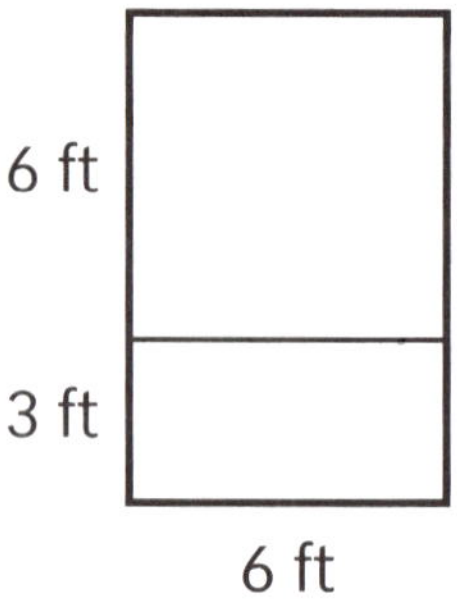

Solution: ______________________________

Dear Family,

This week your child is learning about perimeter and how it relates to area.

Area tells how much space a shape covers. The area of this shape is 8 square centimeters.

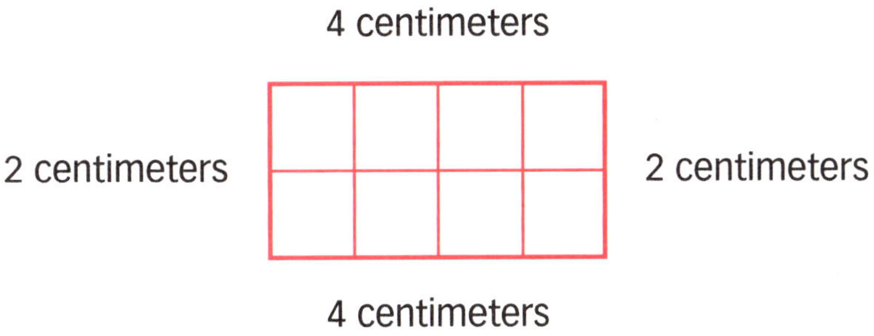

Perimeter tells you the total distance around a shape. You can find the perimeter of a shape by adding the lengths of all the sides:

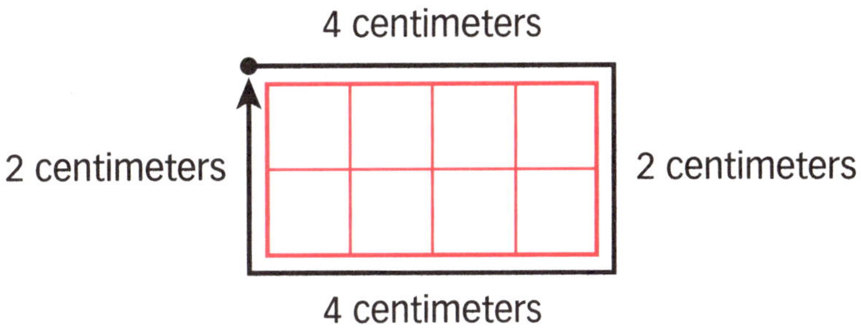

4 + 2 + 4 + 2 = 12

The perimeter of this rectangle is 12 centimeters.

Two rectangles can have the same area but different perimeters.

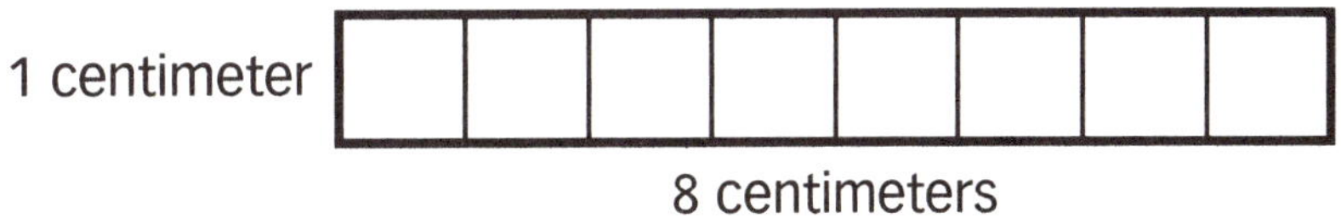

For example, this rectangle also has an area of 8 square centimeters, but the perimeter is 18 centimeters. Also, two rectangles may have different areas, but the same perimeter.

Invite your child to share what he or she knows about connecting area and perimeter by doing the following activity together.

NEXT

Connecting Area and Perimeter Activity

Materials: number cube, pencil, grids below

Help your child explore area and perimeter by doing this activity together.

Part 1 Find rectangles with the same area, but different perimeters.

- Roll the number cube.
- Have your child draw a rectangle on the grid below with a length equal to the number on the cube and a width of 4.
- Together, find the area and the perimeter of the rectangle.
- Now, work together to draw another rectangle that has the *same area* but a *different perimeter*. Is there more than one possibility?

Part 2 Find rectangles with the same perimeter, but different areas.

- Roll the number cube again.
- Again, draw a rectangle on the grid below with a length equal to the number on the cube and a width of 4.
- Together, find the area and the perimeter of the rectangle.
- Now, draw another rectangle that has the *same perimeter* but a *different area*. Is there more than one possibility for this?

Connect Area and Perimeter

Name: ____________________

Prerequisite: Multiply to Find Area

Study the example problem showing how to multiply to find the area of a rectangle. Then solve problems 1–7.

Example

Jared is planting grass in a section of his yard. The diagram shows the length and width of the section. What is the area of this part of Jared's yard?

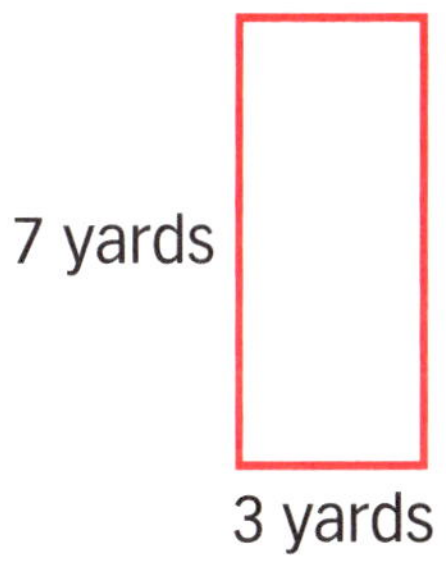

You know the length and width of the rectangle.

You multiply length by width to find the area of a rectangle.

7 yards × 3 yards = 21 square yards

Area = 21 square yards

1 Show how to find the area of rectangle *A*.

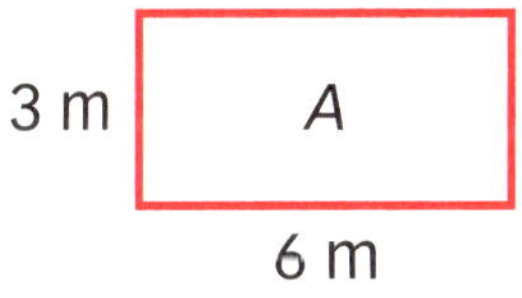

____

2 Write the multiplication sentence you would use to find the area of rectangle *B*.

______ × ______ = ______

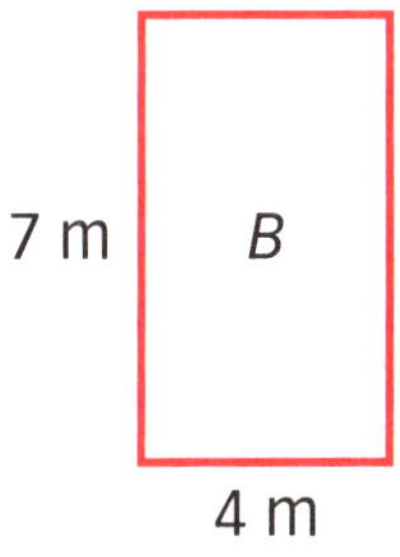

3 Mr. Taro's deck is 5 meters long and 3 meters wide. He has enough stain to cover 18 square meters of wood. Does he have enough stain to cover the deck? Explain.

____

____

____

____

Solve.

4 The diagram shows the floor space of two different tents. Which tent's floor has the greater area?

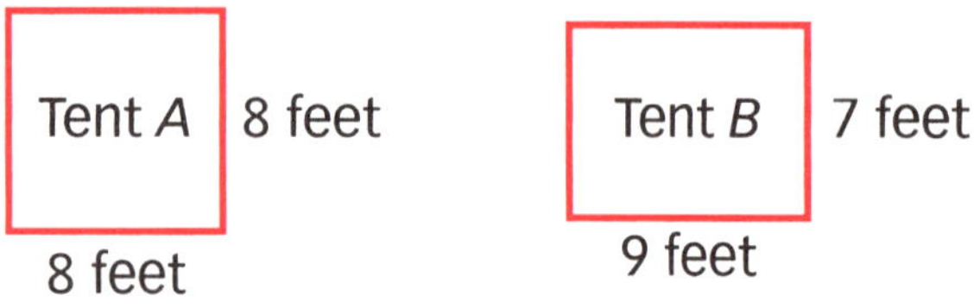

Show your work.

Solution: ______________________________

5 Draw a rectangle that is 5 units long and 4 units wide. Show how to find the area.

____

6 Liv draws a rectangle with the same area as the one you drew for problem 5, but a different length. What is a possible length and width of Liv's rectangle? Explain.

____

____

7 The shaded rectangle is 8 units long and 6 units wide. The larger rectangle is 10 units long and 8 units wide. What is the area of the white space around the shaded rectangle?

Show your work.

Solution: ______________________________

Name: ______________________

Find the Missing Side Length

Study the example problem showing how to use perimeter to find the missing side length of a shape. Then solve problems 1–8.

Example

This is a floor plan of the shed that Sean is going to build. The perimeter of the shed is 16 meters. What is the missing side length?

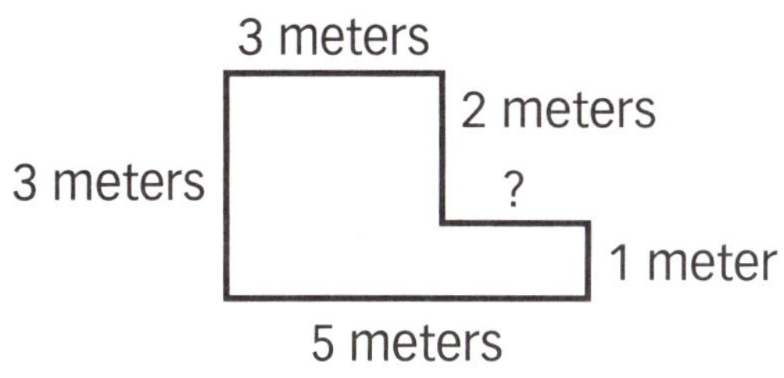

The perimeter is 16 meters. That means that the sum of all the side lengths is 16.

$5 + 3 + 3 + 2 + 1 + ? = 16$

$14 + ? = 16$, so $? = 2$

The missing side length is 2 meters.

1 Write an equation to find the perimeter of this rectangle.

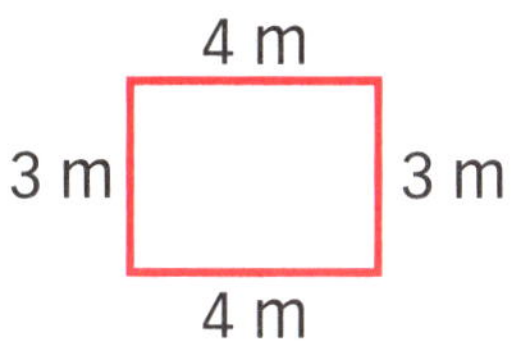

____

2 The perimeter of this triangle is 12 feet. How can you find the missing side length? What is the length?

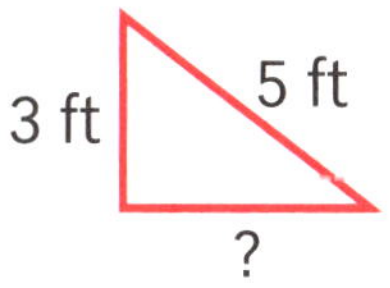

____

____

____

3 A square has a perimeter of 20 inches. Explain how to find the length of each side.

____

____

____

____

Vocabulary

perimeter the distance around a shape; found by finding the sum of the side lengths.

Solve.

4 Lorenzo knows that the perimeter of the trapezoid is 18 centimeters. Show how to find the length of the top side. Write the length in the blank.

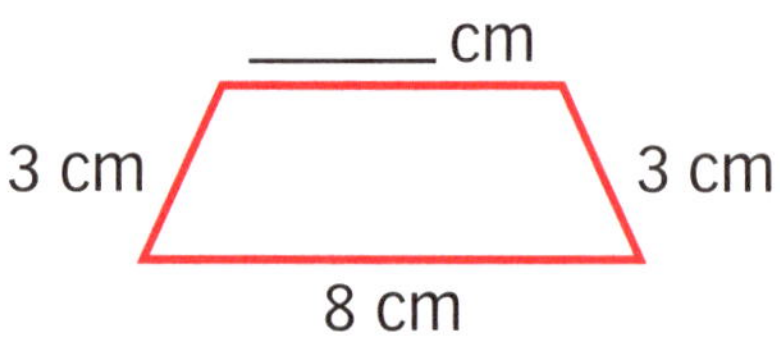

____

5 Nadia makes this sign for her bedroom door. She wants to put a ribbon border around all the edges of the sign. She has 12 inches of ribbon. Is this enough?

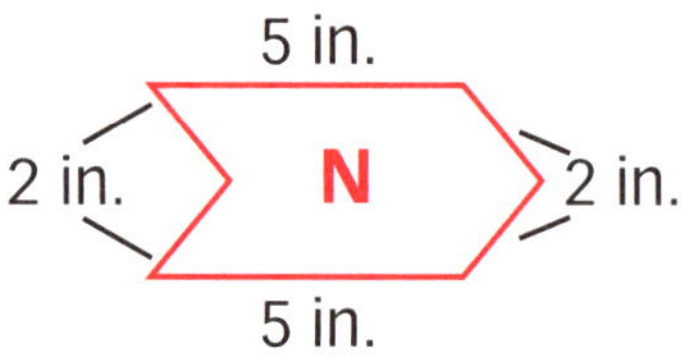

____

____

____

6 The perimeter of this shape is 20 feet. Show how to find the missing side length.

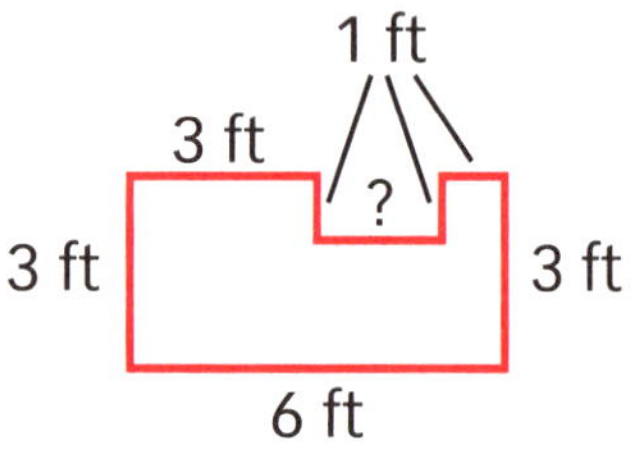

____

____

____

7 Jeff has a garden in the shape of a hexagon. Each of the 6 sides of the hexagon is 6 feet long. What is the perimeter of the garden?

____

____

8 A rectangle has 2 sides that are each 6 centimeters long. The perimeter is 22 centimeters. How long are the other two sides?

Show your work.

Solution: ______________________________

Name: ____________________

Same Area and Different Perimeter

Study the example showing how rectangles with the same area can have different perimeters. Then solve problems 1–5.

Example

Chang has 12 square tiles. He uses the tiles to make two different rectangles that each have an area of 6 square units. Do these rectangles have the same perimeter?

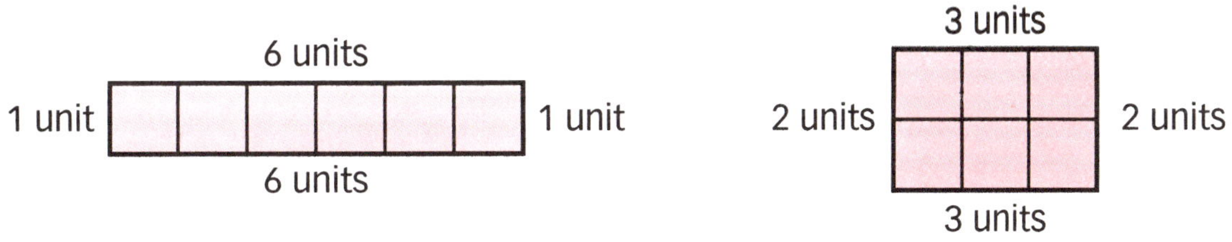

$6 + 1 + 6 + 1 = 14$

perimeter = 14 units

$3 + 2 + 3 + 2 = 10$

perimeter = 10 units

Rectangles with the same area can have different perimeters.

1 Both rectangles on the right have an area of 12 square units. Write the perimeter of each in the table.

Length	Width	Area	Perimeter
12 units	1 unit	12 square units	______ units
4 units	3 units	12 square units	______ units

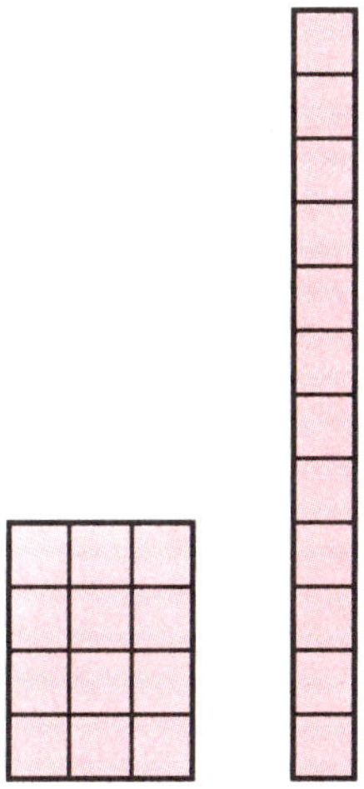

2 Draw two different rectangles that have an area of 10 square units. Write the number of units for each length, width, and perimeter.

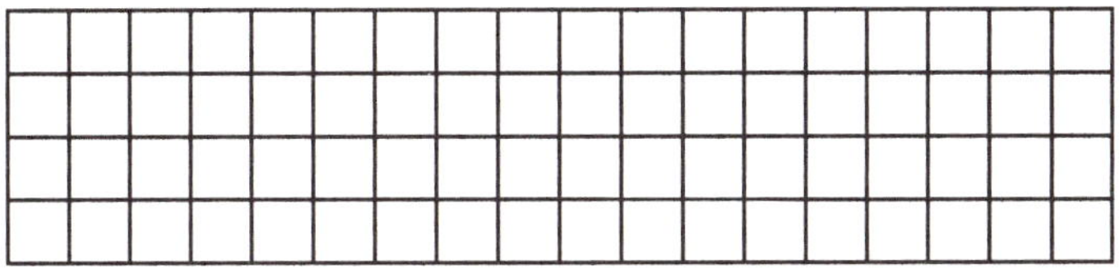

1: length = _____, width = _____, perimeter = _____

2: length = _____, width = _____, perimeter = _____

Vocabulary

perimeter the distance around a shape; found by finding the sum of the side lengths.

Solve.

3 Simone has 16 square-inch tiles. She glues them on cardboard to make two different rectangles, each with the same area. What are the lengths and widths of two rectangles she can make?

Show your work.

Solution: ______________________________

____

____

4 Simone wants to glue colored string around the edges of the two rectangles she made. What is the total length of string she needs for each frame?

Show your work.

Solution: ______________________________

____

____

5 Enrique drew the rectangle at the right. Draw another rectangle with the same area but different side lengths. Which rectangle has the greater perimeter?

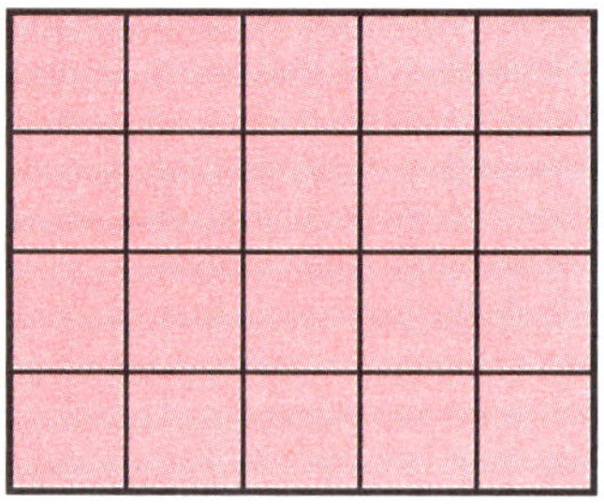

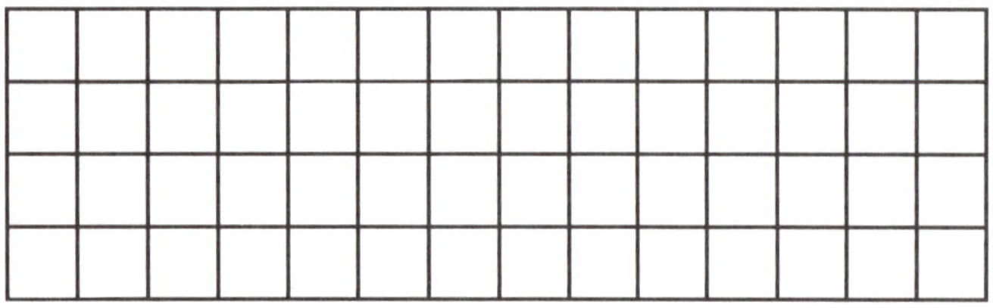

____

____

Name: ______________________

Same Perimeter and Different Area

Study the example showing that rectangles with the same perimeter can have different areas. Then solve problems 1–6.

Example

Kat drew two different rectangles, each with a perimeter of 10 units. Do these rectangles have the same area?

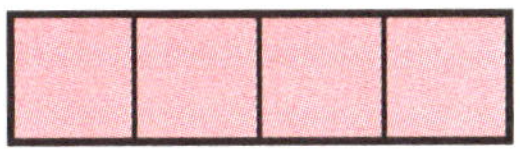

length = 4 units and width = 1 unit
area = 4 square units

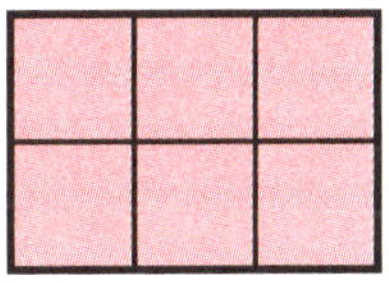

length = 3 units and width = 2 units
area = 6 square units

Rectangles with the same area can have different perimeters.

1 Both rectangles on the right have a perimeter of 14 units. Write the area of each in the table.

Length	Width	Area	Perimeter
6 units	1 unit	______ square units	14 units
5 units	2 units	______ square units	14 units

2 Draw a different rectangle that has a perimeter of 14 units. Write the length, width, and area in the table.

Length	Width	Area	Perimeter
______ units	______ units	______ square units	14 units

Vocabulary

perimeter the distance around a shape; found by finding the sum of the side lengths.

Solve. Use Rectangles *A*, *B*, and *C* for problems 3–5.

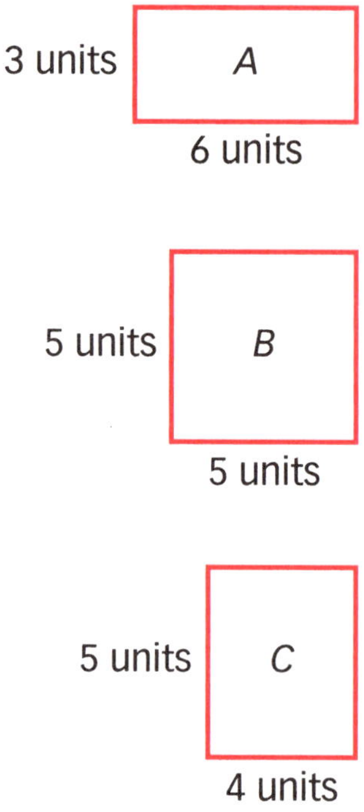

3 Which rectangle has the greatest area?

Show your work.

Solution: ______________________________

4 Which rectangles have the same perimeter?

Show your work.

Solution: ______________________________

5 Draw a rectangle that has the same perimeter as Rectangle *A*. Use different side lengths than the ones in Rectangles *A*, *B*, or *C*. Write the length, width, and area of your rectangle.

length ______________________

width ______________________

area ______________________

6 Find the lengths and widths of two different rectangles that have a perimeter of 20 units. Then find and compare their areas.

____

____

____

____

____

Name: ____________________

Connect Area and Perimeter

Solve the problems.

1 A rectangular rug is 10 feet long and 7 feet wide. What is the perimeter of the rug? Circle the letter of the correct answer.

A 17 feet

B 34 feet

C 68 feet

D 70 feet

Ami chose **D** as the correct answer. How did she get that answer?

____

____

____

2 For which of the following would you find the perimeter? Circle the letter for all that apply.

A the amount of space on a wall to paint

B the amount of fencing needed to go around a yard

C the length of wood needed to frame a picture

D the amount of space a tablecloth covers

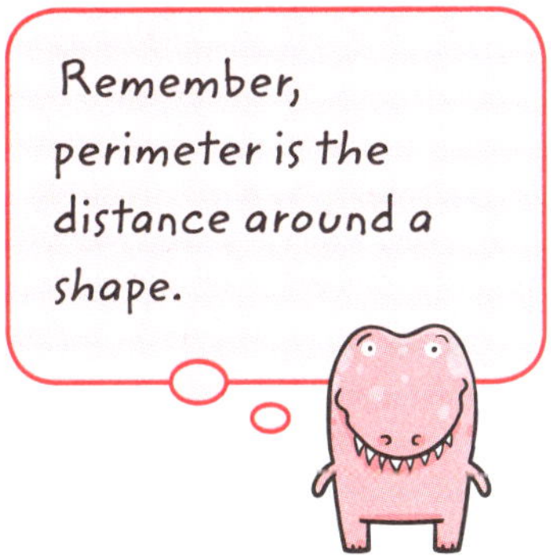

3 Find the perimeter and area of this rectangle.

Show your work.

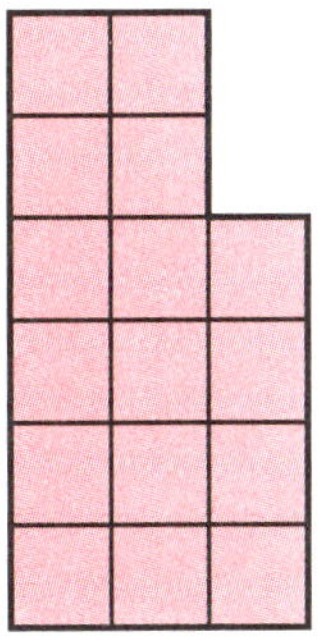

Solution: ____________________

Solve.

4 Find the perimeter and area of the rectangle.

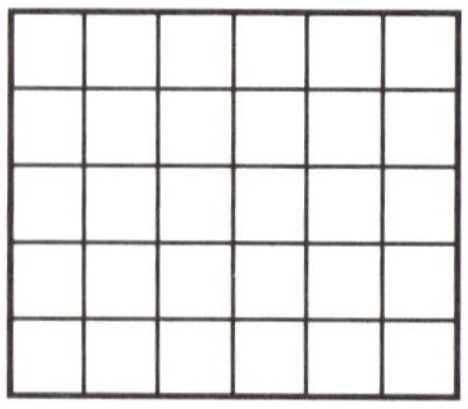

Perimeter: ______________________

Area: ______________________

5 Draw a rectangle that has the same perimeter but a different area than the rectangle in problem 4. Find the perimeter and area of your new rectangle.

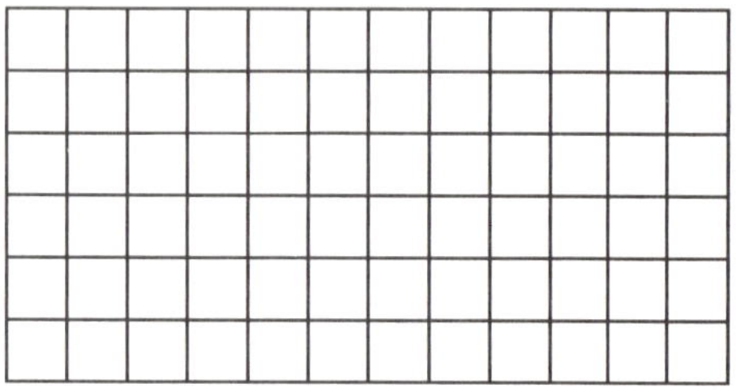

Perimeter: ______________________

Area: ______________________

6 Draw a rectangle that has the same area but a different perimeter than the rectangle in problem 4. Find the perimeter and area of your new rectangle.

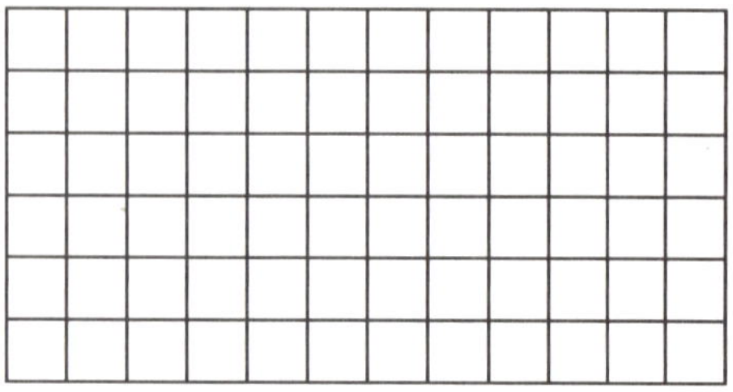

Perimeter: ______________________

Area: ______________________

Unit 5 Game

Name: ____________________

Time Match

What you need: Recording Sheet, Game Cards

Directions

- Mix the Game Cards and place them face down in a pile.
- Take turns. Draw a card. Figure out what time the card asks for.
- Find the clock that shows that time on your Recording Sheet.
- Fill in the blanks to describe the match, and circle *before* or *after*.
- If you can't use the card, return it to the bottom of the pile. Your turn ends.
- The first person to fill three clocks in a row in any direction wins.

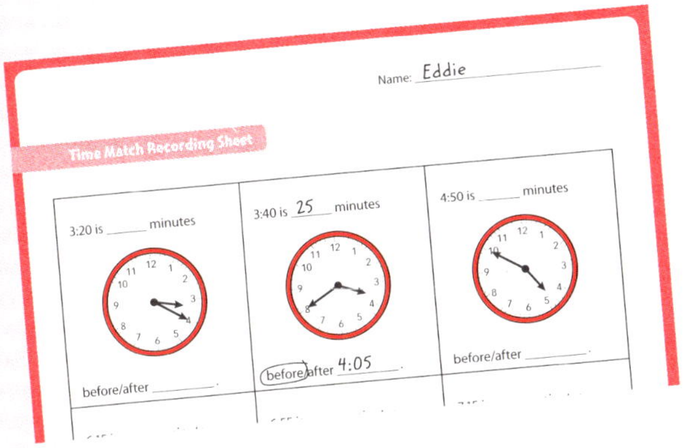

Name: ______________________

Time Match Recording Sheet

3:20 is ______ minutes

before/after __________.

3:40 is ______ minutes

before/after __________.

4:50 is ______ minutes

before/after __________.

6:15 is ______ minutes

before/after __________.

6:55 is ______ minutes

before/after __________.

7:15 is ______ minutes

before/after __________.

7:55 is ______ minutes

before/after __________.

9:30 is ______ minutes

before/after __________.

10:15 is ______ minutes

before/after __________.

Time Match

Game Cards 1

40 minutes after

25 minutes before

15 minutes after

15 minutes before

45 minutes after

15 minutes before

30 minutes after

30 minutes before

10 minutes before

Time Match

Game Cards 2

15 minutes before

40 minutes before

15 minutes after

20 minutes after

20 minutes before

25 minutes before

35 minutes before

30 minutes before

20 minutes after

Unit 5 Practice

Name: ______________________

Measurement and Data

In this unit you learned to:	Lesson
tell and write time on digital clocks and clocks with hands, and solve problems about time.	20, 21
estimate and solve problems about mass and liquid volume.	22, 23
draw and solve problems using pictographs and bar graphs.	24, 25
measure lengths and show data on a line plot.	26
understand area, find areas by multiplying, and add areas.	27, 28, 29
add to find perimeters and find shapes with the same perimeter and different areas or the same area and different perimeters.	30

Use these skills to solve problems 1–5.

1 Read the time, and write it on the digital clock.

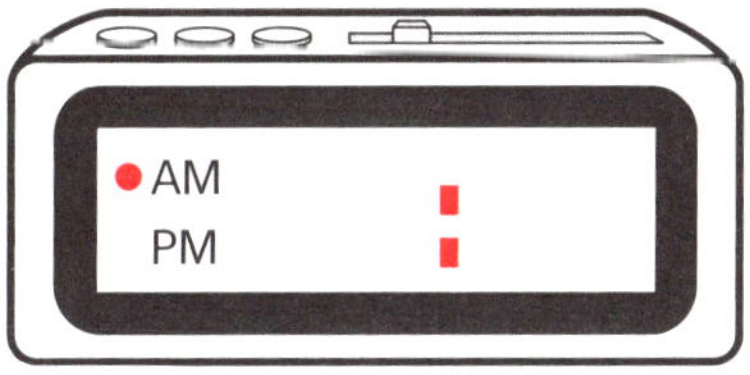

2 Elena takes 3 coolers to her soccer game. Each cooler holds 6 liters of water. How many liters of water does she take to the game?

Show your work.

Solution: ____

3 The Perez family drove 2 hours to get to the zoo. The clock shows what time they started. What time did they arrive?

Solution: ______________________________

4 The owner of The Treasure Corner Toy Store made a pictograph of toys for sale. The pictograph shows how many there are of each toy.

How many skateboards and dolls does the store have in all?

Show your work.

Toys for Sale

Puzzles	* * * * * * *
Yo-yos	* * * * * * * * *
Skateboards	* * * * *
Dolls	* * *

Each * stands for 10 items.

Solution: ______________________________

5 A red blob is covering part of the rectangle.

a. What two numbers will you multiply to find the area of this rectangle? _______ and _______

b. What is the area of this rectangle?

_______ square units

c. What is the perimeter of the rectangle? _______ units

Unit 5 Performance Task

Name: ______________________

Answer the questions and show all your work on separate paper.

There is a new building at the animal shelter. It will hold dog cages. The design must meet the following needs:

- There are two cage sizes. A small cage is 24 square feet. A large cage is 36 square feet.
- All cages are at least 3 feet wide.
- There must be at least 4 cages of each size in the building.
- The floor space of the building is 24 feet long and 24 feet wide.
- There will be a walkway through the middle of the building as shown in the diagram. The door to each cage touches the walkway.
- Extra space that is not used for cages will be made into play areas or used for storage.

Here is one design for the building. The manager of the shelter wants to look at other designs. Make a different plan that meets all of the needs above. Give the total area of all cages. Explain why you chose to design it this way.

Checklist

Did you . . .

- ☐ draw an accurate diagram?
- ☐ make sure your numbers fit the design needs?
- ☐ check that the results make sense?

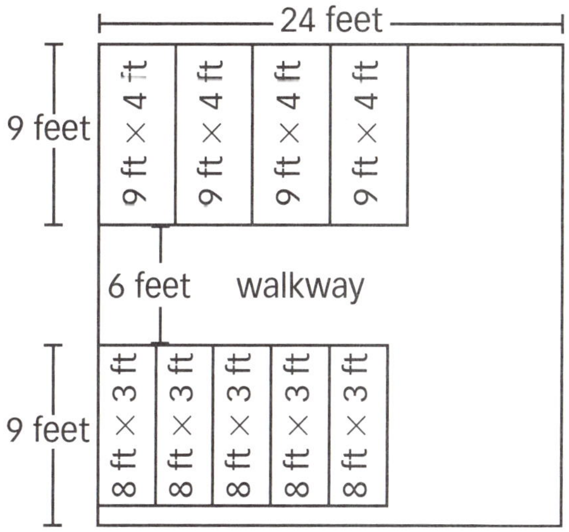

Reflect on Mathematical Practices

1 **Use Models** What models did you use to help you think about the problem?

2 **Explain Your Thinking** Why did you choose the lengths and widths that you used for each size dog pen? Explain any changes you made to the lengths and widths as you worked on the problem.

Performance Task Tips

Word Bank Here are some words that you might use in your answer.

area	length	width
feet	multiply	product
square feet	sum	total

Models Here are some models that you might use to find a solution.

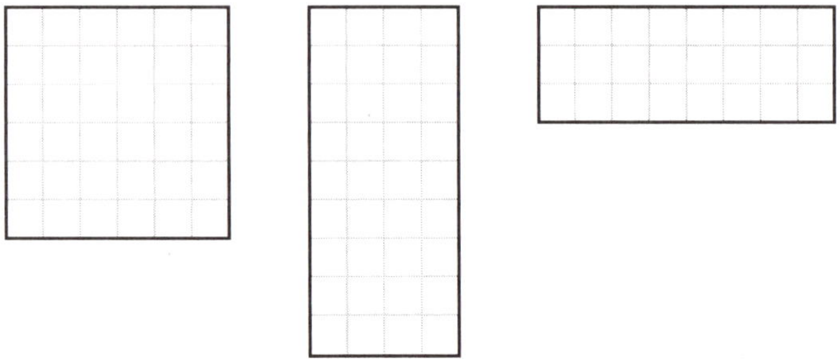

Sentence Starters Here are some sentence starters that might help explain your work.

A possible length and width for ____________________

The total area ____________________

My plan uses ____________________

Unit 5 Vocabulary

Name: ______________________

My Examples

elapsed time

the time that has passed between a start time and an end time

measure

to find how much of something there is

estimate

to give an approximate number or answer

liquid volume

the amount of space a liquid takes up

My Examples

liter

a unit of capacity or liquid volume. Some water bottles hold 1 liter of water.

mass

the amount of matter in an object. Objects with more mass are heavier.

gram

a unit of mass. A paper clip has a mass of about 1 gram.

kilogram

a unit of mass. A kilogram is equal to 1,000 grams.

My Examples

data

a set of collected information

bar graph

a graph using bars to show data

pictograph

a graph using pictures or symbols to show data

key

explanation of what each symbol represents in a pictograph

My Examples

scale

the numbers that show the units used on a graph

line plot

a graph using marks along a number line to show how many objects are in a set

area

the amount of space a shape covers

square unit

a square with a side of 1 unit that is used to measure the area of a figure

My Examples

factor

a number that is multiplied

product

the result of multiplication

perimeter

the distance around a shape, found by finding the sum of the side lengths

My Words

My Words

My Examples

Dear Family,

This week your child is exploring how shapes are named according to their properties.

A **rectangle** is any quadrilateral with 4 square corners, and 2 pairs of opposite sides that are the same length.

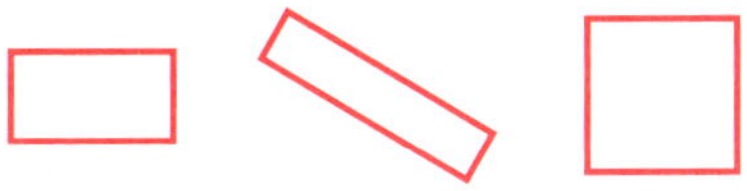

A **rhombus** is any quadrilateral with 4 sides that are all the same length.

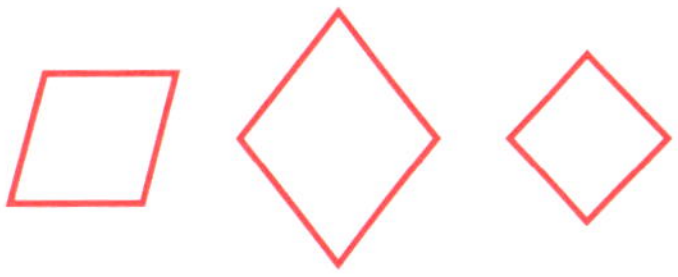

The Venn diagram below shows one way to sort shapes based on a few of their properties. The loop on the left holds shapes that have 4 square corners. The loop on the right holds shapes with 4 sides that are all the same length. This helps you see that a square, which is inside both loops, has properties of both a rectangle and a rhombus.

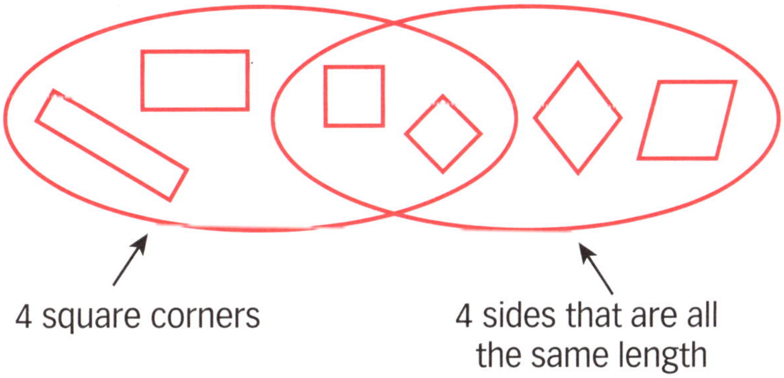

Invite your child to share what he or she knows about properties of shapes by doing the following activity together.

NEXT

Shapes Activity

Support your child as he or she learns to recognize the properties of different shapes by doing this activity together.

Be on the look-out for flat shapes around your home such as mirrors, rugs, tiles, and so forth. As a starting point, look at the shapes in the pictures below.

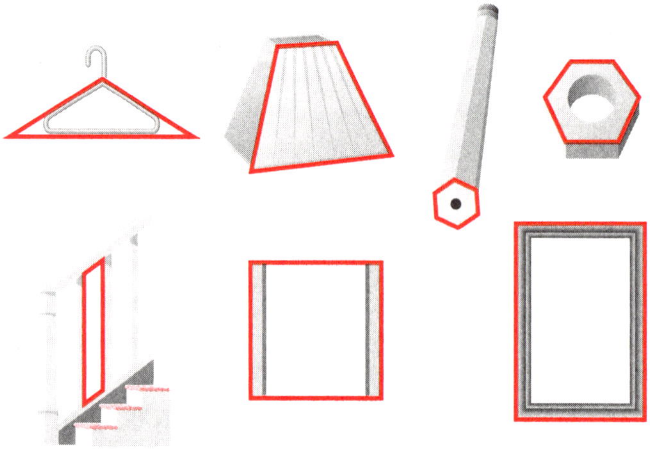

Take turns describing the shapes. For each, describe

- the number of sides
- the lengths of the sides
- the lengths of opposite sides
- the number of angles
- the number of square corners

Then pick two shapes. What properties do they share? What properties make them different?

Now look at similar shapes around your house, and have similar discussions about the properties of the shapes you find.

Understand Properties of Shapes

Name: ___________________________

Prerequisite: How do you know the names of shapes?

Study the example showing how to identify shapes using sides and angles. Then solve problems 1–9.

Example

Which of these shapes are quadrilaterals?

Triangles have 3 sides and 3 angles.
Quadrilaterals have 4 sides and 4 angles.
Pentagons have 5 sides and 5 angles.
Hexagons have 6 sides and 6 angles.

A, *C*, *E*, and *H* are quadrilaterals.

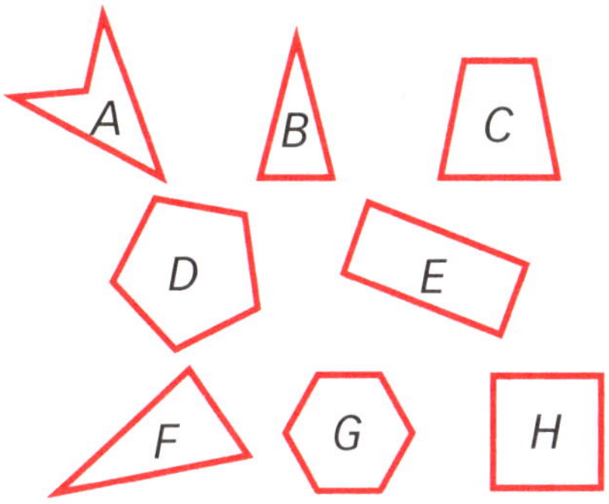

Use the shapes above to solve problems 1–4.

1. Which shapes are triangles?

   Shapes _______ and _______

2. Which shape is a pentagon?

   Shape _______

3. Which shape is a hexagon?

   Shape _______

4. Draw a triangle and a quadrilateral. Make the shapes different than the ones shown above.

Use these shapes to solve problems 5–7.

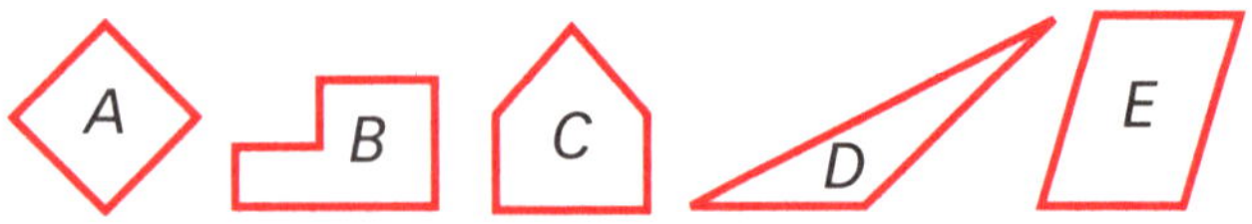

5 Fill in the chart to describe each shape.

Shape	Number of Sides	Number of Angles
A		
B		
C		
D		
E		

6 Write the letters to name each shape shown above.

Triangle ______   Quadrilateral ______

Pentagon ______   Hexagon ______

7 Draw and label a pentagon and a hexagon. Make them different than the shapes shown above.

Use the shapes on the right for problems 8 and 9.

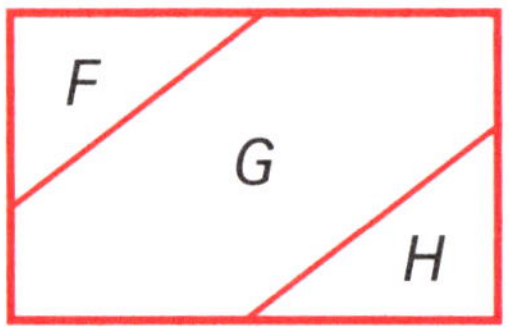

8 Which shapes are triangles?

Shapes ______ and ______

9 What is the name of shape *G*? Tell how you know.

____

____

Name: ______________________________

Compare Shapes

Study the example showing how to compare shapes by the number of square corners and the lengths of sides. Then solve problems 1–8.

Example

Which shapes have at least one square corner?

A square corner is an angle that looks like the corner of a square.

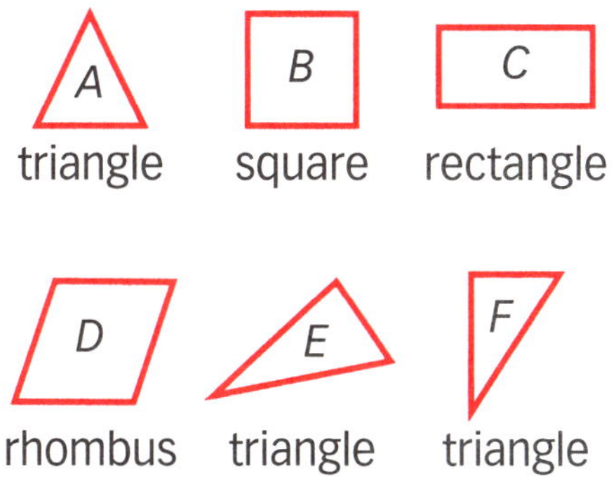

The **square** and **rectangle** have 4 square corners each.

Triangle *F* has 1 square corner.

Use the shapes above to answer problems 1–4.

1. Which shapes have all sides the same length?

____

2. Which shapes have some sides that are the same length and some sides that are different lengths?

____

3. Which shapes have all sides that are different lengths?

____

4. Do all triangles have square corners? Tell how you know.

____

____

____

____

Solve. Use the Venn diagram below for problems 5–7.

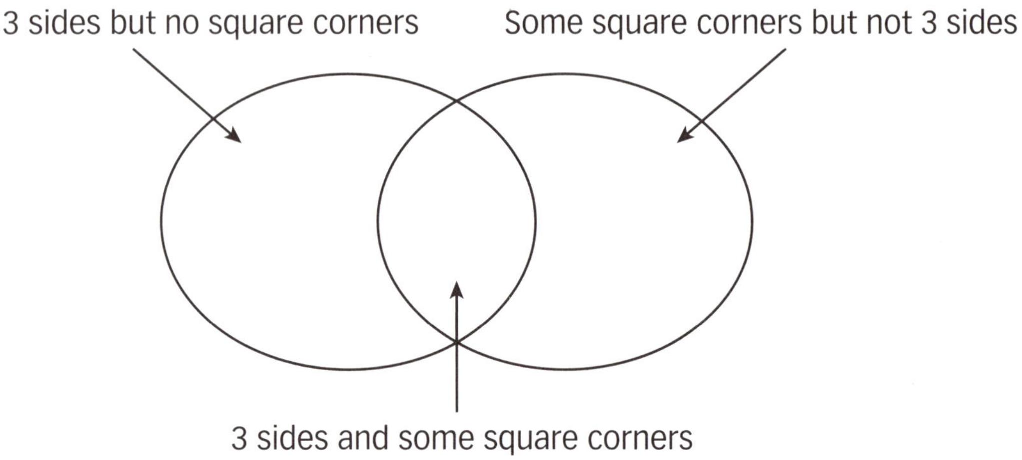

5 Draw each of these shapes in the Venn diagram to show which group or groups it belongs to.

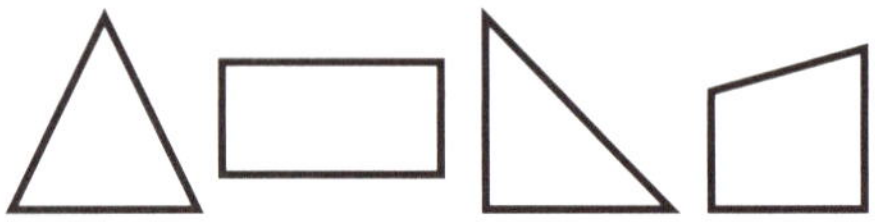

6 Draw in the diagram a different shape that belongs to the group "3 sides but no square corners."

7 Write the name of two different groups that each shape below belongs to.

____

____

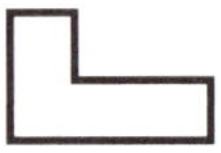

____

____

Vocabulary

Venn diagram a drawing that shows how objects in groups are alike or different.

Name: ______________________________

Reason and Write

Study the example. Underline two parts that you think make it a particularly good answer and a helpful example.

Example

Think about how the shapes in group A, group B, and group C are alike. Write names to describe the shapes in each group. Then look at shape D. Tell where in the diagram it belongs and why.

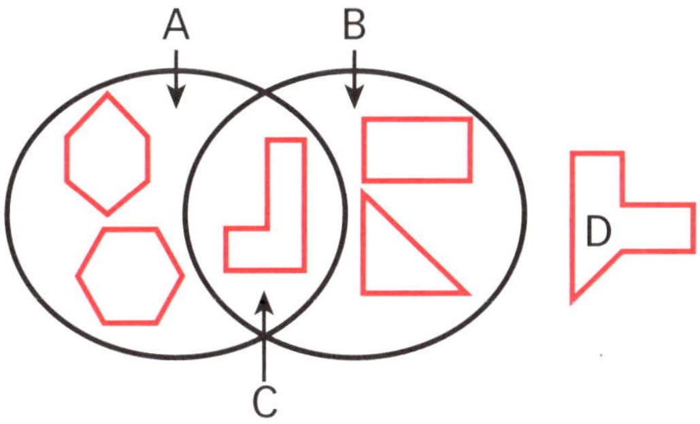

All the shapes in group A have 6 sides. They are hexagons.

All the shapes in group B have at least 1 square corner.

The shape in group C has both 6 sides and at least 1 square corner.

Shape D has 7 sides and some square corners. It belongs in group B.

Where does the example . . .

- write names to describe each group?
- tell where shape D belongs?
- explain why shape D belongs in that group?

Solve the problem. Use what you learned from the example.

Think about how the shapes in group D, group E, and group F are alike. Write names to describe the shapes in each group. Then look at shape G. Tell where in the diagram it belongs and why.

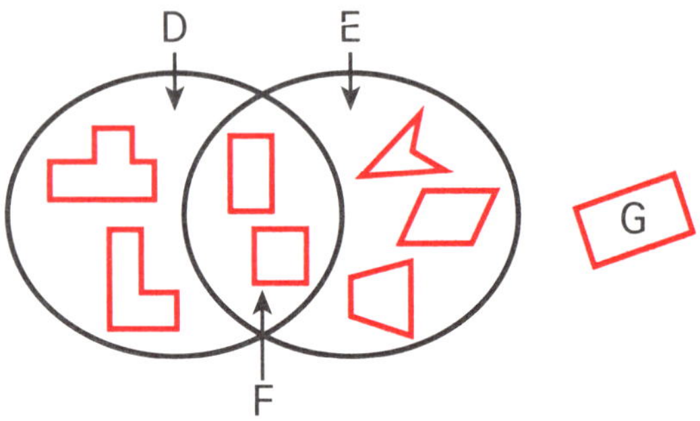

Dear Family,

This week your child is learning to classify quadrilaterals.

A **quadrilateral** is any flat shape with 4 sides and 4 angles. You can use properties to describe a shape, like number of sides, or lengths of sides.

Parallelogram
2 pairs of opposite sides that are the same length

These are parallelograms:

These are not parallelograms:

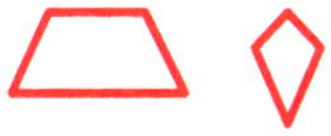

Rectangle
4 square corners
2 pairs of sides that are the same length

These are rectangles:

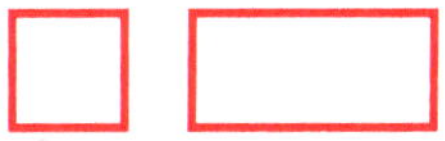

These are not rectangles:

Rhombus
4 sides that are all the same length

These are rhombuses:

These are not rhombuses:

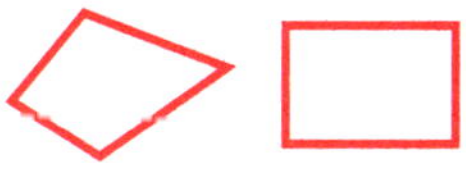

rhombus

parallelogram

rectangle

Invite your child to share what he or she knows about classifying quadrilaterals by doing the following activity together.

NEXT

Classifying Quadrilaterals Activity

Materials: 8 different writing tools such as pens, pencils, markers, crayons (4 should be the same length)

Help your child practice classifying quadrilaterals by doing this activity together.

Invite your child to create a quadrilateral using 4 of the writing tools as the sides of the shape. You create a quadrilateral with the other 4. See below for examples.

Together, describe your quadrilaterals.

- Tell the number of square corners.
- Describe any opposite sides that are the same length.

Now classify both of your quadrilaterals. Is your quadrilateral:

• a rectangle?	yes	no
• a square?	yes	no
• a rhombus?	yes	no
• a parallelogram?	yes	no
• none of the above?	yes	no

If your quadrilateral is none of the above, see if you can figure out what you would need to change in your shape to make it fit at least one of the classifications listed. Try it to check your thinking!

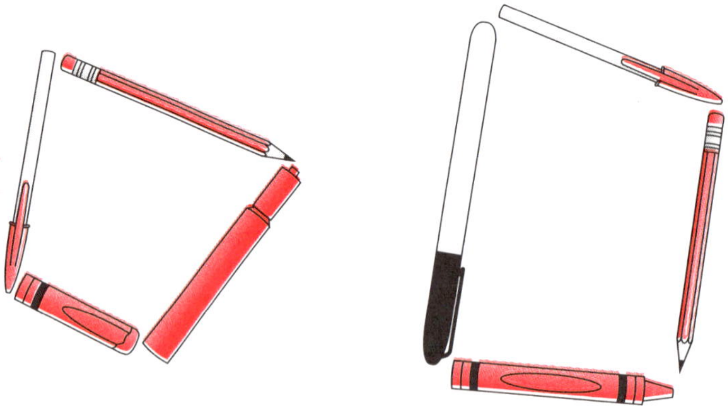

Classify Quadrilaterals

Name: ______________________

Prerequisite: Group Quadrilaterals

Study the example problem showing how to group quadrilaterals. Then solve problems 1–10.

Example

Which quadrilaterals do not have opposite sides that are the same length?

Shape *B* has no opposite sides and the sides are all different lengths.

Shapes *C* and *F* have a pair of opposite sides, but they are not the same length.

Shapes *B*, *C*, and *F* do not belong to the group "opposite sides the same length."

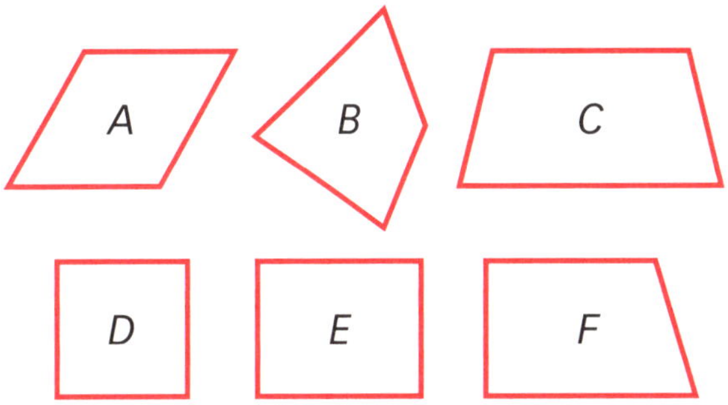

Use the shapes shown above to answer problems 1–5.

1. Which quadrilaterals above have all sides the same length?

____

2. Which quadrilaterals have no square corners?

____

3. Which quadrilaterals have at least 1 square corner?

____

4. Which quadrilaterals have all square corners?

____

5. Name a group that all of the shapes above belong to.

____

Solve. Use the shapes on the right to solve problems 6–8.

parallelogram

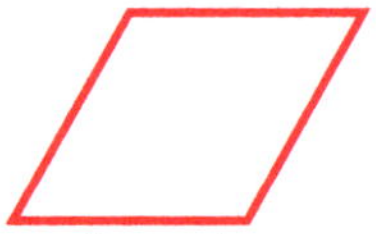

rhombus

6 Which shapes belong to the group "two pairs of opposite sides"?

____

7 Which shapes do not belong to the group "opposite sides are the same length"?

____

8 Write the name of a group that neither shape belongs to. Explain.

____

____

____

____

9 Draw two different quadrilaterals that belong to the group "no sides are the same length."

10 Draw two different quadrilaterals that do not belong to the group "at least 1 square corner."

Vocabulary

rhombus
a quadrilateral with 2 pairs of parallel sides and 4 sides that are the same length.

Name: ______________________

Compare Quadrilaterals

Study the example problem showing how to compare quadrilaterals. Then solve problems 1–7.

Example

Which of these shapes are parallelograms?

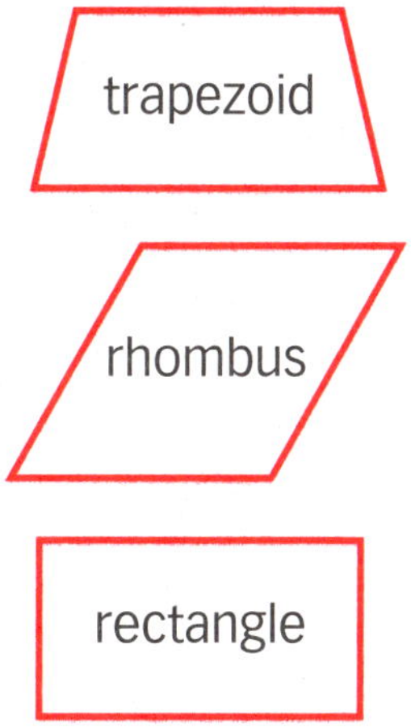

You can list the attributes of a parallelogram in a table. Check if each shape has these attributes.

Attribute	Trapezoid	Rhombus	Rectangle
4 sides	yes	yes	yes
4 angles	yes	yes	yes
2 pairs of parallel sides	no	yes	yes
2 pairs of sides that are the same length	no	yes	yes

A rhombus and a rectangle have all the attributes of a parallelogram.

1 Is shape *A* a parallelogram? Explain.

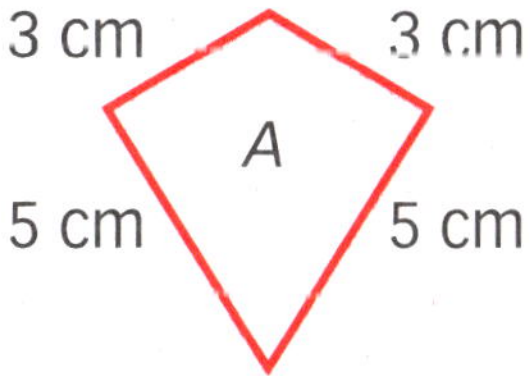

____

____

____

2 What is another kind of quadrilateral that is also a parallelogram? Explain.

____

____

3 Fill in the blanks. Use information from the table above.

Every ________________ is a parallelogram.

Every ________________ is a parallelogram.

Vocabulary

attribute a way to describe a shape, like number of sides or length of sides.

Solve. Use the table to solve problems 4–7.

Attribute	Parallelogram	Rhombus	Rectangle	Square
4 sides 4 angles	yes	yes	yes	yes
4 square corners	sometimes	sometimes	yes	yes
2 pairs of parallel sides	yes	yes	yes	yes
2 pairs of sides that are the same length	yes	yes	yes	yes

4 Circle all the quadrilaterals that are rhombuses.

5 Circle all the quadrilaterals that are rectangles.

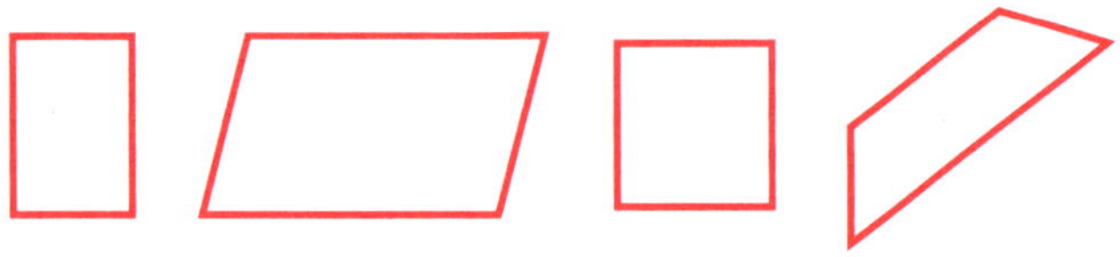

6 Tell whether each sentence is *True* or *False*.

a. All squares are rectangles. ☐ True ☐ False

b. All rectangles are parallelograms. ☐ True ☐ False

c. All parallelograms are rectangles. ☐ True ☐ False

d. All quadrilaterals are parallelograms. ☐ True ☐ False

e. All parallelograms are quadrilaterals. ☐ True ☐ False

7 Jaime says that some rectangles are not squares. Do you agree? Explain.

____

____

Name: ______________________________

Name and Draw Quadrilaterals

Study the example showing how to name a quadrilateral. Then solve problems 1–9.

Example

Justin is drawing a quadrilateral with opposite sides that are the same length. All 4 sides are not the same length. What quadrilaterals can Justin draw?

Make a drawing to see what the quadrilaterals might look like.

Opposite sides are the same length.
The shape has 4 square corners.

Opposite sides are the same length.
The shape has no square corners.

Justin can draw a rectangle or a parallelogram.

Use the shape on the right to answer problems 1–5.

1 One wall of a shed looks like the shape on the right. How many sides and angles does the shape have?

____

2 How many parallel sides does the shape have?

____

3 How many square corners does the shape have?

____

4 Does the shape have 2 pairs of sides the same length?

____

5 Circle all the words you can use to name this shape.

quadrilateral   parallelogram   rectangle

Vocabulary

parallelogram a quadrilateral with 2 pairs of parallel sides and 2 pairs of sides that are the same length.

rectangle a quadrilateral with 4 square corners, 2 pairs of parallel sides, and 2 pairs of sides that are the same length.

Use the clues and shapes *A*–*E* to solve problems 6–8.

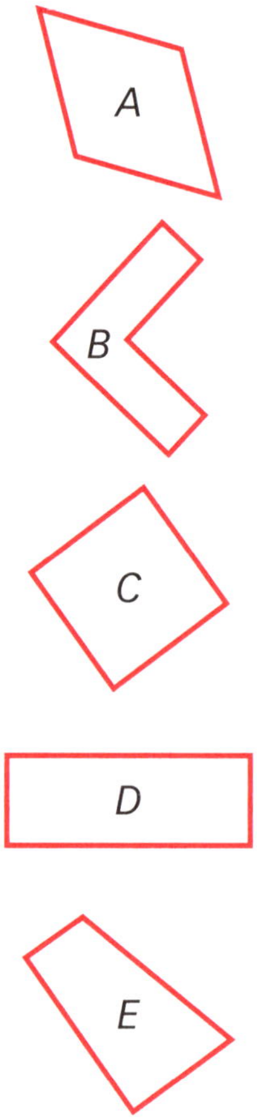

6 I have 4 sides. I am a parallelogram.
I have all square corners.
I am not a square.

I am shape ________ .

I am a __________________________ .

7 I am a quadrilateral.
I do not have any square corners.
My sides are all the same length.

I am shape ________ .

I am a __________________________ .

8 All of my corners are square corners.
Some of my sides are the same length.
I am not a quadrilateral.

I am shape ________ .

I am a __________________________ .

9 Draw a quadrilateral that has at least 3 square corners and 2 pairs of parallel sides. Write all of the possible names for your shape. Tell why the names fit.

____

____

____

____

Name: ____________________

Classify Quadrilaterals

Solve the problems.

1 Which parallelogram is NOT a rectangle?

A

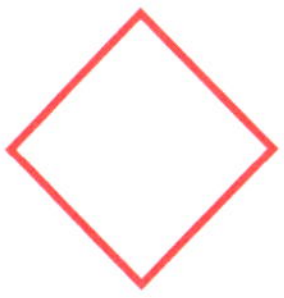

C

B

D

Beth chose **A** as the correct answer. How did she get that answer?

____

____

2 Which of these are attributes of a square? Circle all the correct answers.

A 4 sides and 4 angles

B all sides the same length

C no square corners

D 2 pairs of parallel sides

E opposite sides that are the same length

3 Draw a quadrilateral with 1 pair of parallel sides and no sides the same length.

Solve.

4 Tell whether each sentence is *True* or *False*.

a. All rhombuses are squares. ☐ True ☐ False

b. All squares are rectangles. ☐ True ☐ False

c. All rectangles are parallelograms. ☐ True ☐ False

d. Some quadrilaterals are parallelograms. ☐ True ☐ False

Compare the attributes of both shapes named in each sentence.

5 What one name describes all of these shapes?

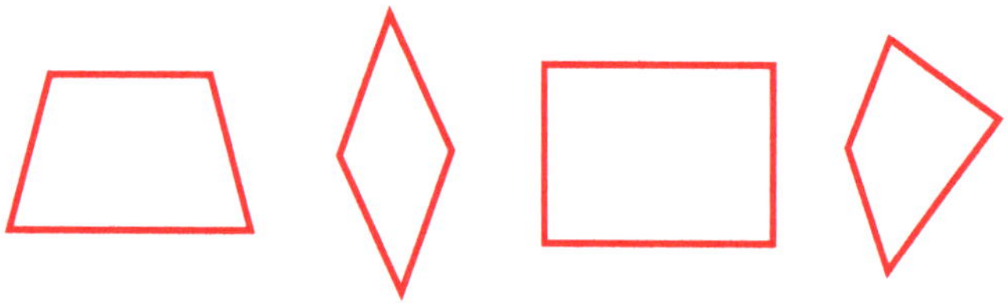

Solution: ______________________________

A shape must have all of the attributes of a kind of shape in order to have its name.

6 Draw a shape that belongs to at least two of these groups: parallelogram, rhombus, or rectangle. Explain why your shape belongs to these groups.

Solution: ______________________________

____

____

____

Think about the attributes of each shape before you draw your shape.

Dear Family,

This week your child is learning about breaking shapes into parts that have equal areas.

Equal parts of a rectangle cover an equal area. Think of these parts as fractions of the whole area.

The parts may have the same shape, or different shapes.

These squares were broken into 4 equal parts. So, the area of one shaded part is $\frac{1}{4}$ of the area of the whole square.

Since all four parts in each square are the same size and shape, each part is $\frac{1}{4}$ of the whole shape.

Here the square was broken into 8 equal parts. So, the area of one part is $\frac{1}{8}$ of the whole.

Invite your child to share what he or she knows about dividing shapes into parts with equal areas by doing the following activity together.

NEXT

Dividing Shapes into Equal Areas Activity

Materials: 2 sheets of paper, crayons or markers

Do this activity with your child to give him or her practice dividing a rectangle into equal parts.

- Work with your child to fold a sheet of paper to make parts with equal areas.
- Begin by helping your child fold a piece of paper in thirds.

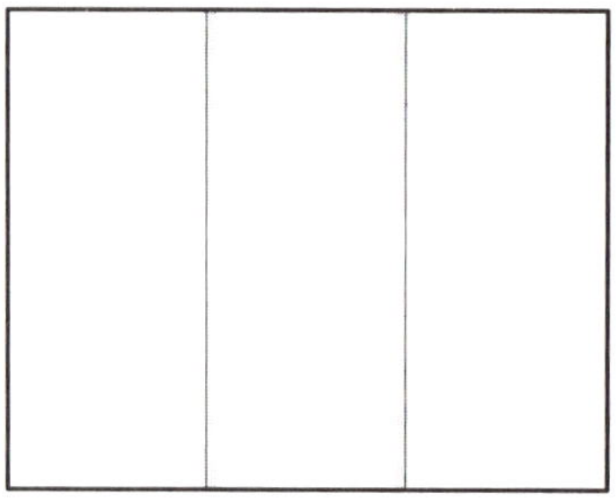

- Guide your child to fold the piece of paper one more time in half.
- Open the sheet of paper. How many equal parts do you see? (6 equal parts)

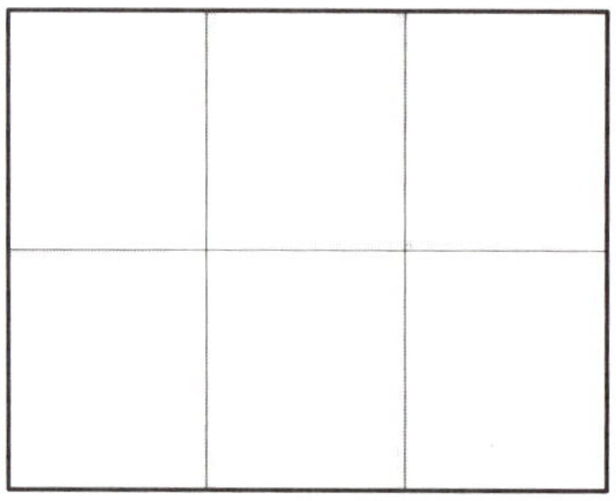

- Have your child name the fraction for one section. ($\frac{1}{6}$) Then, color $\frac{2}{6}$ of the rectangle.
- Now, together fold another sheet of paper in the exact same way.
- Color $\frac{2}{6}$ in a different way.
- Challenge your child to name an equivalent fraction for $\frac{2}{6}$, based on the part of the whole that is colored. ($\frac{1}{3}$ of the rectangle is colored.)

Divide Shapes Into Parts With Equal Areas

Name: ____________________

Prerequisite: Divide Shapes into Two, Three, or Four Equal Parts

Study the example showing how to compare thirds and fourths of the same whole. Then solve problems 1–6.

Example

Mateo and his mom made two same-size rectangular pizzas. They cut one pizza into thirds. They cut the other pizza into fourths. Which pizza has bigger pieces?

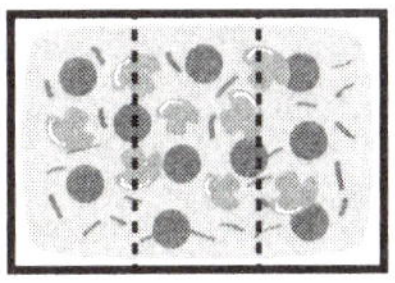

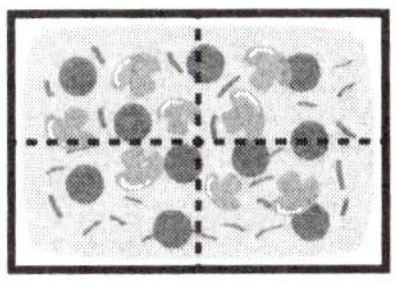

Thirds means 3 equal parts.
Each part is $\frac{1}{3}$ of the whole pizza.

Fourths means 4 equal parts.
Each part is $\frac{1}{4}$ of the whole pizza.

The pizza cut into thirds has bigger pieces. Thirds are fewer parts than fourths. So, thirds take up more space of the same-size whole.

1 Divide this rectangle into 2 equal parts. Then fill in the blank.

Each part is ______ of the whole rectangle.

2 Divide each rectangle into 4 equal parts in different ways. What fraction names each equal part?

____

3 Which rectangle is divided into halves? Explain.

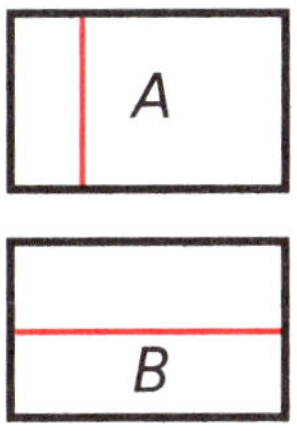

____

____

____

Solve.

4 Divide each rectangle into thirds in a different way.

5 Show three different ways to divide each hexagon into halves.

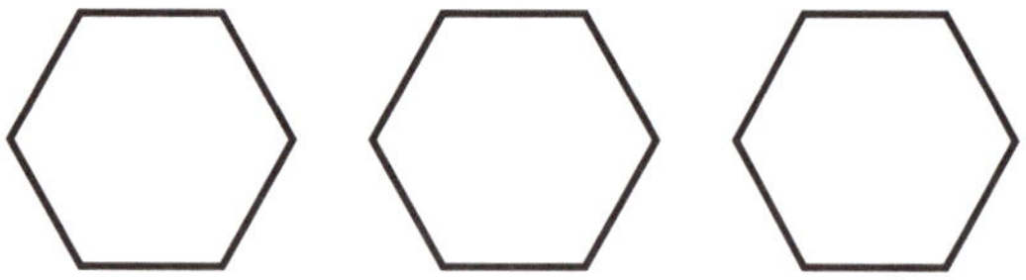

6 Emily drew these rectangles and divided them into 3 parts. She says that since the parts have different shapes, they are not equal. Do you agree? Explain.

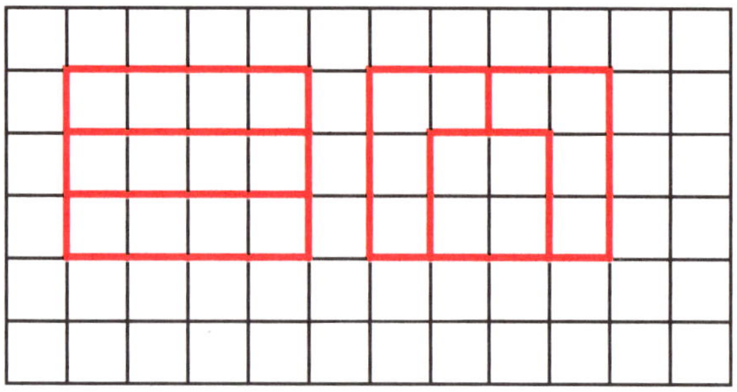

Name: ____________________

Divide Rectangles Into Equal Parts

Study the example problem showing how to divide rectangles into equal parts. Then solve problems 1–10.

Example

Brad and Linda each covered a same-size board with mosaic tiles. Here are the designs they made. What part of Brad's design is red tiles? What part of Linda's design is red tiles?

Brad's Design

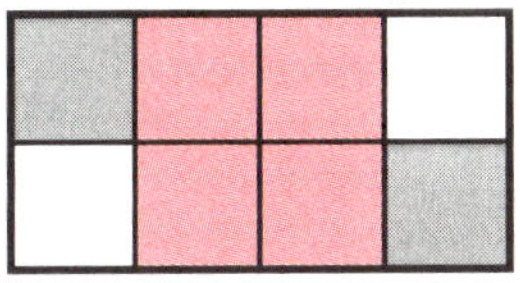

Linda's Design

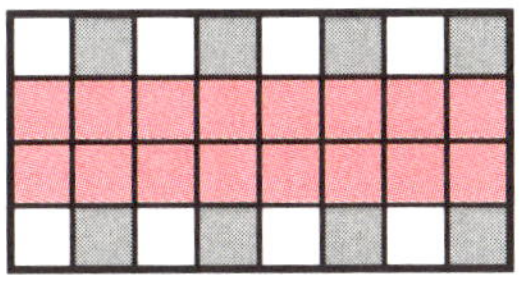

2 rows of 4 tiles = 8 tiles

$\frac{4}{8}$, or $\frac{1}{2}$ of the tiles are red

4 rows of 8 tiles = 32 tiles

$\frac{2}{4}$ of the rows, or $\frac{1}{2}$ of the tiles are red

1 How many equal parts are in rectangle *A*? ______

2 How many rows are in rectangle *A*? ______

3 What fraction of the number of rows is shaded? ______________

A

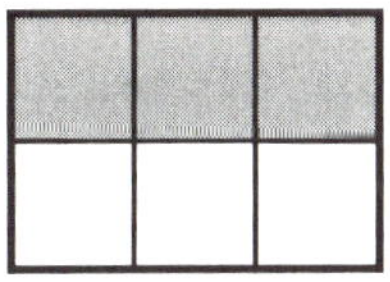

4 Show a different way to divide rectangle *B* into 6 equal parts. What fraction of the whole rectangle is each part?

______

B

5 What fraction of the equal parts in rectangle *C* is shaded? Tell how you know.

____

____

____

C

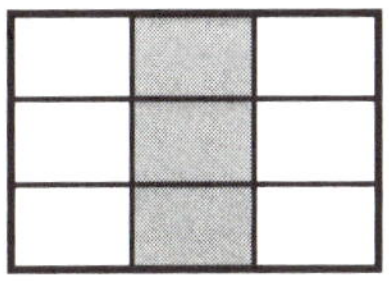

Solve.

6 Square *W* is divided into equal parts. What fraction of the whole square is each part? ______

W

7 Compare squares *X* and *Y*. Tell whether each statement is true or false.

a. $\frac{1}{2}$ of shape *X* is shaded. ☐ True ☐ False

b. $\frac{1}{2}$ of shape *Y* is shaded. ☐ True ☐ False

c. Each row of shape *X* is $\frac{1}{4}$ of the whole square. ☐ True ☐ False

d. Each row of shape *Y* is $\frac{1}{4}$ the whole square. ☐ True ☐ False

X

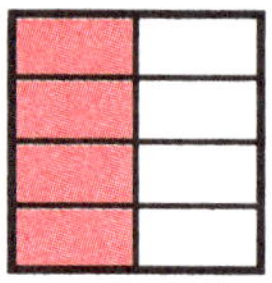

Y

8 Divide rectangle *S* into 4 equal parts and divide rectangle *T* into 8 equal parts.

S

T

9 Shade $\frac{1}{4}$ of each rectangle in problem 8.

10 Show one way to divide this rectangle into 18 equal parts. Then shade $\frac{1}{2}$ or $\frac{1}{3}$ of the rectangle. Tell how you know $\frac{1}{2}$ or $\frac{1}{3}$ of the rectangle is shaded.

____

____

____

____

____

Name: ______________________

Divide Shapes Into Equal Parts

Solve the problems.

1 What fraction of the rectangle is one row?

A $\frac{1}{10}$

B $\frac{1}{5}$

C $\frac{2}{5}$

D $\frac{1}{2}$

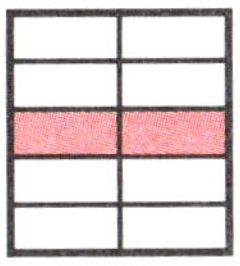

2 A rectangle is divided into 4 rows with 3 equal squares in each row. Each square covers what fraction of the rectangle?

A $\frac{1}{12}$

B $\frac{1}{4}$

C $\frac{1}{3}$

D $\frac{1}{2}$

Bryce chose **B** as the correct answer. How did he get that answer?

____

____

____

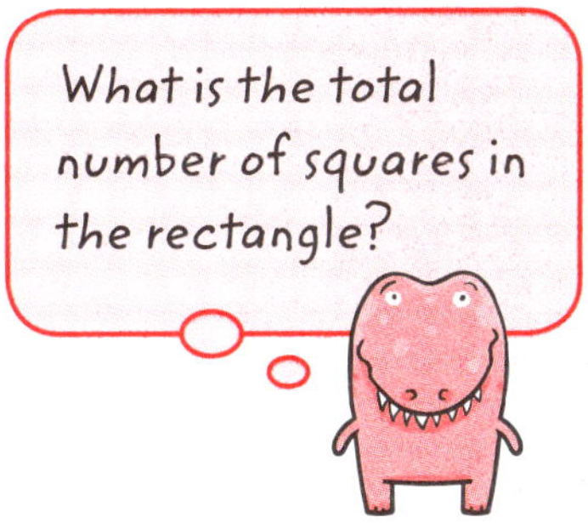

3 A rectangle is divided into equal squares. One row covers $\frac{1}{4}$ of the whole rectangle. Each row has 6 squares. How many squares are in the whole rectangle?

Show your work.

Solution: ______________________________

Solve.

4 Show two different ways to divide these squares into sixths. Then show a different way to shade $\frac{1}{2}$ of each square.

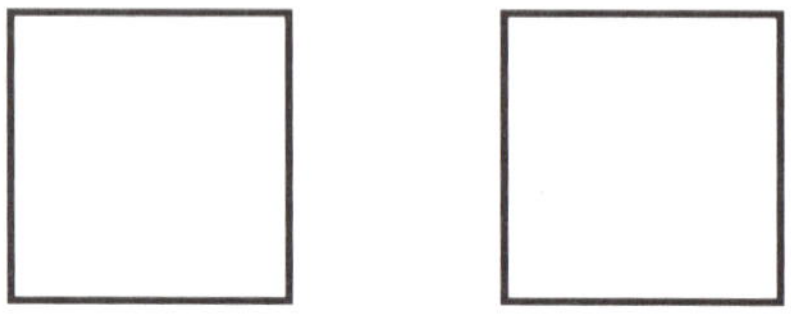

5 Show 3 different ways to divide a rectangle into 24 equal parts.

Make ______ rows of ______ parts.

Make ______ rows of ______ parts.

Make ______ rows of ______ parts.

6 Draw the 3 rectangles you named in problem 5. Shade $\frac{1}{4}$ of one rectangle, $\frac{1}{3}$ of one rectangle, and $\frac{1}{2}$ of one rectangle. Label each with the fraction.

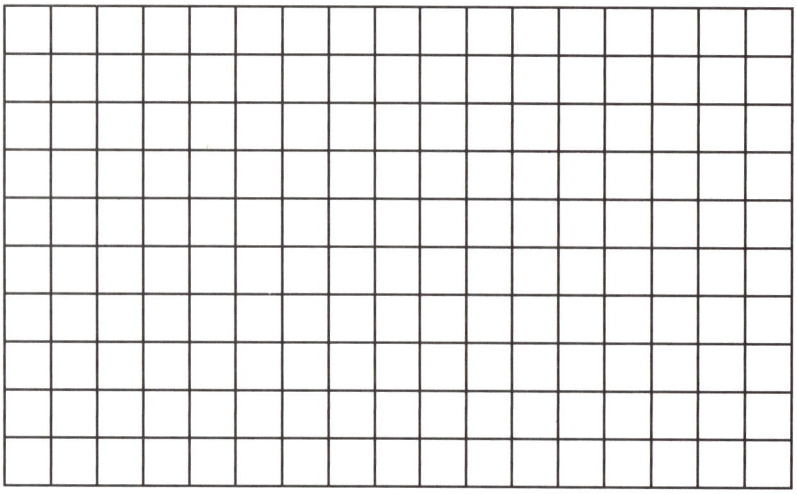

Unit 6 Game

Name: ______________________

Shape Attribute Cover-Up

What you need: Recording Sheet, Game Board (1 for each player), Game Cards, 32 counters (16 for each player)

Directions

- Mix the Game Cards. Place them face down in a pile.
- Take turns. Draw a card. Cover all the remaining shapes on your Game Board that have the attribute on the card with a counter. Place the card in the discard pile.
- Write the attribute on the Recording Sheet. Then draw another shape that has that attribute. Make it different than the shapes you covered.
- If you use all the cards, shuffle the discards and continue playing.
- The first player to cover every shape on the Game Board wins.

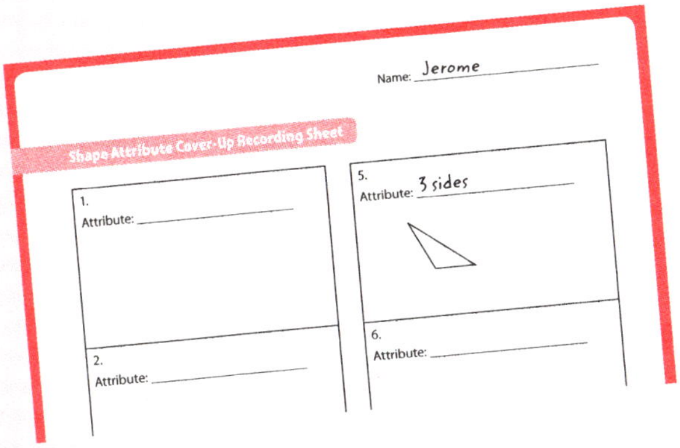

Name: ______________________

Shape Attribute Cover-Up Recording Sheet

1.
Attribute: ______________________

2.
Attribute: ______________________

3.
Attribute: ______________________

4.
Attribute: ______________________

5.
Attribute: ______________________

6.
Attribute: ______________________

7.
Attribute: ______________________

8.
Attribute: ______________________

Shape Attribute Cover-Up

Game Board

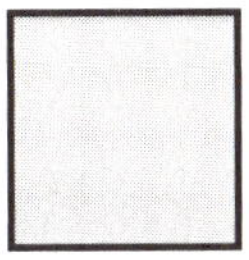 square	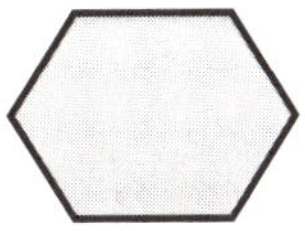 hexagon	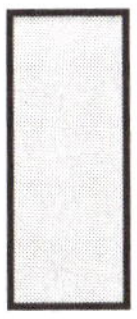 rectangle	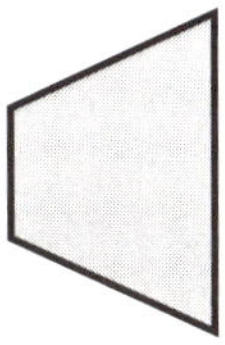 quadrilateral
 pentagon	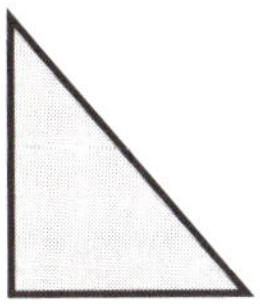 triangle	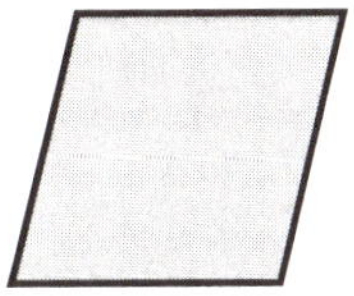 rhombus	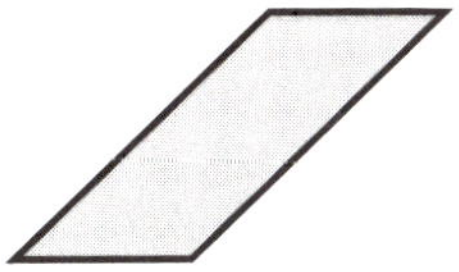 parallelogram
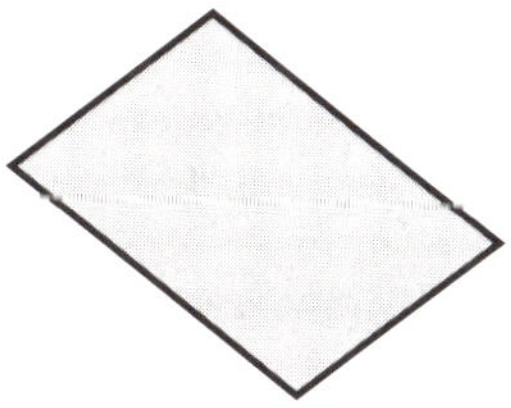 parallelogram	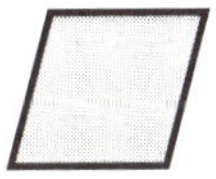 rhombus	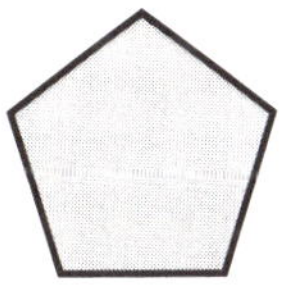 pentagon	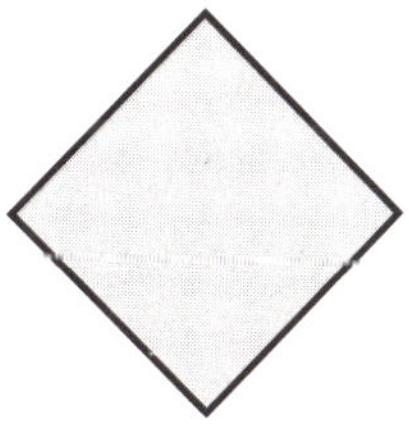 square
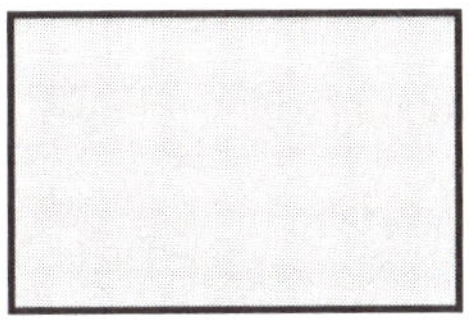 rectangle	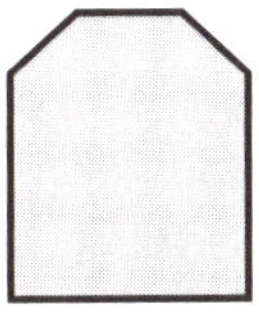 hexagon	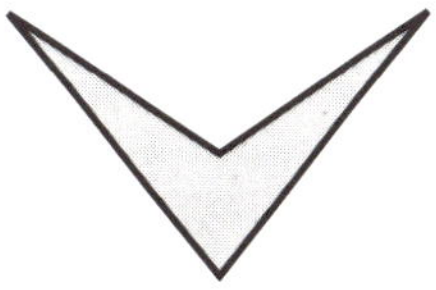 quadrilateral	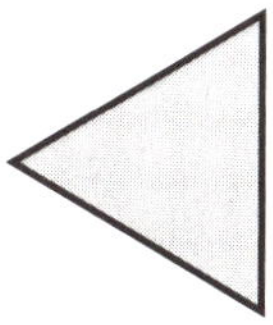 triangle

Shape Attribute Cover-Up

Game Cards

2 square corners	1 square corner	4 square corners	0 square corners
3 sides	0 sides the same length	5 sides	6 sides
exactly 2 pairs of parallel sides	exactly 1 pair of parallel sides	0 pairs of parallel sides	exactly 3 pairs of parallel sides
all sides the same length	exactly 3 sides the same length	exactly 4 sides the same length	exactly 5 sides the same length

Unit 6 Practice

Name: ____________________

Geometry

In this unit you learned to:	Lesson
describe shapes, compare them, and put them in groups that tell how they are alike, for example: by the number of sides or if there are square corners.	31, 32
compare quadrilaterals and put them in groups based on their attributes, for example: all four sides are equal in length or there are two pairs of parallel sides.	32
divide rectangles into equal parts and name the parts using fractions.	33

Use these skills to solve problems 1–6.

1 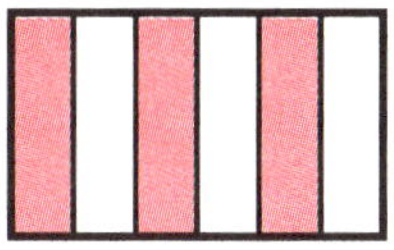

What fraction of the rectangle is each part? ______

What fraction of the rectangle is shaded? ______

2 Name two different groups that both of these shapes belong to.

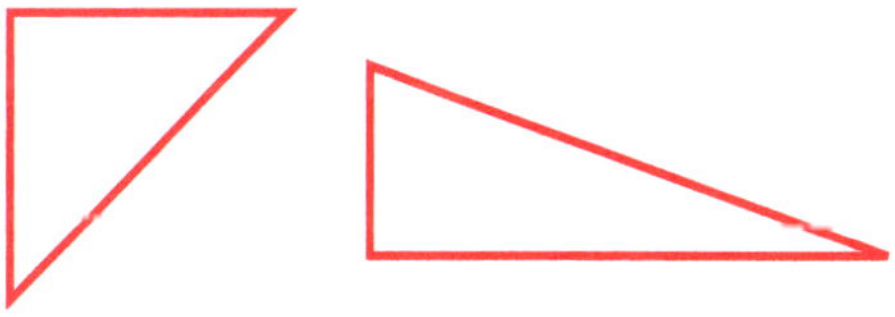

____

____

____

____

____

____

Solve. Use these shapes to solve problems 3–5.

3 I am a quadrilateral with two pairs of parallel sides. All of my sides are not the same length.

Which shape am I? ______________________________

4 Name two attributes that both the square and rectangle have. What are two different names that each shape can be called?

____

____

____

5 Compare the square and rhombus. How are they alike? How are they different? Can one of their names be used to describe both shapes? Explain.

____

____

____

____

6 Draw lines to divide this rectangle to show eighths. Then shade $\frac{1}{2}$ of the rectangle. How many eighths are shaded?

____

Unit 6 Performance Task

Name: ______________________

Answer the questions and show all your work on separate paper.

The third-grade classes in your school are designing a quilt. The quilt will have 9 squares, one for each class. Students want the squares of the quilt to be divided into equal parts. The quilt will be red and yellow, which are the school colors.

Here is your task:

- Draw a diagram to show what the quilt will look like.
- Divide each square into equal parts. Include squares that have 4, 6, and 8 equal parts.
- Color half of each square yellow and half red.
- Describe the design. Use fractions to describe the different squares in your quilt.

Checklist

Did you . . .

- ☐ draw a diagram?
- ☐ include at least one square with 4, 6, and 8 equal parts?
- ☐ use fractions to describe your work?

Reflect on Mathematical Practices

1 **Reason Quantitatively** How did you decide how many parts of each square to make red and yellow?

2 **Use Tools** How can you check that your squares are all divided into equal parts?

Performance Task Tips

Word Bank Here are some words that you might use in your answer.

square	fraction	equal size
half	fourth	sixth
part	eighth	

Models Here is a model that you might use to find a solution.

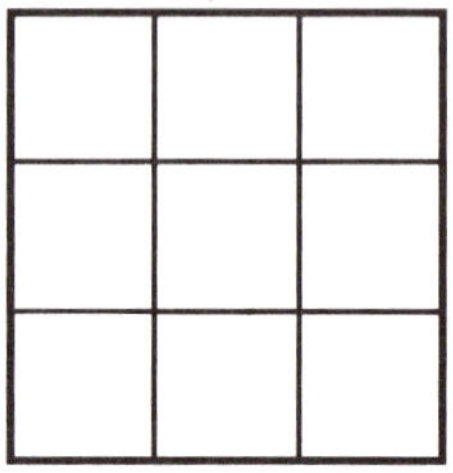

Sentence Starters Here are some sentence starters that might help explain your work.

I divided the square into ______________________________

There are _____ equal parts in ________________________

I colored ______ red and _____ yellow.

Unit 6 Vocabulary

Name: ______________________

My Examples

attribute

a way to describe a shape, like number of sides, or length of sides

quadrilateral

any flat shape with 4 sides and 4 angles

rectangle

a quadrilateral with 4 square corners, 2 pairs of parallel sides, and 2 pairs of sides that are the same length

rhombus

a quadrilateral with 2 pairs of parallel sides and 4 sides that are the same length

My Examples

parallelogram

a quadrilateral with 2 pairs of parallel sides and 2 pairs of sides that are the same length

pentagon

a shape with 5 sides and 5 angles

Venn diagram

a drawing that shows how objects in groups are alike or different

parallel

always the same distance apart

Fluency Table of Contents

Add within 1,000—Skills Practice

Name: ____________________

Add. Regroup if necessary. **Form A**

1 324 + 135	**2** 548 + 314	**3** 253 + 452	**4** 172 + 127	**5** 811 + 96
6 257 + 325	**7** 136 + 61	**8** 564 + 261	**9** 136 + 435	**10** 214 + 214
11 139 + 255	**12** 672 + 121	**13** 188 + 481	**14** 409 + 42	**15** 246 + 138
16 567 + 321	**17** 131 + 182	**18** 412 + 503	**19** 219 + 229	**20** 358 + 436
21 443 + 547	**22** 613 + 43	**23** 172 + 271	**24** 228 + 355	**25** 539 + 190

Add within 1,000—Skills Practice

Name: ____________________

Add. Regroup if necessary. **Form B**

1 $323 + 293$	**2** $148 + 242$	**3** $121 + 456$	**4** $592 + 92$	**5** $253 + 216$
6 $517 + 482$	**7** $674 + 144$	**8** $405 + 375$	**9** $128 + 127$	**10** $234 + 123$
11 $581 + 265$	**12** $447 + 136$	**13** $334 + 595$	**14** $204 + 278$	**15** $111 + 82$
16 $183 + 132$	**17** $571 + 187$	**18** $153 + 144$	**19** $262 + 162$	**20** $347 + 437$
21 $242 + 325$	**22** $610 + 194$	**23** $718 + 78$	**24** $432 + 243$	**25** $519 + 318$

Add within 1,000—Skills Practice

Name: ____________________

Add. Regroup twice if necessary. **Form A**

1 507 + 145	**2** 342 + 647	**3** 184 + 248	**4** 575 + 272	**5** 186 + 365
6 425 + 175	**7** 539 + 374	**8** 246 + 37	**9** 112 + 545	**10** 443 + 263
11 152 + 114	**12** 412 + 432	**13** 253 + 382	**14** 248 + 248	**15** 626 + 89
16 357 + 368	**17** 404 + 107	**18** 137 + 42	**19** 119 + 219	**20** 245 + 254
21 188 + 336	**22** 631 + 283	**23** 192 + 132	**24** 252 + 146	**25** 419 + 382

Add within 1,000—Skills Practice

Name: ______________________

Add. Regroup twice if necessary. **Form B**

1 272 + 242	**2** 269 + 166	**3** 437 + 450	**4** 144 + 192	**5** 128 + 821
6 273 + 378	**7** 175 + 113	**8** 543 + 432	**9** 269 + 69	**10** 354 + 308
11 191 + 471	**12** 225 + 276	**13** 138 + 342	**14** 312 + 444	**15** 137 + 185
16 558 + 158	**17** 121 + 63	**18** 236 + 346	**19** 184 + 675	**20** 136 + 138
21 367 + 477	**22** 103 + 199	**23** 333 + 432	**24** 372 + 32	**25** 159 + 528

Add within 1,000—Repeated Reasoning

Name: ______________________

Find place value patterns with ones and tens.

Set A

1 $101 + 109$

2 $101 + 119$

3 $101 + 129$

4 $201 + 229$

5 $201 + 239$

6 $201 + 249$

7 $301 + 349$

8 $301 + 359$

9 $301 + 369$

10 $401 + 469$

11 $401 + 479$

12 $401 + 489$

Set B

1 401 + 409 = ________

2 401 + 429 = ________

3 402 + 408 = ________

4 402 + 428 = ________

5 403 + 407 = ________

6 403 + 427 = ________

7 404 + 406 = ________

8 404 + 426 = ________

9 405 + 405 = ________

10 405 + 425 = ________

Describe a pattern you see in one of the sets of problems above.

____

____

____

Add within 1,000—Repeated Reasoning

Name: ____________________

Find place value patterns in the hundreds.

Set A

1. $301 + 399$
2. $302 + 398$
3. $303 + 397$
4. $401 + 399$
5. $402 + 398$
6. $403 + 397$
7. $501 + 399$
8. $502 + 398$
9. $503 + 397$

Set B

1. $290 + 210$
2. $280 + 220$
3. $270 + 230$
4. $360 + 340$
5. $350 + 350$
6. $340 + 360$
7. $430 + 470$
8. $420 + 480$
9. $410 + 490$

Describe a pattern you see in one of the sets of problems above.

____

____

____

Subtract within 1,000—Skills Practice

Name: ____________________

Subtract. Regroup if necessary. **Form A**

1 525 − 175	**2** 463 − 251	**3** 317 − 224	**4** 692 − 188	**5** 777 − 543
6 316 − 208	**7** 558 − 62	**8** 634 − 217	**9** 986 − 410	**10** 376 − 158
11 615 − 232	**12** 363 − 131	**13** 820 − 450	**14** 755 − 728	**15** 219 − 158
16 199 − 37	**17** 548 − 514	**18** 560 − 225	**19** 463 − 217	**20** 689 − 299
21 848 − 364	**22** 394 − 145	**23** 870 − 220	**24** 285 − 28	**25** 426 − 193

Subtract within 1,000—Skills Practice

Name: ______________________

Subtract. Regroup if necessary. **Form B**

1 462 − 124	**2** 590 − 340	**3** 359 − 165	**4** 151 − 23	**5** 616 − 552
6 512 − 206	**7** 683 − 542	**8** 294 − 227	**9** 837 − 144	**10** 765 − 255
11 862 − 680	**12** 166 − 71	**13** 999 − 678	**14** 491 − 119	**15** 263 − 105
16 254 − 153	**17** 418 − 64	**18** 784 − 715	**19** 399 − 75	**20** 525 − 250
21 656 − 574	**22** 894 − 361	**23** 413 − 208	**24** 639 − 193	**25** 574 − 236

Subtract within 1,000—Skills Practice

Name: ______________________

Subtract. Regroup twice if necessary.

Form A

1 228 − 194	**2** 615 − 306	**3** 321 − 76	**4** 426 − 115	**5** 846 − 275
6 454 − 127	**7** 987 − 36	**8** 341 − 149	**9** 510 − 250	**10** 258 − 236
11 535 − 137	**12** 466 − 383	**13** 652 − 167	**14** 342 − 132	**15** 573 − 37
16 270 − 244	**17** 751 − 283	**18** 305 − 103	**19** 486 − 93	**20** 765 − 345
21 588 − 370	**22** 329 − 152	**23** 142 − 66	**24** 435 − 219	**25** 853 − 299

Subtract within 1,000—Skills Practice

Name: ______________________

Subtract. Regroup twice if necessary. **Form B**

1 384 − 317	**2** 581 − 92	**3** 480 − 120	**4** 516 − 284	**5** 654 − 432
6 440 − 176	**7** 255 − 123	**8** 629 − 361	**9** 762 − 155	**10** 374 − 288
11 598 − 43	**12** 388 − 139	**13** 555 − 199	**14** 625 − 167	**15** 454 − 380
16 333 − 284	**17** 948 − 73	**18** 459 − 244	**19** 572 − 152	**20** 843 − 482
21 442 − 134	**22** 639 − 413	**23** 867 − 676	**24** 191 − 103	**25** 546 − 69

Subtract within 1,000—Skills Practice

Name: ____________________

Subtract across zeros. **Form A**

1 302 − 143	**2** 505 − 228	**3** 400 − 222	**4** 180 − 126	**5** 600 − 385
6 704 − 372	**7** 300 − 114	**8** 508 − 459	**9** 800 − 65	**10** 206 − 108
11 200 − 112	**12** 803 − 44	**13** 500 − 125	**14** 301 − 142	**15** 450 − 226
16 701 − 78	**17** 160 − 116	**18** 302 − 94	**19** 900 − 470	**20** 200 − 122
21 600 − 305	**22** 404 − 266	**23** 300 − 137	**24** 707 − 378	**25** 209 − 129

Subtract within 1,000—Skills Practice

Name: ____________________

Subtract across zeros. **Form B**

1 206 − 118	**2** 300 − 146	**3** 500 − 230	**4** 600 − 282	**5** 205 − 126
6 500 − 68	**7** 303 − 82	**8** 704 − 397	**9** 407 − 139	**10** 200 − 104
11 306 − 229	**12** 504 − 386	**13** 900 − 555	**14** 400 − 230	**15** 601 − 43
16 400 − 147	**17** 102 − 68	**18** 700 − 375	**19** 608 − 194	**20** 302 − 184
21 204 − 162	**22** 500 − 111	**23** 800 − 83	**24** 305 − 199	**25** 603 − 385

Subtract within 1,000—Repeated Reasoning

Name: ______________________

Find patterns subtracting 1.

Set A

1 $97 - 1 =$ ________

2 $697 - 1 =$ ________

3 $98 - 1 =$ ________

4 $698 - 1 =$ ________

5 $99 - 1 =$ ________

6 $699 - 1 =$ ________

7 $100 - 1 =$ ________

8 $700 - 1 =$ ________

9 $101 - 1 =$ ________

10 $701 - 1 =$ ________

11 $102 - 1 =$ ________

12 $702 - 1 =$ ________

Set B

1 $100 - 1 =$ ________

2 $500 - 1 =$ ________

3 $200 - 1 =$ ________

4 $600 - 1 =$ ________

5 $300 - 1 =$ ________

6 $700 - 1 =$ ________

7 $400 - 1 =$ ________

8 $800 - 1 =$ ________

Describe a pattern you see in one of the sets of problems above.

____

____

Subtract within 1,000—Repeated Reasoning

Name: ____________________

Find place value patterns.

Set A

1. $97 - 2 =$ ______
2. $597 - 2 =$ ______
3. $98 - 2 =$ ______
4. $598 - 2 =$ ______
5. $99 - 2 =$ ______
6. $599 - 2 =$ ______
7. $100 - 2 =$ ______
8. $600 - 2 =$ ______
9. $101 - 2 =$ ______
10. $601 - 2 =$ ______

Set B

1. $200 - 100$
2. $400 - 100$
3. $700 - 100$
4. $200 - 101$
5. $400 - 101$
6. $700 - 101$
7. $200 - 102$
8. $400 - 102$
9. $700 - 102$
10. $200 - 103$
11. $400 - 103$
12. $700 - 103$

Describe a pattern you see in one of the sets of problems above.

____

____

Multiplication Facts—Skills Practice

Name: ______________________

Practice facts up to 5 × 5. **Form A**

1. $2 \times 2 =$ ______
2. $5 \times 4 =$ ______
3. $1 \times 3 =$ ______
4. $5 \times 3 =$ ______
5. $3 \times 3 =$ ______
6. $4 \times 2 =$ ______
7. $5 \times 5 =$ ______
8. $2 \times 3 =$ ______
9. $3 \times 4 =$ ______
10. $2 \times 5 =$ ______
11. $3 \times 2 =$ ______
12. $4 \times 5 =$ ______
13. $3 \times 4 =$ ______
14. $0 \times 0 =$ ______
15. $5 \times 1 =$ ______
16. $4 \times 4 =$ ______
17. $4 \times 5 =$ ______
18. $5 \times 5 =$ ______
19. $2 \times 4 =$ ______
20. $4 \times 4 =$ ______
21. $3 \times 3 =$ ______
22. $5 \times 4 =$ ______
23. $4 \times 3 =$ ______
24. $2 \times 2 =$ ______
25. $5 \times 3 =$ ______
26. $4 \times 4 =$ ______
27. $3 \times 5 =$ ______
28. $2 \times 3 =$ ______
29. $4 \times 3 =$ ______
30. $2 \times 5 =$ ______
31. $4 \times 2 =$ ______
32. $3 \times 5 =$ ______
33. $5 \times 2 =$ ______
34. $4 \times 5 =$ ______
35. $0 \times 2 =$ ______
36. $4 \times 3 =$ ______
37. $2 \times 4 =$ ______
38. $5 \times 2 =$ ______
39. $3 \times 2 =$ ______
40. $4 \times 0 =$ ______
41. $5 \times 3 =$ ______
42. $3 \times 4 =$ ______

Multiplication Facts—Skills Practice

Name: ____________

Practice facts up to 5 × 5. **Form B**

1 $5 \times 2 =$ ____	**2** $3 \times 4 =$ ____	**3** $4 \times 5 =$ ____
4 $2 \times 5 =$ ____	**5** $3 \times 3 =$ ____	**6** $2 \times 3 =$ ____
7 $5 \times 4 =$ ____	**8** $4 \times 3 =$ ____	**9** $3 \times 3 =$ ____
10 $2 \times 5 =$ ____	**11** $5 \times 3 =$ ____	**12** $3 \times 5 =$ ____
13 $2 \times 2 =$ ____	**14** $5 \times 4 =$ ____	**15** $4 \times 4 =$ ____
16 $1 \times 1 =$ ____	**17** $4 \times 3 =$ ____	**18** $0 \times 5 =$ ____
19 $4 \times 5 =$ ____	**20** $2 \times 3 =$ ____	**21** $4 \times 3 =$ ____
22 $2 \times 4 =$ ____	**23** $4 \times 2 =$ ____	**24** $5 \times 5 =$ ____
25 $5 \times 3 =$ ____	**26** $2 \times 2 =$ ____	**27** $4 \times 1 =$ ____
28 $3 \times 2 =$ ____	**29** $5 \times 5 =$ ____	**30** $3 \times 0 =$ ____
31 $3 \times 5 =$ ____	**32** $4 \times 2 =$ ____	**33** $4 \times 5 =$ ____
34 $5 \times 2 =$ ____	**35** $3 \times 2 =$ ____	**36** $4 \times 3 =$ ____
37 $4 \times 4 =$ ____	**38** $3 \times 5 =$ ____	**39** $2 \times 4 =$ ____
40 $4 \times 3 =$ ____	**41** $0 \times 0 =$ ____	**42** $2 \times 2 =$ ____

Multiplication Facts—Skills Practice

Name: ____________________

Multiply by 2, 5, and 10.

Form A

1 $5 \times 6 =$ _______	**2** $9 \times 5 =$ _______	**3** $10 \times 2 =$ _______
4 $9 \times 2 =$ _______	**5** $10 \times 6 =$ _______	**6** $4 \times 5 =$ _______
7 $2 \times 8 =$ _______	**8** $10 \times 4 =$ _______	**9** $3 \times 5 =$ _______
10 $9 \times 10 =$ _______	**11** $8 \times 5 =$ _______	**12** $2 \times 9 =$ _______
13 $5 \times 5 =$ _______	**14** $6 \times 2 =$ _______	**15** $8 \times 2 =$ _______
16 $10 \times 0 =$ _______	**17** $7 \times 2 =$ _______	**18** $2 \times 4 =$ _______
19 $10 \times 8 =$ _______	**20** $2 \times 3 =$ _______	**21** $5 \times 10 =$ _______
22 $3 \times 10 =$ _______	**23** $5 \times 2 =$ _______	**24** $10 \times 5 =$ _______
25 $2 \times 5 =$ _______	**26** $5 \times 8 =$ _______	**27** $2 \times 2 =$ _______
28 $5 \times 9 =$ _______	**29** $7 \times 10 =$ _______	**30** $10 \times 10 =$ _______
31 $10 \times 9 =$ _______	**32** $2 \times 6 =$ _______	**33** $6 \times 5 =$ _______
34 $10 \times 3 =$ _______	**35** $5 \times 3 =$ _______	**36** $5 \times 7 =$ _______
37 $2 \times 10 =$ _______	**38** $7 \times 5 =$ _______	**39** $10 \times 7 =$ _______
40 $6 \times 10 =$ _______	**41** $1 \times 5 =$ _______	**42** $4 \times 2 =$ _______

Multiplication Facts—Skills Practice

Name: ____________________

Multiply by 2, 5, and 10. **Form B**

1 $3 \times 2 =$ ______	**2** $5 \times 8 =$ ______	**3** $7 \times 10 =$ ______
4 $2 \times 6 =$ ______	**5** $2 \times 8 =$ ______	**6** $8 \times 5 =$ ______
7 $10 \times 5 =$ ______	**8** $5 \times 3 =$ ______	**9** $10 \times 10 =$ ______
10 $0 \times 2 =$ ______	**11** $5 \times 4 =$ ______	**12** $4 \times 10 =$ ______
13 $10 \times 7 =$ ______	**14** $2 \times 7 =$ ______	**15** $2 \times 10 =$ ______
16 $4 \times 2 =$ ______	**17** $6 \times 5 =$ ______	**18** $10 \times 9 =$ ______
19 $7 \times 5 =$ ______	**20** $9 \times 5 =$ ______	**21** $2 \times 3 =$ ______
22 $2 \times 9 =$ ______	**23** $5 \times 9 =$ ______	**24** $2 \times 10 =$ ______
25 $5 \times 2 =$ ______	**26** $10 \times 1 =$ ______	**27** $10 \times 3 =$ ______
28 $5 \times 5 =$ ______	**29** $9 \times 2 =$ ______	**30** $8 \times 10 =$ ______
31 $6 \times 10 =$ ______	**32** $5 \times 6 =$ ______	**33** $3 \times 5 =$ ______
34 $4 \times 5 =$ ______	**35** $2 \times 4 =$ ______	**36** $9 \times 10 =$ ______
37 $10 \times 6 =$ ______	**38** $5 \times 7 =$ ______	**39** $2 \times 5 =$ ______
40 $8 \times 2 =$ ______	**41** $7 \times 2 =$ ______	**42** $5 \times 10 =$ ______

Multiplication Facts—Skills Practice

Name: ____________________

Multiply by 3, 4, 6, 7, 8, and 9

Form A

1 $8 \times 3 =$ ______	**2** $6 \times 5 =$ ______	**3** $9 \times 6 =$ ______
4 $4 \times 3 =$ ______	**5** $7 \times 7 =$ ______	**6** $10 \times 8 =$ ______
7 $6 \times 7 =$ ______	**8** $8 \times 5 =$ ______	**9** $7 \times 8 =$ ______
10 $2 \times 7 =$ ______	**11** $10 \times 3 =$ ______	**12** $4 \times 4 =$ ______
13 $8 \times 8 =$ ______	**14** $3 \times 5 =$ ______	**15** $6 \times 9 =$ ______
16 $9 \times 2 =$ ______	**17** $0 \times 7 =$ ______	**18** $9 \times 8 =$ ______
19 $10 \times 9 =$ ______	**20** $8 \times 7 =$ ______	**21** $5 \times 4 =$ ______
22 $3 \times 3 =$ ______	**23** $9 \times 4 =$ ______	**24** $6 \times 1 =$ ______
25 $7 \times 9 =$ ______	**26** $4 \times 6 =$ ______	**27** $9 \times 9 =$ ______
28 $1 \times 4 =$ ______	**29** $7 \times 10 =$ ______	**30** $4 \times 8 =$ ______
31 $6 \times 2 =$ ______	**32** $9 \times 5 =$ ______	**33** $8 \times 6 =$ ______
34 $9 \times 7 =$ ______	**35** $6 \times 6 =$ ______	**36** $3 \times 7 =$ ______
37 $8 \times 9 =$ ______	**38** $5 \times 7 =$ ______	**39** $6 \times 3 =$ ______
40 $7 \times 4 =$ ______	**41** $6 \times 10 =$ ______	**42** $3 \times 9 =$ ______

Multiplication Facts—Skills Practice

Name: ____________________

Multiply by 3, 4, 6, 7, 8, and 9

Form B

1 $6 \times 6 =$ ______	2 $3 \times 4 =$ ______	3 $7 \times 9 =$ ______
4 $7 \times 3 =$ ______	5 $5 \times 6 =$ ______	6 $0 \times 3 =$ ______
7 $7 \times 8 =$ ______	8 $2 \times 4 =$ ______	9 $7 \times 7 =$ ______
10 $3 \times 3 =$ ______	11 $6 \times 4 =$ ______	12 $5 \times 8 =$ ______
13 $9 \times 7 =$ ______	14 $8 \times 2 =$ ______	15 $4 \times 7 =$ ______
16 $10 \times 4 =$ ______	17 $3 \times 8 =$ ______	18 $9 \times 6 =$ ______
19 $8 \times 8 =$ ______	20 $9 \times 10 =$ ______	21 $5 \times 3 =$ ______
22 $7 \times 5 =$ ______	23 $9 \times 8 =$ ______	24 $10 \times 6 =$ ______
25 $3 \times 6 =$ ______	26 $5 \times 9 =$ ______	27 $8 \times 7 =$ ______
28 $4 \times 9 =$ ______	29 $8 \times 0 =$ ______	30 $3 \times 10 =$ ______
31 $7 \times 6 =$ ______	32 $2 \times 9 =$ ______	33 $9 \times 3 =$ ______
34 $10 \times 6 =$ ______	35 $8 \times 9 =$ ______	36 $6 \times 9 =$ ______
37 $6 \times 8 =$ ______	38 $4 \times 4 =$ ______	39 $9 \times 1 =$ ______
40 $9 \times 9 =$ ______	41 $8 \times 4 =$ ______	42 $4 \times 5 =$ ______

Multiplication Facts—Skills Practice

Name: ______________________

Practice facts up to 10 × 10. **Form A**

1 $3 \times 5 =$ ______	2 $6 \times 7 =$ ______	3 $10 \times 10 =$ ______
4 $4 \times 9 =$ ______	5 $8 \times 6 =$ ______	6 $6 \times 4 =$ ______
7 $4 \times 2 =$ ______	8 $7 \times 7 =$ ______	9 $2 \times 3 =$ ______
10 $7 \times 8 =$ ______	11 $1 \times 1 =$ ______	12 $2 \times 8 =$ ______
13 $6 \times 6 =$ ______	14 $10 \times 5 =$ ______	15 $3 \times 7 =$ ______
16 $5 \times 8 =$ ______	17 $9 \times 9 =$ ______	18 $3 \times 3 =$ ______
19 $7 \times 4 =$ ______	20 $5 \times 2 =$ ______	21 $9 \times 5 =$ ______
22 $2 \times 2 =$ ______	23 $8 \times 3 =$ ______	24 $2 \times 6 =$ ______
25 $9 \times 3 =$ ______	26 $1 \times 7 =$ ______	27 $5 \times 4 =$ ______
28 $7 \times 5 =$ ______	29 $4 \times 4 =$ ______	30 $3 \times 6 =$ ______
31 $8 \times 8 =$ ______	32 $6 \times 9 =$ ______	33 $7 \times 2 =$ ______
34 $2 \times 9 =$ ______	35 $8 \times 9 =$ ______	36 $4 \times 3 =$ ______
37 $5 \times 5 =$ ______	38 $4 \times 8 =$ ______	39 $10 \times 1 =$ ______
40 $9 \times 7 =$ ______	41 $5 \times 6 =$ ______	42 $0 \times 8 =$ ______

Multiplication Facts—Skills Practice

Name: ____________________

Practice facts up to 10 × 10. **Form B**

1 $5 \times 9 =$ ______	2 $6 \times 2 =$ ______	3 $3 \times 4 =$ ______
4 $2 \times 2 =$ ______	5 $4 \times 7 =$ ______	6 $6 \times 8 =$ ______
7 $3 \times 8 =$ ______	8 $9 \times 6 =$ ______	9 $3 \times 3 =$ ______
10 $8 \times 8 =$ ______	11 $3 \times 2 =$ ______	12 $1 \times 1 =$ ______
13 $3 \times 9 =$ ______	14 $4 \times 5 =$ ______	15 $8 \times 7 =$ ______
16 $7 \times 6 =$ ______	17 $8 \times 4 =$ ______	18 $8 \times 1 =$ ______
19 $9 \times 2 =$ ______	20 $6 \times 6 =$ ______	21 $8 \times 2 =$ ______
22 $6 \times 3 =$ ______	23 $10 \times 10 =$ ______	24 $4 \times 0 =$ ______
25 $9 \times 8 =$ ______	26 $5 \times 5 =$ ______	27 $4 \times 2 =$ ______
28 $4 \times 4 =$ ______	29 $1 \times 10 =$ ______	30 $8 \times 5 =$ ______
31 $4 \times 6 =$ ______	32 $2 \times 5 =$ ______	33 $7 \times 9 =$ ______
34 $10 \times 9 =$ ______	35 $9 \times 9 =$ ______	36 $2 \times 7 =$ ______
37 $7 \times 3 =$ ______	38 $4 \times 9 =$ ______	39 $6 \times 5 =$ ______
40 $7 \times 7 =$ ______	41 $5 \times 7 =$ ______	42 $3 \times 5 =$ ______

Multiplication Facts—Skills Practice

Name: ______________________________

Practice more facts up to 10 × 10.

Form A

1 5×5	**2** 8×3	**3** 6×9	**4** 2×7	**5** 3×6	**6** 7×4
7 9×7	**8** 8×6	**9** 6×4	**10** 3×3	**11** 9×8	**12** 5×3
13 4×5	**14** 7×7	**15** 5×6	**16** 9×3	**17** 4×4	**18** 6×10
19 9×5	**20** 6×7	**21** 2×8	**22** 0×0	**23** 4×9	**24** 8×8
25 6×6	**26** 4×8	**27** 3×7	**28** 10×10	**29** 8×5	**30** 9×2
31 2×6	**32** 9×9	**33** 1×9	**34** 7×8	**35** 4×3	**36** 7×5

Multiplication Facts—Skills Practice

Name: ______________________________

Practice more facts up to 10 × 10. **Form B**

1 7×3	**2** 8×2	**3** 4×4	**4** 5×9	**5** 8×7	**6** 3×4
7 10×0	**8** 6×8	**9** 4×2	**10** 3×9	**11** 2×5	**12** 4×7
13 8×9	**14** 6×1	**15** 5×8	**16** 2×9	**17** 4×6	**18** 8×8
19 5×4	**20** 6×3	**21** 7×6	**22** 9×9	**23** 5×7	**24** 3×8
25 9×6	**26** 7×7	**27** 8×4	**28** 10×7	**29** 6×5	**30** 2×3
31 6×6	**32** 10×10	**33** 7×9	**34** 5×5	**35** 9×4	**36** 7×2

Multiplication Facts—Repeated Reasoning

Name: ____________________

Find patterns with 4s facts.

Set A

1 $2 \times 1 =$ ______ 2 $2 \times 2 \times 1 =$ ______ 3 $4 \times 1 =$ ______

4 $2 \times 2 =$ ______ 5 $2 \times 2 \times 2 =$ ______ 6 $4 \times 2 =$ ______

7 $2 \times 3 =$ ______ 8 $2 \times 2 \times 3 =$ ______ 9 $4 \times 3 =$ ______

10 $2 \times 4 =$ ______ 11 $2 \times 2 \times 4 =$ ______ 12 $4 \times 4 =$ ______

13 $2 \times 5 =$ ______ 14 $2 \times 2 \times 5 =$ ______ 15 $4 \times 5 =$ ______

Set B

1 $6 \times 2 =$ ______ 2 $(6 \times 2) + (6 \times 2) =$ ______ 3 $6 \times 4 =$ ______

4 $7 \times 2 =$ ______ 5 $(7 \times 2) + (7 \times 2) =$ ______ 6 $7 \times 4 =$ ______

7 $8 \times 2 =$ ______ 8 $(8 \times 2) + (8 \times 2) =$ ______ 9 $8 \times 4 =$ ______

10 $9 \times 2 =$ ______ 11 $(9 \times 2) + (9 \times 2) =$ ______ 12 $9 \times 4 =$ ______

13 $10 \times 2 =$ ______ 14 $(10 \times 2) + (10 \times 2) =$ ______ 15 $10 \times 4 =$ ______

Describe a pattern you see in one of the sets of problems above.

____

____

____

Multiplication Facts—Repeated Reasoning

Name: ____________________

Find patterns with 3s facts.

Set A

1 $2 \times 1 =$ ______	2 $3 \times 1 =$ ______	3 $(2 \times 1) + 1 =$ ______
4 $2 \times 2 =$ ______	5 $3 \times 2 =$ ______	6 $(2 \times 2) + 2 =$ ______
7 $2 \times 3 =$ ______	8 $3 \times 3 =$ ______	9 $(2 \times 3) + 3 =$ ______
10 $2 \times 4 =$ ______	11 $3 \times 4 =$ ______	12 $(2 \times 4) + 4 =$ ______
13 $2 \times 5 =$ ______	14 $3 \times 5 =$ ______	15 $(2 \times 5) + 5 =$ ______

Set B

1 $6 \times 2 =$ ______	2 $(6 \times 2) + 6 =$ ______	3 $6 \times 3 =$ ______
4 $7 \times 2 =$ ______	5 $(7 \times 2) + 7 =$ ______	6 $7 \times 3 =$ ______
7 $8 \times 2 =$ ______	8 $(8 \times 2) + 8 =$ ______	9 $8 \times 3 =$ ______
10 $9 \times 2 =$ ______	11 $(9 \times 2) + 9 =$ ______	12 $9 \times 3 =$ ______
13 $10 \times 2 =$ ______	14 $(10 \times 2) + 10 =$ ______	15 $10 \times 3 =$ ______

Describe a pattern you see in one of the sets of problems above.

____

____

____

Multiplication Facts—Repeated Reasoning

Name: ____________________

Find patterns with 9s facts.

Set A

1 $10 \times 1 =$ ______ 2 $9 \times 1 =$ ______ 3 $(10 \times 1) - 1 =$ ______

4 $10 \times 2 =$ ______ 5 $9 \times 2 =$ ______ 6 $(10 \times 2) - 2 =$ ______

7 $10 \times 3 =$ ______ 8 $9 \times 3 =$ ______ 9 $(10 \times 3) - 3 =$ ______

10 $10 \times 4 =$ ______ 11 $9 \times 4 =$ ______ 12 $(10 \times 4) - 4 =$ ______

13 $10 \times 5 =$ ______ 14 $9 \times 5 =$ ______ 15 $(10 \times 5) - 5 =$ ______

Set B

1 $6 \times 10 =$ ______ 2 $(10 \times 6) - 6 =$ ______ 3 $6 \times 9 =$ ______

4 $7 \times 10 =$ ______ 5 $(10 \times 7) - 7 =$ ______ 6 $7 \times 9 =$ ______

7 $8 \times 10 =$ ______ 8 $(10 \times 8) - 8 =$ ______ 9 $8 \times 9 =$ ______

10 $9 \times 10 =$ ______ 11 $(10 \times 9) - 9 =$ ______ 12 $9 \times 9 =$ ______

13 $10 \times 10 =$ ______ 14 $(10 \times 10) - 10 =$ ______ 15 $10 \times 9 =$ ______

Describe a pattern you see in one of the sets of problems above.

____

____

____

Multiplication Facts—Repeated Reasoning

Name: ______________________

Find patterns with 6s facts.

Set A

1 $5 \times 1 =$ ______	2 $6 \times 1 =$ ______	3 $(6 \times 1) + 1 =$ ______
4 $5 \times 2 =$ ______	5 $6 \times 2 =$ ______	6 $(6 \times 2) + 2 =$ ______
7 $5 \times 3 =$ ______	8 $6 \times 3 =$ ______	9 $(6 \times 3) + 3 =$ ______
10 $5 \times 4 =$ ______	11 $6 \times 4 =$ ______	12 $(6 \times 4) + 4 =$ ______
13 $5 \times 5 =$ ______	14 $6 \times 5 =$ ______	15 $(6 \times 5) + 5 =$ ______

Set B

1 $6 \times 5 =$ ______	2 $(6 \times 5) + 6 =$ ______	3 $6 \times 6 =$ ______
4 $7 \times 5 =$ ______	5 $(7 \times 5) + 7 =$ ______	6 $7 \times 6 =$ ______
7 $8 \times 5 =$ ______	8 $(8 \times 5) + 8 =$ ______	9 $8 \times 6 =$ ______
10 $9 \times 5 =$ ______	11 $(9 \times 5) + 9 =$ ______	12 $9 \times 6 =$ ______
13 $10 \times 5 =$ ______	14 $(10 \times 5) + 10 =$ ______	15 $10 \times 6 =$ ______

Describe a pattern you see in one of the sets of problems above.

____

____

____

Division Facts—Skills Practice

Name: ____________________

Divide up to 25 ÷ 5. **Form A**

1 $16 \div 4 =$ ______	**2** $12 \div 3 =$ ______	**3** $6 \div 3 =$ ______
4 $8 \div 2 =$ ______	**5** $20 \div 5 =$ ______	**6** $9 \div 3 =$ ______
7 $15 \div 3 =$ ______	**8** $4 \div 2 =$ ______	**9** $0 \div 3 =$ ______
10 $10 \div 2 =$ ______	**11** $15 \div 5 =$ ______	**12** $4 \div 4 =$ ______
13 $12 \div 4 =$ ______	**14** $6 \div 2 =$ ______	**15** $10 \div 5 =$ ______
16 $8 \div 4 =$ ______	**17** $20 \div 4 =$ ______	**18** $5 \div 1 =$ ______
19 $15 \div 3 =$ ______	**20** $12 \div 4 =$ ______	**21** $16 \div 4 =$ ______
22 $10 \div 2 =$ ______	**23** $25 \div 5 =$ ______	**24** $0 \div 2 =$ ______
25 $20 \div 5 =$ ______	**26** $15 \div 3 =$ ______	**27** $8 \div 4 =$ ______
28 $12 \div 3 =$ ______	**29** $4 \div 2 =$ ______	**30** $9 \div 3 =$ ______
31 $20 \div 4 =$ ______	**32** $6 \div 3 =$ ______	**33** $12 \div 3 =$ ______
34 $1 \div 1 =$ ______	**35** $25 \div 5 =$ ______	**36** $15 \div 5 =$ ______
37 $10 \div 5 =$ ______	**38** $8 \div 2 =$ ______	**39** $12 \div 4 =$ ______
40 $16 \div 4 =$ ______	**41** $6 \div 2 =$ ______	**42** $20 \div 5 =$ ______

Division Facts—Skills Practice

Name: ____________________

Divide up to 25 ÷ 5.

Form B

1 12 ÷ 3 = ______	**2** 15 ÷ 5 = ______	**3** 8 ÷ 4 = ______
4 20 ÷ 4 = ______	**5** 16 ÷ 4 = ______	**6** 6 ÷ 3 = ______
7 5 ÷ 5 = ______	**8** 8 ÷ 2 = ______	**9** 25 ÷ 5 = ______
10 8 ÷ 4 = ______	**11** 9 ÷ 3 = ______	**12** 20 ÷ 4 = ______
13 15 ÷ 3 = ______	**14** 20 ÷ 5 = ______	**15** 6 ÷ 2 = ______
16 12 ÷ 4 = ______	**17** 0 ÷ 4 = ______	**18** 4 ÷ 2 = ______
19 25 ÷ 5 = ______	**20** 10 ÷ 2 = ______	**21** 15 ÷ 5 = ______
22 0 ÷ 5 = ______	**23** 9 ÷ 3 = ______	**24** 15 ÷ 3 = ______
25 16 ÷ 4 = ______	**26** 6 ÷ 3 = ______	**27** 12 ÷ 3 = ______
28 15 ÷ 3 = ______	**29** 10 ÷ 2 = ______	**30** 3 ÷ 3 = ______
31 12 ÷ 4 = ______	**32** 10 ÷ 5 = ______	**33** 6 ÷ 2 = ______
34 8 ÷ 2 = ______	**35** 20 ÷ 5 = ______	**36** 12 ÷ 3 = ______
37 10 ÷ 5 = ______	**38** 15 ÷ 5 = ______	**39** 4 ÷ 2 = ______
40 12 ÷ 4 = ______	**41** 2 ÷ 1 = ______	**42** 20 ÷ 5 = ______

Division Facts—Skills Practice

Name: ______________________

Divide by 2, 5, or 10.

Form A

1 30 ÷ 5 = ______	**2** 20 ÷ 2 = ______	**3** 45 ÷ 5 = ______
4 18 ÷ 2 = ______	**5** 60 ÷ 10 = ______	**6** 20 ÷ 5 = ______
7 16 ÷ 2 = ______	**8** 40 ÷ 10 = ______	**9** 15 ÷ 5 = ______
10 90 ÷ 10 = ______	**11** 40 ÷ 5 = ______	**12** 8 ÷ 2 = ______
13 12 ÷ 2 = ______	**14** 25 ÷ 5 = ______	**15** 50 ÷ 10 = ______
16 80 ÷ 10 = ______	**17** 14 ÷ 2 = ______	**18** 4 ÷ 2 = ______
19 30 ÷ 10 = ______	**20** 6 ÷ 2 = ______	**21** 100 ÷ 10 = ______
22 18 ÷ 2 = ______	**23** 10 ÷ 2 = ______	**24** 5 ÷ 5 = ______
25 40 ÷ 5 = ______	**26** 10 ÷ 5 = ______	**27** 35 ÷ 5 = ______
28 35 ÷ 5 = ______	**29** 70 ÷ 10 = ______	**30** 45 ÷ 5 = ______

Division Facts—Skills Practice

Name: ____________________

Divide by 2, 5, or 10.

Form B

1. $25 \div 5 =$ ______
2. $45 \div 5 =$ ______
3. $35 \div 5 =$ ______
4. $40 \div 5 =$ ______
5. $8 \div 2 =$ ______
6. $16 \div 2 =$ ______
7. $20 \div 5 =$ ______
8. $10 \div 2 =$ ______
9. $20 \div 5 =$ ______
10. $25 \div 5 =$ ______
11. $14 \div 2 =$ ______
12. $80 \div 10 =$ ______
13. $18 \div 2 =$ ______
14. $6 \div 2 =$ ______
15. $4 \div 2 =$ ______
16. $18 \div 2 =$ ______
17. $40 \div 10 =$ ______
18. $50 \div 5 =$ ______
19. $10 \div 5 =$ ______
20. $40 \div 5 =$ ______
21. $100 \div 10 =$ ______
22. $45 \div 5 =$ ______
23. $12 \div 2 =$ ______
24. $30 \div 5 =$ ______
25. $90 \div 10 =$ ______
26. $15 \div 5 =$ ______
27. $35 \div 5 =$ ______
28. $30 \div 10 =$ ______
29. $16 \div 2 =$ ______
30. $70 \div 10 =$ ______

Division Facts—Skills Practice

Name: ______________________

Divide by 3, 4, 6, 7, 8, and 9.

Form A

1 $56 \div 7 =$ ______	2 $21 \div 3 =$ ______	3 $80 \div 8 =$ ______
4 $18 \div 6 =$ ______	5 $12 \div 4 =$ ______	6 $36 \div 9 =$ ______
7 $35 \div 7 =$ ______	8 $6 \div 6 =$ ______	9 $32 \div 4 =$ ______
10 $24 \div 3 =$ ______	11 $54 \div 9 =$ ______	12 $48 \div 6 =$ ______
13 $64 \div 8 =$ ______	14 $24 \div 6 =$ ______	15 $30 \div 3 =$ ______
16 $63 \div 9 =$ ______	17 $40 \div 8 =$ ______	18 $24 \div 4 =$ ______
19 $54 \div 6 =$ ______	20 $21 \div 7 =$ ______	21 $81 \div 9 =$ ______
22 $70 \div 7 =$ ______	23 $28 \div 4 =$ ______	24 $48 \div 8 =$ ______
25 $24 \div 8 =$ ______	26 $42 \div 7 =$ ______	27 $30 \div 6 =$ ______
28 $36 \div 4 =$ ______	29 $72 \div 9 =$ ______	30 $32 \div 8 =$ ______
31 $16 \div 8 =$ ______	32 $27 \div 3 =$ ______	33 $63 \div 7 =$ ______
34 $56 \div 8 =$ ______	35 $45 \div 9 =$ ______	36 $27 \div 9 =$ ______
37 $20 \div 4 =$ ______	38 $42 \div 6 =$ ______	39 $28 \div 7 =$ ______
40 $72 \div 8 =$ ______	41 $49 \div 7 =$ ______	42 $18 \div 3 =$ ______

Division Facts—Skills Practice

Name: ______________________

Divide by 3, 4, 6, 7, 8, and 9. **Form B**

1 $24 \div 3 =$ ________
2 $42 \div 6 =$ ________
3 $21 \div 7 =$ ________
4 $72 \div 9 =$ ________
5 $30 \div 3 =$ ________
6 $28 \div 4 =$ ________
7 $12 \div 4 =$ ________
8 $48 \div 6 =$ ________
9 $63 \div 7 =$ ________
10 $30 \div 6 =$ ________
11 $27 \div 9 =$ ________
12 $42 \div 7 =$ ________
13 $49 \div 7 =$ ________
14 $21 \div 3 =$ ________
15 $90 \div 9 =$ ________
16 $72 \div 8 =$ ________
17 $48 \div 8 =$ ________
18 $45 \div 9 =$ ________
19 $18 \div 3 =$ ________
20 $28 \div 7 =$ ________
21 $54 \div 6 =$ ________
22 $32 \div 8 =$ ________
23 $32 \div 4 =$ ________
24 $8 \div 8 =$ ________
25 $56 \div 8 =$ ________
26 $24 \div 4 =$ ________
27 $36 \div 4 =$ ________
28 $27 \div 3 =$ ________
29 $81 \div 9 =$ ________
30 $24 \div 8 =$ ________
31 $40 \div 8 =$ ________
32 $54 \div 9 =$ ________
33 $64 \div 8 =$ ________
34 $24 \div 6 =$ ________
35 $56 \div 7 =$ ________
36 $36 \div 9 =$ ________
37 $80 \div 8 =$ ________
38 $20 \div 4 =$ ________
39 $63 \div 9 =$ ________
40 $35 \div 7 =$ ________
41 $18 \div 6 =$ ________
42 $54 \div 6 =$ ________

Division Facts—Skills Practice

Name: ______________________

Divide up to 100 ÷ 10.

Form A

1 48 ÷ 6 = ______	**2** 27 ÷ 3 = ______	**3** 16 ÷ 8 = ______
4 25 ÷ 5 = ______	**5** 14 ÷ 2 = ______	**6** 72 ÷ 8 = ______
7 18 ÷ 6 = ______	**8** 56 ÷ 7 = ______	**9** 6 ÷ 2 = ______
10 28 ÷ 4 = ______	**11** 7 ÷ 1 = ______	**12** 45 ÷ 9 = ______
13 64 ÷ 8 = ______	**14** 15 ÷ 5 = ______	**15** 20 ÷ 2 = ______
16 4 ÷ 2 = ______	**17** 24 ÷ 3 = ______	**18** 63 ÷ 7 = ______
19 12 ÷ 3 = ______	**20** 16 ÷ 4 = ______	**21** 90 ÷ 10 = ______
22 81 ÷ 9 = ______	**23** 36 ÷ 4 = ______	**24** 12 ÷ 2 = ______
25 40 ÷ 8 = ______	**26** 9 ÷ 3 = ______	**27** 49 ÷ 7 = ______
28 30 ÷ 6 = ______	**29** 54 ÷ 9 = ______	**30** 1 ÷ 1 = ______
31 21 ÷ 7 = ______	**32** 8 ÷ 2 = ______	**33** 35 ÷ 5 = ______
34 10 ÷ 10 = ______	**35** 18 ÷ 9 = ______	**36** 36 ÷ 6 = ______
37 10 ÷ 2 = ______	**38** 20 ÷ 4 = ______	**39** 42 ÷ 7 = ______
40 32 ÷ 8 = ______	**41** 50 ÷ 5 = ______	**42** 24 ÷ 6 = ______

Division Facts—Skills Practice

Name: ____________________

Divide up to 100 ÷ 10.

Form B

1. 36 ÷ 6 = ______
2. 16 ÷ 2 = ______
3. 21 ÷ 3 = ______
4. 30 ÷ 5 = ______
5. 56 ÷ 8 = ______
6. 72 ÷ 9 = ______
7. 5 ÷ 1 = ______
8. 18 ÷ 2 = ______
9. 64 ÷ 8 = ______
10. 28 ÷ 7 = ______
11. 8 ÷ 4 = ______
12. 45 ÷ 5 = ______
13. 63 ÷ 9 = ______
14. 15 ÷ 5 = ______
15. 100 ÷ 10 = ______
16. 35 ÷ 7 = ______
17. 4 ÷ 2 = ______
18. 27 ÷ 9 = ______
19. 40 ÷ 5 = ______
20. 81 ÷ 9 = ______
21. 14 ÷ 7 = ______
22. 54 ÷ 6 = ______
23. 25 ÷ 5 = ______
24. 32 ÷ 4 = ______
25. 20 ÷ 5 = ______
26. 42 ÷ 6 = ______
27. 12 ÷ 4 = ______
28. 24 ÷ 8 = ______
29. 60 ÷ 6 = ______
30. 36 ÷ 4 = ______
31. 18 ÷ 3 = ______
32. 49 ÷ 7 = ______
33. 1 ÷ 1 = ______
34. 48 ÷ 8 = ______
35. 16 ÷ 4 = ______
36. 9 ÷ 3 = ______
37. 3 ÷ 3 = ______
38. 6 ÷ 3 = ______
39. 12 ÷ 6 = ______
40. 10 ÷ 5 = ______
41. 24 ÷ 4 = ______
42. 90 ÷ 9 = ______

Division Facts—Repeated Reasoning

Name: ______________________

Find patterns dividing by 2 and 5.

Set A

1 _______ $= 4 \div 2$

2 _______ $= 6 \div 2$

3 _______ $= 8 \div 2$

4 _______ $= 10 \div 2$

5 _______ $= 12 \div 2$

6 $7 =$ _______ $\div 2$

7 $8 =$ _______ $\div 2$

8 $9 =$ _______ $\div 2$

9 $10 =$ _______ $\div 2$

10 $11 =$ _______ $\div 2$

Set B

1 _______ $= 5 \div 5$

2 $2 =$ _______ $\div 5$

3 _______ $= 15 \div 5$

4 $4 =$ _______ $\div 5$

5 _______ $= 25 \div 5$

6 $6 =$ _______ $\div 5$

7 _______ $= 35 \div 5$

8 $8 =$ _______ $\div 5$

9 _______ $= 45 \div 5$

10 $10 =$ _______ $\div 5$

Describe a pattern you see in one of the sets of problems above.

____

____

____

Division Facts—Repeated Reasoning

Name: ______________________

Find patterns in quotients.

Set A

1 6 ÷ 3 = ________

2 6 ÷ 6 = ________

3 12 ÷ 3 = ________

4 12 ÷ 6 = ________

5 18 ÷ 3 = ________

6 18 ÷ 6 = ________

7 24 ÷ 3 = ________

8 24 ÷ 6 = ________

9 30 ÷ 3 = ________

10 30 ÷ 6 = ________

Set B

1 8 ÷ 4 = ________

2 8 ÷ 8 = ________

3 16 ÷ 4 = ________

4 16 ÷ 8 = ________

5 24 ÷ 4 = ________

6 24 ÷ 8 = ________

7 32 ÷ 4 = ________

8 32 ÷ 8 = ________

9 40 ÷ 4 = ________

10 40 ÷ 8 = ________

Describe a pattern you see in one of the sets of problems above.

____

____

____

Multiply by Tens—Skills Practice

Name: ____________________

Use place value to multiply. **Form A**

1 $7 \times 30 =$ ______

2 $40 \times 4 =$ ______

3 $6 \times 80 =$ ______

4 $4 \times 60 =$ ______

5 $90 \times 3 =$ ______

6 $20 \times 3 =$ ______

7 $5 \times 80 =$ ______

8 $6 \times 20 =$ ______

9 $60 \times 9 =$ ______

10 $40 \times 8 =$ ______

11 $2 \times 20 =$ ______

12 $50 \times 2 =$ ______

13 $60 \times 6 =$ ______

14 $9 \times 20 =$ ______

15 $6 \times 80 =$ ______

16 $7 \times 90 =$ ______

17 $3 \times 40 =$ ______

18 $70 \times 5 =$ ______

19 $50 \times 4 =$ ______

20 $70 \times 0 =$ ______

21 $3 \times 80 =$ ______

22 $80 \times 8 =$ ______

23 $6 \times 50 =$ ______

24 $9 \times 90 =$ ______

25 $5 \times 30 =$ ______

26 $70 \times 2 =$ ______

27 $60 \times 5 =$ ______

28 $90 \times 8 =$ ______

29 $6 \times 30 =$ ______

30 $9 \times 40 =$ ______

31 $4 \times 70 =$ ______

32 $7 \times 70 =$ ______

33 $20 \times 8 =$ ______

34 $30 \times 3 =$ ______

35 $9 \times 60 =$ ______

36 $90 \times 5 =$ ______

37 $50 \times 8 =$ ______

38 $2 \times 40 =$ ______

39 $8 \times 70 =$ ______

40 $9 \times 80 =$ ______

41 $50 \times 5 =$ ______

42 $7 \times 60 =$ ______

Multiply by Tens—Skills Practice

Name: ____________________

Use place value to multiply.

Form B

1 $8 \times 30 =$ ______	2 $5 \times 80 =$ ______	3 $40 \times 6 =$ ______
4 $5 \times 60 =$ ______	5 $3 \times 70 =$ ______	6 $80 \times 4 =$ ______
7 $70 \times 9 =$ ______	8 $7 \times 50 =$ ______	9 $60 \times 8 =$ ______
10 $20 \times 5 =$ ______	11 $6 \times 60 =$ ______	12 $90 \times 6 =$ ______
13 $9 \times 40 =$ ______	14 $3 \times 60 =$ ______	15 $40 \times 7 =$ ______
16 $8 \times 80 =$ ______	17 $6 \times 90 =$ ______	18 $20 \times 7 =$ ______
19 $50 \times 0 =$ ______	20 $70 \times 9 =$ ______	21 $5 \times 30 =$ ______
22 $2 \times 30 =$ ______	23 $90 \times 5 =$ ______	24 $4 \times 40 =$ ______
25 $7 \times 80 =$ ______	26 $2 \times 20 =$ ______	27 $90 \times 8 =$ ______
28 $30 \times 4 =$ ______	29 $7 \times 60 =$ ______	30 $90 \times 2 =$ ______
31 $50 \times 9 =$ ______	32 $70 \times 7 =$ ______	33 $8 \times 70 =$ ______
34 $5 \times 70 =$ ______	35 $80 \times 2 =$ ______	36 $3 \times 30 =$ ______
37 $30 \times 9 =$ ______	38 $5 \times 40 =$ ______	39 $70 \times 6 =$ ______
40 $50 \times 5 =$ ______	41 $90 \times 9 =$ ______	42 $40 \times 2 =$ ______